D0882992

The Experience
of
Depression

The Experience
of
Depression

Dorothy Rowe

Principal Psychologist
Lincolnshire Area Health Authority

JOHN WILEY & SONS

Chichester · New York · Brisbane · Toronto

Library of Congress Cataloging in Publication Data:

Rowe, Dorothy.
  The experience of depression.
  Bibliography: p.
  Includes index.
  1. Depression, Mental — Cases, clinical reports,
statistics. I. Title.
RC537.R67   616.8'52   77–9609
ISBN 0 471 99554 1

Typeset by Computacomp (UK) Limited
Fort William, Scotland
and printed by
Unwin Brothers Limited
The Gresham Press
Old Woking, Surrey, England

To my parents
Jack and Ella Conn

Acknowledgments

The author's literary estate, the Hogarth Press, London, and Harcourt Brace Jovanovich, Inc., New York, to quote from *To the Lighthouse* and *The Waves* by Virginia Woolf.

Dr A.C. Woodmansey and the *International Journal of Psychoanalysis* to quote from "The internalization of external conflict", *I.J.P.A.*, Vol. 47, p. 349.

The Oxford University Press to quote from *After Babel* by George Steiner.

Mrs Linda Lockwood to quote her poem "My Experience of Depression".

Dr P. Wakeling to quote his letter to the author.

PREFACE

*"The world of the happy man is a different one
from that of the unhappy man."*
WITTGENSTEIN

This book has grown out of the work which I began in 1968 when Professor F.A. Jenner, Director of the MRC Unit for Metabolic Studies in Psychiatry, University of Sheffield, suggested that I study psychological factors in people who had regular mood changes. What this book sets out to do is to suggest one way in which that phenomenon, commonly labelled "depression", can be considered. The book is not concerned with recording a new form of therapy. If any of the people written about here benefited from their discussions with me it was through their own courage and intelligence that this happened and not through my wisdom. There are many therapists far more skilled than I, and if any of them should read this book they will be aware of how often I was stupid and imperceptive. What I hope to achieve by this book is to promote our understanding of depression in terms of meaning and experience rather than in terms of illness.

This research was made possible by a grant from the Trent Regional Health Authority. I would like to thank Professor Jenner and all the doctors, nurses, psychologists, physiotherapists, occupational therapists and social workers with whom I have worked. The work of transcribing tapes and typing the manuscript was carried out by my research assistant, Ruth Brumby. I hope I have done justice to the nine people I have written about here. I have gained so much from them and from all the people who at one time or another have talked with me about their experience that thanks and expressions of affection seem quite inadequate.

Eagle, Lincolnshire   DOROTHY ROWE
September, 1976

CONTENTS

PART 3 GENERAL CONSIDERATIONS

FOREWORD

Depression — the feeling of being pressed down by the world — is a commonplace of human experience. It is, and seemingly has always been, a recurrent theme of our conversation and our culture. One of the four great humours of mediaeval psychology was the melancholic. The most resonant part of the progress of Bunyan's pilgrim was his sojourn in the Slough of Despond. An entire form of music is simply called "the blues". In our attempts to convey to each other our personal experience of depression we have called upon every kind of metaphor. We have drawn analogies from disease and injury — to be sick at heart, to suffer a broken heart. We enter "the doldrums", the area where no wind of hope or purpose moves us. Depression preys on our mind, we sink into it, we are downcast, we are crestfallen, bowed down, cut up, careworn. Even if we seek the company of others we are the skeleton at the feast. The very vision of the world becomes our metaphor when we experience the "blackness" of despair.

Our everyday "psychology of depression" recognizes its variations in severity, its signs and effects, its origins and its antidotes.

Our account of depression scales it from a mild but burdensome feeling that life is flat, stale, dull and unprofitable to a kind of raging despair. We sense it as a short-lived "mood" or a seemingly endless state.

We note its signs and effects as including feelings of and tendencies towards isolation and withdrawal; a terrible slowing of our thought and action, so that even trivial tasks become too great to be undertaken; we hear ourselves whining and complaining about how badly we are treated, how constipated we are, how little appetite we have; we find our memory bad, our ideas confused, our concentration gone and our thinking impoverished and repetitive; we are agitated, restless, sleepless; we brood on our sins and the sins of others towards us; we sit and stare.

We find, at least speculatively, origins for our depression so that we see it as caused by his death, her rejection, our failure.

We sense that to raise ourselves up we must seek the company of others, find distraction, prove ourselves of at least some worth, sing songs, take holidays, recover our faith, or at least wait for time to heal our wounds.

From time to time persons and cultures redefine their experiences and thereby experience them anew. The experience of depression is one of many aspects of the human condition which, from the mid-nineteenth century onwards, was elaborated in medical terms within the framework of the growing discipline of psychiatry. Psychiatrists attempted to repeat the success of the diagnostic strategies of general medicine within the field of social and psychological phenomena. This was initially not an unreasonable venture. Medicine was increasingly given charge of the multitude of institutions which housed the wretched and the rejected of society and they sought to organize them administratively and intellectually, in terms of the discipline of medicine, as "mental hospitals". Thus they observed the behaviour and talk of their "patients" and gradually saw it as forming clusters of typical manifestations which were then given disease labels. In general medicine such observational cluster analyses of signs and symptoms had often been later vindicated by the growing science of physiology. It seemed reasonable to apply such a strategy as part of the growing concept of "mental illness". Thus was developed the notion of depression as an illness, a *depressive illness*, a *depressive* patient, a *depression*. Two commonly noted aspects of the experience of depression seemed to justify the attempt to see it in medical terms. Firstly depression could clearly be a serious business, equivalent in terms of its impact to a major disease. The wild and sometimes incomprehensible talk of the depressed person, the recurrent tragedy of the man who was so depressed that he killed himself, but only after killing his family so that they should not be left "unprotected", seemed parallel with lethal major ailments. Perhaps more importantly, most of us when we are depressed may reach a point at which the experience seems very like the experience of a disease in the sense that we lose track of personally meaningful causes and become totally absorbed in the intensity of our suffering. It is this that causes us to speak of being *overwhelmed* by depression, *in the grip of* depression. It is this experience that makes us ready to accept that we have been seized by an alien force, an illness, rather than continue to struggle with the idea that it is all to do with the way we have chosen to live our particular and personal life. As the psychiatric notion of depression was elaborated, it tended either to look for physical cause rather than psychological meaning or at least to present the condition as intrinsically mysterious and impersonal. Thus psychiatrists have overwhelmingly used physical treatments as their response to the depressive experience, primarily electroconvulsive therapy and anti-depressant drugs. This again reinforced patients in their view that the condition was as much outside their personal ken or their personal responsibility as a meningitis or a cancer.

Within psychiatry itself there has been a struggle to modify and elaborate concepts of depression in such a way that they would acknowledge the origins of the experience in the life of the patient. One intellectual strategy has been to split depressions into two groups and to speak of reactive or neurotic depression, which is seen as having its source in the lifestyle and problems of the person, and endogenous depression, which is seen as invading the person or at least as having no personally definable cause. What seems to be happening in our culture is that the intellectual strategies of medicine have combined with the personal difficulties we have in dealing with the depressive experience. This inhibits any psychological examination of what is going on when we are in no mood to bear with prolonged questioning or self-inquiry as to how it came about. We are at one with the doctors in seeing the depression as something essentially to be "got rid of" (i.e. treated as an illness) rather than something which we ought to explore because of its significance for our personal life. Moreover it is a commonly noted aspect of the experience of depression that we are involved in the question of guilt, the issue of our wrongdoing, our sin. To reconceptualize the condition as an illness is one way of reordering our view of it so that the issue of responsibility and guilt does not arise either in our minds or in the minds of our relatives and friends.

This book seems to me essentially to take as its starting-point the older, more personal view of depression, namely, that it is a meaningful response on our part to the point at which our life has arrived. Dorothy Rowe has sought to use psychotherapy both as a helpful way of responding to a person's predicament and as a framework within which we can explore the kinds of personal contradiction which, at crisis points, are experienced as depression. The kind of interviewing strategies that Dorothy Rowe has adopted and developed and the use of notions like "construct" and "implication" from personal construct theory seem to me to have served both the clients' purposes and the readers' purposes very well. They have allowed Dorothy Rowe's clients to articulate their life situation very much as they see it, so that we are repeatedly reminded of the unique quality of each person's world. Yet at the same time the author's inquiry is penetrating while gentle, so that at least some of the meaning behind the mystery of each person's situation can be seen and we can draw parallels between their experience and our own.

The book reports a scientific project in that the author has confronted the realities of her subject systematically and with a carefully thought out theoretical approach — these are the hallmarks of science. At the same time she exemplifies that stance in psychology which accepts that our understanding of the person's experience is the only valid basis on which research can be conducted and help given.

It seems to me that we benefit from the kind of venture Dorothy Rowe has undertaken both in our formal comprehension of, and our ability to help, those who are psychologically distressed by what we call "depression". At the same time we are reminded of the fact that depression is part of the human condition and that in understanding it we can come to an understanding of aspects of ourselves.

D. Bannister

PART 1

The Theory

1

CONCEPTS OF DEPRESSION

"O the mind, mind has mountains; cliffs of fall
Frightful, sheer, no-man-fathomed. Hold
them cheap
May who ne'er hung there."
GERARD MANLEY HOPKINS

When Hopkins was appointed Professor of Classics in University College, Dublin, he entered the darkest years of his life; in those years, from 1885 to 1889, he wrote the "terrible sonnets", a record of that experience we call depression. Hopkins died when he was forty-four. Had he lived, he would have seen the start of a great flood of scientific literature on the topic of depression.

Kraepelin began the flood when he called this experience a disease. He used the nineteenth-century model of disease, which was based on the new findings of pathology and bacteriology. He saw disease as something new that had occurred in the life of the patient, although some people, he thought, had a constitution which provided a fertile soil for this disease. He sought to classify diseases in the way that Linnaeus had classified plants.

Freud, while allowing the possibility of a constitutional basis, saw melancholia as a reaction to loss. The extensive psychoanalytic literature on depression (Mendelson, 1974) elaborated this concept of loss and drew attention to the presence of aggressive feelings intertwined with the melancholy.

Karl Jaspers and Henri Ey made learned studies of the symptoms of depression. Adolf Meyer stressed the importance of environmental and cultural influences in depression. Aubrey Lewis and Russell Davis described depression as an adaptation of an intolerable situation.

Once the existence of depression as a disease was accepted by the medical profession, the debate then began as to how many diseases of depression there were and what they should be called. Words proliferated — endogenous and reactive depression, manic depression, psychotic and neurotic depression, retarded and agitated depression, involutional melancholia, affective psychosis, masked depression, senile depression, metabolic depression, unipolar and bipolar depression. Professor Kendell (1976) in a paper called "The classification of depression: a review of contemporary confusion" writes that "The complexity, and the absurdity, of the present situation are vividly illustrated by the fact that almost every classificatory format that is logically possible has been advocated by someone within the last twenty years and some more or less plausible evidence offered in support. There are classifications of depression embracing one, two, three, four, five, six, seven, eight or nine categories .... Some are tiered, others are not. There are also dimensional classifications, with varying numbers of dimensions .... The ninth revision (of the International Classification of Diseases) contains between nine and thirteen different categories to which a depressive illness may now be allocated."

Carney and Sheffield commented that "in the absence of a generally agreed physical basis for depression, responsiveness to treatment is probably the most useful independent criterion of depressive classification that we have". The treatment which gives this *post hoc* diagnosis (that is, if a patient says that he is no longer depressed after this treatment, then he had had an endogenous depression) is electroconvulsive therapy (ECT), which was accidentally discovered by Cerletti in 1938 and which maintains its popularity despite its undoubted damaging effects on memory. Such damage may be counted as worth the risk when put against the agony of a deep depression which ECT can bring to an end, but this damage can hardly be counted as unimportant when ECT is used in the vain hope that it will dissipate the misery of a failed. life, an unhappy marriage or the loneliness and isolation of one who cannot love or be loved.

The discovery of the anti-depressant drugs has ameliorated some of the worst aspects of the experience of depression and has allowed many people to go on with their lives, but it is naive in the extreme to think that the solution to the miseries of this world lies in tinkering with our metabolism. Undoubtedly physiological changes accompany the experience of depression, but this is not surprising, since physiological changes accompany all our profound experiences. Specific physiological changes as necessary precursors to depression have not been found, and the concept of disease, as Kendell (1975) has shown, is no longer as clear and simple as Kraepelin thought.

So, if Hopkins were alive today, all these words, all this knowledge about depression would not cause him to change one word of his terrible sonnets, nor would he consign them to past history, as we have consigned the records of the miseries of scurvy and bubonic plague. What he described is still part of our present experience, an experience hard to endure and difficult to comprehend.

The person who is experiencing depression tries to make sense of his experience and, in doing so, he may look to psychiatry for help, but he soon discovers that there is an enormous gap between his "I am here and this is happening to me" experience and what the psychiatrist calls "depression". He experiences a state of being; the psychiatrist names a thing. "Depression (is) probably the most common presenting symptom of psychiatric patients today," say Slater and Roth, the authors of the bible of British psychiatry (1970). "Organic states are very commonly the prime cause of a depression," they say, in the manner of "Heavy rains are commonly the prime cause of a flood." Even American psychiatrists, who tend to see depression as a response or a state, can be found writing "The variety of ways in which depression manifests itself and the settings in which it can occur raise the question of whether certain central changes in the psychological and behavioral aspects of the individual seem to be consistently associated with depression." (Flach and Draghi, 1975).

The leap from "I am miserable, anxious, guilty" to "You have a depression" is a change in the form of language which sometimes tricks us into thinking we have found something real when all we have done is altered the words we use.

On a stormy day we may have an experience which causes us to exclaim "The lightning flashed." What we saw was simply a flashing light, but in telling our experience we had to put it in a sentence with a subject (lightning) and a verb (flashed). Of course, we know that the lightning and the flashing of the light are the one and the same. We do not waste our time wondering what the lightning does when it is not flashing. But sometimes we are not always so wise.

In Indo-European languages verbs tend to be cumbersome forms of language, while the sentence structure demands a subject and predicate (not all languages are like this, as Cassirer (1953) has shown). We see a friend coughing, sneezing and blowing his nose. We observe all these activities, lump them together and give them a name, "a cold". Then we put "a cold" in a sentence and immediately start to treat it as a real thing. "I see you have a cold," we say. "Don't give your cold to me," as if we can hand round a cold in the way we hand round a plate of cakes. In common parlance we do not doubt the existence of a thing called a cold, even though we know that the necessary conditions which produce the coughing, sneezing and blowing of the nose are extremely complex and variable.

Thus, when we think that there is such a thing as "a cold" we forget that what we have done is to impose a form of our language, a noun, on to a host of different phenomena which we have observed. We have mistaken a form of our language, an idea in our minds, for a thing which exists in reality. We even have a name for this process of turning an idea into a thing — reification, the manufacture of a thing.

It is this process of reification which bedevils so much of the work of psychiatry today. People are observed to behave in different ways and certain regularities, certain groups of behaviours, are identified. These groups are given different names — "depression", "schizophrenia", "psychopathy", are popular ones. Then these convenient names are transmuted into things and in a trice we are wondering about the dimensions of depression, the latency of schizophrenia, the genetic endowment of a psychopathy, all things which in psychiatric parlance take on the undoubted reality of tables and chairs and motor-cars.

"Depression" is a convenient name which we give to a collection of behaviours, feelings, beliefs that we can observe in ourselves and in other people. By making "depression" into a thing with its own set of causes and attributes the psychiatrist makes his experience of the patient's depressive behaviours to be very different from the patient's own experience. Often the patient is obtuse and does not understand that he contains a thing called depression. "Depressive patients," say Slater and Roth, "may show a complete failure of all insight, deny that they are ill, and hold steadfastly to their ideas of guilt and punishment." A sense of guilt and an apprehension of punishment are personal, subjective matters. Slater and Roth warn the student psychiatrist, "It is the objective world in which we live and to which the subjective world must pay deference. It is even more important to know what the facts are than what the patient makes of them."

The facts, for the psychiatrist, are basically the symptoms and signs. Our knowledge of those clusters of symptoms and signs, called syndromes, has been built up over years of careful observation and recording. The validity of observation is always bedevilled by the fact that we tend to see what we expect to see, and the reliability of recording our observations is always spoilt to the extent that the same words can have different meanings for different people. In an attempt to improve the validity and reliability of psychiatric diagnosis and to improve communication among psychiatrists of different nationalities and cultures the "Present State Examination", a most elegant piece of work, was devised as a clearly defined form of clinical interview "with the object of assessing the 'present mental state' of adult patients suffering from one of the neuroses or functional psychoses. The PSE was developed in order to provide reliable and precise data concerning the patient's clinical condition …. This ideal can never be completely attainable because of the difficulties of defining and measuring such complex and often abstract concepts and phenomena." (Wing *et al.*, 1974)

The difference in the perception of the psychiatrist from that of the sufferer comes out clearly when we contrast the definitions of the PSE with Hopkins' poetry. To rate early waking, instructs the PSE, "rate waking one hour before usual time as (1) and two hours before usual time as (2), irrespective of whether the subject is taking sleeping tablets". Hopkins wrote,

> *"I wake and feel the fell of day, not day.*
> *What hours, O what black hours we have spent*
> *This night! what sights you, heart, saw; the ways you went!*
> *And more must, in yet longer light's delay.*
> *With witness I speak this! But where I say*
> *Hours I mean years, mean life. And my lament*
> *Is cries countless, cries like dead letters sent*
> *To dearest him that lives alas! away."*

The PSE says of pathological guilt "the subject blames himself too much for some peccadillo which most people would not take very seriously. He realises that his guilt is exaggerated but he cannot help feeling it all the same." Hopkins says,

> *"My own heart let me more have pity on; let*
> *Me live to my sad self hereafter kind,*
> *Charitable; not live this tormented mind*
> *With this tormented mind tormenting yet."*

A reason for this gap between the psychiatrist's perception of his patient's experience and the patient's perception of his own experience is often found by the critics of psychiatry who charge psychiatrists with being particularly insensitive to the feelings of their patients. This criticism seems to me to be unfounded. Psychiatrists, being human, are no better or worse than any other group of people in empathizing with their fellows. The reason for the gap lies partly in the attempt to meet the demands of scientific objectivity and partly in the way in which words have been confused with things. Unfortunately, when we fail to distinguish words from things we soon become embroiled in disputes like those of the mediaeval scholastics who spent their time arguing about words without ever checking their words against their experiences. It seems that many of the disputes in the study of depression are arguments about words, so much so that the realities, the experiences, are ignored.

Human beings have always seen great power and wisdom as being contained in knowing the right words. Since psychiatrists invented and defined so many of the words in their work, they tend to believe that they are always wiser than their patients. The dialogue between psychiatrists and patients is like that between kind parents, who want their children to depend on them because they feel they know what is best for the children, and children, who feel that they must depend on their parents, for they are the only protection the children have, but know that their parents do not understand them. It is not a dialogue between equals who have a mutual problem to solve. Thus we find a psychiatrist who conceives of depression as a thing, an illness, lodged in the patient's body, will say, with the utmost kindness to the patient, "Don't worry about your depression. Just leave your depression to me to look after." The patient would dearly love to hand over his depression like a rotting tooth or a stone in his kidney, but he knows that the agony he feels is not the agony of toothache or a kidney stone. When he fails to hand over to the doctor's care the thing which is the cause of his misery, he may then be urged to overcome his depression as if it were a disability like poor posture or a cough brought on by too much smoking, a disability which can be overcome by the exercise of the will. When the agony fails to dissipate with increased effort, all that is achieved is that the sufferer feels greater guilt.

Sometimes the psychiatrist will answer the patient's question "Why has this happened to me?" by naming a cause. The kind of cause the particular psychiatrist chooses depends on that psychiatrist's personal beliefs as to the nature of man. If he sees man as a physical machine, ultimately explicable in the language of chemistry and physics, he will choose these kind of words to name a cause. On the other hand, if he sees man as the container of forces which demand expression and which require control, he will choose words from the dynamic theories of psychology and psychoanalysis. Such explanations may satisfy him, for they fit his system whereby he explains the world to himself, but the patient finds that what he knows and believes is disparaged by being described as no more than the result of a bodily change or the predictable outcome of a psychological process.

Depression is a name for an experience. If we want to understand what this experience is, how it arises, what it means and, since it is an unpleasant experience, how to avoid it, then we must examine this experience of depression. For every person it is an individual experience, yet when we look we can see something common in all these experiences.

In his *Spiritual Exercises* St Ignatius wrote of

> *"desolation*

> *... darkness of the soul, disturbance in it,*
> *movement to things low and earthly, the disquiet of different*
> *agitations and temptations, moving to want of confidence,*
> *without hope, without love, when one finds oneself lazy,*
> *tepid, sad, and as if separated from his Creator and Lord."*

Joan Riviere described the total desolation of what the Kleinian psychoanalysts call "the depressive position",

> *"the situation in which all one's loved ones within are dead and destroyed,*
> *all goodness is dispersed, lost, in fragments, wasted and scattered to the*
> *winds; nothing is left within but utter desolation. Love brings sorrow and*
> *sorrow brings guilt, the intolerable tension mounts, there is no escape, one is*
> *utterly alone, there is no one to share or help. Love must die because love is*
> *dead. Besides there would be no one to feed one, and no one whom one could*
> *feed and no food in the world. And more, there would still be magic power in*
> *the underlying persecutors who can never be exterminated — the ghosts.*
> *Death would instantly ensue — and one would choose to die by one's own*
> *hand before such a position could be realized."*

Hopkins said of himself,

> *"I am gall, I am heartburn. God's most deep decree*
> *Bitter would have me taste : my taste was me;*
> *Bones built in me, flesh filled, blood brimmed the curse.*
> *Selfyeast of spirit a dull dough sours. I see*
> *The lost are like this, and their scourge to be*
> *As I am mine, their sweating selves; but worse."*

One woman, whose life and education had equipped her neither to transform her experience into religious ecstasy, nor to fuse it with her intellectual pursuits, nor transmute it into art, said, if she could paint a picture of her experience, she would paint

> *"a very deep pit. Bottomless, well, not entirely bottomless but so steep you*
> *couldn't climb out. Much as you tried, the more you tried to grovel your way*
> *up, the more you would slide. Grey and nothing, like you see when a*
> *volcano's erupted, all the lava, when it's died down, all that sort of clinkery,*
> *burnt-away nothingness, no life, nothing colourful in it at all, no colour or*
> *anything like that. The darker it was, the worse it would be to me."*

Diverse though these descriptions be, they are alike in that they describe an experience where the person is entirely alone, imprisoned, and within this prison is bitterness and isolation. The other thing that these experiences have in common is that they are told in words. Each person describes his experience to himself in his own words; he tells his experience to others in words which he hopes they will understand. Whether the language is that of Hopkins or of the authors of the Present State Examination, it is the words we have to deal with, the words we have to understand.

2

LANGUAGE, CONSTRUCTS, METAPHOR AND MYTH

> *"Genetics*
> *may explain shape, size and posture, but not*
> * why one physique*
> *should be gifted to cogitate about cogitation,*
> *divorcing Form from Matter, and fated to*
> * co-habit*
> *on uneasy terms with its Image, dreading a*
> * double death,*
> *a wisher, a maker of asymmetrical objects,*
> *a linguist who is never at home in Nature's*
> * grammar."*
>
> W.H. AUDEN

Language is the element in which we live. As a fish lives in water and gasps and dies when he is lifted out of the water, so we live in language, and death, so the Psalm says, is when we "go down in silence". Our awareness of our individual self is in and through what Donne called "this dialogue of one", this awareness of a constant stream of impressions and our comments upon these impressions. Our inner dialogue mingles with and is changed by dialogues with others, and to be severed from all conversation with others is to be feared as much as being severed from food or air.

We can communicate with ourselves or with one another by images or by gesture, but such communication does not always allow the discrimination we require. We can feel fear, but to survive we need to formulate this feeling into language, to decide what we are afraid of and what we can do about it. A gesture can convey "I love you", but not "I love you but not in the way that I think you wish that I love you". Language is a necessary condition of reflection and dialogue. Sometimes we wish it were not so and feel with Simone Weil that "The mind enclosed in language is in prison. The mind which has learned to grasp thoughts which are inexpressible ... has reached a point where it is already dwelling in truth." We are aware that we consist of more than our conscious thoughts. As Rilke said, "It seems to me more and more as though our ordinary consciousness dwelt on the summit of a pyramid, whose base broadens out in us and beneath us so much that the more deeply we see ourselves able to penetrate into it the more boundlessly do we seem implicated in those factors of our earthly, and in the widest sense, *worldly* being which are independent of time and space". However, no matter how accurately these statements reflect our experience, for both Simone and Rilke, the only way in which they could clarify these insights and convey their thoughts to others was through the medium of language. We can no more leap out of language than we can leap over our own shadow.

It is through language that we assess the world around us. The scientist looks at the objects of his study and describes them in language which he may have modified for his purpose, but is a language nevertheless. Rocks and atoms can be assessed by a medium separate and different from rocks and atoms, but language can only be assessed in terms of itself. We cannot step outside language to look at it. For this reason the study of human behaviour can never function in the way that physics and chemistry function. Human beings rarely act without thought, and the best way to find out about a person is to talk to him. In the interests of scientific method the psychologist or psychiatrist may decide not to converse with the subject of his study, but he is still forced to rely on some form of communication to get the subject to act inside the experimental situation, and all the while the subject, unlike the rock or the atom, is busily assessing the experimenter and the situation and acting on his assessment. To deny this is to produce experimental results which are nonsense. Human behaviour and language are intimately bound together, and to understand behaviour we must understand language. Even if it is only our bodies that we wish to study we find, as Rilke said, "The body too is body only in the mind."

All races of human beings have language, but what Levi-Strauss called "the mystère suprème" of anthropology is, as George Steiner put it, "Why does *homo sapiens*, whose digestive tract has evolved and functions precisely the same complicated way the world over, whose biochemical fabric and genetic potential are, orthodox science assures us, essentially common, the delicate runnels of whose cortex are wholly akin in all peoples and at every stage of social evolution — why does this unified, though individually unique mammalian species not use *one* common language?"

At present there are some four or five thousand languages in use, a fraction of the number which have been spoken in the past. Linguists tell us that there has been no Darwinian evolution of languages. Dead languages, the languages of primitive tribes, rival in intellectual complexities and subtleties the dominant languages of today.

The difference between one language and another lies not just in the set of sounds that each language uses, but in the way each language divides up reality and responds to it. It is not that the Greek sound for the object in the night sky was "moon" while the Latin sound was "luna", but that the Greeks saw "the measurer" while the Latins saw "the glittering one" (Cassirer, 1953a). Stimuli which can be demonstrated to be almost identical produce different responses in different peoples. Arabic contains over five thousand words for camel. Eskimos have some two hundred names for snow. The gauchos of the Argentine have around two hundred expressions for horses' hides but they have names for no more than four plants. Verbal forms as well as noun forms vary from one language to another. In Kwakiutl the speaker is compelled to say whether a report is based on self-experience, on inference, on hearsay or whether he dreamed it (Cassirer, 1946). How such a verbal form would transform not only our newspapers but our case conferences!

These few examples from the wealth that have been collected by linguists show that we name what we find useful to observe. What we observe depends, in the first instance, on our relative size in this cosmos. "If we were not much larger than an electron," wrote Bertrand Russell (1964), "we should not have this impression of stability, which is only due to the grossness of our senses. Kings Cross, which looks to us solid, would be too vast to be conceived except by a few eccentric mathematicians. The bits of it that we could see would consist of tiny bits of matter, never coming into contact with each other, but perpetually whizzing round each other in an inconceivably rapid ballet dance .... If — to take the opposite extreme — you were as large as the sun and lived as long, with a corresponding slowness of perception, you would again find a higgledy-piggledy universe without permanence — stars and planets would come and go as morning mists, and nothing would remain to a fixed position relative to anything else."

From the size and nature that we are, we are presented with a flux of impressions which we come to see as having certain aspects of performance and stability. What these aspects are vary from one language to another. Language is not just one aspect of reality. It is language which structures reality for us.

This view of language was put forward as long ago as 1725 by Giambattista Vico in his *New Science* when he said, "Minds are formed by the character of language, not language by the minds of those who speak it." Kant considered that he had effected a revolution in philosophy similar to that which Copernicus effected in astronomy when he advanced his reasons to support his view that the external world has no absolute being but that we determine it through the mental forms by which we perceive it. The notion that language is the form by which we structure reality was used by Wilhelm von Humboldt in his comparative study of languages, a study which was much used by Ernst Cassirer in his philosophy of symbolic forms. Cassirer suggested that we should accept "what Kant calls his 'Copernican revolution'. Instead of measuring the content, meaning and truth of intellectual forms by something extraneous which is supposed to be reproduced in them, we must find in these forms themselves the measure and criterion for their truth and intrinsic meaning .... From this point of view, myth, art, language and science appear as symbols; not in the sense of mere figures which refer to some given reality by means of suggestion and allegorical renderings, but in the sense of forces each of which produces and posits a world of its own .... Thus the special symbolic forms are not imitations, but *organs* of reality, since it is solely by their agency that anything real becomes an object for intellectual apprehension and as such is made visible to us." (1953b)

It is through this organ, this instrument of language, that we gain a sense of time, of permanence and change, of past and future. From the work of Piaget and those inspired by him we have come to understand how the realization that recurrences of sets of impressions imply certain permanences in external reality coincides with the beginning of language in a young child. The child that does not acquire this awareness of sameness in flux, this "object permanence", does not acquire language. What the child learns to recognize is not identity but similarity. It is language that provides the sense of identity in similarity which allows us to find again, to recognize that "totally different, spatially and temporally separate phenomena can be understood as manifestations of one and the same subject" (Cassirer, 1953a), that daddy wearing pyjamas in bed in the morning is the same person as daddy wearing a suit in a car in the evening.

For animals everything occurs in present time. Human beings construct a past and a future out of language. "History," says Steiner, "is a speech-act, a selective use of the past tense." (This applies to personal histories as well as to the histories of nations.)

Some animals use tools, but man is the only animal that stores tools for future use. Human beings survive, Steiner contends; because they have the ability "to conceive of, to articulate possibilities beyond the treadmill of organic decay and death .... Man's sensibility endures and transcends the brevity, the haphazard ravages, the physiological programming of individual life because the semantically coded responses of the mind are constantly broader, freer, more inventive than the demands and stimulus of material fact .... Through un-truth, through counter-factuality, man 'violates' an absurd and confining reality; and his ability to do so is at every point artistic, creative. We secrete from within ourselves the grammar, the mythologies of hope, of fantasy, of self-deception without which we would have been arrested at some rung of primate behaviour or would, long since, have destroyed ourselves. It is our syntax, not the physiology of the body or the thermodynamics of the planetary system which is full of tomorrows."

Language is learned through activity and language constantly determines and modifies activity. Distinctions between actions and language are difficult to draw. When we say, "He does not know the meaning of truth," we are commenting at the one time on a man's knowledge of the language, his behaviour and his morality. How indeed do we tell the dancer from the dance?

The statement that "He does not know the meaning of truth" does not have the same implication as the statement "He does not know the meaning of 'teleological' ". The latter statement is a comment on the man's knowledge of a shared public language. The former statement implies that this man's use of the word "truth" differs from generally accepted social usage. He has given "truth" a personal meaning, an idiosyncratic reference. This store of idiosyncratic words and meanings the linguists call an "idiolect". (Similarly, Saussure's "parole" and Chomsky's "linguistic performance".) We all operate inside our idiolects and declare, like Humpty Dumpty, "When I use a word it means just what I choose it to mean — neither more nor less." To understand another person we must come to understand that person's idiolect, which has developed not just from the effects of his actions on his external reality but also from the activity of his inner reality, his imagination. In his study of that master of the imagination, Coleridge, I.A. Richards wrote,

"Because all objects which we can name or otherwise single out — the simplest objects of the senses and the most recondite entities that speculation

14

> *can conjecture, the most abstract constructions of the intellect and the most concrete aims of passion alike — are projections of man's interests; because the Universe as it is known to us is a fabric whose forms, as we alone can know them, have arisen through reflection; and because that reflection, whether made by the intellect in science or by 'the whole soul of man' in poetry, has developed through language — and apart from language, can neither be contained nor maintained — the study of the modes of language becomes, as it attempts to be thorough, the most fundamental and extensive of all inquiries. It is no preliminary or preparation for profounder studies, which though they use language more or less trustfully, may be supposed to be autonomous, uninfluenced by verbal processes. The very formation of the objects which these studies propose to examine takes place through the processes (of which imagination and fantasy are modes) by which the words they use acquire their meanings."*

Thus, if we want to understand the phenomenon which we call depression we must look at the language which we use to select and to describe this phenomenon. The study of language is large and complex, so here we shall examine just three modes of language.

Constructs

> *"It is not the things in themselves which trouble us, but the opinions we have about these things."*
>
> EPICTETUS

Psychologists often play games with their students in order to demonstrate some principle. One game favoured by psychologists who are interested in construct theory is "Three Objects". Here the psychologist asks the student to name three objects, such as three cars or three kinds of food. Let us suppose the student names three cars, for instance, a Rolls-Royce, a Lamborghini Countach and a Ford Popular. Then the psychologist asks the student to tell him one way in which two of these are the same and the other one different. The student could reply in a number of ways. He could say that two are fast and one is slow. or two are elegant and one ordinary, or, two are expensive and one cheap, or two are British and one foreign.

Suppose the student replies that two are fast and one slow. Then the psychologist asks, "Which would you prefer, the fast or the slow?"

Suppose the student replies, "The fast." Then the psychologist asks, "Why is it important for you to have the fast one?"

"Because," the student might reply, "I like driving fast. I feel really alive when I'm driving fast."

"Why," the psychologist will then ask, "is it important to feel really alive?"

"Because I want to make the most of my life while I'm here to enjoy it," says the student, thereby defining an aspect of his philosophy of life.

Another student, choosing the "fast–slow" attributes, might prefer the slow, and when the psychologist asks him why it was important for him to have the slow one he replies, "Because it is safer."

"Why is it important to be safe?" asks the psychologist.

"Because I don't want to die," replies the student.

By asking two simple questions, "Which do you prefer?" and "Why is your preference important to you?", the psychologist reveals some of the general and basic principles by which individuals manage their lives. The student who prefers the elegant car may desire to maintain his individuality, while the student who prefers the ordinary car may want the security of being like everyone else. The student who prefers the expensive car may want a reliable car so that he can be reliable, meet his obligations and so earn the respect of others. The student who prefers the cheap car may stress the necessity of living within one's means and the fear of being disliked as a spendthrift. The student who prefers the British car may stress the safety of belonging to a familiar group, while the student who prefers a foreign car may find safety in reliability or in international cooperation.

Some students find this a painful game to play because to answer the questions they have to formulate statements about their deepest hopes and fears, matters which we do not find easy to talk about to others or sometimes, even, to ourselves. It becomes apparent that the division we habitually make between cognition and affect, intellect and emotion, words and feelings, does not accurately reflect what we experience. Our language structure and our feelings, our emotions, are inextricably bound together. In our search for understanding we can try to look at language and feeling separately, but we need to remember that this is an artificial separation. When we think or say things like "I prefer an expensive car" or "My parents are coming with us on holiday" our statements are accompanied by feelings.

This game illustrates two general concepts about the constructs we use. First, that when two people look at an object they do not necessarily see the same thing, since that object can possess different attributes for each, or where both see the same attributes such attributes may have different values for each. As Blake said, "The tree which moves some to tears of joy is in the eyes of others only a green thing which stands in the way. As a man is, so he sees."

The words which people use to define the attributes of things psychologists call constructs. We use constructs in assessing every aspect of our life, our assessment of objects, people, situations, states of feeling, activities, fantasies, religion, art, science, everything which falls within the realm of language.

Through language we impose forms, structure, on the amorphous mass of sensations that impinge upon us. One form we impose is that of naming, of isolating a set of sensations and giving this set a name, "car", "mountain", "Mary", "anger", "sleeping", "hoping", "going to the shop". We assess these sets of sensations by using constructs. Assessment is the process of evaluating, of making value judgments. That personal language which each of us speaks, our idiolect, is also our morality. We hope that others share our morality as well as our language, but when we find someone who does not we might exclaim, "He does not know the meaning of truth!"

"A morality," said Michael Oakeshott, "is neither a system of general principles nor a code of rules, but a vernacular language .... What has to be learned in moral education is not a theorem such that good conduct is acting fairly or being charitable, nor is it a rule such as 'always tell the truth', but how to speak the language intelligently." A burglar, being interviewed on television, said that, "They say about people getting upset about getting burgled. Half of them ask for it, because they leave doors unlocked and windows open. And they leave those screw locks in windows, they leave the keys in locks, they just leave it there for you to do." (James, 1976) Obviously he had not learned to speak the language intelligently, or at least so those he burgled would think.

We may see expensive cars as good because they are reliable and it is good to be reliable. Or we can see them as bad because expensive cars are extravagant and it is bad to be extravagant. A husband who uses the language "expensive is good" and the wife who uses the language "expensive is bad" will have a breakdown in their communication when the attempt to discuss the purchase of a new car.

The second general concept about constructs concerns the way in which we use our constructs to predict future events. When our experience has taught us to formulate certain constructs, "That expensive car is reliable", "Mother was angry when I was late home from school", we expect that these constructs will apply in the future, "Expensive cars are reliable", "Mother is expecting us for lunch. She will be angry if we are late". To predict we often widen the context to which we apply our constructs, "The more expensive a thing is the more reliable it is", "People whom I love will get angry with me if I don't do what they want". Since some of the constructs we learned in childhood continue to be true throughout our life ("Fire burns", "I must be careful crossing the road") we may expect that all these constructs remain true when in fact they do not. Not all expensive things are reliable. Mothers who demand that their young children arrive home promptly become capable of accepting that their adult children and their families will be late for Sunday lunch. Often we go on using certain constructs to predict without checking whether they are an accurate statement of our reality because we have built them into our system and to change them would mean changing our whole way of living. "I work hard and make a lot of money so that I can surround myself with expensive things. That way I feel secure." "I must *never* do anything to anger the people I love and whom I want to love me."

This system we construct for ourselves and by which we structure and predict our reality Benjamin Lee Whorf called a "thought world", "the microcosm that each man carries within himself by which he measures and understands the macrocosm". Of recent years psychologists, especially in England, have become interested in an approach to these microcosms developed by George Kelly, who was in a philosophical line from Dewey, C.S. Pierce and Kant. This study of microcosms, personal construct theory, offers a way of understanding behaviour using the person's own constructs (Bannister, 1970), while the technique of the repertory grid can delight the hearts of those psychologists who love statistics and computers (Slater, 1976).

One of the problems that arise from the use of computers and statistics is that, since these are techniques which summarize data, the summary is sometimes taken to be a complete picture of what it represents. Thus constructs are sometimes conceived as being no more than single words or, at most, phrases, and the construct system consisting of a set of relationships among words. What is forgotten is that linguistic meaning is found, not in words, but in sentences. It is not that "expensive" implies "reliable", but that "This car is expensive" implies "This car is reliable". "Names," said Wittgenstein, "are points, propositions like arrows — they have sense". That is, propositions have direction, they point and relate. A name can relate to reality only by naming something, by being a significant symbol. If it is not a symbol for something then it is just a sound. But a proposition has sense; we know what would be the case if it were true and if it were false. "Every proposition," said Wittgenstein, "is essentially true–false."

Wilheim von Humboldt had observed what Steiner called "this distinctive binary character of the linguistic process; it shares, it mediates between, the crucial antimonies of inner and outer, subjective and objective, past and future, private and public. Language is far more than communication between speakers. It is a dynamic mediation between those poles of cognition which give human experience its underlying dual and dialectical form. Here Humboldt clearly anticipates both C.K.Ogden's theory of opposition and the binary structuralism of Levi-Strauss." But, of course, all of these people had been anticipated by Lao Tsu who, two thousand years ago, wrote

"Under heaven all can see beauty as beauty because there is ugliness,
All can know good as good only because there is evil.

Therefore having and not having arise together.
Difficult and easy complement each other,
Long and short contrast each other,
High and low rest upon each other,
Voice and sound harmonize each other,
Front and back follow each other."

Whenever we know a proposition, "I love my family", we know its opposite, "I don't love my family", and both are part of our language system.

The computer is equipped to deal with information in binary form, provided our propositions are clearly stated, our constructs clearly defined. But much of our construct system is not like this. Kant once wrote, "However high we may place our concepts and much as we may abstract them from the sensuous world, still images adhere to them .... For how should we give meaning and signification to our concepts if some intuition ... did not underlie them?"

What are these images and intuitions that underlie our clear and literal language?

Metaphor

"When a man is dutifully deceiving himself he
will often admit the truth in his metaphors."

WILLIAM EMPSON

When we make a statement which we hope says exactly what we mean it to say, no more and no less, with no ambiguity, we make what is called a literal statement. "The colour of the moon is silver," we can say, "and the colour of the sun is gold." But sometimes a literal statement cannot manage to carry the meaning we wish to convey, and we must use figurative or metaphorical language, as did Yeats when he said he would,

> *"pluck till time and times are done,*
> *The silver apples of the moon,*
> *The golden apples of the sun."*

"Metaphor" comes from the Greek word *metaphora*, which is made up of *meta* meaning "over" and *pherin*, "to carry". In a metaphor meaning is carried over from one idea to another.

It is extraordinarily difficult to use language in a purely literal way. Scientists try to do this, but even they, perhaps unwittingly, have to resort to metaphors. In the Present State Examination the authors speak of a "physical handicap" and so use a meaning carried-over from "cap in hand", a mediaeval lottery game in which the winners were penalized. They define "worrying" as "a round of painful, unpleasant or uncomfortable thought ... out of proportion to the subject worried about", and so with "round" and "proportion" they build their definition on a spatial metaphor. But when they come to define the degrees of depression, their language is not so much literal as poetic. "The deepest depression," they say, "may be a frozen misery which is beyond tears." (Wing *et al.*, 1974)

According to Max Black, any part of speech, nouns, verbs, adjectives, adverbs, pronouns, even conjunctions, can be used metaphorically and any form of verbal expression can contain what he called "a metaphorical focus". This metaphorical focus causes one word to act upon another so that both change their meaning. Thus the word "frozen" and the word "misery" change when they come together in "frozen misery".

There are many ways that misery can be experienced and can be observed in others, so to observe the misery of "deepest depression" accurately and to name it a word must be found which already has a meaning some aspect of which can be carried over to naming this observation. Rilke once said that seeing a thing truly means naming it, and naming it means making a connection, finding an analogy between the object and something within the mind. Foucault wrote, "To look for the meaning of something is to discover what it resembles." (The poet and the scientist have no choice but to use the tool of language in the same way.) The process of creating a metaphor is one of analysis and synthesis, of analysing the new observation and of synthesizing elements of this analysis with images of certain past experience to create a new whole, a new image. The process of creating a metaphor need not be, in fact rarely is, a fully conscious one, mainly because the process can operate so quickly, but sometimes because the metaphor is drawn from a past experience which the person prefers to forget. Since a metaphor moves from the known to the new and since, as small children, we came to know of our bodies before we learnt of a world outside our immediate experience, many of our metaphors relate to our bodies. The anthropologist Mary Douglas has argued that our organic system provides us with an analogy for the social system. Experience of one's body provides individual, private metaphors as well as shared, public ones, as the psychoanalysts have shown.

It is from the metaphors which we create that we develop our idiolect, our individual language. By metaphor we can name experiences for which there is no adequate name available in the public, shared language. By metaphor we can name and describe those inner experiences that no one else can share. Everyone who has experienced depression has a metaphor for that experience, sometimes expressed only in one's private language, sometimes in the language that one shares with another, as Winston Churchill used his metaphor of the black dog to let his wife know into what state he had been plunged.

By metaphor we create our world anew. According to T.S. Eliot, "When a poet's mind is perfectly equipped for his work, it is consistently amalgamating disparate experiences; the ordinary man's experience is chaotic, irregular, fragmentary. The latter falls in love, or reads Spinoza, and these two experiences have nothing to do with each other, or with the noise of the typewriter or the smell of cooking; in the mind of the poet these experiences are already forming new wholes." (1932) Eliot would have been more accurate if he had said that the poet is better than the ordinary person in creating new metaphors rather than that the ordinary person does not create them at all. We are all born poets, but most of us are soon taught to keep our images to ourselves and perhaps even to become ashamed of this ability to create these metaphors. In the interests of society many of us give up being individuals, being poets. Eliot described this more accurately in his poem *The Love Song of J. Alfred Prufrock*,

> *"We have lingered in the chambers of the sea*
> *By sea-girls wreathed with seaweed red and brown*
> *Till human voices wake us, and we drown."*

Even those of us who are, like Prufrock, drowned poets, can remember in our childhood how every aspect of our lives had a vitality, a significance that went deeper than the objective meaning of tables and chairs and cats and dogs. Such things became people to us. Even the letters of the alphabet had a reality far beyond their shapes on the page. Rimbaud remembered this when he wrote,

> *"You vowels, A the black, E white, green U, blue O,*
> *Some day I will reveal your hidden identities."*

As we grow older those inanimate objects which were of importance in our lives still seem to possess personalities. Recently, an old man who, when young, had helped to build the "Titanic" was asked in a television interview how he had felt when he heard of the loss of that ship. "It was," he said, "like a death in the family." Hard-headed scientists give their computers human names and may even be drawn into serious discussions of the now popular myth that computers may one day take over the world. Through metaphor we change reality from something which is supremely indifferent to our existence into something which is human like ourselves.

Metaphor at one and the same time oversimplifies and extends meaning. It oversimplifies in that it discards the detail that it finds irrelevant. When we use the metaphor "the leg of a table" we have discarded the details that legs commonly move and are made of animal tissue, but we have extended the meaning by implying that the leg of the table is not just a piece of wood or metal but supports something and can be expected to be found standing and not flying. Like constructs, metaphors contain implications and predictions, and we sometimes act on the implications and predictions of our metaphor without realizing that we are doing so. The belief that senna-pod tea drives impurities from the body can metamorphose into the belief that ECT drives out impure thoughts from the mind. Metaphors like "the leg of a table", "the face of a clock", have been used so many times that they appear to be inert, to have lost the wealth of associations that the newly coined metaphor possesses, but even they still rest on assumptions and imply predictions. The depressed person who is told to "pull yourself together" hears in this metaphor the implication that he has disintegrated and that he is expected to do something impossible, to repair himself, like a broken plate to stick itself together again. The metaphor "pull yourself together" contains the notion of a human will which stands outside reality but can still influence it. If the broken plate had a will of its own it could repair itself. When we are committed to a particular metaphor we think that anything that does not fit the metaphor cannot be true. If we believe that the metaphor of the human will is a true picture of reality then, when the person we have advised to use his will says that he cannot do this, we think that he is lying or being wilfully obstructive. That he does not share our metaphor may not occur to us. Similarly, those psychiatrists who are committed to the metaphor of the "medical model" to explain depression and the like regard data which do not fit the medical model as simply untrue. We imprison ourselves by regarding our metaphors as absolute realities instead of relative descriptions.

Much of the discord both in science and in ordinary interactions comes from different metaphors being used by different people. In the Middle Ages the world was explained by the metaphor that the world was a book written by God. Galileo tried only to extend this metaphor, to say that the "book of nature" is written in mathematical language and can be read only through mathematical cyphers, but he was punished for this. Jung described the metaphor of the communist state as "the time-hallowed archetypal dream of a Golden Age, where everything is provided in abundance for everyone, and a great, just and wise chief rules over a human kindergarten". Those people who accept this metaphor as reality would find it hard to understand those people who do not conceive of the worthwhile life as being part of a human kindergarten. Many of us, when we view another nation, simply do not understand the metaphors by which that nation is understood by its inhabitants. In the same way, we find Elizabethan poetry obscure because we do not understand the elaborate metaphor of "The Chain of Being" by which the Elizabethans explained their world to themselves.

A metaphor requires a response, an act of completion from the listener. To communicate successfully we need a common background of metaphor. Where this does not exist serious misunderstandings will arise. When Cheadle and Morgan wondered, "Does the chronic psychiatric patient understand plain English?" they came to the conclusion that he does not. They asked a group of ninety patients the meaning of a number of metaphorical phrases commonly used by the staff in talking with the patients and found that, "When told, 'You want it served up on a plate,' 28 patients knew what this meant, 62 did not, and of those 62, 39 thought it meant 'nicely cooked' ". Other most popular wrong answers were "get you in a photograph" in answer to "put you in the picture", "a bookmark" in answer to "a turnup for the book", "go skating" in answer to "break the ice", and "sharpen your sense of smell" in answer to "keep your nose to the grindstone". The authors commented that, "When a patient does not take advice, we often put it down to some manifestation of his illness. The fact that he may not understand our perfectly good, plain English is worthy of consideration."

It is not only the chronic patient who does not always understand the "good, plain English" of the doctor and nurse, and sometimes the doctor and nurse do not understand the "good, plain English" of the patient. If we are to understand another person we must come to understand his metaphors. The important metaphors by which we order our lives comprise more than just a phrase or so. It was Vico who said that, "Every metaphor so formed is fable in brief." A fable or a myth.

Myth

"human kind
Cannot bear very much reality."

T.S. ELIOT

A myth is a story which has been created not just to entertain but to explain, to give an answer to what Rilke called that "great dynasty of questions" which present themselves to every human being, since human beings do not simply live but reflect upon their living. "Who am I?" we ask, "How was I created? What will happen to me when I die? How was the world created? Is there a reason for my existence?" All these questions and more are part of the one question, as framed by Rilke, "How is it possible to live when the fundamentals of this our life are so completely incomprehensible?"

To those parts of our experience which we feel we can comprehend and, through our comprehension, in some way control or, at least, predict we apply our reason, our logical and scientific thought. To those parts of our experience which are beyond our comprehension, yet we must in some way explain if we are to overcome our terror, we apply our myth-making ability.

Our early ancestors, like present-day primitive tribesmen, were not devoid of reasoning ability. They thought logically about many matters, in creating tools, providing food, organizing their community. Where reason could frame no answers they created myths. The progress of science is simply the extension of those areas of experience where we can feel less frightened, where we can look at certain matters as being amenable to logic and reason. We no longer need to explain changes in the weather in terms of the desires and emotions of our gods nor our health in terms of bodily humours. Nevertheless, all our powers of reason cannot supply a proven true answer to Rilke's question. The fundamentals of our life are still completely incomprehensible, and like ancient and primitive man we create myths to explain, predict and comfort.

The distinction between mythical and scientific thinking is easier to draw in theory than to observe in practice. The object of myth, as of science, is to explain the world and to make its phenomena intelligible. Because we can never know reality directly, but only the structures we make, we can only create myths about the ultimate nature of reality. (Bertrand Russell described us as musicians who were born deaf, who have constructed a musical notation, which we can manipulate in a variety of ways according to the rules which we devise, to create a musical score which we hope relates to the music, but as we cannot hear we cannot know how the music actually sounds. It may be sublime; it may be chaos (1964).) Thus science itself is built on myth, on unprovable guesses about the nature of reality.

Science and myth are alike in that both have a faith in the order and unity of nature. As Frazer said in *The Golden Bough*, "The magician does not doubt that the same cause produces the same effects." Through our ability to see what we expect to see, we often see a pattern which we think we have observed objectively and deduced logically when in fact we have observed and deduced in terms of our myth. History books and clinical case histories furnish many examples of this. Again, while we can distinguish mythical thinking as being concerned with only the beginning and end of a process and reason as seeking out all the intervening steps (comparing, for instance, the first book of Genesis with the science of geology), in our hurry to obtain a satisfying explanation we are often blind to possible intervening steps and alternative explanations.

To use our reason, to think logically, scientifically, we try to be objective, that is, to stand aside from what we are considering and to see it as separate from our own needs, hopes and fears. In mythical thinking we view an object in terms of ourselves, how it meets our needs, fulfills our hopes, dispels or inspires our fears. In myth man is the centre of the universe, the sun, the planets and the stars revolve around the earth and man is created in God's likeness. As Copernicus, Kepler and Darwin found, science is the enemy when it decreases our significance and increases our fears. Myth, in itself, is invulnerable, since it is impervious to rational arguments and cannot be refuted by syllogisms. It is vulnerable only when it is recognized as myth.

The processes of rational thought have been the object of much study. Cassirer is one of the few philosophers who was concerned with the processes of mythical thinking, which he regarded as one of the organs or tools by which we create a structure "from the ever-flowing, ever uniform stream of impressions which strike our senses or arise from the autonomous processes of the mind" (1953a). Cassirer drew on the work of Usener, whose study of mythical ideas showed that "such ideas, no matter how manifold, how varied, how heterogeneous they may appear at first sight, have their own inner lawfulness; they do not arise from a boundless caprice of the imagination, but move in definite avenues of feeling and thought"

(1953a). Usener described how early man created "momentary gods" when some object became of sudden and immense importance to him, such as a tree he climbed when pursued or a spring of water which suddenly flowed from a barren field. In such an experience the tree or the spring is no longer part of ordinary reality; it takes on a significance which is derived from the man's inner world. This way of perceiving objects the psychoanalysts call "projection", when the person projects part of his inner world on to an object outside himself and then acts as if what was part of himself actually belongs to the object. Cassirer gave a marvellous description of the moment when such a projection occurs. "It is," he wrote, "as though the whole world were simply annihilated; the immediate content, whatever it be, that commands his religious interest, so completely fills his consciousness that nothing else can exist beside and apart from it. The ego is spending all its energy on this single object, lives in it, losed itself in it. Instead of a widening of intuitive experience, we find here its extreme limitation; instead of expansion that would lead through greater and greater spheres of being, we have here an impulse toward concentration; instead of extensive distribution, intensive compression. This focusing of all forces on a single point is the prequisite for all mythical thinking and mythical formulation. When, on the one hand, the entire self is given up to a single impression, is 'possessed' by it and, on the other hand, there is the utmost tension between the subject and its object, the outer world; when external reality is not merely viewed and contemplated, but overcomes a man in sheer immediacy, with emotions of fear and hope, terror or wish fulfilment: then the spark jumps somehow across, the tension finds release, as the subjective excitement becomes objectified, and confronts the mind as god or daemon." (1953b)

It is not just god or daemon that is created in this way. "As soon as the spark has jumped across, as soon as the tension and emotion of the moment has found its discharge in the word or the mythical image, a sort of turning point has occurred in human mentality: the inner excitement which was a mere subjective state has vanished, and has been resolved into the objective form of myth and speech."

This is what happens when a person suddenly falls in love. Then, one realizes in a flash of inspiration that another person is no longer just an ordinary human being but is the repository of all one's hopes and dreams, and so exerts the power and fascination of a god or daemon. With the realization "I am in love", the object then becomes part of those private fantasies that one has been building all one's life, fantasies that relate to private, individual hopes and fears and to the public myths that one has learned — myths like Prince Charming, Sleeping Beauty, "love makes the world go round", "happily ever after", and so on.

We forget how frequently this experience of projection and myth-making occurred when we were small children, but we can observe how children have favourite fairy stories and how readily they see animals and objects as people like themselves. Falling in love is usually a glorious experience and the myths we create from it are usually glorious too. (Sadness comes when the promise of the myth is not fulfilled.) Children who are happy project happy aspects of themselves on to the world and so create happy myths. It is the child who is frightened and insecure who lives in a world of dangerous giants and evil witches. Traditional fairy stories remain popular because they give assurance that the small, weak, and unloved child will survive and triumph — Cinderella will become a loved princess and Jack will defeat the giant.

A favourite fairy story can become the plot of the story which a child believes will be his life story. Many young girls expect that one day Prince Charming will come and they will fall in love and live happily ever after. Some boys are equally bound to a myth of one true love. Others have sworn to be Jack the Giant killer, to defeat daddy and all giants like him. That form of therapy called Transactional Analysis calls this myth "a script", and people who enter into Transactional Analysis are usually shocked to discover that they were living their lives according to a script which they had created when they were young. Sometimes the realization that one is living a particular myth is sufficient to free one from it.

The myth we construct to live our lives by contains an account of what we expect death will mean to us. Birth and death are the main subjects of myth. Some myths try to overcome the fear of personal annihilation by describing some kind of eternal life, but then, as Wittgenstein said, "Is some riddle solved by my surviving for ever? Is not this eternal life as much of a riddle as our present life?" If we see death as a mere doorway to another life, we then have the problem of leading a life on this earth which meets the requirements of the next. If we see death as the end, with no afterlife, we then have the problem of obtaining adequate happiness and satisfaction in this life.

The ancient Greek philosopher Xenophanes commented that the Ethiopians made their gods black and snub-nosed while the Thracians gave them blue eyes and red hair. People have not ceased to create their gods in their own image. When we believe in God, whether the God of the Roman Catholic Church or the Church of England, whether we call him Allah or Jehovah, we, as individuals, invest Him with those personal qualities we most value. But personal qualities, like everything else in this world, are always a mixed blessing. If we see in our God the power and authority to protect us, He may use that power and authority against us. If we see His goodness and love, then we may not deserve to share this goodness and love. If He is all-seeing, then there is nothing we can do that is not observed. If He is omniscient and benevolent, then why is life so full of suffering? If one must suffer to be saved, how much suffering is enough?

We create myths to give ourselves an explanation that satisfies, but once we apply our reason to our myths our satisfaction is dispelled. We preserve our myths by thinking in a magical way about anything that touches on them. In myth emotion is turned into an image, but the image in not known as an image. We regard these images not as symbols but as realities which cannot be rejected or criticized.

In magical thinking nothing happens by accident and the person relates everything that happens to himself. The child feels that the spark from the fire deliberately burnt him and the moon shines to give him company at night. The grandiosity of magical thinking is seen in the adult who declares, "I am responsible for my family's happiness." That a person is responsible for his own happiness and that much that happens in this world is beyond our control are facts which conflict with this kind of magical thinking.

In magical thought there is no clear distinction between a word and what it means. We are forbidden to address certain people directly by their names but must use titles, else something terrible will happen. While the taboos on names and on those words we call swear words have been removed or modified of recent years, we still, in a magical way, give power to those people who know the names. The person who calls a child's inability to read "dyslexia" is seen as more powerful than the parent who says, "My kid can't read." We sometimes think that an illness has been explained once it has simply been given a name. Words are powerful, but in magical thinking they take on a power far in excess of what reason would allow them.

Myth is not something that childlike, ancient or primitive people indulged in and that we have discarded. Myth is still and always will be an integral part of our life. Every time we read a newspaper or watch television we are sharing in the current myths of our society. We preserve our myths by magical thinking and we transform our myths into art. We cannot live by reason alone any more than we can live by myth alone. Myth is always part of the system by which each person structures his world.

Conclusion

"The limits of my language *mean the limits of my world.*"
WITTGENSTEIN

Each of us, through our individual language, through a system of constructs arising from reason, metaphor and myth, structures and evaluates our individual world. The world we create is a world of meaning. Everything we perceive has a meaning, even if the meaning we give something is "this thing has no meaning". The fundamental attribute of human beings is that they create meaning. Not to do so is impossible, even when we know that there is no way that we can prove the truth of the meaning that we impose. To have the capacity to impose meaning on what may be ultimately and forever meaningless is a terrible irony.

Try as we may to see our world as solid and real,

"we don't feel very securely at home in this interpreted world." (Rilke, 1968)

Day by day we may feel that the world we have constructed is secure, so secure that we have lost all awareness that it is constructed and we take it for solid reality. Then something happens, something which destroys or threatens to destroy the hopes, the satisfactions, that we have created — it may be the death or defection a loved one, or the dashing of our hopes, our reason for living, by something of which we were unaware — and suddenly our world shifts, tilts, we put out a hand to steady ourselves and there is nothing there to brace against. Gone is the solid world, and we see that we rest on a fragile raft. When we peep over the edge we see emptiness, emptiness more vast and frightening than the emptiness of the universe.

Fear clutches our hearts. Hastily we try to reconstruct our world, perhaps by denying that anything has changed and by trying to use the same materials, the same ideas, we had used in the past, or perhaps we try to find new materials, new ideas, to construct a world which will be safe against assault. But the memory of the terror remains.

Yet the cause of this terror also gives us our freedom. Because we construct our world we are free to construct it in an infinite variety of ways. We can move freely in a spacious world, or we can build ourselves a prison.

3

THE EXPERIENCE OF DEPRESSION: AN HYPOTHESIS

> *"Human beings awake to consciousness to find themselves in chaos. They then try to impose order on this chaos in order to make life endurable .... We cannot verify whether the chart that we make of the mysterious universe corresponds to elusive reality; but, in order to live, we have to make this chart, realising it is an act of faith which is also an act of self-preservation."*
>
> ARNOLD TOYNBEE

Each of us lives in our own small world, a microcosm where we are aware of what goes on inside ourselves and outside ourselves, an inner and outer reality. We organize our microcosm by means of our individual language, which is a system or structure of propositions. These propositions may be brought clearly into awareness in the process of reasoning or they may be less consciously used in the process of mythical or magical thinking. Both processes, in their use and development, rely on metaphor.

The concept of structure has been found to be very useful in a number of scientific disciplines. Piaget defined structure as "a system of transformations ... the notion of structure is comprised of three key ideas: the idea of wholeness, the idea of transformation, and the idea of self-regulation".

The idea of wholeness refers to the observation that a structure is more than the sum of its parts and that each part is subordinated to the whole. For instance, a pile of blocks is just an aggregate, but when placed in a particular pattern according to a certain rule or law they form a structure, an arch, which is a whole, a unity which is more than the sum of its parts. The idea of transformation refers to the rules or laws of the structure which brings about the changes. Transformations both structure and are structured. Each block of the arch both holds up the arch and is held up by it. The idea of self-regulation refers to the notion that the transformations in a structure maintain that structure and never go beyond it. The relationships between the blocks of an arch maintain the structure but do not go beyond it, although the arch itself can be part of another whole.

The illustration of an arch as a structure is a rather static one and perhaps does not convey the notion of movement that is contained in many structures. The notion of movement is seen clearly in the theory relating to mathematical structures or groups. In group theory what is looked at is not a property which has been abstracted from things which have that property (e.g. "intelligence" abstracted from the behaviour of a number of people) but "from our ways of *acting on things*, the operations we perform on them; perhaps, rather, from the various fundamental ways of *co-ordinating* such acts or operations — 'uniting', 'ordering', 'placing in one–one correspondence' and so on. Thus, when we analyse the concept of groups, we come upon the following very general co-ordinations among operations:

(1) the condition that a 'return to the starting point' always be possible.

(2) the condition that the same 'goal' or 'terminus' be attainable by alternative routes and without the itinerary's affecting the point of arrival." (Piaget, 1971)

Transformations within a group do not mean total change but rather a self-sameness connected with change. Thus, a lorry driver can travel from London to Leeds on the M1 or the A1 roads. He can reach his destinations by various routes (transformations) but on arrival he and his lorry are still recognizably the same. A return to the starting-point is possible.

This concept of sameness and change within a group is particularly important when we try to understand ourselves. Watzlawick, Weakland and Fisch applied this concept very wittily to problem formation and resolution in their book *Change*. However, here we are concerned with the structure of an individual's language, which itself structures that individual's world. Such a structure is more complex, more various in its outcomes than the groups of behaviour described by Watzlawick and company. To deal with the structure of an individual's language we need to incorporate in our notion of structure the idea from contemporary physics that structure is the set of *possible* states and the transformation that actually occurs is a special case. "The actual is now interpreted or explained as an instance of the possible." (Piaget, 1971) By using this concept we can account for the fact that for every proposition that we know we also know its opposite. The salmon can only swim up its river to spawn, but we can say, "I shall be home in time for tea" or "I shall not be home in time for tea".

The idea of our individual language structure as being a set of possible groups also accounts for the fact that since our individual language develops through our interaction with our environment we acquire a set of groups of transformations and outcomes which vary in their probability of use. As a small child we might have discovered that, "If I lie on the floor and scream she'll give me what I want", but, while we never forget this (or any other transformation) entirely, we learn to use it less frequently since it is not so effective with our wife or employer. Of course, such a transformation can itself be transformed into persistent nagging or aggrieved silence with the same desired result.

The total set of possible groups form that sense of sameness in flux, that sense of uniqueness, which we call "I". Since we have the ability to make infinite discriminations, we can discriminate one self or a number of selves, and see in these a wide variety of attributes and their converse. We ask the question "Who am I?" and seek the answer by finding propositions that can be applied to "I".

Change can come about in two ways. Through our interaction with our environment (physical activity, talking with others, reading books, etc.) we can modify our individual language structure by learning something new. "I can ride a bike." Or we can alter the probability of a particular transformation occurring. "I am too old to ride a bike."

Cassirer (1953a) records that "according to Humboldt, language was made possible by address and response, by a tension which arises between I and thou and which is resolved in the act of speech". Research in child development is proving Humboldt to have been right. John and Elizabeth Newson, in a paper on the origin or symbolic functioning, stress the importance of the word "intersubjectivity" which "draws attention to the general principle that human cognitive understanding arises from a process of *negotiation* between two or more human beings; and it suggests that it may not be sensible to seek the roots of those shared understandings which constitute human knowledge within the action patterns of any one individual viewed in isolation". They conclude that "the origin of symbolic functioning should be sought, not in the child's activities with inanimate objects, but rather in those idiosyncratic but shared understandings which he first evolves during his earliest social encounters with familiar human beings who are themselves steeped in human culture".

It seems, then, that the structure by which a person organizes his world originates in the baby's interaction not just with his physical environment but, more importantly, in his interaction with other people. The structure develops and changes, transforms through continued interaction with others. The child plays, imitates, talks, learns to read, observes others, thinks about others, contrasts himself with others. The whole process is one where the child is both receptive to others and reaches out to others. As he gets older, the ways in which he interacts with others change but not his desire to be in contact with others.

The interaction of human beings with one another seems to be more than just a pleasurable or useful activity. It seems to be a necessary condition of life, as necessary as eating and breathing. Loneliness is painful. Solitary confinement is torture. Reports by prisoners who have experienced long periods of solitary confinement and experiments where the subject is deprived of all sensory exchange show that the person's whole being, body and mind, is affected by this isolation. It would seem that we cannot help but be unpleasantly affected when circumstances cut us off from interaction with our fellows.

Yet none of us interact uninhibitedly with all of those around us. When we were small babies we looked at the world with uncritical interest, but we soon learned to be cautious with strangers, to be careful about what we touched, to inhibit our feelings, to withdraw, to distrust and fear others. We learned to structure our world by means of propositions which limited our interactions with others. "I keep myself to myself." "It's no use talking to my father. He never understands." "The people in my village are so nosey, I never talk to them except to say good-day."

These kinds of propositions are like bricks in the wall that each person builds around him. Some people build low walls, or walls with special gaps, and they can reach others easily across these walls. But some of us build walls which are high and difficult to climb, and when we make these walls too high, quite impassable, then we start to suffer a torture which is even worse than that suffered by the solitary prisoner facing an indeterminate sentence.

In my discussions with people who have experienced the torture of depression it has become clear that each of them has built such a wall. Or, to return to the concept of the structure by which we each organize our world, the person who experiences depression has in his language structure a group of propositions each of which concerns a way in which he separates himself from other people. For each of these propositions he knows its opposite. To take a simple example, a man's language structure may include "I love my wife/I don't love my wife", "I trust my boss/I don't trust my boss", "I forgive my father/I don't forgive my father", "Other people like me/Other people don't like me". On those occasions when he operates on the group of propositions "I love my wife. I trust my boss. I forgive my father. Other people like me" he feels comfortable in himself and interacts easily with others. On those occasions when he operates on the group of propositions "I love my wife. I don't trust my boss. I shall never forgive my father. Other people like me" he can interact easily with his wife and friends, but he has a barrier between himself and his boss and father. But on those occasions when he operates on the group of propositions "I don't love my wife. I don't trust my boss. I shall never forgive my father. Other people don't like me" he has surrounded himself with a wall and cut himself off from all important interaction with others. In such a state he cannot be happy.

In referring to a particular language structure as the building of a wall around oneself I am not merely using a metaphor to describe an abstract concept. While different people describe their experience of depression in different ways, there is one feature that all share. Each person describes the experience as one of being enclosed. Some say it is like being in a dark prison cell, some say it is like being at the bottom of a deep hole, some say it is like being wrapped in an impenetrable cloth, some say it is like being unable to move in the middle of a vast and empty desert, some say it is like being enclosed by thick, soundproofed glass. The images vary, but the underlying concept is the same. The person is in solitary confinement. And as the days pass, the torture grows worse.

Depression is that experience which accompanies the selection from the set of possible states of a person's language structure that particular state or system of propositions whereby the person sees himself as being cut off from and as choosing to be cut off from interaction with others, both people in his external reality (e.g. wife, friends) and figures in his internal reality (e.g. his God, happy memories of his dead mother, his good self, his successful future). It is likely that such a state will always be accompanied by physiological changes which increase in their profundity the longer the person operates with this particular structure of propositions.

A person can operate with very little active awareness of his own language system (he can assume that all right-thinking people think the same as he and that those who do not are either mad or bad). What awareness a person has of his own language system is what we call insight, while the awareness we have of another's language system we call understanding or empathy. As every psychotherapist knows, insight and understanding, though excellent things in themselves, are often not enough to help a person change. This resistance to change in a person who is suffering and who is asking for help is puzzling until we consider his predicament in terms of his language system.

As we have noted, for every proposition contained in a language system its opposite is also present. While a person may wish to change a particular proposition he may be reluctant to change the opposite of his proposition and its implications. Proust suffered greatly from an illness which he recognized as being psychosomatic, but he would not relinquish those aspects of himself which gave him pain since, as he wrote, "It is among those who belong to the magnificent, the lamentable family of neurotics that we find the salt of the earth. They it is, and not others, who have founded religions and achieved masterpieces. The world will never know how much it owes to them, nor yet what they have suffered in the act of giving". (1962) When it was suggested to Rilke that he should enter into psychoanalysis to help him gain peace of mind he decided to struggle on alone, since "if my devils were driven out my angels would receive a slight, a very slight (shall we say) shock, and, you see, I cannot let it come to that pass at any price". We all prefer to keep our devils than risk losing our angels.

We try to deflect from us anything that would compel us to change our language system and so our lives because we are afraid of the unknown. Whenever we glimpse the possibilities of a world which we ourselves structure or the possibilities within ourselves, often only seen in the extremes of emotion, we draw back from an unknown which we see as chaos (or the madness which the depressed person fears). We can risk change when we have some understanding of this chaos. Rilke wrote of this, "Our conflicts have always been part of our riches, and when we are terrified of their violence we are only terrified of the unsuspected possibilities and tensions of our own strength; and chaos, if we can but win a little detachment from it, instantly evokes in us the foreknowledge of new orders and, in so far as our courage can have any share in such prefiguration, the curiosity and desire to accomplish that still inscrutable future order."

Change in our construct system comes through our interaction with others, sometimes in the action of work and play together; sometimes the interaction is through something another person has produced, books, newspapers, pictures, films, music, sculpture, scientific discoveries, technological creations. In every area where we work and play, we change and develop, acquire knowledge by discussion. A scientist or an artist may advance the sum of human knowledge and experience by work which he does on his own, but he prepares for that work through discussion with others and the significance of his work becomes effective when he tells others of it.

The seeking of knowledge through question and answer is sometimes called the Socratic method of dialectic. Socrates considered that the only way that human nature could be known and understood was through dialectic and that the value of life lay in man's ability to scrutinize the conditions of his existence. "The unexamined life," said Socrates, "is not worth living."

This book contains studies of nine people who at least at one time in their lives thought that life was not worth living but who nevertheless spent many hours with me examining their lives and mine. These people spent some time in the wards or in the outpatient department of a large, old psychiatric hospital which was typical of the kind that lies on the outskirts of each English city.

When I first became interested in the question of why certain people became depressed I also began working with what was then a new technique for answering questions, the repertory grid. This technique is now used by psychologists in a wide variety of ways. I have used it to look at how an individual sees himself and his relationships with others. I would begin by asking the person to draw up a list of the people who played or had played an important part in his life. This list would include himself and his ideal self, the person he would like to be. (The "important people" were not necessarily real people. Here Joe included his pets in his list; Helen included disparate aspects of herself.) Then I would ask the person, in his own words, to describe himself and the people in his list. From this I drew up a list of personal constructs. I would then take each construct in turn and ask the person to rate on this construct, using a seven point-scale, each of the people in his list. Working systematically, we would construct a grid of numbers. Figure 1 shows part of Mary's grid. A computer analysis of this grid would then show the relationship between the ideas in the grid. Figure 2 shows how such ideas can be set out in a graph.

Shortly after I had begun to work with grids I met a woman whose depression had not responded to many years of excellent psychiatric treatment. On her grid she showed that she divided her world into good and bad people. She placed herself and

Figure 1. Part of Mary's repertory grid

	SELF	IDEAL SELF	MOTHER	FATHER	SISTER
Happy	1	7	2	5	6
Self-conscious	7	4	6	1	1
Bothers about people	7	4	6	1	1
Careful with money	7	4	6	1	1
Depressed	7	1	6	1	1
Does things right	1	7	4	4	5
Pig-headed	5	2	1	6	4

Figure 2.   Graph of the analysis of Mary's first grid

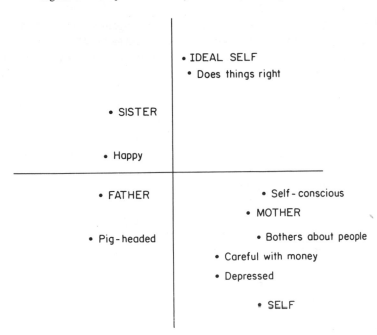

the people she loved among the good people, and all would have been fine except for one thing. The good people were "poorly"; and the bad people were well. So all attempts by psychiatrists to make her well were also, for her, attempts to make her into a bad person, to make her different from those she loved. It was no wonder that she remained depressed (Rowe, 1971).

As my work progressed I became increasingly aware of how limited and artificial the grid technique was in seeking answers to the questions I was asking. I came to see it as useful only as a signpost, pointing the way to further exploration (Rowe, 1976). I looked for the implications of the constructs the person had given me and so began to understand how one construct has both good and bad implications, how the presence of one construct implies the presence of its opposite, how constructs exist, not merely in clear, logical language but in metaphor, image and myth. They cannot always be captured in repertory grids but they can be glimpsed in conversation.

So, we put our conversations on tape and my research assistant transcribed these into what amounted to many hundreds of pages of typescript. Much had to be omitted, but as far as possible the accounts given here are in the words of the actual discussion. I have not set out to describe each person in the way a novelist describes a character or in the way a psychologist writes a report of his assessment of a person. This is actual conversation, and so it lacks both the dramatic succinctness of a play or novel and the objective brevity of a scientific report. Melvyn Bragg, when he presented the accounts of their lives given by people of Wigton, suggested that his readers should "adopt a 'hearing mode' when reading". This advice would apply here.

I have selected from the transcription of the taped conversations those portions which state or imply those propositions which serve to isolate the person. My part in the dialogue was usually to ask questions in order to make clear to myself what the person was saying. I would sometimes put forward my own propositions in order to improve our mutual understanding and to show that there are always alternative ways of viewing a situation. As there is no visual record of our conversations, the account given here does not include the expressions and gestures by which we communicated and which were often the reason for what we said to one another. Our talks were filled with misery, anger, fear, bitterness, affection and laughter. I hope the record of what was said conveys some of this feeling. Each person read and commented upon the first draft of his own chapter.

In Chapter 13 I have listed for each person the group of propositions which served to isolate that person. The propositions in each set were linked to one another in various and often subtle ways. It took months for me to acquaint myself with all of these propositions and I never felt that the list was complete. Nevertheless, each person's set of propositions formed a closed group which, no matter what path one followed in the discussion, had only one outcome, "I am isolated and depressed". When each person became able to change certain propositions, his group of propositions changed in its composition and outcome.

PART 2

The People

4

JOAN

"Seek the way of martyrdom, make yourself
   the lowest
On earth, to be high in heaven.
And see far off below you, where the gulf is
   fixed,
Your persecutors, in timeless torment,
Parched passion beyond expiation."
                                    T.S. ELIOT

A nurse had written in Joan's notes, "She has a nice home, happy and healthy husband and children and she can't see any point in living further."

Joan had been in the care of a psychiatrist for some six years when he wrote to me to ask me to see her. He said, "She cannot say clearly what her problem is. She is not a good talker but she has got to know me over the years and I do not think she is frightened of discussing her life with me. I wondered if a repertory grid would help to throw light on any sources of anxiety that this woman is not consciously aware of."

Accordingly I sent her an appointment, then found I had another appointment on that day, wrote and cancelled the appointment and offered her another time. She came without demur. She was an ordinary housewife, a little plump, her prettiness fading, dowdily dressed, the sort of woman one passes in the street a hundred times and never remembers.

She seemed shy but accepting. We talked and did the grid and when she was leaving I asked her if she would like to come again to see the results of the grid. She said that she would. After the session in which we talked about the grid I asked her if she would like to go on talking and she said that she would. We arranged a time to meet then, but after that I left it to her to phone me when she wanted to see me again. For the first two months our meetings were almost weekly, with her husband coming along for five of these sessions. In August I went away, and in September and October Joan and I met four times. In November she phoned to say that she had not been in touch with me because she felt happy and settled in herself. However, Christmas with all her family proved too much for her and the Sunday after Christmas she phoned me at home in a state of great distress. We met four times in

January, and on the fourth occasion she came simply to discuss what she could to to make her life more interesting.

A repertory grid can tell us no more than what a person is prepared to say on the occasion he does the grid. Sometimes I do not realize until much later how very guarded the person was over certain issues. At other times certain omissions are immediately apparent as being significant. Both of these happened with Joan. I was made aware of how few people were in her life — no one outside the immediate family. She did not disclose, however, what she really thought of her husband and her mother-in-law.

A grid can never reveal "the truth" about a person, since a person doing it has to simplify and compromise to meet the demands of the technique. The computer analysis is another simplification, and when this analysis is expressed in the form of a graph, the graph itself is no more an accurate picture of the person than a map of England is an accurate picture of the country. Joan's graph was similar to the graphs of other depressed people. There was a large gap between self and ideal self, the person she would like to be. Self is well away from all the other people in her graph but close to the negative, unpleasant ideas contained in the grid. She put her mother at the extreme of being possessive yet not concerned about her. She described her husband and her mother-in-law in reasonably favourable terms, but, as we were to find from later conversations, such a description was not entirely true.

At our next meeting we looked at the graph of the grid and then examined the ways in which Joan had used some of the constructs. She had described her husband as "seeing things in black and white" and herself as not seeing things in black and white but wishing that she did so. I asked her why she would prefer to see things in black and white. "Well, it just makes life easier," she said, "just to believe what you see and not wonder about what people tell you."

Q. "Why isn't it a good idea to wonder about what people tell you?" A. "You wonder whether they are telling the truth. I usually find that they are not."

So this ideal of seeing other people in a simple way was one which, in fact, she did not wish to emulate since this would involve trusting other people, something which she knew was too dangerous to do. Her resolute determination not to trust other people was a constant theme in our discussions, as was the theme of her fear of her anger.

Her difficulties over her anger were made very clear at our first meeting when she had said that she felt that if she showed her anger people would not like her.

Q. "How do you feel when you suspect that someone doesn't like you?" A. "Terrible — very — the opposite of self-confident — very unsure of myself — as though there's something wrong with me that they do — it must be my fault." Q. "That it's your fault that somebody dislikes you. You don't feel that they could be mistaken?" A. "No — I think it must be me."

I asked her how she felt if someone got angry with her. "Suppose a shop assistant gets angry with you?" "I should be hurt, and I wouldn't go in that shop again .... If I know someone who's nice and then they're angry, I don't want to know them any more." This was how she proved her prediction that if she became angry with a person that person would reject her.

I posed her a problem with which we are sometimes presented in life. "Suppose you are faced with a situation in which you can act in one of two ways. If you act in one way you will respect yourself but people won't like you. If you act in the other way people will like you but you won't respect yourself. Which would you choose to do, to be liked or to respect yourself?"

Joan said that while she would like to be able to respect herself, she would compromise her principles to retain other people's liking for her. "It depends on the situation. I don't think I'd shoot somebody just to get the admiration of other people. I think I'd go pretty far, actually, to keep other people's admiration." I asked her how she felt about compromising herself in this way. "Angry. I'd like to be natural."

Q. "When you get angry like this, what do you do with that anger?" A. "I suppress it most of the time."

At the beginning of our third meeting she had said, "If I could choose to be depressed I could snap out of it, couldn't I? When I feel depressed it comes out of the blue. I don't go round deliberately trying to start feeling depressed. I feel perfectly happy. It's just like a black cloud coming over." But later, as we went on talking about anger, she said, "It's with concealing this anger that I get depressed. If I could say what I felt I shouldn't get depressed."

She found it very difficult to talk about her anger, since, as she said, if you talk about your anger "you'd feel a greater resentment than you already do, you know. You might start showing it. You'd think it would be bound to be felt by the other person, wouldn't you?" How much the other person would feel of her anger worried her very much. When I was saying that I did not think that there was anything wrong with having angry thoughts Joan objected, "Well, it depends how far the thoughts go, doesn't it? It sounds stupid, honestly — there was a knife in the kitchen, and I could have picked it up, and stuck it into my mother. And I thought I'm going to do it one day — it was easy though — it was frightening at the time — I should have liked to have gone outside the house."

Although Joan was frightened of revealing her anger, there was one person with whom it was safe to get angry and that was her husband. "Occasionally, not very often, something does set me off and I do lose my temper. It isn't very often," she said. "I seem to lose all control. Go beserk nearly. Fortunately it doesn't happen very often. I don't let it. I'll get hold of anything that's in front of me and just throw it."

Q. "How do you feel afterwards?" A. "Better. Guilty that I'd lost my temper. I always feel sorry after."

The group of propositions to do with anger, guilt, rejection and depression that

Joan used can be put in a diagram (Figure 3) which shows the transformations within this set of propositions. The outcome of either showing anger or concealing anger or simply talking about her angry feelings is to feel depressed.

Figure 3.   Transformations within a group of propositions

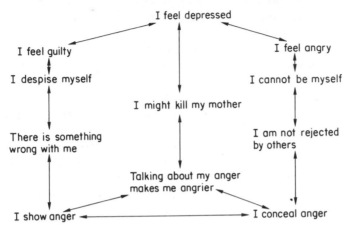

I had asked her in our second meeting, "Do you feel that getting depressed is a sign you're a bad person?" "It's a sign that I'm not what I should be."

> Q. "What is that?"   A. "An ordinary, nice wife and mother."   Q. "So if you were patient, nice and ordinary you wouldn't be depressed?"   A. "If I was ordinary I wouldn't be. I associate ordinary with nothing to do with depression."   Q. "So am I right in thinking that being depressed in some way means to you that you're a bad person?"   A. "Yes."

As Joan saw it, if she were really a good person she would never get angry, she would never need to conceal her anger and therefore she would not get depressed. So she must feel guilty about getting depressed.

For Joan, not to be a person who got to be depressed was to be an ordinary person. In her grid she had described herself as a person who "acts different parts". In a conversation two months later she remarked, "I just visualise everybody being different to me." I commented that, "When I talk to some patients here I find that they don't want to think of themselves as being just ordinary. It's not only patients who feel like this — it's all people, I guess. We'd rather be unhappy and have the impression that we are rare souls, different, something special, than just be one of a collection of rather ordinary people. To be an individual. That's much better than being just run of the mill." To which Joan said, "I've wondered that. I wonder how much I dramatize and how much is real."

Important though the concealment of anger may be in Joan's way of living, it is not sufficient to explain the continuance of her depression. Knowing the relationship between concealing anger and being depressed, she could have found more outlets for her anger than simply throwing things at her husband, and so she could have ended the agony of depression. Similarly, she could have found other satisfying ways of expressing her individuality. What was important in the creation and maintenance of her depression was not just the concealing of anger but her fear of what would happen if she did not conceal it. This fear, in turn, was only a small part of the immense fear which permeated her whole life.

Joan lived her life in the constant expectation that the outcome of every situation would be bad. If she went on a car journey with her husband she expected not to arrive safely. Numerous safe arrivals had not ameliorated her pessimism. "I think if I go over a bridge it will collapse. I think I should stay in bed all day if that's the things I always think. I always think that something bad is going to happen."

Joan's expectation of something bad was not directed solely at her environment. Within herself was something bad as well. She said, "Some people get depressed, say, for ten years and then get back to how they were before. Now all my life, even as a child, I've had psychiatrists, you know. You see I can never go back to how I was before, because there wasn't before. I've never been normal." When I asked about all the psychiatrists she had seen she said, "I don't know — it seems a lifetime. I can't really remember. I remember nightmares and sleeping in a bed on my own. I would sleep with mother and father and I can remember my father sitting up with me during the night. I was nine. I can remember thinking that there was something in the bed. They would strip the bed every night to prove that there wasn't anything there. I can remember them remaking the bed and I remember something crawling up the bed and touching me. I was frightened of the dark. I had a light on. Sometimes now I'm frightened of the dark and put the light on. My husband knows it and it annoys him because he doesn't like sleeping with the light on."

In our conversations Joan often referred to her depression as if it were a thing, not an action — she had a depression rather than she was depressed. I commented on this and she said that she did think of her depression as being a thing. I asker her if she could picture this depression as a person and, if so, what sort of person it would be. She said, "A terrible person — frightening. All I can see in my mind is a black shape — a person as a black shape .... An egg-timer shape. It is quite close, facing me."

Q. "What makes it frightening?" A. "Sounds strange — the fact that it's black." Q. "What if you change places, you go inside it and have a look at yourself. What do you see?" A. "The black shape is bigger than the female person. It's standing up and the female person is sitting down — this sounds barmy — the black shape is just two-dimensional." Q. "What is the other person saying to the black shape?" A. "She is just looking at it." Q. "If she were to say something, what could she say?" A. "I should tell it to go away." Q. "If she told the black shape to go away, what would it say?" A. "I sort of get the feeling that it would go away because it hadn't thought she could tell it to go away and when she did, that frightened it. Up till then it had the power, and with her telling it to go away it lost its power so it went away." Q. "Why doesn't she say, 'Go away' to it?" A. "Oh dear — uh — she's content to sit there and look at it. She doesn't want to move because it would take too much effort." *Q*. "The black thing, does it know it's frightening her?" *A*. "Yes." *Q*. "Does it want to go on frightening the girl?" *A*. "Yes." *Q*. "How would it feel if the girl told it to go away?" *A*. "Surprised." *Q*. "Where would it go?" *A*. "Just walk out of sight." *Q*. "So perhaps the girl doesn't want it to go away?" *A*. "Mm." *Q*. "Why doesn't she want it to go?" *A*. "Sounds ridiculous. I can see it happening, but we are talking about something that's not there. If I said — I think she'd be lonely without it if it went — be just her on her own, you know." *Q*. "Is this all the company she has ever had?"*A*. "Mm." *Q*. "So it's better than nothing. Sometimes, does the black thing get a lot closer to her and sometimes does it move further away?" *A*. "It doesn't move — I've a feeling that if it moved closer, she'd be a lot more frightened. But it doesn't move, it just stands there. She'd be a lot more frightened if it moved closer, but if it moved further away she'd be upset." *Q*. "This image — when you're depressed does it seem any different? Does the black thing seem closer or is the image always the same?" *A*. "I've never seen this image before. I've never looked at it like this before. It's something that's come and I've never thought."

As she was getting ready to leave at the end of this session Joan said, "You know, one day you might feel better than another. One day last week I was sitting watching television, and, with depression, you know, when it comes I think that I'm still on top of it, can still control it, to a certain extent I can understand it. This feeling came over me then, I felt as if I was going barmy, and I had no control over it — I couldn't stop it. I came out in a hot perspiration and — it was still there. I went to the shop — I thought I'd be better in a bit — but I couldn't go in the shop — I was so terrified. I thought, shall I go in the shop and tell someone? Can I make it home again? The day after that it had gone! I really thought I was going mad. I was afraid I would."

The next time we met I asked Joan to picture this experience. She described it as a grey cloud which hovered beyond the black shape. This grey cloud behaved like a teasing, tormenting child. "Why is it tormenting?" I asked. "Just because it enjoys it. Because it is more powerful than the girl. She can't retaliate. It enjoys power."

Q. "Why is it more powerful?" *A*. "Because it's a substance that can get all round everything." *Q*. "How does the cloud feel about the girl?" *A*. "In a way it feels sorry for her." *Q*. "Then why doesn't it stop tormenting her?" *A*. "Because that part — rules over the other feelings." *Q*. "Is there anything the girl can do to stop it?" *A*. "No, no. If she tries it rears up on her." *Q*. "How does it feel about the black shape?" *A*. "I don't know. Contemptuous, perhaps." *Q*. "Does it tease the black shape?" *A*. "It ignores it." *Q*. "What does the grey cloud want?" *A*. "I don't think it wants anything. It's just enjoying itself as it is." *Q*. "How does the girl feel about you?" *A*. "Contemptuous. Because she has all the attention. And she knows it." *Q*. "I see, she's really in the centre of all this. How do you feel about the girl?" *A*. "Envious. When I'm out walking no one takes any notice of me. All the attention is on the girl." *Q*. "How would you feel if they turned their attention onto you?" *A*. "Frightened! I sort of envy the girl because she's not frightened of them. I really don't know — she's a friend to me." *Q*. "But you're still frightened of the girl?" *A*. "I don't know — envious of her — not frightened in a physical sense, but frightened in that she could make me look ridiculous in front of the rest." *Q*. "How could she do this?" *A*. "Oh dear — by drawing attention to me — everyone ignores me and she could draw attention to me. And make me look ridiculous in some way. I can see her in my own mind as small and dainty. I see the person who comes in me as very big, ugly and odd. Big and wonky, that's all." *Q*. "The black shape, how does it feel about the girl?" *A*. "It feels power over the girl." *Q*. "Does the black shape feel proud of having this power?" *A*. "Yes — it likes having power over somebody else." *Q*. "So, if the girl banished the black shape where would that shape go to?" *A*. "It would just go away." *Q*. "How would the girl feel then?" *A*. "I can see the cloud in the room, and if the black shape went she would turn to it. She would expect it to make up for her being left." *Q*. "How would it do that?" *A*. "Oh, I have this picture of the cloud closing in and filling the gap."

Since the cloud behaved as a dangerous, tormenting child such a change was not entirely welcome, even though it means that the girl would not be left alone. So it seemed that the depression pictured as a black shape was necessary to keep some sort of experience of internal chaos, pictured as a grey cloud, at bay. The depression, too, was in some way necessary to this aspect of herself which she pictured as a young girl and which she valued. This image contained a good deal of fear, but it also reflected a balance of forces which Joan would be reluctant to upset.

Our conversations during the first few months were very much taken up with discussions of her relationship with her mother, whom Joan found to be cold, rejecting and very critical of her. Being under the same roof as her mother produced in Joan feelings of anger and depression, so her mother's announcement that upon her husband's imminent retirement they would be moving from a town three hundred miles away from Joan's village to a house in Joan's street created a crisis which seemed to call for some sort of action. Joan said that she was not strong enough to confront her mother on any issue and that her husband would not assist by taking any decisive action — like emigrating — but would weakly acquiesce, desiring to avoid unpleasantness at all costs. Since this was an issue that involved him as much as Joan, I asked her if he would like to come with her next time she came to see me. She thought that he would, and he continued to come for several sessions. The issue of Joan's mother provided no more than a brief introduction to the main theme of these talks, which was the nature of the relationship between Joan and Bill. The crisis about mother faded from view and she reappeared in our talks only briefly when Joan, now largely free of her depression, said that she no longer saw her mother as some dangerous, powerful, love-demanding but love-withholding important figure, but as a little old lady for whom Joan felt sorry.

In our first conversations Joan had described her husband as easygoing. She said that he gave no indication of what he thought, but acquiesced in situations where he expected he might be opposed. She had said that she wished he would say what he thought, but when he was given the chance to say what he thought by joining Joan and me she saw this, so he said, as "horning in on my act". The first conversation of the three of us made it quite clear that if Bill did assert himself Joan would either demolish him or ignore him.

In the discussion about Joan's mother Joan said that if she had to choose between hurting her mother and hurting her husband and children she would not hurt her mother. I queried this in the light of what she had said, that she preferred to suffer this pain than to avoid it by doing things she thought were wrong. "Because I am virtuous I must die," I said. "Of course," she replied.

Joan said that if she did anything to stop her mother from coming to live near her the guilt she would feel would be intolerable. I asked if she did stop her mother from coming what would be the very worst thing that would happen. "She would refuse to ever see me again," Joan said. I suggested that perhaps her refusal to rebuff her mother was not so much a fear of the guilt she would feel but a refusal to give up the hope that one day her mother would show her love. She agreed that this was so. I told them that I wondered whether she had married her husband in the hope that he would give her the love that she had not got from her mother, but, of course, he could only love her in his way, not her mother's way. When he offered his kind of love she said, "Thanks very much, but it's not quite what I wanted." They both laughed at this and agreed that it was so.

Bill's idea of what he wanted from his marriage was clear and simple — a normal family life and a wife who was "loving and generous". His placidity proved to be a pride in not giving way to anger, since his rage was a thing to be feared, so he thought. The scenes in which Joan hurled abuse and objects at him seemed to me to be a game which they both won, she by feeling relieved of her frustration and he by confirming his belief in his self-control.

Joan talked about the married life she had wanted when I asked her, "When you were small did you plan the future, daydream about what you were going to do?" "I didn't plan what I was going to do," she said, "I used to dream about what it would be like. Daydreams always sound daft when you talk about it. I think I used to fantasize a lot — I used to imagine I'd marry a chap who was one of a large number of brothers and sisters, had a nice, friendly, typical, plump, cuddly mum. But I married an only child."

We had been talking about how meaningless her life was to her, so I asked her, "What sort of thing would have to happen now to make you feel that life is worth living?" "Nothing that could happen. I'd like to have a family round me, adult family, brothers, sisters." Joan worked part-time and was never depressed at work. I asked, "Does the group of people you work with at the café — are they somewhat like what you imagine grown-up brothers and sisters would be like?" "Yes." Working at the café also met another need. As she said, "Bill gets upset if I work an

44

extra night, so I do, mainly because I like the work, but partly because I can get at him. I think I'm dying to tell him about the extra night because I know it upsets him. I get the feeling I'm paying him back."

This seemed to explain how Joan could manage to work in the café even when she was very depressed and it led me to think that she had close friends among the other workers there, but later it became clear that the people in the café were no more than casual acquaintances, people, like the patrons of the café, who provided a pleasant contact with no possibility of a closer, more demanding, relationship. Joan set very firm limits on how close her relationships were to be. She said, "I get this feeling with everybody. I know it's there all the time. I remember when we first got married, I remember thinking the most important thing was I mustn't get too fond of him, because tomorrow he might drop dead. It was the same with the children. I mustn't get too attached to them. They might get run over. I wouldn't get too fond of animals in case anything happened to them .... I've never loved anybody enough so that if anything happened to them it would hurt."

> Q. "Do you mean that if your husband or your kids died you wouldn't feel hurt?" A. "Well, I've trained myself that any of them could die any day. What would happen if they really did I don't know. I only know I've taught myself how I hope I'll be. When I'm depressed I think that I would like to go first in case they died and then it would hurt."

The next time Joan and I met, without Bill, I said to her, "Perhaps your marriage is a lot more to you than you know." "I can't visualize life without it. But I can't make it as happy as it should be because I can't put enough love into it. I've thought about it over the years and wondered whether it was natural to feel like this. I remember feeling when I first met Bill, I'm not going to get too involved. Even after we were married, he was never going to have the satisfaction of knowing I depended on him, no one would have that satisfaction. It's gone to the other extreme now, I show it and do it in everyday things."

> Q. "Why don't you want him to have the satisfaction of your depending on him?" A. "It gives people certain power over you." Q. "So you see loving somebody as being dependent on that person?" A. "Yes." Q. "Could you conceive of loving somebody and not being dependent on that person?" A. "No. If you love someone, your emotions are involved, aren't they? You give someone the right to play with your emotions. You're dependent on them to look after your emotions." Q. "When you love the children, in that love do you feel you're dependent on them?" A. "I feel that, I don't know, if they said, 'Mum, we don't love you any more, we're going down the road to Mrs. So and So,' I wouldn't care because I'd expected it all along." Q. "So you expect that anyone you depend on, that person will reject you." A. "I suppose so."

At a later meeting Joan described her husband as seeing things in black and white and implied that she saw this as a desirable trait. I asked her, "Why is it good to see things in black and white?" "Well, it's easier. It makes life easier. You're not all the time looking for motives."

Q. "Why is it important to take things at face value?" A. "You can get let down." Q. "But to be like that you have to be pretty sure people are telling the truth." A. "Yes." Q. "What makes you sure they're telling the truth?" A. "Well, just taking my husband and his mother. If she tells him anything he believes her. Now I'm not sure he believes her because he knows she's telling the truth, or whether he just doesn't care if she's telling the truth or not." Q. "So he's either single-minded or uncaring?" A. "Yes." Q. "Which would you prefer to be, single-minded or uncaring?" A. "Uncaring. If you don't care, nothing can hurt or affect you." Q. "Do you think he sees the world in black and white because he doesn't want to get hurt?" A. "I don't know. I think he is in a little world of his own. Nothing can touch him." Q. "Which would you rather he was, single-minded, a nice simple man who sees the best in everybody, or a person afraid of getting hurt?" A. "Single-minded. I don't want him to have to build up a defence because then I should feel guilty." Q. "So when you say to him, 'Oh, you live in a world of your own' you're really excluded from that world. If you could, if you did break through these defences, do you think you would find a vulnerable person, someone who would get hurt?" A. "I can't imagine him any different." Q. "How would you feel if something happened to him that did hurt?" A. "It would depend who did it. If it was my fault I'd wish that I'd never done it. If someone else had done it I should be angry with them." Q. "How would you feel towards him? Would you feel more close to him, love him more?" A. "Er — mm — yes." Q. "When you say, 'I wish I saw things in black and white,' this is what you're saying, 'I wish this was a defence I had'. When you see your husband use that defence so effectively, this makes you feel shut off. When you say, 'I can't imagine him without it' this means you've been married to a man that you've never really met — you don't know what he's really like. How do you feel about being married to a man who is in a shell — is that too hard a way to put it?" A. "No — er — frustrated. Lacking something. There's something missing. Yes."

I asked, "Who can you talk to in your life, that when you talk to them you feel that they are really there?" "Nobody."

Q. "Do you feel that I am here when I talk with you?" A. "Yes." Q. "What sort of person do you think I am?"

Joan laughed, "What sort of a person? Mm. Well, I suppose you can always throw me out. You want my honest opinion?"

Q. "Yes." *A.* "Oh dear! Basically someone who's doing a job and getting paid for it. You sit and listen to everybody else's problems. Sort of try to help them up." *Q.* "What else do you know about me?" *A.* "Umm — nothing much."

(We had, at this stage, been meeting over seven months, during which I had talked a great deal about my marriage and divorce, my son, my sinusitis, my holidays and, extensively, on how my views of the world differed from hers.)

Q. "If you had to describe me, what words would you use?" *A.* "Oh dear! I could only say about your job." *Q.* "What you're saying is that if I wasn't paid for doing this job I wouldn't be doing it?" *A.* "Yes." *Q.* "So by doing so you effectively block me off. This prevents close contact with me. You've put a label on me. You've put me in a category. And anything I do you will label as 'Her being a psychologist'. Labelling me makes me much safer." *A.* "Yes." *Q.* "What you're describing is a way of being safe from everybody, isn't it? You can put us all into a category, like 'My husband lives in a world of his own'. We get no pain if we think like that." *A.* "Mm." *Q.* "Why is it important to you to see people in their role and in their category? I'll put it this way, would you rather come to see me thinking I was in my role doing the job I'm paid to do, or come and see me as you would if you were visiting a friend? Which would you rather? Would you rather see me as a psychologist or as a friend?" *A.* "Psychologist." *Q.* "Why is it important to see me as a psychologist?" *A.* "If you had a friend and er — I mean I haven't told them anything, and I know that one day I'll never see you again and you'll forget." *Q.* "So what you are saying is that as long as you can see me enclosed in this category you are not in danger of being rejected by me? But if you saw me outside this role, as another human being that you know, then you would be in danger of being rejected by me." *A.* "That's nearly right. The first bit where you said, 'not being rejected by you', well, in my mind you do even now. It's like a friend saying that I don't want to see you again. Yes." *Q.* "That was a very dangerous question when I said, 'What do you think of me?' Whatever you said I could take the wrong way." *A.* "Yes." *Q.* "So rather than risk rejection you prefer to live in a world where you're not close to anyone." *A.* "Yes." *Q.* "If a person chooses to avoid the pain of rejection by not forming any close relationships then he is avoiding pain, but in doing so he collects a lot of other pain — the pain of loneliness." *A.* "I should have thought this preferable." *Q.* "Well, you're in a position to know. You know what it is like to be depressed." *A.* "Yes ... and I would rather stay that way." *Q.* "Being depressed?" *A.* "Rather than form close relationships. I just feel it's the preferable of the two." *Q.* "What do you think would happen if you formed a close relationship?" *A.* "I shall end up getting hurt and having more pain, more depression." *Q.* "Can't you conceive that you might have a relationship that won't bring depression?" *A.* "No." *Q.* "Why can you be so sure that you are always going to be rejected?" *A.* "I just know." *Q.* "Is it something in the rest of us? Or is it something about you that all other human beings reject?" *A.* "I don't think I could live up to other people's expectations. They would expect more from me than they got." *Q.* "What sort of things would people expect from you?" *A.* "Oh dear — I think they would — expect me to give up being myself." *Q.* "Do you think you would lose your identity?" *A.* "Yes. They would want me to be a shadow of them." *Q.* "The threat of losing your identity is a terrible threat. — Do you get this feeling that you would just be wiped out?" *A.* "Yes. They would sort of devour me." *Q.* "Do you think I could devour you?" *A.* "No, I haven't thought of that. No — I don't think that." *Q.* "All along I've been presenting as 'I see the world like this'. I sit in this room, a sort of authority, irrespective of what sort of person I am. You see me as having power, as having power over you. So on the one hand you can see me as being good and on the other as being powerful. Although you think I might be able to do you some good, I might be able also to have a sort of power over you and damage you in some way. If you don't keep me at a distance there's this danger that I might take away your identity. I'm expecting you to change, to be like me." *A.* "No, no. It was all right until the last bit." *Q.* "What, expecting you to be like me?" *A.* "Yes." *Q.* "There's a danger that you'll stop existing and that I shall wipe you out?" *A.* "I just can't see anything beyond that. You were saying about being good or powerful — if you had stopped just before that it would make sense, but I can't see that." *Q.* "But I am a threat?" *A.* "No, no." *Q.* "But could I be a threat?" *A.* "Yes, exactly." *Q.* "But could I only be a threat insofar as you can see yourself as being weaker than me?" *A.* "I think — er — yes. Everybody, yourself included — if you let yourself be bullied." *Q.* "Do you see yourself on the losing side if you go into someone else's power? You're stronger on your own?" *A.* "Yes." *Q.* "In a relationship is one person always in power over the other one?" *A.* "All the time. Everybody has these relationships." *Q.* "So you're saying that the matter of power always turns up? You say that a question of power won't arise because I won't get into a relationship. But can you conceive of a relationship where there isn't the question of power?" *A.* "No, no." *Q.* "So you see relationships as, if you go into a close relationship with a person then you're under that person's power?" *A.* "Yes. If it's been any two people, any, then one will always try to have more strength than the other. One person always tries to destroy the other." *Q.* "You can't see a relationship where this doesn't happen?" *A.* "No." *Q.* "Do you see this with your relationship with your husband?" *A.* "I think if I got closer he would destroy me." *Q.* "How would he destroy you?" *A.* "I've got that devouring image again."

Later in this conversation I asker her, "Why is your husband so threatening?" "I don't know. I just thought it was because of me."

> Q. "You fail to see the sort of expectations he has of you?" A. "I don't know what he sees in me." Q. "How would he devour you?" A. "I just get the picture of someone like in a foreign country where the woman walks several paces behind the man. I can picture him becoming one of those types." Q. "Have you ever put this to him? Have you ever said, 'You want me to be behind you, and do whatever you want me to do'?" A. "Well, I — he knows he doesn't stand a chance." Q. "But you still think this liking is lurking within him?" A. "Yes. I have a defence against it all the time."

On a number of occasions Joan showed very clearly how much she despised herself for having to come to me and ask me to help her through a bad patch of depression. On one such occasion she described how meaningless her life was and how much she wished to die. "I was just stood there the other day and, I know this sounds dramatic, but I thought, 'Well, I could just lay down and die', and then I thought, 'That would be lovely, you know, really lovely' — I mean just to have lain down and died."

> Q. "How do you picture death?" A. "It's nothing. Black, lovely, beautiful — getting away from life." Q. "Do you picture blackness and with you inside it?" A. "I don't know. When I think about it, all I'm thinking about is getting away from now. There's nothing at the other end."

When we explored how people, especially her children, could be affected by her death it emerged that she wanted to be forgotten so that she would not feel responsible for her children being hurt. Feeling responsible meant feeling guilty. I asker her, "What's so bad about feeling guilty? What does it mean to you?" "I don't know how to describe it. It's not really a bad feeling. It's like carrying a heavy weight around. You'd like to be free of it."

> Q. "So guilt is a weight — a burden?" A. "Yes." Q. "Suppose you saw yourself as carrying this burden of guilt — how would you carry it? What sort of burden is it?" A. "Like a big box. I can see somebody staggering along with this enormous load on their shoulders." Q. "Now if this box gets bigger and heavier and heavier what's going to happen to the person carrying it?" A. "Just sort of crumble up into nothing. Just be so squashed underneath that you can't see them."

So it seemed that anything which threatened to increase her sense of guilt was also a threat to her sense of her own individuality. Death, which she pictured as 'Nothing. It's the end. Final', was as dangerous as it was desirable. She said, "I feel that if the desire was that great, I should have done it before now. But there are days when I would really love to, and I just couldn't do it. My kids are all great, but there's the little one — I think I use her as an excuse. I mean, at her age — I think of someone looking after her and think they might not love her as much as I love her. I see my husband — he doesn't show his affection very much." So she could not die, as much as she wanted to. That left a meaningless life to be lived. "I just cannot see any point in life," Joan said. "What's the point of getting up every morning? You go to bed just so that you can get through another day. You know, I can't understand other people doing it."

When Joan talked about her relationships with her family and her loneliness she would say something like "I feel I don't love anyone. I feel there are too many people demanding things of me — clinging to me." But we had established very early in our conversation that people demanding things of her was not entirely unacceptable. In our fourth conversation she had said, "Suppose you enjoy seeing things in the way you know is wrong. I'm thinking of one particular thing, actually. My mother-in-law is in hospital. She should be out soon, so my husband said we'll bring her back to our house. I can wallow in a terrible sense of injustice. Now if he said we won't bring her I should feel terribly let down because I wouldn't be able to carry on with this feeling. That's the wrong way to look at it, surely, but I do."

Q. "You enjoy being a martyr." A. "Yes, I do. I don't go around thinking I'm a martyr, you know. I think to myself that I'm hard done by. If I enjoy something I'm not going to change, am I? How do you persuade yourself to stop enjoying it and be miserable doing it the right way." Q. "Unless you can think of another way which doesn't involve being a martyr but yet you get some enjoyment out of it — " A. "I suppose if the family don't come on holiday with us I shall be robbed of something, the fact that I shall not be able to feel sorry for myself. It proves I must be nuts." Q. "Does it? If you go back over history, all the vast numbers of martyrs. There was never any shortage of people ready to turn up and be burned by the Inquisition." A. "That cause was a bit different to mine." Q. "They were martyrs and they could go to the stake believing that they were wonderful and different people. They weren't just like ordinary, everyday people were they? They were special .... This is an aspect of depression which I think is the hardest thing for any therapist to try to shift in anybody. It's quite easy when a person is suffering the pain of depression for the therapist to offer all sorts of acceptable advice about getting rid of the pain. But, when the therapist starts to make suggestions which involve not only losing the pain but the status, the difference that goes along with it, when the therapist starts to make an attack on the vanity of the person, this is when the person says, 'No, I don't want to change.' For human beings it is terribly important to be an individual, to know yourself as being different from other people, special. If you can't be different and special in terms of being exceptionally great and powerful and beautiful and intelligent and all those sort of things — " A. "You choose this way!" *Q.* "Yes, you choose this way. This is special. So when the therapist says, 'Shift away from being a martyr' you think, well, I can't move right up the other end, I can't become the greatest, most beautiful, most intelligent person. It means I've got to shift down to this ordinary place, to be like the other how many millions in the world. We don't like to change, we'd rather be different, though it's painful, than to be the same as others, to be ordinary." *A.* "So if you don't want to change, in your own heart, you won't change.'

Joan may have accepted that she was choosing to be hard done by, but she did not accept, from this conversation, that she would decide to choose differently, as a later conversation showed.

When her husband was present she described him as "a Victorian-type father". She went on, "He sits in a chair opposite the garden — he's up and down all the time — it distresses him to see the children and their friends in the garden, walking on the lawn. If, like the other day, Susan is going round to a friend's place, Bill said, 'Where are you going?' She said, 'I'm going to a friend.' He said, 'Don't bring her back here,' and I immediately stepped in and said, 'Now Susan, you can bring back any friend you like.' I immediately defend her against him — she knows this and can come to me." I turned to Bill and asked, "Is this true you don't like the children to bring their friends back home?" "I don't mind, but we made a rule that one night a week they don't bring their friends home." "You said every night — be honest," said Joan. "I did at the time. But it doesn't worry me, doesn't really." "You could have fooled me," said Joan. "That one can be a bit noisy." "Well, I wouldn't ban her from the house." "They still come a lot." "I make sure they do." "Well, everybody's happy," said Bill. "Are you happy?" I asked, "It seems your authority is being undermined all the time." "I get used to it," he said. "Doesn't worry me, that part of it. I think they know if I really say anything." "You feel that when it comes to the point the children know what you say goes," I asked. "I think they realize that I really mean it, they do it."

I asked, "How do you feel when the house gets in a mess?" There was a long pause and then Bill said, "Get annoyed at times. I often tidy up when the kids have gone to bed and Joan's out. Then Joan comes in and says, 'This place looks like a tip.' She hasn't seen it before I've tidied it up. It looks quite reasonable, mind you."

"You've got the wrong question there," Joan said to me. "If Bill gets annoyed because it's untidy it's for my sake, because I always seem to be tidying up. If the house is untidy it doesn't bother him, not as much as it does me. But the fact that I'm going to start tidying up again instead of settling down. He says, 'Why don't you leave it?' and I say, 'It looks like a bomb's hit the place.' He'd quite cheerfully leave it. It doesn't worry him personally." "So," I said, "You have it both ways, do you? The children make a mess and you think that's what children ought to do, and then at the same time you complain because the house is in a mess and you've got to tidy it up?" "Yes, I'm being a martyr, you see," said Joan. "I like feeling hard done by. I enjoy it. I like to think you're sitting down and I'm working. I know if I sit down and somebody else does the work I feel guilty."

Q. "What happens when you're not feeling hard done by? How do you feel then?" A. "Can't think when I'm not feeling hard done by. I'm like that when I get up in the morning. I've got to get out of bed for a start — and from then on everything I do is with an air of martyrdom throughout the day."

That feeling hard done by was a way of avoiding a feeling of guilt was implied here, but not made clear. Why it was so important to her to avoid an increase in her feeling of guilt was not clarified until some two months later when she described her feeling of guilt as a burden which, if increased, would annihilate her.

In the conversations with the three of us present Bill was usually very mild and placatory. Whenever he made an assertive statement, he immediately modified or withdrew it. Only once did he ever say he felt "a little annoyed" and that was when I asked him how he felt when Joan said that she wanted to be free. He could not afford to challenge Joan too openly since, as she said, "If he opposes me on something I'll do it." To the extent that feeling depressed is the opposite of feeling active and independent, it was actually to his advantage for her to be depressed. Bill objected to Joan working in the café, the one activity during which she did not feel depressed. When I asked why he objected Joan said, "I don't know whether it's true but I think it's because I enjoy myself." "We've argued this before," said Bill, "there's nothing I can blame it on to, honestly." "But on the whole you're not terribly happy about her working," I said. "Don't really know. I think if I was honest I'd say I wouldn't want her to work." "Why?" I asked. "I don't know. I'd say, on the other hand, we don't go out much, I agree." "We don't go out at all," said Joan.

Joan said that Bill had tried to stop her working last year. He said that he was simply following the doctor's instructions that she should not work. Joan said that the doctor had told her that she should continue working. There was no way of resolving this, since each had obviously heard what each wanted to hear. I asked Bill why he did not want Joan to work. "I can't answer that — the only thing I can think of is that I like her around when I'm there." "To my mind," said Joan, "Bill doesn't like to see me or the children enjoying ourselves. He's always happier when we're miserable." "What do you think?" I asked Bill. "I don't know," he said. I went on, "How does this tie in with what we worked out last time that if Joan stopped being depressed and became active and independent she might want to leave. So you said it was in your interest for her to be depressed because while she's depressed she won't leave you. Those weren't your exact words, but that was what we worked out." "I personally haven't seen that at all. When she gets depressed — ." "You're quite happy," said Joan. "Thank you," said Bill. "How do you say he reacts when you're depressed?" I asked. "Different to when I'm not," said Joan, "When I'm not depressed he's moody and miserable and when I'm depressed he changes." "In what way?" I asked. "Becomes more friendly, talkative ...."

Q. "More the sort of person you'd like him to be?" A. "Yes."

"Were you aware of this?" I asked Bill. "She tells me this, but I'm not aware of it."

Q. "How do you feel when she's depressed?" *A.* "I think I feel a bit down. I never settle at work for one thing." *Q.* "How do you feel at home?" *Q.* "I'm always unsettled, even at home." *Q.* "Do you talk to her more, or do more things?" *A.* "Well, things like I talk to her more or do more things." *Q.* "So you behave differently when she's depressed. You say you behave differently because you've been warned about her illness, you feel unsettled,"

I turned to Joan, "And are you saying you think he behaves differently because he prefers to see you depressed?" "Yes," said Joan. "We've argued this out as well," said Bill, "It's not a good thing to go to work, or to drive a car when you're unsettled." "So you're saying you don't want her to be depressed because it stops you working?" I asked Bill. "Yes," said Bill. I asked Joan, "Can you describe some of the things he does that gives you the impression that he doesn't want you and the children to be happy?" "Does? That implies that he physically does something, whereas to my mind it is more his mood. He doesn't do anything." "That is a fairly serious charge," I said. "I'll stick by it," said Joan. "I get moody, I know I do," said Bill.

Getting moody may have been his way of getting her to fulfil the role he wanted her to play. When they first married, he told me, Joan had been "the ideal wife". I asked him what was for him the ideal wife. "Loving and generous," he said. On hearing this Joan said, "I have to be the perfect mother, the perfect wife, the perfect daughter, the perfect daughter-in-law, when all I want to be is me."

For Joan "being me" might mean feeling hard done by, but it also meant wanting to be free. This need for freedom had not been created by her conversations with me. She had spoken of it when we had been exploring the implications of the constructs she had used in her grid. One of these constructs was "possessive". I had asked her, "What for you is the opposite of possessive?" "Unpossessive."

Q. "Which would you prefer to be, a possessive person or an unpossessive person?" *A.* "Unpossessive." *Q.* "Why is it important not to be a possessive person?" *A.* "I don't want my children to think of me as I think of my mother. I want them to feel free. To live their lives as they want them." *Q.* "Why is it important for people to live their own lives?" *A.* "Make your own mistakes — find your own happiness the way you want it."

Being free, being able to choose one's way of life, was important to her, but she saw her children being able to do this, not herself. Her way of life had been chosen for her by others, her depression had been thrust upon her. At our third meeting she said, "When I feel depressed it comes out of the blue — I don't go around deliberately trying to feel depressed. I feel perfectly happy. It's just like a black cloud coming over." Three months later, two months after Joan had personified and described her image of depression, we returned to her concept of depression and looked at it in relation to the concept of choice. Joan had said, "I do try to get rid of these things, you know. They do go away on their own sometimes and that's great." I commented, "When you say these things go away, it seems as if these things just happen to you. These *are* things that you've got some choice about. Whether they're good or bad, you've decided to be this way. These worries and depressions you see as visitors on you from somewhere." "Yes, that's the way I see it. The come and they go. I try. I try."

> *Q.* "Do you have more will-power at one time than another?" *A.* "I don't know. It would depend with what it was connected. Can you cure depression with will-power then?"

"Well, will-power's a pretty vague sort of term. To do something, if you say, 'I have decided to do something,' supposing that something was in your power to do, like you've decided to make a cake, you've decided because you know how to do it. But if you say, 'I will get over my depression,' well, you haven't the power to do that, because at the moment you don't know how to overcome your depression. When we feel that some things happen to us, something happens out of the blue, — well, on the whole, things just don't happen out of the blue, do they? There's a stream of events leading up to something. If you cross the road and get knocked down by a car, that seems to be out of the blue, but someone has planned to drive there and has done so. He just doesn't appear from nowhere and just knock you down. I'm just saying that if you get depressed the depression doesn't come from nowhere. It's just that it's a bit harder to find where it came from. If you get knocked down while crossing the road, when you come to think, 'The car came round the bend too fast,' or 'I didn't look'. If something happens suddenly you can think about it afterwards and work out what happened. But there's something about depression that stops us from being able to work it out. It's almost as if we don't want to find out. I notice when you and other people talk to me about depression you always talk about something that has happened to you and not something you have done yourself. You can say, 'I didn't look. I got run over because I didn't look.' But you don't talk about being depressed in the same way."

"It's true, yes. Does there have to be a reason why you get depressed? I mean, can events lead to — I usually let things get on top of me, and then I start getting depressed, you know. I let things get on top and the depression automatically follows. Then I work through the depression, get over it, and then things start building up again."

"You sort of think that you're something petty that things happen to?"

"Sort of being made that way, you know."

"Well, this is one way of looking at it. Human beings are made in different ways. If they're made one way they end up getting diabetes. You've got no choice about the things you are born with. A person can be born with a faulty body, like with diabetes or epilepsy or shortsightedness, and this is the same way of thinking about people in a passive way. They are made in that way. A lot of psychiatrists look at mental illness in this way, as something passive. People have the physical make-up that makes them depressed. They look at the make-up that makes depression, and out of this way of looking at depression comes a very passive way of treatment for it. Take ECT — you lie down on the bed and have ECT. If you think of depression as being passive, then you will treat it in a passive way. Well, you've had lots of tablets and ECT, your depression has been treated as being something that just happened to you. What do you think about that?"

"I still can't see an answer. You always take the next thing that is offered to you and hope that this is it. If it's a lot of new tablets, you know?"

"Well, it depends. A lot of people get depressed once. They take some tablets and feel a lot better. And then they get depressed again. They never thought much about why they get depressed, they just accept. This kind of treatment works in a limited sort of sense. There's another way of looking at mental illness, and it's inside every psychiatric patient there's another person just waiting to get out. And what you've got to do is to give these people the right pills and then this normal person will appear. If you sit in case conferences you hear the doctors sometimes talking about various patients making 'a breakthrough'. This normal person who is inside this abnormal person — and it always seems to me, when I read the case notes right back from birth that it seems incredible to me that there is a normal person inside, waiting. Is there ever such a thing as a normal person? But again you hear this — about going back to being a normal person when you know you'll never be her. In any case, not one of us can go back. Nobody can go back. I suppose it only makes you worse hearing people talking about going back to normal."

"I just visualize everybody being different to me." Joan was well aware that there was no ordinary person inside her, waiting to be released, but the notion that the depression was visited upon her was too delightful to give up easily, since such a notion had the corollary that something which had been visited upon her by some other agency could be taken away by that agency, without any effort by her. As she said at our next meeting, "I've just got this feeling you know, that I've got to do something or say something. You know, you've done it, or you've said it, and you're cured. Like come here and say the password and do this thing and you're OK. That's it."

Q. "Like some sort of magic?" A. "Yes, yes."

Being free means choosing between alternatives, and this notion of choice Joan found very hard to accept. This question arose when we were discussing her feeling of being hard done by. I asked, "What would happen if your life changed so that you weren't able to feel hard done by?" "The reason I feel hard done by is because there seems to be so much to do in so few hours, so if I didn't feel hard done by I'd have less to do and more hours to do it in which would be great."

Q. "That would mean you would have greater freedom to choose, wouldn't it?" A. "Mm." Q. "Though sometimes when we realize that something could happen and we'd have greater freedom, there'd be lots more choices — we could make perhaps unlimited choice. Sometimes this seems very pleasurable. The idea of freedom seems very pleasurable when we're hard pressed, but sometimes when we're faced with it we don't always feel it's so good. Have you ever been in this situation where you haven't got anyone pressing you? Suppose your husband and children were away and you were alone. Have you ever been in that situation where you've been on your own?" *A.* "No, I've tried to visualize it — daydream about it — I can imagine after a day it would wear a bit thin." *Q.* "Yes, while we all think how lovely it would be to be perfectly free without any ties of any kind the notion of complete freedom is for many people very frightening and we keep away from this fear by keeping ourselves busy by creating things for us to do. We collect our own burdens, and the mere fact of having lots of things to do stops us from having to face the emptiness which is inside yourself as well as outside. Complete freedom is a pretty terrifying notion." *A.* "Does this mean everyone reacts like this?" *Q.* "I'm not sure everyone reacts like this. I think it goes something like this — we have got to in some way define ourselves — to say I am this sort of person, I do these sort of things, I have these sorts of relationships. So we have to make the choices and stick to these choices. Everybody does that, but some people take up more burdens, keep themselves busier, turn themselves into martyrs more than others do. I think that women are terribly prone to this, because a woman's work is never done. If you want to collect unlimited burdens, become a wife and mother, because you've always got the children that always need something doing for them, and the house always needs cleaning so you can never come to the end of your burdens." *A.* "What do you do if you want to throw them off?" *Q.* "Well, it's a sort of conflict, isn't it? One part of you wants the burdens around you and the other part realizes that this is too much." *A.* "There's no answer to that, is there?"

"There's probably an answer in coming to recognize it. I mean, I think you've made progress in that you're able to joke about the fact that you need to be a martyr. Lots of people don't even get that far. They haven't even recognized in themselves that they've always been martyrs. I think that a person can be able to face up to being alone, accepting how much freedom a human being actually has. Sometimes we deny that we have any freedom at all. We say that all these things have been thrust upon us — like, I've got to carry out my duties, I have no freedom — but, if you think about it, everybody's got a choice — you chose to get married, you chose to have three children, you were collecting those burdens, now you've got a choice, you can choose to devote every minute of your day to your housework and children or you can choose something else. You can choose to do less housework and be less involved with your children." "But housework's housework," Joan said.

Q. "Yes, well, it's a question of how important it is, why do you need it. You can say, 'I can choose. It's important to me to have a spotlessly clean house,' or else — some women don't believe they've got a choice. They believe they've got to go ahead and keep cleaning the house." *A.* "I don't believe I've got a choice, really. You can't choose whether to cook them a meal or not. You've got to feed them all the time or else they'll go hungry." *Q.* "Yes, but you can choose whether you're going to cook a three-course meal or open a tin." *A.* "I don't cook three-course meals, but three meals a day take up a certain amount of time. And you've got to make beds, haven't you? You can't choose." *Q.* "There are limits to what we can choose. We've got no choice over when we're born and when we die, usually, and within each situation there are various sorts of limits to what we can do. But within each situation we've got a fair amount of choice and sometimes we can choose to see we've got a choice, and other times we can choose to say we've got no choice at all." *A.* "I can't choose whether I spend two hours a day walking my daughter to school. I've no choice there." *Q.* "But you made a choice about it some time ago. You made the set of choices that led up to this." *A.* "So I've got no choice now, I've still got to take her to school. I can't change that. I'm stuck with that." *Q.* "You're stuck with some of your choices." *A.* "All these things I'm stuck with last me twenty-four hours a day." *Q.* "There again you could work this out. What you're actually saying is that you've chosen this way because the other choices available have outcomes which you would find unpleasant." *A.* "You can say it that way, or you can say it my way." *Q.* "Yes you can." *A.* "So you can say that, but I've got no choice." *Q.* "There are other alternatives — some people do let their children go to school on their own." *A.* "Are you saying I should let her go to school on her own and then I'd be a better person?" *Q.* "No, I'm not saying that at all. What I'm trying to get you to see is that all your actions are choices and not things forced upon you. If you take the attitude that you have no choices then you have the right to be a martyr, because things are being put upon you, but if you say that the things that I do are the outcome of choices I've made then you can't feel put upon." *A.* "I still maintain I don't have a choice."

Bill talked about how he hated coming home to an empty house, and this led us back to the topic of how Joan limited her affection for her family. I said, "Coming back to the question of your enjoying being a martyr and when you say you limit your affection — these seem to be positions of tremendous importance to you — central to your safety. I wonder if they are also central to being depressed. In choosing these positions you are also choosing depression." "Depression is a form of escapism," said Joan. "What do you mean — escapism?" I asked. "I don't really know — when life gets too complicated," she said, "I wish there was a magic cure."

Q. "A magic cure means something you don't have to do anything about. Controlling it yourself means something you do to yourself." *A.* "It's all right saying that so long as you know what will control it."

I talked about how choosing to be a martyr and choosing to limit her affection could lead to her being depressed. "So to stop being depressed I've got to love everybody and to stop being a martyr."

She said this rather angrily and I felt I had pushed her too hard. I said, "Both these situations involve a lot of risk, because if you stop limiting your affection the pain of loss is going to be something you can't control, and if you stop being a martyr you're going to have the problem of what you are going to do with all this freedom. You might not even get it, but just the thought that you might be free." "So as far as I can see I'm going to remain depressed — not limit my affections, I can't do that after all these years."

> Q. "Well, you can keep it on more honest terms. What I mean is that before you saw depression as something that just happened to you. If you accept that there is a link between these two important areas and depression, then you can say, 'Well, I'll get depressed.' And then you can say that you've made the sort of choices that have led you to being depressed."

I talked about how a person can learn to live with his depression, to find ways of coping with it. "At home," said Joan, "I think if only I could shut myself away in the bedroom." "Why not?" I asked. "Well, if she did that all the kids would immediately dash into that bedroom," said Bill, "What I say is that they should still wait there until you answered, shouldn't they? I tell them to go to bed. This is one of the areas where I try to get them to take notice of me. I try to bring them away from Joan, but this only makes it worse. That's when I try to put my foot down, but they won't take any notice of me then." So the fact that Joan had undermined her husband's authority with the children meant that she could not get the peace and quiet she needed when she was depressed. Depression may be a form of escapism for her, but she had nowhere to escape to.

At the end of this discussion it seemed to me that Joan had not budged an inch on the question of whether she had a choice, whether she should accept responsibility for being depressed. However, two months later I was talking to her about how what we expect determines what we do, and I mentioned, "If you're born a girl you're programmed to do this, to grow up and get married and have a family — " and she commented, "But surely you've got a choice!"

Later in the same discussion she described her feeling of guilt as a burden, a heavy box which threatened to crush her. I said, "By now you should know what size box and what weight of box you can carry. If you could judge this you wouldn't take on extra burdens." "But," she asked, "what makes a person who has the choice of whether to carry the burden or not, carry it?"

> Q. "I suppose he decides there are certain things to do and not to do." A. "You make it sound so easy." Q. "I was just sitting here thinking that it's not so long ago that I was saying to you that you have a choice and you said, 'Oh no, I don't have any choice.' I was just thinking that here you are

58

telling me that you do have a choice. So somewhere along the line, in between that conversation and now, you've changed. You've changed, and you see choice in the world. Do you agree you have a choice?" *A*. "Yes — the thing is you've got two choices. The choice of being as you are or changing."

Six months before, on the second time we met, she had said, "I'm sure that to change you've got to be born again. I think you're there and that's how you're made."

Some months later when Joan and I were discussing how she saw her husband, I said, "One thing that always bothers me when I start talking to someone like yourself who's been depressed is — if your depression is tied up with the person you are, that means that if we change the depression we change you. And if this happens, how much does this change your relationship? This happens to a lot of girls, who at home are trained to be good, quiet girls, and then when they're older these girls get the impression that they're not terribly good people, there is something defective about them and they feel not valuable. Then some day they get married and they don't expect a great day with Prince Charming. I mean, when such a girl grows up she marries someone she quite likes. He is not as good as she wanted, but he's as good as the girl expects. A girl with a low opinion of herself tends to marry somebody — she just feels grateful for getting him, she doesn't expect very much. Then as she gets older she gets to thinking that she could have married someone else or done something else. I think this is one of the things I'm concerned about. I wonder how much this sorting out is going to change your marriage." "I haven't got an answer for that. Oh dear! Everything you've said makes sense. The thing is I never know how much of it is true and how much of it I imagine to be true. I have a feeling sometimes that if you told me it was my next-door neighbour who caused my depression or something like that it would all fall into a pattern. A lot of my life makes sense now, and now you're talking about my husband and that makes sense now." I answered this by saying that I could only draw on my own experiences and was not claiming to know the truth, and I said then that whenever I put up a proposition which did not fit her case she was very quick to point this out.

Again, on another occasion when we were talking about her feeling for her husband she said, "I know that if he suddenly walked out it would leave a gap, but I don't know whether it's because I got used to him."

Q. "Well, you can't live with someone for ten years and have three children without being attached." *A.* "I don't know. Once upon a time I would have said, 'Yes, of course.' I don't know that I know what it is. What I mean by loving someone. I know what it is for the children, but that's a different kind of love. Now I'm starting to realize that maybe what I felt wasn't love." *Q.* "Do you feel just indifferent?" *A.* "I think it's a bit late now to start worrying. — I always feel there's something missing. Isn't this the way all married couples feel?" *Q.* "What do you think is missing?" *Q.* "Some great beautiful thing. Does it actually happen in life? The everyday, ordinary housewife, when you see her in the street, does she look like something wonderful has happened?"

We were looking at what words mean to us, what expectancies are built into these words and how our reactions to a situation are determined by the terms we use to describe ourselves. At our third meeting, when she had said that to change she would have to be born again, I said, "Well, there's a lot you can't change, like your body, for instance. But it is possible for us to make changes in ourselves. This is because we have a language which we can use to think about things that aren't present. Because we've got language we can abstract qualities of things and situations. When we talk about a blue sky we can talk about the blueness. We talk about a person's smile, yet a smile cannot exist without a person. Because we've got a language we're quite different from other animals. So with our language we can make changes in the way we behave. We can use different words to describe the same thing. For instance, you described your mother as being possessive. This isn't a good way for her to be. You couldn't have described her as being very close, could you?" "No."

Q. "If I said to your mother, 'Are you possessive or close and concerned?' she would say, 'Close and concerned, of course'. We have the power to change because we are able to redefine. We say we thought it was that, but now we see it as something else. We may not redefine to its total opposite, but we may say, 'When I was a child I thought my mother to be totally possessive, but now I'm older I think she must have clung to me because she had such an unhappy marriage.' Then it's just a slight change. There's a change in words, and a change in the way of looking at things." A. "I see your point. I see what you mean. I can see that way of looking at it. But all these ways of doing it, leaves the fact of doing it. It will mean a tremendous effort. It seems easier to let life go on as it is."

However, she took the harder way of looking at the implications of the concepts she used. I would often contrast my concepts with hers. One day, when she was talking about how she limited her affection she said, "Well, if you love someone, your emotions are involved, aren't they? You give someone the right to play with your emotions. You're dependent on them to look after your emotions."

Q. "So you expect that anyone you depend on, that person will reject you." A. "I suppose so." Q. "You've got three separate ideas — idea is the wrong word, it's ideas and feelings — you put altogether in one group — love, dependency and fear of rejection. So you can say to yourself if I love somebody I'm dependent on that person and that person will reject me — this is all together in one notion. But these are three separate things. It is possible to love somebody without any notion of dependency. That feeling of love is a pleasurable feeling, a warm feeling, a strong feeling, it goes out towards the other person, it carries a feeling of continuing concern and interest, but it doesn't have to have a feeling of dependency." *A*. "When you offer love, as when you offer a gift to anyone, anything at all, surely you are depending on them to accept it, and not get it back from them. Surely you can offer nothing without this feeling — depending on them to accept it." *Q*. "But that's the next stage. You have the feeling first, and then you show the feeling and hope that the other person will accept it. You can't make an offer till you've got something to offer. So the three things come in different stages — love, dependency, and possible rejection. They come in an order. You see them necessarily connected. I'm saying that they are not necessarily connected. It is possible for human beings to love one another without being dependent on one another. It is possible to feel love for someone in whom you have no dependency at all." *A*. "I can understand you could feel love so long as you didn't go to offer it." *Q*. "Now it seems here is another sort of idea, that it seems as if you were saying that when you offer someone love you are putting yourself in a weak, dangerous position." *A*. "I would never offer anybody anything unless I was sure they wanted it in the first place." *Q*. "Because you see the act of offering as a weak position, because you can be rejected. Some people regard being in love as a strength, a strong position." *A*. "I don't see it like this." *Q*. "This is another way of seeing it." *A*. "I can usually see things in another way, I can usually see another point of view, but this I can't see." *Q*. "It seems that you've been taught that loving is dangerous because loving is a weakness where you can get hurt. Other people who've had different childhoods see loving as good, as a strength, and it doesn't matter if you get rejected if you love another person because if you really love another person you care what happens to that person and want good things for that person, even if the good things for that person don't include you." *A*. "I've heard that before, but it doesn't necessarily apply to human nature." *Q*. "I think that human salvation lies in the capacity of human beings to love one another, and their damnation lies in their capacity to hate one another. The terrible thing that happens to human beings is that they are never allowed to feel the completeness, the openness, the warmth that you feel when you're loved, and the child who doesn't experience this doesn't know how to love someone in return, but a child who has experienced it has no problem in loving. It's easy as anything, like breathing."

I went on to say that some people had the notion that each of us was born with a limited amount of love and we had to dole it out carefully, else we should run out of it, when, in fact, a human being could feel an unlimited amount of love. Killing off one's capacity to love deforms a person, making that person less than he or she could be. I said that I considered the essential part of what I did in therapy was the feeling of love that I had for the people I talked with, and if I did not have this then the rest of what I did was no more than "tinkling cymbals and sounding brass". When Joan got up to leave she said that she had come to see me that day to see if I could convince her that life was worth living, and if I failed to do this she was going home to kill herself, but I had convinced her. She left looking quite happy. This conversation took place after Joan had telephoned me to say that she felt terrible and to ask if she could see me that afternoon. As her husband had already left for work she got to my office by riding her bicycle several miles and pushing it up a long steep hill, with a gale blowing against her. At least some part of her was prepared to be convinced by me.

Over the next two months the periods of depression became much fewer and we began to look at the question of what else she might do with her time. Joan wondered, "Does everyone plan their lives? Don't they take it from day to day?"

Q. "Some people do live day to day. But some don't — they have quite a strong concept of the future. If they didn't, insurance companies wouldn't flourish, would they?" A. "I don't think you can plan the future. I mean — it's no good planning something that might never happen. It's tempting fate." Q. "What you're really saying is that if you make plans then it's asking for them not to come true." A. "Yes, mm. I could plan something — ." Q. "Do you expect to be disappointed?" A. "When we start the car I never expect to arrive at the other end." Q. "How do you feel when you do get to the other end?" A. "Relieved! Just a little relieved, but I really just accept that we're there." Q. "You've made an awful lot of car journeys." A. "Well, yes." Q. "There are a lot of people in the world who will make a plan and expect to carry it out." A. "That's being optimistic. How can you expect to do something tomorrow if you don't know if you're going to be here tomorrow?" Q. "The only thing you can go on is past experience, you know. If your plans have always turned out all right, well, then you can expect they will in the future." A. "Mm — I can't really think that way." Q. "There's no certainty that anything will happen in the future just because it happened in the past, but if you've not been disappointed in the past much you expect not to be disappointed much in the future. If you've been disappointed a lot in the past then you expect that in the future." A. "Mm — it's very difficult when you think one way to imagine everyone thinking the other way." Q. "So long as you keep expecting the worst — ." A. "You're never disappointed when it happens." Q. "So this is a way of avoiding disappointment?" A. "It's surprising how often it turns out to be right." Q. "Does it cheer you up? Do you think, 'Ah, I was right'?" A. "No, no. Well, I'm glad I didn't expect any better." Q. "Or you would have been disappointed?" A. "Yes." Q. "So by expecting it to be bad you've avoided pain. Whereas if you expected the best you'd feel happy while you were expecting the best, but you'd get the pain if you were disappointed." A. "Yes." Q. "I suppose it has its place in the system as long as it doesn't stop you from acting at all, and just do nothing." A. "Yes, that's it. I never make any plans." Q. "So you live from day to day — it's a safe system, but it doesn't make a happy life, does it?" *A*. "What's the alternative? The alternative is to go around being optimistic about everything, isn't it?" *Q*. "You might get let down sometimes, but not a hundred percent of the time. You don't get knocked down every time you go out or have an accident." *A*. "No, no." *Q*. "Then you do make plans and those plans turn out well. Like you made a plan to go to Norwich for a holiday and you came back all right. So there is some chance of things turning out well. But you're living as if things turning out badly is a certainty. It's only a possibility." *A*. "I shall have to try to think optimistically." *Q*. "Nothing — if you would agree with me — nothing is certain in life. You can be no more certain of things turning out badly than them turning out well." *A*. "I don't know. I've often thought things would turn out well and they've turned out badly. It's always turned out badly. I've expected nice surprises and all I've got is nasty surprises." *Q*. "Did you expect when you first came to talk to me that this would turn out badly?" *A*. "I didn't know what to expect but I hoped it would help." *Q*. "You still expected the worst?" *A*. "I didn't see how you could help me." *Q*. "So in some respects it turned out all right? And then you had some hopes that turned out all right? I suppose when you hope there's some sort of probability, rather than certainty." *A*. "I suppose so, I must have had hope, or I wouldn't have come." *Q*. "There's this problem, when we talk about disappointment and our expectations, there are things we have no control over. Like we expect the sun to rise tomorrow, and our expectations and hopes have nothing to do with whether it does or it doesn't. Whereas, the expectation 'I'm going to the pictures tonight, but I'm sure I won't enjoy it', you make sure that prophecy comes true. It's right within your control." *A*. "I don't see that. I mean, I've been to the pictures with this feeling and it's been a jolly good film. Or it's been *vice versa*." *Q*. "Yes, well, what I meant, you go off hoping it will turn out nice, and sometimes it does, and sometimes it doesn't. We can also make sure that something turns out the way we expect it to. You can say, 'I'm going to a party and I know I'm going to hate it', and then you behave in such a way that nobody talks to you. And then you could say, 'I know I'm going to enjoy this party', and then behave in a friendly way to everyone there. Or you can go to the pictures and say, 'I'm not going to enjoy this film.' You sit there thinking all the time of unhappy things that have happened to you that day."

Joan went on to talk about how she always expects her mother-in-law to say hurtful things and she always does. She was never the kind, understanding person Joan wanted her to be. We discussed this, sat in silence for a while, and then I said, "This question of what we can control is terribly important. There are lots of things in this world over which we've no control. But there are lots of things we do have control of. Often we don't realize that we've got control. Another way of thinking can bring something under our control. If you can think of your mother-in-law in a different way — I mean, you can think of her as you have done in the past as a person having power over her family, or you can think of her as someone very close to you — who can ruin you, or you can think of her as somebody over there, away from you, who has no power over you, so she has become unimportant to you. This is the sort of person she is and always will be, so you can think, 'I'll chat to her and do my duty by her but I'll keep her away and not let her come so close that she can hurt me.' "

"That's probably because I expect her to — I suppose, I mean I wanted her to be the ideal mother. So if I do what you say, and sort of push her to one side of my life, then I am giving up my ideas, aren't I? I know it will have to change, but I'm not sure how I shall do it."

"Giving up your illusions can be very painful — I suppose that as long as you expect to fulfil this dream you're going to go on expecting something from your mother and mother-in-law they can never give. So you're sort of in a situation where you're going to have to go on trying to get from them something that they can't give. So you can go on being disappointed by them or you can give up the dream of finding a perfect mother. You could say, 'Well, that's something I've missed out on.' Both are pretty painful processes. But in the first one if you continue to try to find the perfect mother in your mother and mother-in-law then you're going to be disappointed. By wanting these two persons to be perfect mothers you're finding the hurt. If you can manage to give up this dream it means giving up hope of something very beautiful and wonderful, the hope of something that's been with you for as long as you've been alive. So it's an enormous thing to give up. If you can manage, then once you've lived through this and got over it you won't be going on getting hurt."

When, at our third meeting, Joan had said, "It seems easier to let life go on as it is," I replied, "If you believe that people don't change you can make that prediction come true. There are things we don't want to change. You said, 'It's easier to let life go on as it is.' But is it easy to get angry and have these murderous impulses? But perhaps part of you, perhaps the little girl inside of you doesn't want to give up these murderous impulses. Perhaps there is pleasure in that. If, when you were tiny and your mother had control over you, you got so angry, then you could go to bed and have a lovely daydream about how lovely it would be when your mother had gone, and in this fantasy you'd have some pleasure in punishing her for being so terrible. You got away with it and so now you won't want to give up that part. If you were frightened that such thoughts had come into your head, you'd give them up."

"That's true. I suppose that's true. I don't want to give it up, then I won't give it up."

Q. "One part of you won't give them up and the other part of you feels guilty. You've got a choice. You can give up these fantasies or stop feeling guilty. Enjoy them!"

Joan laughed. "I don't see how you can enjoy that type of fantasy. If you give them up, you've no sort of — what's the word — revenge, I suppose. It's inside yourself, so no one else knows about it."

Q. "Secret revenge?" *A.* "Yes." *Q.* "That's the reason people survive many terrible things. They daren't revenge themselves in real life, but they get the fun out of fantasy." *A.* "You don't feel guilty about it? It's all right then. It's all right then. It's not sort of — oh dear — ridiculous?" *Q.* "Everybody, if you got them to tell you what their fantasies are, they'd all be ridiculous. And we'd all be as good and bad as the others. No great difference in the fantasies. Some are for revenge, some for achievement. But this is how human beings survive. Fantasies are a safety-valve and a way of working things out. Like when you were a little girl you didn't go and kill your mother because you knew it would be very inconvenient if next morning there was no one there to cook breakfast." *A.* "I see now. Oh dear."

Over the months when we were meeting, Joan's depression steadily decreased. She gave up taking anti-depressants and became more active. She returned to driving the car and enrolled in a further education class. In summer for the first time in her marriage she took a holiday without her husband and children and without feeling guilty about doing so. A month before Christmas she telephoned just to tell me she was well and happy. Then Christmas came and she had her parents and mother-in-law to stay. This she found was too much. A week later she was still depressed and we had a long talk in which I went over many of the things we had discussed, but nothing seemed to make any difference to her. Then I said to her, "You're not depressed when you go into the café to work. You're just being yourself there. Other times you set yourself standards and then when you don't live up to them you feel guilty. It's like just now when you said you ought to be home minding the family. I think you are creating responsibilities that aren't really necessary. You think they are necessary. But when we get into a situation where we are watching, observing ourselves, this is when we fail by not living up to the standards we set ourselves. We become unhappy because we can't maintain the standards. We need to be in a situation where we are just ourselves. We don't fail these standards if we don't set them in the first place. We are being spontaneous. We are not splitting ourselves in two. We are not controlling ourselves by observing ourselves. I mean, when we make the split it is an artificial split — we are still one person. You can't make yourself feel affection. One side of you can't say to the other side, 'Be affectionate.' You just can't do this. Affection arises — it's there — just the way you feel about your children. You're worse when you try to fight your depression. You're worse because you say 'I ought not to be depressed.' That makes you worse. If you could say, 'Well this is how I feel today,' that's not so bad then. Just be yourself. Admit you feel depressed some days. This is as much you as anything else."

"It's quite a nice thought actually — mm — I didn't realize before but you do feel worse because you feel you shouldn't be depressed." As Joan said this her face changed. The pressure which had been bearing down on her brows and mouth suddenly lifted and she no longer looked depressed. "I suppose it's something you might as well enjoy," I said and we both laughed, "This is something you choose. It's not inflicted on you. Today is the day you chose to be depressed." "What a nice thought. It appeals to me."

After this Joan no longer came to see me, but she would telephone occasionally to say she was happy, was still doing "the same old things" but enjoying it. I sent her the first draft of this chapter and later called at her home to talk about it. Joan said, "It's awfully difficult to remember how you felt — I mean, I can't imagine, feeling now like I do, I can't imagine sort of ever visiting the hospital as an outpatient. If somebody said to me, 'Would you like to come for an appointment tomorrow', no chance, I'm not going up there. But before I couldn't wait to get up there. It's two totally different people. It used to be, my whole world was just hanging on to the next time to go there. I just lived through the week until I had to go. I mean, I just wouldn't entertain it now."

Q. "Do you feel that you're still a martyr, that you're hard done by?" A. "Occasionally, I must admit. No more than most people. It doesn't bother me as much as it did. I took everything seriously. I can laugh about most of it now." Q. "Does your mother look different to you now?" A. "Um, well, before, I don't think I ever stopped thinking about her and about the past, it was there all the time. I suppose in a way I enjoyed it, having been hard done by. I was all the time thinking about her, all the things that had happened. It used to pass the day away, just thinking about it all day long." Q. "How much do you think about her now?" A. "I can't say not at all, but I don't think of her like that. Just normally, I should say." Q. "So when you think of her now you think in terms of what's happening now?" A. "Yes. It's as if it's all been washed away. It's as if I haven't got time to think about the past now. I can't be bothered. I can't imagine ever getting depressed. If it came back again, it would be a hell of a shock. I'm just confident that it's going to stay away. This time, in all the years of having it, you know, it's cleared up, say for a few weeks, but during those weeks I was always conscious of the fact that it was there somewhere and I was waiting for the next time — oh well, I've done three weeks, it's bound to come again soon and it always did. But this time it's the first time, after ten or eleven years, when it's gone and I can't imagine it coming back."

Later in the conversation Joan said, "I think that when you're depressed you're in a little world of your own, where everybody else is sort of getting at you, and whatever they say or do, they're doing it to do you some harm. Your interest revolves sort of totally around yourself. It amazes me now to think back to think how self-centred I was. I only thought of me and all the little harms that had been done to me. It's like coming out of prison."

Q. "What have you found now that you're out of prison?" A. "Freedom. Everything is totally different." Q. "How's Bill different?" A. "I wasn't thinking of him. I was thinking of people I know." Q. "How have they changed?" *A.* "It wasn't them. It was me. I'd rather sit at home all day and feel sorry for myself. I didn't go anywhere, but, I mean, those same people I sort of imagined that they didn't want to have anything to do with me and I can't get rid of them now. Before somebody would say, 'Come for a cup of tea,' and I would say, 'I can't, I'm too busy' and then I would sit at home thinking, 'They didn't want me anyway.' But now I find I'm a bit snowed under with folk. I'm amazed at how many people are friendly, they really are. I go round and I quite enjoy complaining that I haven't got any time to myself. There's always somebody coming round or I'm going somewhere. Before I was sitting at home thinking everyone's in their own little world, they don't want to know, but when I came out of mine they did .... When you're not depressed it all seems so petty but, as you say, when you are depressed everything's a major thing. Even the time that Bill used to come home at night. He left work at half-past four so he was in here by twenty to five. I used to do my nut if he was three minutes late. I'd be saying, 'If you thought enough of me!' Now if he bowls in at a quarter-past five, I'm too busy to notice. I used to make a great thing out of it if he was three minutes late, yet anything could have happened, the traffic lights could have held him up. It's things like that, though, when you're not depressed, you don't have time to worry, not so much of the time, you couldn't be bothered. You just look for something. If he'd come in dead on the dot every night I should have found something else. Before I used to let anything he said get at me. I used to shrivel up inside and nurse the grievance for days, but now it sort of goes in one ear. I can just laugh it off." *Q.* "You used to say that he liked to see you down and the children quiet and not enjoying themselves." *A.* "I still think this, but I realize that he's got no chance now, no chance at all. I can soon change his mood for him, whereas before I used to, it made me miserable then. It used to create an atmosphere and it used to rub off on all of us, but now I tell him to snap out of it."

I commented that in all our conversations it seemed to me that we had not uncovered any deep, unconscious motives and anxieties but had simply talked about aspects of herself which she knew well. Joan agreed and said, "I've been thinking, as you say, you need time to talk about it. But apart from that, before you get to someone you can talk to you are blocked off so many times that you don't expect anyone to talk to you in the end. I mean, when you're depressed you just want to talk to someone and you can't go to your friends because I think you yourself would find it embarrassing and I don't think they would know how to handle it. I think you seek professional help so you start going to your GP, well, that's a two-minute job and he gives you tablets, take these three times a day. You don't talk to him, do you? He hasn't got the time. I've been to the GP, up and down to him. Then I went to the Samaritans. I wanted someone to talk to, and the person they sent was unfortunate, she only wanted to talk about herself and when you're depressed you're so self-centred, all you want to do is talk about yourself. You want to find somebody to listen. And then you go from one to the other, you keep going from the GP to the Samaritans, to the hospital and to Dr A. I mean, I liked him ever so much, but I can't say he ever listened. I found myself outside the door before I could say anything. And you get blocked off so many times. You want to talk to somebody but you can't find anyone that wants to listen. So when you do eventually get to someone who wants to listen you just can't see it, because you don't expect them to listen. You feel as if you're sort of testing them for so long — I'll sit here a couple of hours then I'll sit another hour, I'm still here, I'm not saying anything yet, I'm just going to see how long they're going to hold out, until they say, 'Go on, whizz off.' "

"How long did it take you to feel some sort of certainty that you could talk to me?"

"Oh I was amazed. I mean, the first day I honestly thought it might be a two-minute job, so I didn't come in prepared to say anything. I thought there'd be somebody there who'd say, 'How are you? Fine. Well come back in six weeks' time!' This is what I expected. You appeared to be in no hurry, all the time. I couldn't believe it. At first I thought, even after spending a couple of hours, I thought that must have been a fluke. You mustn't have had anything else to do that afternoon. It won't happen again. And then when it happened the next time I began to believe in it. It was amazing at first, it was. I think this is partly because this has happened to you in your search for someone to help you. When you eventually come to someone, you don't believe it. It's too good to be true. It's like having a raging toothache and no dentist will take your tooth out and then one says, 'I'll take your tooth out.' "

I asked Joan whether knowing something about the person she talked to was helpful.

"It would help the patient," she said, "or, I mean, it would help me to know that the other person knew what I was talking about. If I talk to Bill about it, he's never felt depressed and he hasn't a clue. I couldn't explain how I felt to somebody who'd never felt it themselves. I think you've got to feel depressed to understand how it feels. And to know that the other person knows how you feel, you feel that you're putting over to them somehow .... It's terribly difficult to explain that enclosed feeling. You can't actually explain it unless you know somebody else that you're talking to has experienced it and you know that they know what you are talking about. You don't feel that you can explain it. You just want people to know what you mean without having to explain."

5

MARY

One of the fascinating things about being in England is that I keep meeting people whose portraits I have seen in the history books I used to read in Australia. Mary was one of these people. I had seen her when she was a mediaeval princess, tall and slender, her long hair framing an oval face of delicate strength, her blue eyes looking at the world with wonder and reserve. Now she was a bank clerk. Her father was a builder and her boyfriend mended cars.

I first met Mary when she was referred to me by her psychiatrist for assessment of her intelligence and personality and to ascertain whether she was "suitable for psychotherapy". This was Mary's second admission to hospital. She had first been admitted when she was sixteen. Her clinical notes described her as very withdrawn. She was given ECT, after which she became more outgoing and she was discharged. The diagnosis was "reactive depression in a girl of sixteen years following abortion and resultant guilt feelings". Not quite two years later she was admitted to hospital again in a very depressed state, very withdrawn and seen by her consultant as suffering extreme guilt. This time the diagnosis was "endogenous depression". Again she was given a course of ECT.

At this time I was engaged in setting up a department of clinical psychology. This took a great deal of time and energy, so I did not want to make any long-term commitments to individual patients. However, Mary's doctor used some successful guilt-arousing tactics to persuade me to see her regularly. He said that he and the nursing staff were concerned about her, since, even though she had responded to ECT, she had "surrounded herself with a defensive wall".

So Mary and I met once a week or a fortnight for an hour or two. We drank coffee and sat quietly while she told me about her family, her job and the plans for her wedding. When her wedding day and my summer holidays drew near we both felt that we had dutifully met one another as we had been instructed by the doctor and now we could part. I wished her well and told her that she could get in touch with me at any time. I sent her a wedding present and received a thank-you note. In the months following her marriage she wrote to me twice, letters which were simple accounts of what she was doing. Each time a letter arrived I wondered if it contained a plea for help, but there was nothing in each to which I could respond by asking her to come to see me. Then one day, nine months after her wedding, she phoned me to say that she felt very depressed. I told her that I would drive up to her village to see her that afternoon.

When I finally arrived at Mary's home, she seemed much better than she had sounded on the telephone. Mary said that she would like to see me again, regularly, so we made arrangements for this (not an easy thing to do in a large county which is almost bereft of public transport).

When we met, five days later, I explained to Mary that I thought that from then on our relationship would be different. I said, "When we first met we were both forced to meet one another. Dr Smith said to you, 'I want you to go and see Dr Rowe,' and he said to me, 'I want you to see this girl,' and at that stage I was working hard at setting up this department. I wasn't going to get involved in any relationship with anybody, because all my time and effort was going into getting things going. But Dr Smith was going to retire and he said to me, 'You can't let this young girl down,' so you see neither you nor I had much choice about it. We might never have chosen to meet if we had been given the option. So I felt it never went anywhere, although we got to know one another a little bit. I thought that possibly you had made a choice, it was something you wanted to do when you rang me up, when you said you didn't feel very well. Now I think we both feel this is a different relationship."

"I'm always frightened when I do things on the spur of the moment," said Mary. "I think I'm going to get told off for doing it. When I phoned you up I was saying, 'Have I done the right thing?' If I do something myself I always think there will be someone who will get mad at me."

So Mary and I met every fortnight for six months. By then her pregnancy made it too difficult for her to travel the twenty miles by bus. She seemed very happy, so I visited her at home only twice, but we kept in touch by letter and telephone and I went to see her after her baby was born.

Shortly before Mary was married she and I had spent an afternoon doing a repertory grid. As well as herself and her ideal self, she considered her parents and sister Fay, her fiancé Robert, her boss, her grandmother, grandfather and me. The words she chose to describe these people were "depressed", "careful with money", "bothers about people", "likes quiet", "self-conscious", "shy", "does things right", "happy", and "pig-headed". The analysis of the grid showed "self" as very isolated, the opposite to "sister" and associated with the ideas of "depressed", "careful with money" and "bothers about people". "Ideal self" was far away from "self" and close to the idea of "does things right". Her father, boss and grandfather were close to "pig-headed".

Nearly a year later, when she started coming to see me again, Mary repeated this grid. On the first grid Mary saw herself as being very isolated, but now she saw herself as much closer to other people. On the first grid she used "does things right" as an important construct, but on the second it was much less important. In all, she saw her world in much the same way as she had done a year before, but she was less extreme in her description of it.

On the first occasion when Mary did a grid, I spent time asking her about the implications of some of the constructs she had used. We began with "not careful with money". "People who are not careful with money," Mary said, "borrow from other people and soon owe a fortune. Owing money makes me uneasy. On the other hand, people who are 'careful with money' and 'mean', they 'don't bother about other people' they 'are not concerned with what people think or whether they are hurt'. This 'makes people upset' and so 'people don't like you'." She would prefer not to be "mean", and "to buy people presents", "to bother about people", but she found that when she bothered about people this "makes me miserable". So, as she saw it, if she was careful with her money people did not like her, and if she was not careful with her money she became miserable and uneasy.

For Mary the opposite of "self-conscious" was "not bothered with doing something the right way". Being "self-conscious" meant that she "worried about what people think", since, "I want to keep on the right side of everybody," and "I feel guilty if I upset anybody." Not bothering with doing something in the right way meant "not bothering what people think of you". Such people were like her sister Fay. She saw herself as being not like Fay, but that her parents "used to treat Fay and me as being the same" and this she felt was "not fair". "People," she said, "take no notice of what Fay does," and that too was "not fair". Whereas "people notice what I do. People wouldn't like me to behave like Fay," and if she did, "Dad would tell me off." So again the implications of both alternative were unhappy ones. She was left feeling guilty, or fearing rejection and her father's anger, or feeling that she was not being treated fairly.

When we finished the second grid, a year later, I asked her, "You would describe your father as someone who didn't care about people — what for you is the opposite of 'bothers about people'?" "They don't care if they upset someone."

Q. "Why is it important to be bothered about people?" A. "Well, you can't bother too much, or else you won't do anything for yourself. But if you bother about other people, they will bother about you. If you are ill they will come round and cheer you up." Q. "What would happen if you bothered too much?" A. "If you bother too much they will come to expect it, and you won't have time for yourself." Q. "Why is it important to have time for yourself?"

Mary thought for a while and then said, "To do the things you want to do."

Q. "Do you mean to be yourself, an individual?" A. "Yes, in a way. I'm not very good at explaining myself. If you bother about other people too much, and don't think about yourself at all, you don't become an individual and they become dependent on you. People can be inclined to use you." *A.* "So, if you bother too much, people will use you. If you don't bother at all, what happens?" *A.* "People won't do anything for you, because you won't do anything in return. People think they're not appreciated and say, 'Why should I do it?' " *Q.* "If you bother too much about people you'll just sort of be a doormat, a nobody. If you don't care at all people won't like you?" *A.* "Yes, that's right. They think, 'Well I'll get nothing back' — that sort of thing." *Q.* "You would like to be somewhere in between?" *A.* "Yes. Being concerned about people makes you depressed."

A little later in this talk I said to Mary, "Now this is a problem I have been setting people and getting some interesting answers. Here is a situation (and situations like this do arise at times) which you can't avoid and there are only two ways in which you can act. If you act in one way people will like you but they won't respect you, but if you act in the other way people will respect you but they won't like you. Which would you choose? Do you want people to respect you or to like you?"

"I don't know. Whatever was the easiest way out, knowing me. If it was somebody I thought a lot about I would like them to respect me. I suppose. Yes. Some people aren't bothered whether they like me or not. But not having so many friends I wouldn't want to lose their friendship. It's like a joint effort between me and Robert. I'm not very good at making decisions on my own."

"This is the sort of problem we were talking about when we worked out that if you bother too much about people you become a doormat and people don't respect you, and if you don't bother at all people don't like you. Suppose we changed the problem round and said the situation was like this — suppose you had to face this situation and if you acted one way people would like you, but you wouldn't respect yourself. If you acted the other way people wouldn't like you but you would respect yourself. If you had to choose between people liking you and self-respect?" "People liking me."

Q. "So you would give up your own self-respect? You want people to like you even if you gave up your self-respect?" *A.* "It depresses me." *Q.* "Is this one way of describing what happens when you get depressed? You're pushed into a situation where you've got to make this choice, and you end up doing something you don't approve of?" *A.* "Yes. It's more a case of relying on other people's opinions too much. I'm always asking people what I should do." *Q.* "Then at the same time you have some ideas about what is the right or wrong thing to do?" *A.* "I always know what I would like to do, but I always ask somebody." *Q.* "Who are the people you ask?" *A.* "Generally Robert, sometimes my sister, if she is in one of her serious grown-up moods. It's usually Robert. I try and get an answer out of him sometimes. Then sometimes I still don't know what to do. Well, I can usually tell, if he's for it he doesn't say anything, but if he's against it he'll say. I can't make decisions myself. I sort of tag along." *Q.*

"But sometimes you end up tagging along and doing things you don't want to do. You've had a lot of things done to you, haven't you?" *A*. "Yes. I don't blame anyone else — I blame myself." *Q*. "Do you blame yourself because you couldn't make your own decisions?" *A*. "I suppose so. I wish I could have done what I wanted. Everyone else seemed to think I did right."

We talked about one decision she had made for herself, that of getting in touch with me again. Mary talked of how she feared that if she did anything herself people would get angry with her. Then she said, "I can't talk to anybody else because they've got funny ideas, different to mine. I think they think I'm a crackpot .... My mum won't listen, and I'm frightened of upsetting my mum. Sometimes you can talk to her and sometimes you can't. And Robert, you can't talk to him. His way of thinking is so different. He really can't see why you're depressed. He tries to understand but he just can't see it. He thinks I'm better off talking to someone who can understand me. But usually what I get is, 'Oh no, not that again.' He just can't understand."

Q. "When he says he can't understand, do you feel he doesn't want to?" *A*. "Yes, I do sometimes. I think he doesn't try. I think it's something he's never met before. His family is so happy-go-lucky sort of thing. It seems so unimportant to him."

We talked about her family and then I said, "Well, if you were able to make your own decisions you wouldn't be forced into situations where you did things you didn't want to do, then you wouldn't get depressed. So what you need are some pills to make you stand up for yourself — but we don't have those sort of pills because they would start a revolution." "It's just that I get put upon. People will say, 'Oh, Mary will do it.' In the bank I keep changing my job to get the hang of the work, and it's surprising how many things follow me round from job to job. I get things like that." Mary went on to describe how everyone used her as a doormat, "I don't like to say no."

Q. "What would happen if you did?" *A*. "I'd feel guilty. Other people think if anything wants doing, 'Mary will do it.' I'm afraid of upsetting people if I refuse." *Q*. "Does Robert think you're a doormat?" *A*. "Sometimes he does, though he does things for me sometimes."

Her mother did not see her as a doormat. "She'd never ask for anything unless it was important. She gives me things. Mum buys things for herself, she says, and then finds they don't fit her, so she gives them to me. Dad says she's not to buy me things. I get given a lot of things other people don't want. My sister gives me make-up she doesn't want. People give me clothes that's too small for them. I don't want them but I can't say no. I feel awful if they find out I don't wear them."

Q. "Do you feel put down by these presents?" *A.* "I feel put down."

Three months later, when we had returned to this question of her fearing to upset other people, I asked, "When somebody gets angry with you, do you feel this person hates you, dislikes you?" "Yes, I do a bit. I always tell Robert nobody loves me."

Q. "You don't feel that somebody could get angry with you about something you had done, but that person would still care for you?" *A.* "I suppose if I stop and think about it I'd think so, but I get carried away — they shout at me and I think they don't like me."

I said that many people felt like this, but in fact it was possible to be angry and still love the person who angered you. 'Do you stop loving Robert when you get angry with him?" I asked. "No, but that doesn't make any difference. I get this idea in my head and I can't shift it."

Q. "When you feel that someone dislikes you, do you feel that it's that person's fault or yours?" *A.* "It's my fault. I wonder what I've done to upset them." *Q.* "Yet it could be the other person's fault." *A.* "It could be, but I've got this feeling that I'm useless. I always think that I'm in the wrong when the boss sends for me." *Q.* "Do you get told off as much now as you did when you were a little girl?" *A.* "I don't get told off much at all. I'm just convinced that I'm going to be all the time." *Q.* "Robert distinguishes between what you do and what you are." *A.* "But Robert often complains. I really think he's making a joke, but I take it far more seriously."

Mary's case notes had stated that she had "no difficulty in getting on with her parents", and that she "gets on well with her father", but, when interviewed then, she must have been more loyal than honest. This was, in fact, a very unhappy family.

Mary's father was a large, domineering man who saw himself in charge of his wife and daughters and who did not spare himself in giving advice and instruction, most of which was unwanted by Mary. But she dare not oppose or criticize him since she was still as frightened of him as she had always been. When she was small the family lived in a house on a busy road. She said, "According to my dad, when I was about two I used to go out of the gate and run up and down the path. One night he was giving me a lecture on it (I was only two) and the next day he was driving past, and I saw his van and waved, and he saw me and got out of the van, put me inside the gate and gave me such a good hiding — I never went out of that gate again. I think that is where my fear of him came from although I don't actually remember it myself. My dad thinks it's such a clever story to tell." "It taught you to be frightened of him and frightened of roads," I commented. (Mary was terrified of walking down the main street and especially of crossing the road.)

Once I asked her if she ever did the opposite to what her father said. "I'd like to," she said, "but I'm frightened of him. I always thought he would find out. I'd be in tears if he shouted at me. I've usually done what he said. I used to think he was God, he'd find out if I did anything."

Q. "How old were you when you found out that he didn't know everything you did?" A. "Not long ago. It was Robert more than anyone who convinced me he wasn't God .... Dad took everything I did so seriously, so much that he took the enjoyment out of things — like when I took art at school, he was always so critical of everything I did. Dad thought I was a great artist — same with English, he used to look in the dictionary for long words. He wanted me to come first. I would have enjoyed it if he hadn't been pushing me. I didn't get on with men teachers who were just like my dad. I got on better with teachers that were like my mum. They seemed to have more patience. When I went to high school there was a shed between the boys' and girls' schools. He warned me if I went behind the shed with a boy he'd find out — the school caretaker would tell him. He was more pleased about me passing the Eleven Plus than I was. I was his little girl. He told everybody that. He expected me to stay little and his. When you're little they think it's funny for you to have boyfriends. When you're older they don't like it. I didn't like grammar school, I was pushed all the time. I think by the time I was finished they were glad to get rid of me."

"Were you depressed then?" I asked. "I was in my second year. I wouldn't go to school. There was a group of us always being pushed to do better than the others. My mother didn't push, my dad did, the teachers as well."

Q. "You had your father pushing you to be something special and different. When I was at your place the other day, you said that you wanted to be ordinary. Why is it important to you to be ordinary?" A. "I don't like people who think they are better than they are and look down on other people. Usually the sort that are a bit above themselves aren't nice. I don't like people who look down on you. My dad looks down on people." Q. "So has your father been trying to push you to be somebody special so you can be the sort of person that looks down on other people? He doesn't put that bit in, but is this the way you've felt it? If he makes me be somebody special then I'll end up like one of those nasty people that look down on other people?" A. "Yes. He has great ideas about what I'm going to be." Q. "So he'd say he was trying to make you into the sort of person he wanted you to be, and you'd say he was trying to make you into the sort of person he was." A. "Dad's a great believer in education. It broke his heart when I left school. He thought I was going to do something important when I left school." Q. "How do you feel when someone says you're something special?" A. "I don't feel special. Dad wanted me to do those things to make him look better. I knew Robert when I was in the third year at school. By the time I was in the fifth year we were thinking of getting engaged." *Q.* "How old were you when you decided not to be what your father wanted you to be?" *A.* "Fifteen. At Christmas. We'd had a bit of a row over Robert. He was trying to split us up. He'd decided Robert wasn't good enough. He'd only been to a secondary modern school. I think that was the first time I really went against him. Up till then I didn't see much wrong with him. He had it in his power to split us up."

Just how important her father had been to her was shown when Mary said, "I can't remember my mum when I was little but I can remember my dad. I can't remember what my mum looked like, but I can remember what my dad looked like. Very tall and slim and black hair. When my sister was born, so I wouldn't be left out, dad used to take me out a lot."

Q. "Did you have good times as well as bad with your dad?" *A.* "A mixture of both. I remember him introducing me to people — he was so proud. He took me with him when he went to work .... Dad never talked to Robert. Robert couldn't come to the house — he'd come there when only mum was there. He's got such funny ideas. He's got all the answers, but you know it's a lot of rubbish. He thinks he's brought me up to talk to him. He'd do anything for me, but I can't talk to him. He has funny ideas about my mum. She can't talk to him."

Her father's attitude to Robert had not got any friendlier after their marriage. As Mary said, "He's extremely jealous of anything we've got that he hasn't. He thinks we ought to struggle. He's frightened we'll get a house better than his. Anything we've got that's better, he'll try to pull down. It wouldn't have been like this if I'd stayed at school, single, he could have boasted about me."

Q. "He could have taken the credit?" *A.* "Yes. He thinks it's wrong that we should want to better ourselves. We should be thankful for what we've got. He thought it funny when Robert failed his driving test. Any bad point he can find, he'll come straight round to tell us. He wants to think that Robert is lazy, doesn't want to work. He thinks that Robert doesn't think enough about me. He thinks Robert didn't want to marry me. My dad thinks he is the boss. And we let him think it as well. He tells me what to do and what not to do. Robert says he is the only man who knows everything."

Mary often talked of how angry her father made her. She sometimes vented this anger against Robert. "I just take it out on Robert," she said, "I know it's dad but I take it out on Robert."

Q. "Would you feel guilty if you took it out on your father?" *A.* "I don't know what to say. I think he would feel guilty, but I don't think I should ever do it." *Q.* "Why would you never do it?" *A.* "Because I'm supposed to do what he says." *Q.* "Do you mean that fathers should always be obeyed?" *A.* "I don't know why I think that, but I do. I don't think he is right, and I don't think I should take any notice of him, so — I suppose parents know best."

Two months later I said to her, "You're not as bothered by your father now as you were when you were a little girl. As you get older you'll stop being bothered by him. What he says to you won't have the same power to upset you." "I find I can stand so much and after that I get so angry. Sometimes I come home from my dad's and I'm so mad."

Q. "Have you ever answered him back?" *A.* "No." *Q.* "What would happen if you did?" *A.* "I don't know as if much would happen, but I don't think I dare do it. I just get all sorts of threats about what would happen if I answered him back. There would be so much trouble." *Q.* "What would he threaten to do to you?" *A.* "Belt me." *Q.* "Well, he can't do that now." *A.* "I get very close sometimes to answering him back. I get these little remarks in now and again. I come out feeling so good if I managed to get one in, you know. If I say something I've got to get out pretty quick."

But she was not likely to answer him back very strongly or often for, as she said, "I feel sorry for him because I know he cares and that he would do anything for any of us."

Although her father wanted her to do well at school, Mary said that he would never go to any of the school functions. "Did you want him to go?" I asked. "No. He always made out he knew everything. I was in a concert once. He didn't come but my mother did. He wanted me to get on but he wouldn't come to meetings or concerts. Mum used to come. Mum used to feel out of place — a lot of people talked posh at that school."

Another time Mary said of her parents, "My dad's more forceful than my mum. She's very quiet with him. She won't put on anybody."

Q. "Were you frightened of your mother?" *A.* "I don't think so. The only thing I was frightened of was if I did anything wrong she would tell my dad. She couldn't hit me as hard as he could." *Q.* "How did she feel about your father hitting you?" *A.* "I don't really know. I can't really remember her being there. She used to say, 'If you tell the truth I won't punish you.' I really can't remember her being about." *Q.* "But sometimes she would be the cause of you getting punished because she would tell your father." *A.* "Yes. Most of the time she would just threaten. She'd usually say, 'Wait till your father comes home,' when we'd done something wrong. Then we'd go and hide. I remember being told off for doing nothing wrong, or nothing I could think of."

Here, I talked about how, in effect, a child never has one good parent and one bad parent for, in the child's eyes, if the good parent does not protect the child from the bad parent then the child has two bad parents. Mary's comment was, "Mum wouldn't dare interfere. She'd get into trouble if she went against him. It's very seldom that my mother will stand up to my dad. I can remember them once having an argument about two years ago when I was at home and that's the only argument I can remember them ever having. She won't even answer him back. She always sides with him."

> Q. "If it was something where you were involved, would she side with him then?" A. "I think she would try not to get involved then. But if she had to take a side, I think she would take my dad's."

This was, Mary said, because her mother was frightened of her father. "If she has bought any new clothes, she won't tell him. She puts them in the wardrobe. If he says, 'Where's that come from?' she'll say, 'Oh, I've had that ages.' She won't tell him she's bought anything."

One day, when Mary was telling me how she often cannot tell whether Robert is angry with her or just joking, she said that she had never really learned about jokes because there were very few jokes ever made in her home. Robert's parents laugh a lot but hers never do. I asked her, "How do you feel when you're with people who laugh a lot?" "All right after I get used to them."

> Q. "Why are your parents so serious?" A. "They're ones for doing things properly — they're proud of doing things properly." Q. "But, are you putting these two ideas together — people who take things serious do things properly? And so people who laugh don't do things properly?" A. "Well, yes, I hadn't thought of the last part." Q. "Every attitude we take has an advantage as well as a disadvantage. Taking things seriously has obvious disadvantages, but this seems to be the advantage. Would it be possible to laugh a lot and do things properly?" A. "I suppose it would, but ...." Q. "You've never considered it?" A. "No, I think that mum and dad took little things that didn't matter seriously." Q. "I suppose that I consider that I laugh a lot and that I do things properly. I might be wrong, but that's how I see myself. I wouldn't want to live a life where I didn't laugh a lot." A. "I enjoy being with Robert's parents, but I feel guilty because I'm with them, enjoying myself." Q. "Why do you feel guilty?" A. "I don't like to tell my mum I've been out having a good time. My mum's been awfully depressed lately and I feel guilty about having a good time." Q. "If you tell her you've been enjoying yourself what does she say?" A. "She always says she's pleased for me, but I always feel so rotten." Q. "You don't think it makes her happy to know that you're happy?" A. "I know, but I still feel guilty. My dad's so peculiar, you can't go out and have a good time with him." Q. "Do you feel it's up to you to make sure your mother's happy?" A. "It seems to

me as if it is." *Q.* "Does your father make you feel guilty about being happy?" *A.* "I don't let him bother me too much — he's often jealous." *Q.* "On the whole it's not a good idea to turn up at your parents' place when you're happy." *A.* "Yes." *Q.* "Was it safe to be happy when you were little?" *A.* "I can't remember. I can't remember any particular good times we had. I can't remember many happy times. I can remember mum letting us play mud-pies once in our best dresses. That was the best day of my life. It was only because we were growing out of our best dresses, but I didn't realize it at the time. If ever mum slapped us round the ankles he had to get in on the act and take over. I remember I caught fire once and mum was trying to beat out the flames, and he looked through the window and thought she was belting me and he came in and took over — my sister had found a box of matches and set fire to me — he was so big — that's my dad's trouble." *Q.* "So by taking seriously things you avoid situations of having to feel pity for your mother and making your father jealous and you also do things properly. There's a lot of advantages about taking things seriously." *A.* "I suppose there is."

Mary often contrasted herself and her sister. Her parents saw her "always as a quiet little girl" who "played with dolls quietly" while, "My sister was a tomboy. She gets more attention than I have ever done — more clothes, more toys. Mum's always careful not to leave her out, make sure she's wanted. I wouldn't say she was unhappy. She expects to be like me without being like me. Because she's so like dad they clash so much. She always comes off worst. Dad sees to that …. When she was little she wanted to be like me. We were always dressed the same."

Q. "Why does she want to be like you?" *A.* "I don't know. I'd like to be like her in a way." *Q.* "In what way would you like to be like her?" *A.* "More easygoing. Wish I'd gone to her school. She always seemed happy at school. Nothing much bothers her. If anyone upsets her, she tells them so — too much — there are times when you should keep quiet." *Q.* "When you were tiny, did your parents see you as alike or different?" *A.* "Alike, I think, as far as I can remember. Both dressed the same." *Q.* "How did you feel about this?" *A.* "I was mad — I had to wait two and a half years longer for anything that Fay did. We got everything together — got prams the same Christmas — identical dolls — We never used to play together. She played with children down the street but there was nobody my age. I stayed home making dirty pastry or something like that. I used to read a lot when I was little. Things like *Black Beauty*. Fay didn't learn to read as quickly as I did. I didn't think my mum and dad could ever understand why Fay wasn't as clever as I was." *Q.* "How did they feel about this?" *A.* "They got angry and would shout at her. They just sort of gave up in the end." *Q.* "This must have been worrying for her." *A.* "I suppose it must have been. I've never thought about it."

Mary had met Robert when they were at school and had fallen in love with him. He protected her against her fears and was a bulwark against her depression. He stood by her when she became pregnant by him at fifteen and her family insisted on an abortion. They were engaged and married by the time she was nineteen and it seemed to me that Robert cared as much for Mary as she cared for him.

But loving someone rarely means understanding that person. Mary loved the way Robert would laugh and joke, but she thought that so much laughing and joking was a sign that he did not take serious matters seriously. Such a refusal meant to her that he was not greatly concerned about her. The fact that he was strong and independent and could make decisions meant that she thought she should always ask his opinion about the smallest household matter and that she should ask his permission for everything that she did. "I say to Robert, 'Can I go out?' and he says, 'You don't have to ask me, of course you can.' He thinks it's funny because I think he won't let me go out."

Robert came to one of our sessions and no amount of laughing and joking on his part could hide the fact that he was very nervous. I pointed this out to Mary who said to Robert, "You don't get bothered." "I get bothered and don't show it," he said. "Do you get bothered about Mary and not show it?" I asked. "Yes," he said. "I don't believe it," she said.

Just as she shut him out by believing that he did not worry about her, she shut him out by refusing to tell him what was wrong when she was depressed. "You won't tell me anything," he said. So it seemed that the one time she wanted him to show concern, when she was depressed, was the one time when she refused to respond to any sign of concern from him. He would ask her what was wrong and she would say, "Nothing." "Why won't you tell him?" I asked. "The words won't just come out," she said.

It was not surprising to me that she could not describe to him what was happening to her. It was only by getting her to talk about her private imagery that I could come to any understanding of her experience of depression. When I had asked her to describe her image of being depressed she had said, "Me shut off from the rest of the world, all on my own. That's how I feel. When I talk about depression I always see me on my bed and nobody else."

> Q. "Where is your bed?" A. "In the flat where it is now — Robert sat in front of the telly not caring. He's thinking, 'What a daft thing she is'. I could get up and go out but I'm frightened that people are going to look at me." Q. "Why are you frightened of people looking at you?" A. "I'd think 'What's happened now?' At work when anyone comes up to me I think, 'What on earth have I done now?' They tell me off at work. They say I should have a better opinion of myself. But when I was off work a few weeks ago I felt completely safe in that flat. Nothing could hurt me there."

I commented, "I think this is something in depression that just isn't understood. Depressed people are seen as just being down. I hadn't understood this until I saw it happening to someone. He just couldn't get out the door. It was just too frightening." "Yes, I'm like that for some reason. It's peculiar really. I open the door and close it behind me and think, 'I'm safe at last.' "

Q. "It's easier to say to people, 'I feel dreadful, I can't go out,' because if you say to them I'm frightened to go out ...." A. "It's stupid. I don't feel so bad if I go out with Robert, but I don't stop out long. I want to go home again, but I feel safer if I go out with him than if I go out on my own — that he'll look after me. He wants to stop out longer than I do — then I want to go home again. He calls me a stick-in-the-mud. I'd be quite content if he went out on his own and I stayed home on my own." Q. "You say you feel like this most of the time?" A. "I do really, yes." Q. "How do you manage when you've got to come to see me?" A. "I don't think about it. I busy my mind with other things and the next thing I know I'm in the bus. That's how I am. My mind's always full of things, I'm always thinking of what I've got to do. If I ever sat down and thought about it I'd never get here." Q. "Is it like this every day when you've got to go to work?" A. "Yes, I dread getting up. Some days are worse than others. No one can do the shopping faster than I can. I whizz round the shops and back into the bank again, in the rest-room — funny I feel safe in the rest-room — not as safe as home — but safer than outside. Some days I can't even cross the road. I won't cross until the road is absolutely empty. Other days I'll be in a dream and wander across and wonder why everyone's braking like mad. I'm in a dream. I get to work and think, 'I can't remember leaving home'. Before I was married my bedroom was the only room I liked. I used to sit up there always. At home I used to be terrified at night alone, but it never bothers me to be alone in the flat at night. I used to think there was a ghost in that house. The ghost of an old woman. I never saw her. One night one of my pin-ups fell down. I was convinced she'd pulled it off. I used to dread being in the house on my own. I used to creep down the stairs and hear funny noises. I'd never go in the attic alone. The first time I saw that house I didn't like it. If ever I went to bed alone in that house I'd make sure my head was under the covers so she couldn't get me. Right until I left home last year I kept my head under the pillows." Q. "Would you say that the worst part of being depressed is your fear of going outside?" A. "Yes. When I was off work I was perfectly happy." Q. "You didn't feel depressed?" A. "I felt safe."

Earlier Mary had said that when she was really down she tried to stop herself thinking of all the things that upset her. Now I asked, "When you feel safe do you still go on thinking those terrible thoughts?" "I think of them, but they don't hurt me so much because I'm safe."

Q. "Do you have times when you're not thinking these terrible thoughts and can go out?" A. "There are times but they don't last long.

Sometimes I look forward to going out and when I get out I want to go home." *Q*. "How long have you had this fear of going out?" *A*. "It started when I first didn't want to go to school. Mum used to push me through the school gates. I'd stand outside the front door. If she got me to the gate usually I'd go in. When I got to high school that's when she realized, when she took me to the doctor's for the first time. I wouldn't go to school. I used to walk up the road and then come back again." *Q*. "Does Robert understand how you feel?" *A*. "I don't think so. He says I'm a spoilsport, like a wet weekend, but I'm not as bad as I used to be. I used to affect everyone. I try not to let is show. Sometimes I think I have done well because I felt so awful, then he'll say, 'You were awful. What's wrong with you?' I'm terrible with people I don't know. Robert's marvellous to have when you're on the verge, half and half, never a dull moment, but sometimes I don't appreciate it. He's always bounding with energy. He tells me I sleep too much."

The next week, when Mary arrived, I asked her, "How did you manage to get out of the house and down here?" "Last night I didn't think I was going to make it."

Q. "People don't realize how brave you are." *A*. "It's not so bad if there are not many people about. If the bus is full I can't wait to get off. I look to see how many people are in the High Street. I couldn't get to sleep last night, worrying about coming here. It's not so bad at work these days. I dread going to work and coming home. I dread the party next Saturday. I daren't tell Robert. He'd call me a miserable old so-and-so." *Q*. "What makes you frightened at the party?" *A*. "So many people there, that's what worries me the most. I've been frightened of parties when I've known everyone there." *Q*. "When you feel frightened like this, can you attach the fear to something like, 'I feel frightened of something, like being bitten by a dog, or getting run over.' Do you attach something to your fear or just get frightened?" *A*. "When I'm at home I'm convinced that there's a big bogeyman watching for me outside. I get convinced that if I go outside something's going to happen to me. At home I feel completely safe as if nothing can harm me. I get very frightened of roads." *Q*. "When you can't get outside — the bogeyman — is that the image you have in your mind? But what sort of thing? If you had to draw a picture of it, what would it look like?" *A*. "A big black person to get me. If I think about it, it looks like my dad — sounds daft. I imagine him all dirty, his hands all dirty, his face dirty. He's always like that. I admit he's got a mucky job, but I think he could be a bit cleaner. Most fellows come home dirty, but he washes his hands and they're still dirty." *Q*. "So what will the black shape do if you go outside?" *A*. "Just being there is bad enough, never mind him doing anything — he thinks he can do as he wants all the time. When I said we might be going to town to see my Gran and then we didn't go, and when I went round later to see my dad I got into ever so much trouble because I hadn't let him know I hadn't been. He still thinks that I should tell him of all my movements ...."

She went on talking about her visits to her grandmother and she rushed on to tell me a story which she had told me before, how when she was fifteen, her father had suddenly announced that all the family were going on holiday immediately and it was only with difficulty that she could persuade him to let her run round to Robert's house to tell him that she was going away. "When he speaks we've got to move."

I said, "This fear you've got of going outside is so great that you can't talk about it. We start to talk about it, then you go off on to something else." "Yes, I know." There was a long pause and then I said, "If you describe it as something that is waiting for you, something that looks like your father when he's very dirty, it's more than that, because if it were just your father, you've got ways of dealing with him in the here and now, so it's not your father at present." "It's like Robert says, I live in a world of my own and nobody else can get in. When I'm at home I feel nobody can hurt me or anything. When I go out it's ... it might hurt."

Q. "What sort of hurt can people do to you?" A. "I don't know — people can be unkind — people can say horrible things that can upset you."

We went on to talk about one thing that people can talk about and upset her — babies. The following week Robert came with her and the week after that we talked about how she behaved like a little girl with Robert and with me to avert our anger. So we did not return to the question of her fearful images until the next week.

As Mary came down the corridor to my room a dog bounced out of the coffee-room and ran up to her. Later I asked her, "How did you feel when you were standing out there and Harry's dog came down the hall?" "Awful — it's cats I don't like. They're all right as long as they don't come near me. If it sits on my knee I can't move."

Q. "What do you fear will happen?" A. "I don't know — I'm frightened of all of them — mice, birds, cats, anything. They're all right as long as they don't come near me. I don't know why."

We talked about her fear and Mary said, "It's hard to put it into words what I feel and think. Like a feeling you can't describe. It's like something that takes over you."

Q. "It takes you over?" A. "It seems to. Like a space programme when people from outer space take over, like that, you know." Q. "Yes, well, what does it look like?" A. "I know last time I said it looked like my dad, but I don't know. Whether it's because my dad gives me the same sort of feeling, I don't know." Q. "If you had to draw a picture of it, what would it look like?" A. "It's a bit like one of those invisible barriers you see on television — you just put your hand out — it's a bit like that. It's at the door of our flat." *Q.* "What happens if you walk up to it?" *A.* "If I insist that I am going out I can walk through it — but it seems to make me change my mind that I want to go out." *Q.* "How does it do this?" *A.* "I just start to think, well, do I really need to go out, or else I — if it's something like work, well, I think I have to go, I can't keep having time off, and I manage to persuade myself that I have to go out, but if it's shopping, I think, well, can I last until tomorrow, I sort of go on thinking if Robert's home tomorrow he can take me, things like that." *Q.* "You can get through the barrier with Robert?" *A.* "Yes. I don't like stopping out long. I like to get back. I feel so uncomfortable. I don't know why but I am. When I'm in the pub or anywhere I feel so uncomfortable after a while." *Q.* "You've got to be back behind your barrier?" *A.* "Yes. I think, 'I'm not going to say anything,' and I don't realize that I've done it — I just stop speaking, we'll come out and Robert will say, 'I thought we'd better come, you've gone all quiet and awkward again.' I'm not awkward, I just sort of shut up. I feel like sort of hiding in a corner." *Q.* "Was this barrier at home when you lived there?" *A.* "Yes. I could sit for hours in my bedroom and that never bothered me — that was safe but I never really felt comfortable anywhere else in the house." *Q.* "So, when you're behind the invisible barrier you feel safe, but at the same time you feel that this invisible barrier in some way controls you?" *A.* "Yes."

"If the invisible barrier was a person what sort of person would it be?" "I suppose, a very protective one, one that's sort of, I suppose, I always imagine that outside is always dangerous. The barrier keeps me away from all this danger, I suppose."

Q. "How would you describe a protective person?" *A.* "Always holding my hand, and I don't know, sort of — something that won't let anything touch me, if you know what I mean, some sort of harm could come to me in the flat, but that doesn't bother me. I can't picture the barrier as a person. It's more like a cloud that you can't get through and out." *Q.* "Can it move round with you?" *A.* "I don't know. I've never thought of taking it with me." *Q.* "How does this cloud feel about you?" *A.* "I suppose it must be very possessive, it doesn't want me to leave it, I suppose." *Q.* "Does it feel loving?" *A.* "I suppose it must in its own way. It doesn't want anything to hurt me so it must like me." *Q.* "How does it feel when you go away and leave it?" *A.* "Sort of — its voice — I can always hear its voice calling me back." *Q.* "But is it calling you in a sort of ordering way, or is it plaintive and lost or is it ...?" *A.* "Pleading, I think. It's upset that I've gone, that's the only way to describe it. Because I was on holiday for two weeks and I only went out three times, and twice I was only out for half an hour. It's always calling me to get back and when I have to go out ...." *Q.* "How do you feel about the cloud?" *A.* "I don't want to hurt its feelings, but I don't want it. I should love just to be able to get out and wander about without sort of being nervous and frightened." *Q*. "Why don't you want to hurt its feelings?" *A*. "Because I don't want to hurt anyone's feelings — I'm always frightened of upsetting anybody and anything. Even if I don't like them I shouldn't want to hurt them." *Q*. "What would happen if you upset the cloud — hurt its feelings?" *A*. "Probably it wouldn't hurt the cloud at all — probably hurt me. I should feel guilty." *Q*. "So everytime you go out you have the cloud behind and it's pleading with you to come back. The longer you stay out the guiltier you feel, and so when you go home and stay home, while you might not be doing a lot of the things you'd like to be doing you haven't got the cloud pleading?" *A*. "No, it feels sort of content and ...." *Q*. "You don't feel guilty then?" *A*. "Yes — things upset me easily when I'm out, but it takes a lot to upset me when I'm at home. I sort of feel, 'Well, it's my territory, this bit.' " *Q*. "How long have you known this cloud?" *A*. "I suppose practically all my life, I don't know." *Q*. "Can you remember when it started?" *A*. "I think it started when we moved to the house we've got now, because I can't remember the other place — mind you, I liked that house, and didn't want to leave that house so maybe it was there then — I don't know. But it seemed to get worse when we moved into the house we're in now that I really started not wanting to go to school, things like that." *Q*. "Was the cloud waiting outside when you had to go to school?" *A*. "I could never get out the door — I used to walk up the road and come back again. Mum used to get ever so mad — I used to tell her she didn't love me. She wouldn't make me go to school if she loved me, I used to say." *Q*. "Is the cloud more like your father or more like your mother or more like Robert?" *A*. "I suppose in a way it's mainly like Robert — but mainly like my mum with my dad waiting on the other side of it — the great dirty man waiting outside, on the other side of the cloud." *Q*. "Does the cloud tell you that the outside world is dangerous?" *A*. "It makes me feel that it is." *Q*. "How does it do this?" *A*. "I get frightened of roads and traffic and people. I can't stand crowds. I won't go in shops if there's a lot in there. If there's a lot of people in the shop it's going to be a lot longer before I get back. I don't know." *Q*. "Can you summon up the cloud — get it to come here?" *A*. "I hope not. I've never tried it. It's all right at home." *Q*. "But what would happen if the cloud could move around?" *A*. "I suppose if it could move around permanently, I could go where I want, take it with me." *Q*. "If you did, you'd be safe wherever you went." *A*. "No, because it couldn't protect me, I mean, I'm sure a ten-ton lorry is stronger than it is. It couldn't actually protect me, it wants to stop me going out where I could get hurt, if you see what I mean. It wouldn't help if it could come with me. It's people more than barriers or cars — particularly some people. I get very edgy when I'm with them." *Q*. "How would you feel if you woke up one morning and found that the cloud was gone?" *A*. "Probably very lonely. I don't know. It would be a new experience." *Q.* "Would you be frightened?" *A.* "I can't imagine myself being frightened at home, and that's the only place where it is." *Q.* "What if — what if you were out — suppose next Saturday night you're sitting in the pub and you suddenly realized that the cloud has gone, how would you feel then?" *A.* "I'd probably enjoy myself. If I suddenly realized that I didn't want to go home." *Q.* "Do you talk to the cloud at all?" *A.* "I talk to myself. I don't talk to the cloud. I tell myself I'm daft when I don't want to go out." *Q.* "How would the cloud feel if you went out to it and said, 'Go away, I don't need you any more'?" *A.* "It would have to find somebody else." *Q.* "You feel it needs somebody?" *A.* "Yes." *Q.* "If you said that to it, would it pack up and go?" *A.* "No, it wouldn't. I'd have to convince myself that it's gone. It's only in my imagination anyway. It wouldn't go — I'd have to convince myself that it's gone." *Q.* "You remember when we talked about you being depressed and you described this image of you lying on your bed and Robert being in the next room. Does that link with the cloud in any way?" *A.* "I think it's stronger — I get worse about going out when I get depressed. I don't manage to get to work when I'm depressed. I don't know whether the cloud gets stronger or whether I don't have as much power to say that I'm going to work." *Q.* "Would you describe your relationship with the cloud as something of a battle?" *A.* "I suppose it is in a way." *Q.* "When you're depressed is that when the cloud is winning?" *A.* "It wins easier. I wouldn't say it's winning." *Q.* "What would happen if it won?" *A.* "I should never get out, never at all." *Q.* "When you were so depressed that they sent you to hospital, was this when the cloud was at its strongest?" *A.* "Yes. Mum couldn't even get me out the door to go to work or anything. She dragged me up one morning and said either you go to work or to the doctor's. I'd do anything rather than go out, but I wasn't happy at being home either — I was fighting a losing battle all the time."

The next time I saw Mary she was very happy. Her doctor had confirmed that she was pregnant. She told me her news as soon as she arrived. We discussed this for a while and then I asked, "So, being happy like this, how did you feel about coming out this morning?" "No, I'm not bothered. I had to come out — I had to tell somebody. The chap on the radio wouldn't listen to me this morning."

"Last week we talked about the images that have made you frightened. Now that we've talked about it, did it make any difference?" "I think I felt better afterwards, not so bothered. Some bit bothered, but not as bothered, I think. I sat thinking about it and it seemed daft and silly."

Q. "You described this cloud as telling you not to go outside. What are some of the dangers that you feel out there?" *A.* "I don't know — it's just — I sort of get these feelings — don't know what might happen. Don't really know what — I suppose the end of the world will come. I remember when I was at school, I thought that the end of the world would come when I went to school. I couldn't believe it when I came home at night and I was all right. It's nothing in particular — I don't know." *Q*. "Well, it really is something in particular isn't it?" *A*. "It's not that anything in particular was going to happen to me — it's feeling that something was going to happen." *Q*. "What is it that happens to all of us?" *A*. "I suppose we die." *Q*. "How much do you think about death?" *A*. "Not much about myself. I think about Robert. If someone talks about it I say, 'When it comes, it comes,' but I've often worried about Robert. I'm frightened of being on my own when I wake up in heaven. I wonder what it would be like to be a ghost." *Q*. "So when you were thinking of death then you were thinking of it in terms of you still being around, of there being another life beyond?" *A*. "Yes." *Q*. "But you feel that you could be frightened, that whatever it is, it's some place where you'll be on your own?" *A*. "Yes." *Q*. "When you're depressed do you think more about death?" *A*. "When I'm depressed I often wish I was dead myself, though I don't know what good it will do. I feel everybody would be better off without me — but it's got to be quick. I mean I couldn't bear to hurt myself — there's all sorts of things I couldn't do. I've thought of running under a lorry but knowing my luck they'd miss me." *Q*. "When you think they'd all be better off without me, what sort of picture comes in your mind? Do you get a picture of them being better off without you, or do you get a picture of you somewhere else?" *A*. "It's a picture of them carrying on as if I've never existed. I imagine Robert going back to his mum's." *Q*. "Do they talk about you?" *A*. "No, mum and dad and my sister, carrying on as they are doing now, just as if I've never lived there." *Q*. "You don't get a picture of them being all sorry?" *A*. "No." *Q*. "That's death to the *n*th degree, isn't it? What people have always done about death is to build memorials, so the people who are still alive can think they won't be forgotten because there'll be the gravestones, the memorial tablet, the statue that will make people remember." *A*. "I can imagine my grave being overrun with weeds and people not remembering — I can't imagine Robert at a funeral, not even mine. I can imagine him all laughing and cheerful. He hates people crying all over the place." *Q*. "Perhaps Robert always jokes most about the things that upset him the most." *A*. "When his dad was ill, he didn't seem bothered at all. He reckons he did, like, but he didn't show it. It's impossible he'll get upset if I die." *Q*. "Well, he doesn't let you see him get upset, but this doesn't mean he isn't upset." *A*. "I can't see Robert getting upset." *Q*. "I think you do Robert a grave injustice when you say those sort of things because, if you thought about it, the things he does ...." *A*. "I know, but I just can't picture him. I've never seen him upset, so I don't know what he'd look like. It's something I can't picture. His mum's just the opposite. She just reads about somebody dying in the daily newspaper and she's in tears." *Q*. "Well, this is probably why he doesn't show much, he's probably fed up with her."

Mary agreed that there might be something in this idea. I said that I thought that after all she and Robert had been to one another, it was unlikely, that, if she died or ran off with the milkman, he would forget her. Then I said, "I've got a picture of you after your death. There they are, all busy, going ahead, and you can see them as you're drifting round there and you're thinking, 'They've all forgotten all about me.' Is this the sort of picture that you get when you think about it?" "Yes. I imagine them carrying on as usual — I suppose they would. It's as if I'd never existed at all. As if I'm completely forgotten."

Q. "What would you prefer, that they forgot you when you died, or that they remembered you?" A. "I should like to be remembered. I don't suppose I'd like them crying all over the place or anything like that. It would be awful if you died and they just forgot you. May as well not have lived to start with." Q. "Why do you think they don't remember?" A. "I don't know. I suppose my mum would be ever so upset, but I can't imagine her being upset. I've caused so much trouble for them — they don't want any more trouble." Q. "You know how you often say, "I feel awful if I upset people,' would you feel awful in the same way if you were dead and knew they were upset?" A. "Yes. It's the same sort of thing. I want to say, 'Don't worry.' " Q. "So when you think of dying and not being around any more, if you think of your family mourning your death, which shows they cared for you — this has a good implication — because they mourn you, therefore they care about you, but it's also got the bad implication that you can't stand other people being upset." A. "I'd feel awful." Q. "So the other alternative is that you die and your family don't mourn you?" A. "They just forget me." Q. "They just forget you has the bad implication that nobody loves you, you may as well not have lived. Nobody ever took any notice." A. "I can't win." Q. "At the same time it has the good implication that they're not upset, and you don't feel guilty about making them upset. It's also this sort of conflict that is all the way through your relationship with Robert, so that if Robert gets upset you feel guilty, and if he doesn't get upset you feel unloved."

I asked Mary why it was important for her not to upset people. "I just don't like upsetting people."

Q. "What do you think will happen if you upset people?" A. "They won't love me — get cross with me. I'm terrified people will get angry with me — Sometimes I worry about things I've said that don't upset people but I think they might do. They don't appear to be upset, but I wonder when I've said something I don't really mean, and I think I've upset them even if they don't appear to be upset, and I'm always worried in case they are — and I get upset so easily. I think everybody's like me. Nobody has to shout at me to make me really upset. I take things the wrong way. I suppose everybody is just like me." Q. "Do you get any

> sense that this fear of angering people is out of proportion of what actually happens?" *A*. "I often tell myself that I'm being daft. I know it's out of proportion but I can't convince myself." *Q*. "Do you think that if somebody loves you that person will be less likely or more likely to get angry with you or no difference?" *A*. "I don't know. It doesn't seem to make much difference. I still worry about Robert as I do about my boss at work." *Q*. "Are you saying that even though Robert loves you that doesn't make any difference, he can still get angry with you?" *A*. "Yes, but he doesn't. I always imagine he will do." *Q*. "When I asked you whether you expect a person who loves you to get more angry with you, I was answering to myself what to expect. I would expect that anyone who loved me would very rarely get angry with me. People who don't love me are more likely to get angry with me." *A*. "Robert doesn't get angry with me very often, but I'm always expecting it. He makes it a huge joke, but I feel a bit sick." *Q*. "So the fact that a person loves you isn't a sort of protection against that person's anger. Does that cloud protect you from other people's anger?" *A*. "Yes, usually because other people's anger is on the other side of the cloud and visitors are usually polite. Robert doesn't get very angry anyway." *Q*. "Because he loves you?" *A*. "This seems impossible to believe anyway. He doesn't mind what I do more or less. If I want to go out I can go out. I don't have to ask him or anything. If I want something I can buy it. I always do ask him. Once I bought something and I was absolutely terrified he'd tell me off for buying it, and he didn't mind. I've never bought anything since without asking him."

The world that Mary looked upon was filled with animals which could harm her in mysterious ways and was traversed by roads where traffic moved in dangerously random ways. The people in this world might appear charming and friendly, but they were likely to interpret her slightest word or gesture as an attack upon themselves and so at any moment they might turn on her and rend her with their anger. This was the world she had known all her life. When she was fifteen a real disaster entered her life and she had no defence against it. She got pregnant.

I asked her, "Who decided that you should have an abortion?" "I went to the doctor with my mum. My mum just turned round and said yes. The doctor said it was the right thing to do. I went home and everybody said it was the right thing to do. I was on a lot of tablets — being treated for depression — so perhaps it was just as well."

> *Q*. "How long had you been depressed?" *A*. "A good while." *Q*. "Do you wish you had the baby now?" *A*. "I still do." *Q*. "How far gone were you when you had the abortion?" *A*. "About — just over four months." *Q*. "How did they do it?" *A*. "With a drip. There were two others on drips. They called us the three drips. The nurses were all right. The doctor was horrible — she upset me — ever so cross and angry." *Q*. "Did she treat you like you were wicked?" *A*. "Yes. The other doctors

were all right." *Q.* "When you were in labour were you on your own?" *A.* "Not on my own. It was night time. They had to call one of the doctors out. I don't think he was pleased." *Q.* "Was it very painful?" *A.* "It was rather ...." *Q.* "Did they say anything about what had been born?" *A.* "No." *Q.* "Did you wonder?" *A.* "Yes ... They couldn't get the drip in me. It used to come out." *Q.* "Was it explained to you beforehand what was going to happen?" *A.* "No." *Q.* "Were you frightened?" *A.* Terrified." *Q.* "Did your parents know what was going to happen?" *A.* "I don't think so." *Q.* "Do you think your mother would have really known because she'd children?" *A.* "She was rather frightened that the neighbours would find out." *Q.* "Was she more concerned about the neighbours than what was going to happen to you?" *A.* "I think it concerned my dad more than my mum. As soon as he found out he was going to send me away." *Q.* "There was no possibility of your mother keeping the baby, and bringing it up?" *A.* "I think she would but at the time it was so confusing. Everything happened so fast. She's influenced by my dad. Just does what he says. He said I ought to be grateful because he wasn't going to court. A few people he did tell said he seemed to be proud." *Q.* "What would Robert have liked?" *A.* "I haven't a clue." *Q.* "Was he able to give you much support?" *A.* "Yes. He came every night to see me. Brought me chocolates. Dad wasn't very nice to him but he used to come." *Q.* "Do you think that having an abortion has had any long-term effects?" *A.* "I think about it a lot. It's something I shall never do again." *Q.* "How did you feel when you came out? Were you still depressed?" *A.* "Not when I came out. It didn't sink in, not until afterwards. I was all right until the time came when it should have been born." *Q.* "Did you think of the baby as a boy or as a girl?" *A.* "A boy." *Q.* "Did you give him a name?" *A.* "Yes, Mark." *Q.* "Have you still got Mark with you?" *A.* "Yes." *Q.* "How old is he now?" *A.* "Four in September." *Q.* "So every time you see a four-year-old — did you get badly depressed in the same time of the year the second time you got depressed?" *A.* "Yes. The first time — I was here on Mother's Day. Mark often seems to be around. I could turn round and expect to see him stood there. It's a peculiar feeling." *Q.* "What does he look like?" *A.* "About so big, blond hair — "

One day when we were talking about why Mary liked to stay at home she said, "When I'm at home I feel nobody can hurt me or anything. When I go out it's — I might get hurt."

Q. "What sort of hurt can people do to you?" *A.* "People can be so unkind. People can say horrible things that can upset you." *Q.* "What sort of thing do you find upsetting?" *A.* "I can't stand anyone talking about children or babies. When anybody brings one to show me, I never know what to do. I can't stand anyone putting one on my knee and anything like that. I'll start crying." *Q.* "Do you think of yourself as being good enough to be a mother?" *A.* "I don't know. I've thought a lot about it lately." *Q.* "What sort of person should a mother be?" *A.* "I don't know, but I think I'm probably too possessive." *Q.* "Possessive like your father's possessive?" *A.* "Not sort of possessive like he's possessive, but I shouldn't like anybody else to have anything to do with it. It's mine and you can't have it." *Q.* "But why would you be so possessive?" *A.* "I suppose it's because I think that they're going to take the baby from me."

Once when we were talking about how Mary was afraid of other people's anger, she said, "I don't know how to protect myself. I just don't know how to cope with it." But as time went by it seemed as if she was learning some effective ways of protecting herself. On the last occasion she came to see me before her baby was born I asked her, "How much of it is that you come down here because you don't want to offend me by saying, 'I don't want to come so often'?" "It's not that I don't want to come. It's a long bus ride."

Q. "What do you think is the point in coming?" *A.* "I have found out a lot about myself that I hadn't known about." *Q.* "Having thought about it now, do you feel it's made any difference? Do you act and feel differently?" *A.* "Yes. I find myself thinking about why I am doing something. When I don't want to go out I know why now. I can go out a bit better."

Some weeks later I arranged to meet Mary one evening after she had finished work. I had been waiting for some time in my car outside the bank when she dashed out and said that she could not leave work as some money had been lost and would I mind waiting. So I waited and eventually she came out and got in the car. She laughed as she told me how the money, some hundreds of pounds, had eventually been found in the money drawer where she had been working as a teller. "It's their fault for not teaching me the job properly before they put me on it," she said. I remembered how she used to agonize over the possibility of making the smallest error in her accounts and how meticulously punctual she used to be, all to avoid upsetting people.

When I visited her after her baby was born, a large healthy, blond, blue-eyed boy, she told me that at the christening she had scolded her father for giving the baby some chocolate cake. Since it is well known among animals a mother is fiercest when defending her young, this change in Mary is not remarkable. Such a defence of her young may stem from the mother's possessiveness, something in herself that Mary had feared, but it seemed that Mary had no difficulty in sharing her baby with Robert. Indeed, she was immensely pleased about Robert's delight in his child.

6

JOHN

"If a man has one person, just one in his life,
To whom he is willing to confess everything —
And that includes, mind you, not only things
criminal,
Not only turpitude, meanness and cowardice,
But also situations which are simply ridiculous,
When he has played the fool (and who has not?)
Then he loves that person, and his love will
save him."

                                                    T.S. ELIOT

When Dr A wrote to me to suggest that I see John he said, "Mr J complains of feeling depressed, both night and morning, of fears of going out because of giddiness, and other symptoms of anxiety. His appetite is poor, he has difficulty in dropping off to sleep at night, and there is some loss of interest and concentration. These symptoms date from about seven months ago when a friend died of cancer."

John was a man in his early thirties. When he came to see me he was not merely tidily dressed but his clothes had that kind of informality that requires hours of forethought and planning to achieve. His informality was conventional. The only unusual feature was that he wore two watches, one on each wrist. One of these had belonged to his friend who had died.

His smile was quick and warm but it carried with it a sense of being grateful that I was talking to him. He was accompanied by a young woman whom I took to be his wife but later I found that she was the widow of his friend, Paul. Our sessions were never less than two hours. Jan would wait all that time, and when we finally emerged she would never look bored or impatient but rather with immediate concern to see whether John was happy or sad.

At the first meeting we did a repertory grid where John talked about himself, the person he would like to be (his ideal self), his mother and father, his wife and children, his brother Peter and his friends Jan and Paul. When the grid was analysed it showed a wide space between "self" and "ideal self". The person closest to "ideal self" was Jan.

At our next meeting I showed him the results of the analysis and then asked him about the implications of some of his constructs. First I asked him about "having pride in his home". The opposite of this was to have a home which was "untidy and dirty". He said that he took a pride in his home because people would reject him if his home was not neat and tidy. "It would frighten me a bit if I was rejected because of my appearance. To me it's just one of those things that come automatically. It's a case of a man taking longer than the wife to get ready to go out." John described how his mother set an example of neat dress but when John tried to dress the way his friends did his father would complain and would say, "Go and get your hair cut. If you don't, you can pack your bags and go." But John wanted to dress like his friends, since "I like their friendship. I can't think of anything worse than people not wanting to have anything to do with you."

John described his father as "domineering", "wanting attention, to be carried about", while he himself was "quiet", "worried" and "depressed". I asked him, "Do you think there is any advantage to worrying? There are obvious disadvantages like feeling miserable, but do you see any advantages in being the type of person who worries?" John thought there was. "If you worry about a person you don't want them to carry you about." "Does that mean," I asked, "that a person who worries is a person who cares?" John agreed that it did. "Now the thing is," I said, "the way that it has come out on the grid here, the notion of worrying is something that you ought to be because caring seems the right way and being quiet, not domineering, and keeping your home neat and tidy is the way to get on with other people. You lead that sort of life. These ideas are close together, but in between them is 'depressed'. So to be a good person you have to be a caring person. To be a caring person you worry — " "So, when you're worried and quiet you are automatically depressed," said John.

John always spoke about his mother in a warm and concerned way. However, his father, "would come home from work, have his tea and go straight out drinking. I think that was why I never took to drinking. I remember when dad was out of work and we really had it rough, we had one set of clothes for the winter and one for the summer and that was the lot." He described how at his school poor children were made to feel inferior.

A month later, when we were discussing how John felt when he was depressed, I asked him to try and form an image and to desribe it. The image that came was of two people, his friend Paul and his brother Peter, who seemed to have given up in despair when his marriage proved to be unhappy. "I suppose I am putting myself partly in their place. Especially with Peter. What comes into my mind is that if we had left him — he was in such a state. I wondered what it must have felt to have lived like that. I was lucky."

I had wondered about just how happy his marriage was, but he had made no comment. That he was not prepared to talk about it came out very clearly in this conversation. I asked, "What makes your life so close to Peter's life?" John replied, "I think this fright inside me is that I could go and do something like him. I went to the house and found him lying in bed. I asked him why he had put up with it and he said, 'Just to keep the peace'." I asked John whether he did things to keep the peace and he said that he disliked arguments and disliked being used. His father often succeeded in using him since his father could be nasty in an argument. "Dad tends to take it out on Mum. So I tread carefully there. If you have an argument with him and he knows he's wrong, he's really stuck. He just can't say he's wrong. He will start taking it out on other people. I don't like to argue. I don't mind a friendly discussion. But you can't have a straightforward argument with him. As soon as you have got a point he starts being nasty. He knows the point where he can get you to back off. My sister is stronger. She can fight back. My wife — she can also square him up."

I asked if Peter's wife was like his father and John said that she was. I commented that we often manage to marry people that remind us of our parents. John agreed and lapsed into deep thought for a long while. Finally he roused himself and said, "I shall probably get it off my chest and — I wish I could clear my mind, start to think for myself and proceed to work." Again he was silent. I waited, then said, "When we are in a situation where we keep on wishing we could stop feeling and thinking like this, I think there is something in the total situation that maintains these feelings. The sort of thing I am thinking about is how your father makes you feel, this feeling that you might despair like Peter. That's what made me say about how we usually marry someone like our parents. You said, 'Yes, my sister-in-law is like my father,' and I wondered about your relationship with your wife, and if within this relationship she was like your father?" "No, not really, because she is very understanding. Strict, very strict. She doesn't try to use me. But if a person, like my dad, had a go then she really can get back at him. She could give him it back, but the next day she will have forgot about it. I couldn't just turn it off. It would be in the back of my mind all the time, even if he didn't bring that argument up. It would still be in the back of my mind."

We went on talking about how arguing upset him and we did not mention his wife again in that session or the next two sessions. At our next meeting he told me that he had left his wife and had gone to live with Jan's parents. The family were in uproar. Only his father gave him any support. "I've been talking it over with Dad. He'd stood by me more this time than he has on other things." John often described how important it was to him that he could talk to Jan about Paul. Now he said, "I thought the wife understood. I thought she understood that I needed Jan to talk to. She was the only person I could talk to. I said I wasn't prepared to stop seeing Jan. She said, 'You're not bothered about us.' I thought that was a bit unfair. She said, 'About what time will you be home?' I said I shouldn't be too late. Suddenly she shot up in the air and started saying 'I think you'd rather be down there than at home.' Well, I said that to be fair, you don't really want to talk to me about it. I said, 'There's not just Paul, there's Peter.' She said, 'Well, if you go, don't bother to come back,' and then I didn't know really where I was at the time. I said 'I shall go and see Jan to tell her what has happened, and then go on to see Mum and Dad.' I told Jan and she didn't know what to make of it. Then I went to see Mum and Dad and they couldn't understand it. I said, 'We'll have to get my sister.' She came and then she just turned round and said, 'You're obsessed with Paul's death, just obsessed', and then they suddenly flew at me, you know. It was a madhouse and I didn't know what to say."

In that session he described all the activity his action had provoked in his family, and all I could do was to reassure him that this behaviour on the part of his loved ones was not unusual. Most families behave like this when two of their members end their marriage. At the next session he talked about the painful events that take place when the practical arrangements for maintenance and the care of the children have to be made. He said that his wife was very bitter. I asked how easily he could talk to his wife before Paul's death. He said that he had talked quite easily then but things had changed after Paul had died. "She just couldn't understand why. The way she looks at it, when a person's gone, he's gone, so that's that. She turned round and said, 'Well, he's only a friend.' I just couldn't shut it out, not after eight years of friendship. I couldn't push it back, and every time I tried to talk it over I would get so far and — There is such a lot I want to get off my chest. I wanted to talk about things. I wanted to talk about what I've been through coming up to see you. Up here I used to feel that I had got it out more or less, but when I got home I would clam up again. I mean, I couldn't talk all the time about the same thing. She didn't want to know what happened up here, she just didn't want to listen."

> *Q.* When your wife would say that it was a waste of time to come here and that you ought to be back at work, was she saying, 'I don't believe there is anything wrong with you'?" *A.* "That's what I took it to mean anyway. She said that she couldn't see the point. I said, 'Well, you haven't given me the chance to explain. You won't listen when I try to get things off my chest. I have to go outside the family to talk.' Her excuses were that it's either late or she doesn't feel like it. It's mostly late at night when I want to talk, to put things right before I go to bed. She seemed to think it was a waste of time. That is why now I think I have been able to get off the sleeping tablets. I can pop round and see Jan, and if I want to talk about it, I can to Jan. Then I'm okay."

John talked about how it upset him that some members of his family had not been entirely truthful with him. He knew that I had once been in the position his wife was now in, so I wondered whether he thought that I was more sympathetic to his wife than I was telling him. I asked him, "Do you think I am saying what I am thinking? Do you think there are things about you that I think and don't tell you?" "I don't think there is any point. I mean, if I didn't have any trust in you after two or three goes I should have said that it was a waste of time coming up here. She used to say it was a waste of time. But I needed someone to talk to after getting so tensed up. I have to get out what I can. I can say that it is nice to know that there is someone prepared to listen and hear my views about getting over it and getting better. She couldn't accept that. She said that unless I am taking tablets it's a waste of time. Whereas I feel better these last few days since I have been off the tablets. I was just getting sick and fed up of taking tablets. I knew I was really going the wrong way. I was getting more and more tablets put at me. The doctor, all he was doing was prescribing more and more tablets. They just keep you calm. They don't cure. This is where I get some help from Jan. When I get depressed I don't know if it shows but she knows. On Saturday night I was low again. I couldn't talk. I was hopeless."

We talked about the burdens his family were placing on him and I asked why he still accepted these burdens when he could leave the family now. "I don't want to be outside the family," he said, "because on my side the love is still there. The point is that I still think I am right in what I've done. If I did say, 'Okay, it's all over' you sort of wash your hands of the family, so that you can't return. I couldn't, not once I'd gone." I asked if he was told that "if you left your family you would never be depressed or frightened again" which would he choose. He thought that at the moment he would get out but might regret it. Twelve months ago he would have answered that he would stay inside the family.

In saying that he would stay with his family in preference to overcoming his depression John was showing just how highly he valued his family. When he said this we had already spent a considerable time in discussing the depression and anxiety that he experienced. At our second session he had said, "That's one thing I would hate — to be on my own. I just can't sit there in an empty house. I get irritable, I can't sit on my own and watch TV. I've got to have company." "I'm the opposite of you," I said, "If I'm with people a lot and have no time on my own, I get this feeling of things coming over my head, bearing down on me and I feel harassed and irritable. I have to get off on my own. I get irritable if I get too many people around. I get the image of all this" (I gestured towards the walls and ceiling) "coming in — all this noise and stuff. I can't think straight as well. So how do you feel when you're on your own?" "I wouldn't say it's close to fright. Really tough. But I can't really explain. When I like to go into town, I go into a shop, as I am today I would be okay but tomorrow I couldn't do it. Frightened! I walked into Smith and Jones and I got halfway up the stairs, going on to the first floor, and a sort of queer sensation of everything going away, then as if everybody was shouting to get out of it. I just had to get out of the shop and I sat quiet for a bit and was all right."

Q. "What were the people shouting?"   *A.* "There was no voice sound, just a shouting. What reminded me was when you were saying that the thing was coming over you. That's how I feel. It's hard to explain, and this is the trouble. If anyone asks me — I get to the stage — I feel so panic stricken. But then I have to hold myself, because if you do panic — well, the average person can't — It's just, for the first few seconds, just as if everything has gone away. I try to resist it, that's the only word I can use. I'm just gone completely. I've never fainted. The way people describe fainting — well, that's the nearest I've been to how they describe fainting, but I have never fainted. Sort of I've got to grip. When I feel it coming on, I've got to grip and I feel cold, my hands are always cold. But the sweat is rolling. When I did tell the doctor about this he said that it was part of the anxiety. Then the shouting comes in. It's as if everybody's shouting. They just shout. You can't really make any words out. It's frightening at the time. Then I go outside and pull myself together, but I won't go back. I got to the stage when I couldn't go in certain places, because I had that happen to me. I won't go near Smith and Jones now for a long time. I had it, I was turning into Church Street and I was on my motorbike and I had it happen there. I wanted to get off and throw my bike down. I just couldn't help it for those few seconds. Then I got the shouting. All I can do then is get in the house."

The feeling that accompanied the shouting was a numbness which went close to the feeling of no longer existing. John saw these panic attacks not as something visited on him from outside but as part of himself.

> Q. "Do you get some sort of warning that it's going to happen?" A. "Yes. It's not just a sudden thing I feel. I just feel sort of miserable. Then I get very edgy and it sort of builds up from there. What I can't understand is what happened in Smith and Jones. I felt all trembly afterwards. I just go about and I'm okay but if somebody said, 'Are you going to pop up to Smith and Jones with me?', well, then I would use all sorts of excuses not to go." Q. "What's the earliest you can remember having this?" A. "When I was eleven or twelve years old. It was near the river, near the locks, and it came on then. I can remember running home. I did fall in the river once when it happened. I remember being pulled out. It was lucky someone was there. There was some rafts and we were jumping from one to another and they were moving apart and I fell. I went quite some time then before I had another. Then it came on again. Some weeks I am quite happy, and then sometimes it's every day. Then a week, a fortnight, okay. It's that bit I can't understand."

This experience had left John with a fear of water and he was unable to go swimming. He was also afraid of heights or even just of looking at tall buildings. He could not travel in lifts or look over the edge of a cliff.

A few weeks later John described a dream he had had when he had been under anaesthetic at the dentist's. "I dreamt about there was this circle with all these people and I had to put all these people in certain positions and there was a voice in the background saying, 'If you don't get it right you won't come round.' Before I went to the dentist I had this fear that I wouldn't come round. When I did come round I had just got this pattern sorted out. It happened just as I came round. He said, 'I had a heck of a time with you.' "

> Q. "This nightmare is very similar to the panic, isn't it?" A. "Yes." Q. "It's a kind of death, isn't it?" A. "The more you talk about it the more these things seem to drop into line. With the dentist — I kept on wondering about. Afterwards when you talk like this it all ties up."

About two months later John said that he had been very interested in a play he had seen on television the previous evening about the patients and staff of a psychiatric hospital. "There was a chap in that who reacted a lot like I did. I wondered if he was took from real life. His worry was his wife had cancer and he couldn't cope with it and he wanted to run away from it all the time. He felt that he had to run away and he kept threatening to run away and in the end he did. Well, he got as far as the doors and then they stopped him. I could see myself in parts of him where it built up and built up and all he wanted was to run away from it. There were parts where I could see what he was feeling like and I could have switched off, but I had to see what he did in the end"

Q. "What happened in the end?" A. "He just calmed down and accepted it. The pity of it was from my point of view the play was really concentrating on the charge nurse and he wanted to get out because of the money. It just wasn't enough for him. He went on to the factory floor. They were concentrating more on his side than on the patients." Q. "When you wanted to run, what did you want to do?" A. "I just wanted to run. That's why I wanted to know what would happen after he had run. But really what I do is the same as him. I just calm down and then it all builds up again. Because it fitted in with how I felt — that's why I thought it was a true story. Afterwards when you have calmed down you don't know what you'd have gained by running. You think you'll run away from it all and afterwards when you sit down and think, you think, well, who would you run to?" Q. "In the minutes that you feel you have to run what do you feel?" A. "Fright. It's the same sort of fright that I explained to you I got when I went into Smith and Jones. You begin by sweating and then you tense up, and it feels as if everyone is shouting at you. Say I am at home and everything seems to be going away. You feel as though you don't exist. And then you just sort of click. It only lasts a few seconds." Q. "You feel that you are running away from this world but that you would still be existing." A. "Yes. Then you sit down and think about it. It's this running bit that I can't understand — why you have this feeling that you've got to run. When you sit down and think sensibly about it you can't run."

The reason he could not run was that he had nowhere to run to. "When I was at home before I got married I used to have bad arguments with Dad. I used to come out and meet the lads I used to knock around with. That helped me at the time to control it. Once I was married I couldn't do this. I would panic and go into the bedroom and be quiet."

Q. "Do you feel that if you ran out of the house you couldn't go back again?" A. "It's the first thing I think about. I have a picture that I should be running round in circles but I wouldn't be getting anywhere." Q. "This is the same as the other day when you were really down and you said, 'I shouldn't be going back, I should be progressing.' You see yourself as going in a straight line. If you go round in circles, then that is bad. So if you rush out of the house, you're not going anywhere, you might not be allowed back in again and you'll be running round in circles." A. "That's right."

We often talked of Paul's death and John would say how frightened he was to think of it. On one occasion he could not hold back his tears. He said, "I find it impossible to do this with other people." "I think it's better to cry than to not." I sat with him, and after some while I said, "You know, when someone dies like that, when we think of them, we are really thinking about ourselves. It's our own death. When you said something to me the other week about cremation — you said you were frightened. What I thought you were saying was that this fear of cremation came from the thought that it might be you and you might not be dead. That it's both Paul and you."

John had a recurring nightmare about Paul's cremation. "It starts where the coffin is just coming in. Then it sort of builds up from there. The noise gets louder and louder. The shouting is in the background, then it seems to build up and — it's really unbearable. It's like the shouting in a panic attack, but I can make out the words in this one, because Paul's mother kept on saying, 'Bury him, bury him'. The voice gets louder and louder, and then suddenly I'm awake. I get out of bed and have a walk around, and then I get back into bed. I lay there — and that's when I usually break and cry." I asked John to imagine what would happen in the dream if he had not woken at that point. Reluctantly, he thought about this, "I think I would see the burning — all I can imagine is that he is still alive, you see." I asked him to imagine that he was the person in the coffin. He said that he would be fighting to get out but would not be able to do this because it would be too late.

We talked about the discussion he and Paul had had about cremation. "It wasn't a light-hearted discussion," he said, "When Paul died so suddenly it came back to me — me disagreeing with him." John was against cremation, "because there's nothing there. Nothing to show respect to. You can go back to a grave. You can carry on the love side, the respect. Whereas with the cremation it's final. There's not anything left. Everybody just wanted to push him away." Paul had been in favour of cremation. "His argument was that the same thing happened with an ordinary burial. I said, 'Cremation means that you are just wiped out, and the majority of people forget.' "

"If you are cremated it's as if you've never lived," I said, "Why is it important that people should remember you?" "To show respect and love. You gave your love and that's a way they can show it in return." John pictured his death as "When they came to look after the grave I should be there watching. In that way I could accept it. I could if I was there. But with cremation — you can't."

> *Q.* "So when you picture yourself being buried you picture yourself stood there and seeing it?" *A.* "Yes. I do, actually." *Q.* "This image, does it convey to you that you haven't died and that you as a person still exist? You're not in the form that other people can see as still existing. Whereas with cremation the person that you know no longer exists. So when you have this dream, the person is still alive in the coffin. It's more that you in your body being burnt to death, it's you as a person that is able to exist forever that's being wiped out." *A.* "I was thinking, when you were tying two things up together a minute ago, about the cremation and when

I get a panic attack. You asked me last time when I had a panic attack and I go numb. For those few seconds while it's come on I feel I don't exist — then it comes back. I think this and it's too late." *Q.* "Is this why you can't go back to where you've had a panic attack? Next time it might last longer?" *A.* "Yes."

It seemed to me that the reason he needed to demonstrate that he had not forgotten Paul was to try and disprove his belief that the cremation of a person meant that he was forgotten. But John knew that even burial did not ensure that the person would be remembered. "If you go to the graveyard you see so many graves neglected. Another thing I don't like, say a pensioner dies, people will say, 'Well, he had a good innings,' well, it's just not on. I don't like that. Death — it's selfish — I just like things to carry on. People, I wish they could just carry on." In his talks with Jan about Paul John sought assurance that Paul had had good times. But there was nothing that would make Paul's death or his own acceptable to him. "I think back on the religious side and wonder what it can all mean. I was that way minded when I was younger. I've been thinking about it again since there was all this trouble in Ireland. That's all religion. If you do this and that you'll be all right. It's a type of disappointment. You're taught in Sunday School and church that if you're kind and do good things you'll live a long life, well, it's not so."

At our third meeting I had asked John which was worse, being depressed or being frightened. He replied, "Depressed. The frightening bit — I know I can get out of it. But depression — I can be talking and it comes and I can't clear it out of my mind like I can the fright. The frightening sensation lasts a few seconds, where the depression drags on and I can't pull away from it. I need someone to talk to. I have to talk about it. I just feel as if I'm going to break all the time. I try to hold it back, until I just can't and I cry. But it doesn't seem right for a man to cry. I still can't accept that."

Two months later, when John's unhappiness in his marriage was now quite clear, I said to him, "Time and time again you come back to saying, 'I tried to talk to my wife but she wouldn't listen.' It's something that was tremendously important to you. A husband could say a lot of things about a wife he isn't getting on with, but this is the only thing you say about your wife, 'I tried to talk to her but she wouldn't listen.' This seems to be the most important thing." "Yes, because if anything is bothering me during the day and I can get it off my chest at night — . When I started to talk to Jan about Paul I found it was easier to talk things out. I felt more relaxed. It was better than just keep on taking tablets."

Q. "But you've got this great heavy weight that you are carrying and you say to your wife, 'Help me put this down,' and she'd say, 'Take a tablet,' and leave you there still holding it. And you can't put it down."

John saw himself as collecting many burdens and his family as taking the attitude that he should carry these burdens unaided. "I get the feeling from the family 'You sorted Peter out last year, so now you can sort yourself out this year'. I don't want them to do anything. I just want to talk to them." What made the burdens heavier was that "I always tend to look on the black side until things are sorted out. I expect things to turn out badly until it's explained to me, or I have heard someone else's opinion."

John said that he would get depressed before Paul had died. "Things would seem out of proportion — I would worry the night before if we had a meeting the next day. In the morning I didn't want to go and face it. I used to get really tensed up — But with Paul and Peter I think it all came together. I should have got everything sorted out — but I can talk about it more now." John was silent for a while and then he said, "What I can't understand is that I can go two or three days feeling okay. If I had a reason to feel down I could understand it."

> Q. "When you say you can't understand it, are you saying you can't accept it? Sometimes when people tell me about being depressed they also say they feel guilty about being depressed." A. "Yes, I think that as well. I'd like to say I'm feeling depressed because of so and so. But if I've no reason and there's a conversation going on, I feel so miserable." Q. "So if you come here and you're not talking much you think I am thinking that you're a miserable devil because he's not talking much." A. "Yes, it's always there and the trouble is I know it's always there at the back of my mind. It was going through my mind last night." Q. "You know, we always have expectations of other people. In the first sessions it's quite easy for a person to talk because there is quite a lot to tell me and I can ask a lot of questions, and after a time you get through all that and this is the stage where we need to look at what is happening and say what our expectations are. It's always a problem to me when someone is silent, I don't know what is the best thing to do. Sometimes it seems appropriate to sit in silence, and sometimes we will have sessions where we don't speak a word to one another but that seems to be the right thing to do on that occasion. Other times I get a question inside me and I want to ask it, but when I ask questions I don't think I have the right to demand answers. You could say, 'I don't feel like talking today.'" A. "Yes, I do feel like that today because — I can't really explain. I can't explain how I do feel — maybe I expect too much. You know, too much when I come up here. I want you to help me and say, 'The reason you feel like this is because of this.'" Q. "You want me to wave a magic wand. You're hoping that when I give you an explanation then everything will feel all right." A. "Yes, I'm hoping."

I asked him what would happen if he "just sat there being depressed". "I should break. I don't like to break down in front of people. You can't do that all the time."

> Q. "What you're saying is that you can't break down in front of me."

John whispered, 'Yes, that's it — I'm frightened of going back to where we started from."

Q. "So you feel that we have made some progress and that if you started to cry as you did when I first saw you you would feel that you had slipped right back to where we started, and that that would mean that neither of us had achieved anything. Do you think I would think the less of you if you came here and broke down?" *A.* "No, I don't think that. Most days I feel a lot better from having talked to you. It's just that I don't want to go back to where I started from."

John described his experience of depression as "nothing seems to interest me. I try to cover up, but I don't want to talk. When people try to make conversation you don't feel like it. You think to yourself, 'Oh, I wish they'd shut up'. You feel that they are trying to boost you up. I can get one day where I am really cheerful and we can be ragging one another, and then the next day you get them trying to set you up to do it again. They keep coming at you. You try to avoid them all the time. I suppose you could offend people. I don't want to do that because the next day when you're all right you feel such an idiot. You can't very easily say that you didn't feel very well yesterday. I think it's unfair to take it out on other people. And then it's such a hard thing to explain, unless somebody has been through it themselves."

I asked him to form an image of his depression. He said, "All I can think of is a crowd of people arguing — men — dressed in black. I am stood watching — I am in danger — the men are nasty, very nasty. Sort of similar to the riots that you see where they have a go at one another. Eventually they will start on me and I wouldn't be able to fight back. It's in a big hall. I am sort of looking down on the hall. I am waiting for them to finish arguing. I am at the back of the hall, looking down on them. I've never really thought about it like that before — not until just now. I haven't pictured that sort of thing. That's what it's like when I'm really depressed. You can't really listen to people. Say if I was getting on to the children about something I should just walk away. I would go into another room. I seem to want to avoid all that sort of thing. I always have done. I suppose I am always avoiding arguments, I do as much as possible."

Q. "Now this image that you've got — while you're high up looking down on those people, actually the whole image is you, and this feeling has come from inside you, hasn't it? You say that you hate these people who are arguing and yet they are part of you. Can you imagine it now and you are one of the people?" *A.* "Yes, there would be a big high stage with just one person stood up. We are arguing about money. They are all blaming one person."

John was silent for a while and then he said, "I think the reason that the money side is coming over so strong is — it's been a big talking point — through our married life. It's still happening now in a way — I mean my wife wanted the money for the children, she wanted money for herself — it seemed to be top priority. I am looking at it now from the outside of it."

Q. "She valued you for the money you could earn and not for the person that you were?"   *A.* "I think so."

John went on to talk about the money problems that had arisen with his leaving home. "Did your parents argue about money?" I asked. "Yes, well, Dad did. The set-up there was different to what my wife and I had. We never had separate money. It was put into a cup in the cupboard and just left there. All I ever wanted was cigarettes and some petrol for the motor-bike, and the rest of it was left there. I never gave her a set amount. Dad gave Mum a certain amount. I always thought that the way we did the money was the best way. It was trusting in one another. There was no secrets about it."

Q. "So was your father not trusting your mother with any money? Or was that the way it looked to you?"   *A.* "I thought it was greed on his part. If she was short he would make sure he had enough money for his drink. He used to bet every day. He had to have money for that regardless of what else anyone needed. I always said I would never follow his ways."   *Q.* "So the way you handle money within a marriage, you used to say to your wife 'I trust you', and now she is showing you that she doesn't trust you."   *A.* "Yes."   *Q.* "Why is it important to have money?"   *A.* "I suppose to live comfortably. I like to be as comfortable as possible. Happiness — I don't think you can buy that."   *Q.* "Do you think that money is good or bad?"   *A.* "It's nice to live in comfort, but I think it would be a bad thing to have too much. You could tend to be greedy."   *Q.* "Why is it bad to be greedy?"   *A.* "I mean that some people will get money and keep on banking it and then it becomes an obsession."   *Q.* "Does your wife save it or spend it?"   *A.* "She prefers to save it. Her views are opposite to mine. She would say, 'Well you don't know when we're going to need it.' I used to say, 'You need it now, and you might as well spend it on clothes and food and things for the home.' My wife would always be on about money. It was ridiculous."

The second time we met John had said, "I really dislike arguing with people. It upsets me, so I think it's unfair for me to go and upset somebody else. I go round any way to avoid an argument." I asked, "When you upset somebody, are you hurting this person?" "Yes. I don't suppose it's wrong to hurt another person if you've no consideration for other people. But I just don't. I think it also makes you feel uncomfortable. I don't, because it's hard to carry on a normal conversation after a really serious argument." We returned to discussing his anxiety about arguments four months later when he had weathered the worst of the storms that had blown up after he had separated from his wife. "I think I have found it easier to ignore gossip since all this blew up," he said. "Six months ago I couldn't have done that. If I knew I was right I couldn't say, 'Well, let them gossip'. The only thing that worries me is that I've changed so much." John was worried that he might be becoming more like his father. "I've always looked down on my dad for his temper and things like that.

It is in the back of my mind that I could possibly go like that. That's why I avoided drink. I think I look at things entirely different now. I don't think I shall take people for granted the way he does. I'm really taking things a lot easier than he would. I definitely wouldn't want his temper. It upsets too many people. When he was in a temper he would upset people unnecessarily and it was impossible for him to apologize. I think it helps to have a certain amount of temper, which I didn't agree with a bit ago. I have found it easier to argue. I used to have to sit and think about arguments. I used to think too much. I think the reason I disliked the bad temper bit is it reminds me of the bullying at school." John described how he had been bullied by a gang of boys because he came from a poor area of the city. "I remember one lad, he used to be the worst. He would push and push me, and — there was this cycle shed and he accused me of touching his bike and he was prodding me with his finger, and I made his nose bleed, and he went and told the headmaster and I got caned. So you were tied down and couldn't protect yourself. I can remember the headmaster as well. I never liked him. It wasn't just me, though. Anyone from our area was treated the same. We were good lads when the football team was needed, but apart from that they didn't want to know. If you didn't have the right school uniform it was a black mark. I stopped in short trousers longer than anyone else. I could never understand why those people had to pick on someone who wasn't so nicely dressed. That annoyed me as much as the bullying. I would feel inferior because I couldn't dress so well."

Q. "So by accepting their bullying you were agreeing with them that you were an inferior person, and if you fought back you were in danger of being punished by the headmaster." A. "It was ridiculous because they push and push you until you fought back, and when you did fight back you felt sorry for them."

I asked how his father behaved when someone got angry with him. "He usually has flashes in front of his eyes or his feet are playing him up. That's his usual excuse for losing his temper. He uses that so it saves him having to apologize."

Q. "It sounds like if you get like your dad you won't be able to use such an excuse because you've seen through your dad." A. "Yes, but I don't want to get like him." Q. "This question of how you deal with anger is coming up all the time. We're often faced with the question of what to do about our anger. If you never express the anger that you feel, or if you turn it inside yourself, sooner or later you begin to suffer for it. Then you've got the problem of how you do express it. It seems to me that to deal with your own anger takes courage, because if you're angry with a person and you show that person your anger you've got to take the consequences and sometimes those consequences can be really bad, and it's a chance that you've got to take, you don't know what the outcome is going to be. You've got to be brave when you do it. The way you described your father, it seems that he is only brave up to a point. When the consequence of his anger is that someone gets angry back then he turns tail." *A*. "Yes, yes. There have been cases when I have wished that I could lose my temper. But there is something there that tells me to keep calm. It's like you said, you just don't know what you are going to do afterwards, whether you feel you're going to be able to face that person because you feel such a fool. I always try to think what the other person is thinking. When I was a shop steward I would often sit there wondering and thinking about the job. If we had a meeting, say, the next day, I would often sit there several hours thinking things out. I would sort of cross-question myself. I would be the management and think of the things they would ask me. I would try to work it out, and when I got in the office next day they would say something entirely different. I used to envy those people who could come straight back at a person. But you can put yourself in a bad position then, way out of proportion. I try to avoid arguments. I think, 'Is it worth arguing about?' If you don't like arguments it's hard to get any satisfaction because you are pulling somebody down. If you have a go at somebody and even if you know you are right, you don't feel good because you have won. You tend to feel more hurt than you have actually hurt them." *Q*. "Why is it important not to hurt people?" *A*. "Well, look what it's done to me. You feel so helpless." *Q*. "I get a picture of you arguing with a person, but actually you're playing both parts. You're hurt by winning and you're hurt by losing." *A*. "I think the closer you are to a person the more you try to avoid arguments, because of that feeling and the hurt afterwards."

Leaving his family brought many changes to John. He remarked on how easygoing Jan's parents were, "You're not tied down. When I first moved in it was a bit of a joke when I'd say, 'I'm just popping over to see Mum,' and they'd say, 'Oh, you needn't keep on telling us what you're doing.' Jan's father said, 'You've thrown your clock card away now.' All this sort of thing has relaxed me. While I have been away the things that I used to take for granted — like helping with the washing up or tidying the bedroom — they keep saying, 'Leave it,' I say, 'Well, I have always done it.' I'm doing more or less the same things at Jan's mum's as what I was doing at home. But it's — I feel as if I want to do it."

He decided to change his job. In the past he had accepted his family's advice to take a job which did not interest him but which paid good money. Now he would take a job where "I am concentrating more on the job than on the money. Looking back on my life, everything was a set routine. Getting up, going to work, coming home, helping round the house. My wife and I accepted that this was the way that you went on. I felt I got into a rut and I couldn't see any way out. Now I have the freedom and I can go back to how I wanted to be — that was when I was seventeen, when I could get out. I used to get out, have a lot of freedom."

Q. "Why is it important to have freedom?" *A*. "I used to get so tensed up and miserable — everything used to be routine." *Q*. "But a lot of people like that sort of thing. A lot of people don't want their freedom. Why for you is it important?" *A*. "To be happy. I'm doing more or less what I want to do. You can make your own decisions. If you change routine all the time, there's variety. I am more relaxed. The change means no boredom. You never know what's coming next. Looking back on my marriage now I can see a lot of faults that I couldn't see before. You were on about once — well, I was saying about how it was important to keep the house tidy, everything in its place, and you said, 'Wouldn't it be easier to just come home, and kick your shoes off and sit down?' At that time I couldn't agree, but now I can see that you had a point there. Tidying up is just a waste of time. Now I can do something that I really want to do, not that set routine. I think the hardest part to me was when we were at home it was such a set routine, even down to meals. There was a time and a set meal for each day. I more or less followed that on from when I got married. Now I don't know what I am going to be doing from one day to the next. I seem a lot happier that way." *Q*. "You mean that being married was just like a continuation of being at home before you were married?" *A*. "Yes — now I am on the outside and able to look at it. I mean, I thought that was right." *Q*. "You said something about freedom to make your own decisions. To do that you've got to have confidence in yourself, haven't you? Very often people who haven't got confidence in themselves will create a routine. It's sort of artificial confidence because you know what you are going to do. If you stick in the routine then all your decisions are made." *A*. "Yes, you go for the easy way. Instead I can get up in the morning and say, 'What shall I do today? Shall I go here or shall I go there?' "

I asked, "Do you still take as long to get dressed?" "Not quite. Yes, I'm still bad with clothes, and now I can't buy as many as I did before. If I had more money I should like some more clothes. That's another thing. When we went somewhere I had to dress in a certain way, collar and tie. Now I can go about without a tie."

Q. "When you were little and were being taught all these things and how to dress, what was the message there? What would happen if you weren't always neat and tidy?" *A*. "We used to get into serious trouble. If we got our clothes torn we were punished and that's why we kept ourselves tidy as possible. We would get into such trouble. We didn't have a lot of clothes .... At school I always did feel conscious of my dress. If I didn't feel right — I would prefer not to go out if I didn't — when I was at school I had to make do with what we had. With my brother being older than me I used to have all his clothes. I resented that. When I started work I bought my own clothes and I really, well, I got too many. I always made my mind up that when I was in a position to buy my own clothes I would buy a lot. I was always tied by what I could wear." *Q*. "So having the right clothes was part of your freedom?" *A*. "Yes, when I started work and started to buy my own clothes I would try to keep up with the fashion. My dad would get at me about this, but if you weren't interested in the fashion you didn't get a girlfriend." *Q*. "How much did it mean to you to be neat and tidy and wear the right clothes and be accepted by others?" *A*. "I think it did a lot, really."

Several months later I was shopping in the market and saw a young couple whom I did not immediately recognize. They were both laughing. John's hair was blowing in the wind and his sweater and trousers looked like they had been the first clothes that had come to hand when he got dressed that morning.

7

ROSE

"What shall I do, singer and first-born, in a
world where the deepest black is grey,
and inspiration is kept in   a thermos?
with all this immensity
in a measured world?"

MARINA TSVETAYEVA

The doctor who looked after Rose when she was in hospital wrote in his notes about her,

"Admitted from Out Patient Clinic, informally. GP made urgent appointment for her. She has become very depressed during the past two weeks. She has lost interest in her surroundings and expresses morbid and suicidal ideas. She is restless, anxious and depressed, tearful during conversation. She was one of ten siblings. She was married at twenty-three. Her husband was a bricklayer. Four children, all are married and quite happy. Her childhood was quite happy. She left school at fourteen, had various jobs as a housemaid. Marriage happy. Then he joined the army during the war. He was cruel and used to go out with another woman. He left in 1958. He used to beat her up. She obtained a legal separation. She went to work and brought up her four children. Slowly her children got married and left home. Since her youngest, her son, got married five years ago she has suffered from depression off and on. Earlier this year she gave up her job and became more depressed. During the past two weeks she has become very depressed. She cries at home, has lost interest in everything, appetite diminished, sleeps poorly. She has at times felt 'there is no point in living any more'. *Personality*. Active, very helpful to other people. She always liked mixing and talking to neighbours and friends. She has always been a happy person. *Diagnosis*. Endogenous depression."

I had mentioned to the doctor that I was doing research in depression and that I would be interested in seeing a patient who was clearly endogenously depressed. He suggested that I see Rose, who had recovered after a course of ECT and who was now an outpatient. On the morning she had come to the hospital to see the doctor I went round to the ward and introduced myself to her and asked if she would like to come and talk to me about herself.

Rose was a short, grey-haired woman of sixty whose sturdiness had not quite been reduced to frailty by her illness. She had no difficulty in talking, indeed, quite the reverse. I abandoned my usual practice of learning about a person by giving a repertory grid and instead simply listened to her talk, only occasionally asking a question or making a comment.

On the first occasion she came to see me I asked her if she would like to change herself in any way. "Oh, I wouldn't change myself," she said, "Because I prefer the way I have been brought up. My father and my mother — well, they were good. I wouldn't change my father and mother for anything. Jolly good. Strict, yes, we had to be in by nine o'clock and all those things. You daren't speak at the table. When he had had enough he used to get very cross. He was strict, but he was kind. My mother was very dainty and I never saw her untidy. My father had been married before so it was against her parents' wishes. He had had a big family by his first wife. He was twenty years older than mother. They got married and as I tell you she had ten children. We would go home from school, and in those days we didn't have lino, and we had to help wash the kitchen floor. Every day she had a clean apron on and she was a good reader."

When I had asked her what sort of a person she was she replied, "Well, I like to be honest. I like to be able to pay my way. I wouldn't do a dirty trick. I wouldn't do anything nasty. I would always stick up for myself and I wouldn't mince words, I mean, I don't like lies anyway. I would never lie and I would try to be like my parents brought me up. I don't go to church as much as we used to do. We used to go to church three times a day."

Rose often talked about her parents and her childhood. "Mother would have a little chair that she used to bathe the children on near the fire, and we had a shovel. Do you know what a shovel is?"

"Yes."

"We used it for making up the fire, and we even had to scrub the handle of that, and scrub even the brushes, the sweeping brush. We scrubbed our Sunday boots and the box we put them away in, and the outside toilet. We had pegged rugs on the floor and my eldest sister would help my mother. They would scrub the floor together because it was a big floor. You had to pump all your water. There was no water on tap. I mean, you had lamps — that's all mother had. At ten years old I was up at half-past six in the morning, doing a milk round for half-past seven. They wouldn't allow that today. Our house was there and the school was down the road, and so I had a minute to get to school. I was good at dictation, good at arithmetic and I loved reading, but as for drawing I was hopeless, but if you'd been out all those hours before you went to school, you'd be ready for a rest. The one who got home from school first laid the table, and the one who didn't do anything had to collect the pots up for mother. When I got home and had had my tea, I had to go out on the milk round again. There were no bottles in those days, it was all measured out."

I had commented to Rose that people who got depressed were often very truthful people. "My father told us that we were never to tell lies," she said. "We daren't tell lies."

Q. "If you did something that he told you not to do how would he punish you?" *A*. "We would perhaps get a good smack." *Q*. "Often when you have parents who are very strict you grow up to be very strict with yourself. You have high standards and you make yourself work hard." *A*. "It's very silly but I think you do." *Q*. "You do more than you need to do." *A*. "Oh yes. He did his job well, and we had such a large family, but the younger ones, they had an easier life. My elder sister and I knew what we had to do. It wasn't a case of what you wanted to do, but what you had to do. Mind you, we always had a nice home, and all that. I was fourteen when I left school and then I was away. I would go home for the holiday or half days and anything like that. My mother was lenient, you know. She would give way where father wouldn't. With being such a big family there was always plenty to do." *Q*. "What happened if you didn't do what you were told?" *A*. "I don't know because you daren't do no other." *Q*. "Would you have got belted?" *A*. "Well, she would have told father when he got home, but I don't think he ever hit me. I know my eldest sister got it, and I know so did my brother. I remember that whenever I was told not to do a thing I would never do it. When father was shaving we daren't move. He had one of those cut-throat razors. We wouldn't dare pass his chair. We would stop in that one place while he had finished. Once he had got it done then you could move. That's what I call the past — discipline! We would go into the garden and help him, and we would always go for a walk on Sundays. He would wear this great, big, stiff collar and we would go for a walk on Sunday evening with him. He would play an accordion and we would sing hymns. We had Sunday clothes in those days and then they would be put away and you would never see them again until the next Sunday. Mother had this wooden locker for our Sunday shoes, and as your turn came around you had to clean them all ready for Sunday coming round again. We had to clean everybody's."

"When did you have time to play?"

"When did we have time to play! Well, first of all I had the milk round and then school and then the milk round again, and I would get finished maybe after six some time, and then if the nights were light we would have time. But in the winter we would be in bed by half-past seven. Mother would play cards and dominoes a bit with us. Father would lock the door at nine o'clock. There was the baby to see to and then there was packing father's lunch. They would take us to bed with a candle and then bring it down again with them so there was no chance to read. Anyway, candlelight wasn't very good. Mother would have let us do more of what we wanted to do, but she couldn't do that because she was afraid of father. We had to go to church three times every Sunday and I had to take the milk round before I went to church. I managed to get my daughters to church but I used to have to smack my son before he would go. I had to belt him to get him to go. My father was a man who was liked. If ever he went down to the public-house — well, he didn't often go because he hadn't the money — everyone would treat him to a drink. He was nasty when he had a drink. I remember when I was fourteen and he had been out and someone had treated him to a drink or two he came home and mother said something to him and he was going to hit her, and I picked up the great big poker and I said, 'If you touch mother I shall hit you with this.' That made him sit down like. 'Oh, my goodness,' I thought, 'I shall never live with a man who drinks.' That really upset me. It was rare that he was like this, but then we didn't want it many times. If we took his lunch out to him in the fields at harvest time he would always give you a drink of his tea or a bit of his pudding. He was good but he was so strict. I left home when I was fourteen, and I said, 'I'm going where there are no more children.' Anyway, I went where there were five. I was a daily and I had to walk one and a half miles, night and morning. Anyway, coming home I would try to catch up with my brother because I was terrified of walking home in the dark. This lady I worked for had had a baby about the same time as my mother and I thought to myself, 'I thought you said you were going where there were no more children.' Anyway, she went funny. She was going to drown herself and her husband missed her, and she was going to throw herself into the pond. Anyway, her husband saved her and I stayed on there for ten months and after that I never worked where there were children. It was because there were so many of us. I like children, but my eldest sister and I didn't have the chances the younger ones had. It really did get you a bit. There was always a baby in the house. Mind you, there was one baby and she was dumb and she couldn't sit up and she only lived eighteen months. She never cried. She never made a sound or anything. She died on a Wednesday. I know that because my brother had just come home for a half day and mother was giving her some orange juice and then she got the mirror to see if she was breathing and she was dead by three o'clock. I remember the police came and I said to him, 'Would you like to see our Emily?' and he said, 'Oh no, I don't like seeing people when they are dead,' and I said, 'Well, she's only a baby, she won't hurt you.' Anyway, he wouldn't come and look at her. I mean, she was only a baby."

"How did your mother feel about losing the baby?"

"She was upset at the time but she got over it. And then when I knew that there was another coming — oh, gosh! My eldest sister had a good job and she had to give it up to come home and look after my mother. There weren't nurses like there are today. My mother got this other one and I wouldn't look at it. Well, the midwife didn't take away the afterbirth and she was so ill we had to get a doctor and she was in bed three months. That was the start of mother's illness. It played on her nerves a terrible lot, you see. Then she had two more children and I think that's what did her."

"You had to stick up for yourself in those days," Rose said. "There was a bully at our school and he set about my brother who was bigger and able to look after himself. Anyway, when I came out of class I interfered and my brother said, 'Get out of the way and let me fight my own fights,' but you see I didn't want anyone to hit my brother."

Q. "Didn't you think your brother could look after himself?" A. "Oh, I couldn't see why the bully should hit him. We did have some good times, and especially in the summer holidays. We seemed to get summers when you never needed a coat. Father would be taking in the harvest. It would be a long job in those days. He would have to cut the corn, stack it, put it in stooks and then cart it to the farm to be threshed. The one who didn't have a job would take father his tea. Father was frightened of thunderstorms. If one was about you would be able to see him coming across the fields and he would be death white. We had to cover every looking-glass up and he would get in the darkest corner. I could never understand a man like that being afraid of a thunderstorm. It would be as if he was going to die. Have you ever seen a thunderbolt? Well, one dropped in the park up there and at that time we weren't even allowed to speak. He was terrified and he made us terrified."

"I suppose your father was afraid of dying." "Yes, I suppose he could have been. I suppose he thought he might get struck and just die there. You couldn't believe it was the same man when there was a storm."

Q. "You must have been wondering about him. He was so strict and right in everything and then when he was drunk he got so angry." . A. "It was a rare thing that he would go down to the pub on a Saturday night. After a day harvesting we would have to go to the back door of the pub and get him a pint of beer. You could serve children at the back door in them days. You can't now though. We always had a well-stocked garden of vegetables and all that. We always killed a pig which we had in the sty every year, and then my brother had chickens."

I asked, "Do you remember telling me how, when you were ill, you were very frightened when you woke up in the morning? I was wondering if this fear was anything like the fear your father experienced."

"It could have been, yes. I was only a child of ten when I had to get up at half-past six, and that was all through winter too. It was too much. I didn't agree with that really. I earned half a crown and that was a lot then. We hadn't got a piano at that time but the lady I took the milk for had and I had piano lessons for two years. I paid for two lessons a week and the schoolmaster would let me out to get my practice in, but as soon as I was fourteen I went away and had to give it all up. I was getting on fine with the piano. I got on really well."

Q. "Would you have liked to stay on learning?" A. "Oh, I would have loved to have stayed on learning. But you see, I couldn't. I loved those piano lessons." Q. "Would you have liked to have stayed on at school?" A. "I would have liked to, so would my sister."

After her first job Rose went to work in Surrey. "This lady wrote from Surrey and asked me if I would like a holiday. I went for a month and then she asked me if I would like to live there. I said I wouldn't mind at all. I worked at a chemist's. I stayed there six months. I started my periods when I was fourteen, but I used to bleed at the nose and never — you know. They took me to the doctor and he said, 'There is only one thing for you — you'll have to go back home.' I came back home and I don't know whether the air was too strong or what but my periods became all right after that. I was so upset, I did like it down there."

"With all that strict upbringing, did your mother tell you where babies came from?" "Oh no. I'll tell you what — when I was going to work she gave me these, you know what, they weren't like they are today, she said, 'You'll want these' and she never explained it to us. All she said was, 'Don't bring trouble home.' "

"If there hadn't been so many children and you could have done what you wanted to do, what would you have done?" "I don't know what I'd have done. I've always thought, 'Well, I'm a woman, and I've never got that sorted out, I know I'm not a man, but I would have liked to have been an engine-driver. I never got myself sorted out. I don't know what I would have taken on. I like being out in the open."

> Q. "There are a lot of things you would have liked to have done?" A. "But, you see, we didn't have a chance. I mean, we knew what we had to do. We couldn't be what we wanted. My sister and I had to do the work we didn't want to do."

Rose told me about her brothers and sisters and showed me their photographs. One of these was half a wedding photograph with the bride missing. "This one is a picture of my brother," she explained, "I didn't like his wife so I cut her off." Rose's brothers all seemed to have had good jobs. I commented, "The boys always seemed to have the better chances." "Well, mother loved boys. She liked us girls' help, but she loved the boys. Her boys were everything to my mother. She would do anything for them. She helped them. She liked us girls but the boys came first. We always had to get our jobs ourselves whereas she always went with the boys to make sure their jobs were good ones."

> Q. "How did you feel about it — that your mother preferred the boys?" A. "I didn't think it was fair. Yet, mind you, I knew my mother had a family and I never went home without I took something with me. I wasn't that bitter, but I just didn't think it right .... When I came back from Surrey my mother was ever so cross. Then I got this job near Boxton. It was at a vicar's house and his wife was Irish. We used to have prayers every morning in the drawing-room. Whenever I cleaned in the drawing-room she always came with me and she would stay with me while I did my work and when I had finished she would come out with me and lock it." Q. "Did she help or did she just stand there?" A. "Oh, she just watched me. Well, one night, it was a Thursday, I heard her laughing, she kept on laughing, and there she was stood in front of a mirror. She had come to see if I was all right because there was such a storm overhead. There she stood in her white nightgown and her mob-cap with a candle in her hand and, oh, it did give me a fright. I couldn't hear no storm so I

decided she was a bit funny, so I decided that I would leave, but I didn't know how to do it because I had two great big suitcases and I couldn't manage all my things. The next day she went off to town and I had a word with the gardener and I told him that she had terrified me the night before and that I wasn't going to stop any more. She left me to clean the silver, so I put all that away, and the gardener tied one case on the handlebars and I had to get away before she got back. On my way from there I ran into a flock of sheep and I was wishing they would get out of the way. I had some relations living in Boxton at the time, so I went to my aunt's and asked her if I could stay a while. I told her that I had run away from the rectory and that I had no money. She gave me my dinner and she lent me some money to get home and I promised her to send it back and also some money to send my bicycle back. My mother! Oh, was she cross! She said, 'What have you run away for?' Well, it was only because I was so frightened. I never did get any money but I got my bicycle back and I went to work at Hayslope." Q. "How old were you then?" A. "I was only sixteen. At Hayslope I was trying to be a parlourmaid. Every time the daughter went hunting I had to light her a fire in her room and heat the water for her to have a bath when she came home and all those sort of jobs. Then the head housemaid left to get married and so I got her job. I was there for three years and then the housekeeper left and they got a new cook. She was ever so good, but one of those secret drinkers."

"When you left the job near Boxton was your mother very angry with you?" "Oh yes — she was angry because I had no pay, you see. The first thing she said when I got home was, 'You'd better get yourself another job.' I said that I needed some money to repay my aunt and then there was my bike, but she hadn't any money and I didn't realize this. It was because she had so many children."

Q. "Did your father think that you were right to leave that job?" A. "Well, he was fairer. But I didn't care what they thought because I daren't stay in that job." Q. "Did they understand that you were frightened?" A. "Father did, but mother had the other children, and I don't think she realized how much it had upset me. I went into the Labour Exchange and I got a job straight away. My sister had a bad leg and my mother was ever so cross when they sent her home. And yet she gave up her job and came home to look after mother whenever she had one of her babies." Q. "Would your mother ever say 'Thank you' to her for doing that?" A. "What, thank you for looking after her? Well, I don't know as if she would say thank you. Once, mother had done a crossword in the paper. She got two hundred pounds and that set her on her feet for a bit. I would take her over some bacon for her and children to eat whenever I visited. When she won this money she gave all her children three pounds except me, and she gave me two pounds. I asked her why she had only given me two pounds and she said that would do for me, and I said, 'I want three pounds please'. My sister had gone to a shop in the High Street and got a new coat and she got a hat free with it, and I said, 'If they have all got three pounds then I want three pounds too,' and anyway she went and fetched it and gave it to me. My sister and I went into town and she got the dark coat and I got the light coat and then we got these free hats."

One day Rose told me how she came to meet her future husband. "I wasn't bothered about young men," she said, "From sixteen to twenty I never bothered with men and then I went with one or two and then I got the wrong one.

Q. "What did you like about him then?" *A.* "Well, he's got that wheedling manner. He was one of those persons that could charm a snake and you didn't realize. He'd take you out, to tea, he'd pull out your chair, open the door. I thought, 'He's got manners,' never thinking of him completely changing like he did. While we were courting, his manners, he'd do all those things for you, push my bike up the hill, and, naturally, when you've been brought up to do so much for yourself and you get somebody that would open a door and pull your chair out, you thought you've got someone that's going to look after you, never thinking what a woman's man he was going to be .... He was a marvellous workman, he could build and ice cakes — wonderful for working. He could have been well off. But I'm not going to puzzle any more. He should have had more sense, shouldn't he? He knew he could earn good money and he had the chance. He could do anything. He had the offer of a house. In those days he could have had it for fifty pounds. I would have helped him in his business, but he just wouldn't do it. If he had gone about it the right way he and the children would have benefited. That is what I feel I have lost. But he loved going dancing. Being spoilt was in his family. He never had responsibility and I had because we were a big family and we learnt responsibility. I don't know why he did it. Maybe we weren't suited. But he wouldn't make a go. I can't understand it though. I suppose, in the war he got his freedom. I know he had women then. He was always talking about his women. When he got home he still stuck to his women. He had one in this place and one in Belguim. He told me he had one in York. She was married though, and her husband was in the RAF."

"How did you feel about it when he told you?"
"Well, the nurse sent for him because my third daughter was a breech, and I got the nurse early. It was winter and she was ever so cross with me. Anyway, she realized about twelve o'clock that Kathy was coming feet first. I didn't have the sort of pains that you ought to have. She ran to the butcher's phone and told the doctor to come at once. I thought I was going to die, I can tell you. They said that I should have to have my husband home and, I mean, I didn't say no. When he came he said, 'What have I come home for?' He said, 'She's your daughter!' I said, 'You ought to come. She's your daughter.' He said he should have stayed in York with this woman.

He said he had things to do for her. Kathy was his daughter, and, anyway, we didn't part very good company. We had a row. He said he never ought to be sent for and, of course, I, even as bad as I was, I had to stick up for myself. We parted and I didn't speak. I thought he would get over it. It's all built up from when he was demobbed. My son was born in 1946, in the September, and he was demobbed in the June and took this caretaker job and got on with this woman. He wouldn't listen to me. He used to threaten me more than anything. You see, I didn't want the children to have to go away. I wanted to look after them. I wanted him to be a father to them as well — but not like he was. He didn't get much money being a caretaker and when he added his books up he was always short. Well, I got thirty shillings a week and he would say he was so much short. We paid six shillings rent and the rest we had to live on. He would go into the sweet shop and buy things there, but I would feed him all right. But when he had to make up the caretaker money I knew we were off on the wrong foot then. But when he used to come home smelling of scent like he did — I mean, he would reek of this scent, and if I said anything I was wrong, you see. It grew and grew and grew. He would dance and I was there with the children. I couldn't go because of them, but he had to go because he was the caretaker. I got so fed up with arguing, it got on my head like a record, it did."

Q. "Why do you think he turned against you?" A. "Well, he had other women during the war." Q. "Yes, but lots of men did. I was wondering why he turned against you." A. "He turned round once and said I was the vilest woman on earth. I don't know why he said it. He always wanted his way. I wanted to help him with his work. He would come home and ooh! The smell of scent, it was terrible! Those eight months were awful. He would never acknowledge that it was him that was doing it. He didn't think he was doing wrong. She wanted this wall altering in her house and so he went and did the job and from then on it started. She could make herself up to look glamorous. I used to shake as I went past her. I had to pass her house because I lived down there. And yet I don't understand her. Where's her conscience? I know it happens, but I don't understand people."

I asked her why she had not divorced him. "I ought to have done. I took him to court the first time — that was 1947 — yes, it was 1947 because my son was born in 1946. My husband's father was alive then and he went with him to court. It was over money matters, you see. I didn't have enough money to pay the butcher's bills and that. My husband said that if I couldn't pay I should go to another shop and get some there, but I had never been used to living like that. His father paid his fine and they told him not to go down to this woman and he said, 'Well, I'm not going down there anymore,' and he went out of court, got on a bus and went straight down. I felt infuriated — when you know how you feel when someone promises not to go and then goes straight away. He went down there and then came back to my house and he got drunk two nights, and I never went back, I never slept with him after that. It was like a cat and dog life, if you can understand. He tells so many lies — I mean, I didn't want to go to court. After that he would give me three pounds a week, no more than that. I should have gone to court again, but I couldn't go because he would have lied and I would have failed. I mean, I couldn't stand it. It was his lies. I was afraid of him telling lies and getting away with it. Jack was three weeks off being a year old when he went out that night and got drunk. I thought afterwards that I should have pushed him down the stairs. He wouldn't have known anything about it with being so drunk. I should have ended up in jail but I wouldn't care. I often thought afterwards that's what I should have done. The social worker told me to get a new dress and get made up, and I said, 'Well, I haven't the money to do it and I've got the children to feed.' I wasn't one of those people who bought new dresses when I've the children to feed. When she had gone I said, 'Well, thank you for your lies!' I wrote a letter to the social somebody and said that we were going to try to make a go of it, but it just wouldn't work. He went down there. So what could I do? Constant lies and with the children, and I wanted to look after the children. I mean, we had so many arguments I got that I couldn't fall out any more. I hated to fall out if the children were there because it wasn't good for them. I don't know how they got to be as good as they are. They've got good jobs and good husbands. I thought, 'I'll never fall out any more.' Mind you, if I've got anything to say, I'll say it. I do! You see, I'm a fighter, and while I'm fighting I'm all right .... I've always been good at money. I can always manage money. If I couldn't have managed money I couldn't have brought up my children. My husband would go to one shop and then to another. My mother never owed a penny. He wanted money to go with other women. When we got the letter about the house he got me by the throat. At one time I had to have police protection. He had got hold of Jack when he was only three and took him all round the house and told him that his mother was a murderer. Fancy saying that to a child! At one time he was going to burn all the house down. He made this heap of stuff in the middle of the room, and burnt it. He burnt every photograph. Anyway, I had the police out that night, I stood up to him and that is why I think I suffered both mental and physical. I wouldn't give in, you see. Then he used to get the carving knife, well, I knew if he did do anything I should have hurled a chair or something. I never showed that I was frightened. I always stood my guns there, whether I felt bad afterwards, which I did, many a time, but I stuck up to him and when he used to sleep downstairs, he'd get a cold and he'd come, 'Will you get me some milk?' and, I know it was hard for the children, but I wouldn't. I wouldn't give it. 'If you want milk, you want to get it down there and if you die, you die, because you're not much good to me.' Eventually he went there and never came home for his meals. He used to come home on a Sunday but he didn't have his dinner with us. I would cook the children's dinners — it was on the primus, we didn't have electricity. He would come home and ask for food and of course I used to get quite cross. I would do him an egg or something. I said, 'If you're going to keep on coming I might as well cook the dinner and you can have some of mine,' but he would never sit with us like. He would have his dinner and then he would go. No matter how frightened I felt I stood up to him .... There were three girls and me and Jack in two bedrooms, and I didn't want the boy sleeping with the girls. Then I got the letter to say I could have this house. I said, 'Are you coming?' he said, 'No, I'm staying here.' So I went and took a few knives, plates, cups and saucers and he put a lock on the door, so I went. He stayed there a year, and then the owner made him leave because he hadn't paid the rent .... People ask, 'Why haven't you married again?' I would say that I was busy bringing the children up and I never found anyone. Well, to tell the truth, I had no feelings. The shock had taken away all my feelings. You could stick anything in me and I wouldn't have felt it. The shock was really great. No, I had no feelings. It took ages for my feelings to come back, it really did. But to get your life spoilt through someone else, that's awful. That's the tragic part of it."

"Does it make you a bit envious when you see someone get a good husband?" "I suppose there is a sadness there — do you understand? It makes you wonder why. I mean, you have only the one life, and it does really touch you. I love home life. I've gone without a meal when I've given it to the children. I wouldn't get into debt. My brothers and sisters have been good and have helped. I sometimes wanted to cry for the children's sakes. It seemed so hard to think he came home from war and went off like that. I know I'm a person who would work so hard that I'd make myself ill. But as soon as I was better I'd be working again. I was always hoping. I never gave up hope. Without hope I should never have got through. I thought, well, he might come back. He might realize that his home was there. I lived on hope, you see. I used to think, 'Why should he go there when she's got a man?' I used to think, 'What the heck does she want two for?' I used to hope and think he might come back. He did. He came back for a week. He slept downstairs for a week and then he packed his bags and went. Then I didn't hope for him coming back. I hoped that I would get through and that I would always have work. I mean, people always came to me for help .... But, I tell you, I was always running away in my mind and packing my case and I never got anywhere. It's a horrible feeling. I felt I must run away, you know. I never got my case packed, mind you. But that was how my mind was working. Then when I got down to that house I felt better, because I never saw my husband going down the lane. I could have left the children, the same as he left me, but I didn't want to leave. My principle was different. I loved them. I would think, 'I'll pack my case and go.' I never got anywhere, but, oh, I couldn't leave them. I wasn't that kind of person. I would have felt so guilty. I had a lot of patience. I would be in the potato fields all day and come home and get them a hot tea and then I'd get them off to school next day. I couldn't have left them. I mean, where would I have gone and what would I have done? If I had just had the two perhaps I could have got away and got a job and kept the two, but I had the four. No, I couldn't have left, no. What had they done? Why should they suffer for what their father had done? I begged him to stay with us, but he wouldn't. I wouldn't have left them at any cost. I used to bathe them in the old wooden tub. I would start with Jack and work my way up. They always had clean clothes for the weekend. I would patch and darn. I would wash their hair. I would start at six and I would finish bathing at nine o'clock. That was my Saturday night. Everything had to be kept clean, and besides, the children hadn't done nothing wrong. Why should they suffer? He'd done that. Why should I suffer? But that's just it. I got hurt so much, that I'd no feeling. In the end you could have stuck pins in me after all that. All I wanted to do was feed the children and keep them warm. It was hard work, trying to guard the children from them who would talk to them about their parents. I never stopped them talking to their father, but he would never take them to the sea. He took this woman and her two girls, but he never offered to take my children. They would go on the Sunday School outing which we had, and I used to take them for walks and picnics. My friend Mrs Richards and I have taken them for lovely picnics. I used to walk miles and miles with them."

Once, when Rose was describing the hardships of her own childhood, she said, "When I was a child I thought that when I grow up my children aren't going to live like I do. They'll have a better life. I would never be as strict as my father. I would have this strap to threaten them with but I never used it. Anyway, one day when I wanted this strap it was missing .... Margaret had broken it down because she didn't want no strap. I outed it after that. On the whole they were really good. We would chop sticks and go sticking. We would take the pram and get loads of sticks. It was in the war and we had coupons ahd we would walk three miles for the two eggs we were allowed. I remember being down to my last sixpence and that would buy a bread loaf for the children and I lost it in the snow. My friend was with me and she was short of money too and she helped me look for it and I wouldn't leave the place until I found this sixpence. She couldn't lend me sixpence because she hadn't any money either."

> Q. "Do you think it's a good idea that children should be frightened of their parents?" A. "No, I think no child should be afraid of his parents. That's wrong. I think they should be able to come to you and tell you their side of the story." Q. "Did you give more to your boy like your mother gave more to your brothers?" A. "No. The girls thought I did, but he couldn't wear their clothes. He had to have new clothes where they had handmedowns. I worried over my son being like his father, but I needn't have worried. He's not like him in his ways at all. I was working at the fish shop at the time, and while I was away my husband used to come down to the house which was annoying really but there again he was entitled to because we weren't separated or anything legal then. Say Jack was playing up, well, I would want to hit him, and he would turn round and say, 'Don't touch him'. I did use to square him up, but if I had have smacked him he might have told his father. Mind you, I wasn't frightened of him because by then I had got used to him."

Rose had coped with the children's various illnesses, including Jack's tonsil operation. "He went in on the Sunday and we went in on the bus to fetch him home on the Wednesday. He said, 'What on earth have you left me here for, mother?' and, of course, he hadn't realized that he had had his tonsils out. I stayed home with him for a week. I went back into the fields a week later. We were down below Boxton Castle. There was an awful storm and I was terrified and I got him in the van and then they had to have a tractor to pull us out like. We would weed the wheatfields. I used to like the potato-picking because they were lighter. As the year went on they seemed to get heavier. My friend from the village was very good and she would help me carry the baskets. We would get the children off to school and we would be picked up at nine o'clock. We were home again at half-past three when the children came home and then, of course, we would set to and start to cook dinner. We got a pound a day. We were called the ladies' gang. Then when some plants were little you had to go down the rows and chop out some, say, for every four plants you would leave only one. Now they have a machine which doesn't set so much seed. That was tedious work. We worked all up the rows and then back again. Then I would go pea and bean pulling too. You had to fill so many bags before you got your money. I was pulling beans one day and that finished me. I felt something go and I had pulled every muscle in my body. Then I went into housework and that was boring, really. It was to me, anyway. I used to love having my sandwiches out there in the fields. One man would light us a fire if it was a bit cold, and then there was one man who would bring us out scones. One boss would bring the children out sweets and chocolates. I liked being out but I didn't like all the dirt. It was all right when the sun was shining. I really enjoyed that. Then I took to washing and everything I could think of. Then I went into housework and that was the worst thing I ever did. Mrs Halifax broke her thigh and they couldn't get anyone so I said I would go and give her a hand. I've never seen so many cobwebs in all my life. I stayed there seven years." As well as doing housework Rose took on a job in the fish shop. "I had been ill and I met Mrs Brown in the fish shop and she said, 'Do you feel like work again?' and I said, 'Well, I shall have to do something,' and she said, 'You could come and give me a hand.' So I went to help and gradually I got better. Oh, Mrs Brown was a friend to me. She was a lovely person. Her husband died three weeks after I went there. Then she had her father with her and she said that he was never going into hospital while he dies, and then, he was getting a big age but he was fine one night and he got out of bed and then he died. We knew she wasn't well and we said to her, 'Why don't you take a fortnight off?' Anyway, Mrs Brown and I went to see a neighbour who wasn't well and afterwards Mrs Brown said, 'I'm not very well but Mrs Jones is worse than me' and when we had had our tea she asked me to go and see if there was anything I could do to help Mrs Jones, so I asked if I could and I mended the fire for her and then I went back to help Mrs Brown. She was going to turn the fish over — well, they just got her a chair and they just got her to sit down and she said to me, 'Carry on with the fish' and I'd fried chips but I hadn't got to frying fish. Mrs Brown was in the back of the shop and she was ever so bad and then we got the doctor and she said, 'Carry on frying' so we did until it was time to finish. We took her home and the doctor was there. She was sat in a chair and I sat there for a long while and I thought that the doctor might send her to hospital but he didn't. Next morning she was dead. So that finished that. She really was good to me. She was goodness itself. I thought how terrible it was to die."

In all the years Rose worked and brought up her children she did not attempt to divorce her husband. He paid a small maintenance. "The children went for the money and I thought that must have been a terrible thing for them to do. I keep on seeing my mistakes and I know now what I should have done." It was not until the children were grown up that she took her husband to court. "I put on a paper that he hadn't given me anything for seven weeks. I went to see the solicitor with my friend, Mrs Richards. Then we were called into court and I was here and he was there and I was horrified. How I gave my evidence I don't know, but I thought I did it quite well. When it was his turn he had no solicitor and no friends, and he said that he owed lots of money to the insurance people and so on and it sounded so sad. Anyway, the magistrates never questioned me, but they did him. That was it. He had to pay so much a week. That was it, you see. I shouldn't have left it so long. I didn't want to fail – I couldn't be let down again …. The worst night I ever had was when I got the separation. My son was engaged then. Jack said to me, 'Where are you going, mother?' I said, 'I'm going to bed. I've had enough for one day. I just can't stand any more.' When I got my separation order from him I knew he wouldn't come back. I mean, his life was different. She liked a gay life and he liked a gay life. I think it hurt his pride when he had to pay after I had got my separation."

Q. "Did you think that he had come to dislike you?" A. I began to think that he never did like me. I mean, he never bothered. I always hoped that I would have work and then be able to keep going."

By the time the legal separation had been settled Rose's three daughters had married and left home. Rose said, "My children are good to me. When the family were home I would get up early and get them hot breakfasts and yet when they had gone I felt I couldn't have gone on. But I never, never thought the day would come when the house would be empty, because the house was always full."

Q. "You never thought ahead that this might happen?" A. "No never. My son was married in the June and their bungalow wasn't ready until October and of course my son and his wife stayed with me. They went on the Saturday, but that's the one thing I never got myself built up for — for being on my own. I know friends pop in and all that, but I never thought there would be no one to look after. I couldn't believe it was true. When my son was doing his apprenticeship he never went out because he hadn't the money. He went out with his pals and he met the girl and that was it. It's natural. But I never thought I would be on my own." Q. "You didn't think about the future?" A. "That's one part of my life that I didn't sort out. I was so busy looking after them that I never visualised that part. I should have done, but I didn't. I suppose you can't think of everything." Q. "Yet you must be a person who plans and organizes to have coped the way you have done. You never organized into the future?" A. "No, I never did organize myself. I've organized money. I've never got into debt. I never organized my life. I don't know why I never did. My son would say, 'I shall never marry!' He would go out at weekends and I didn't feel really well, if you know what I mean. Things used to upset me. And even then I never got myself sorted out for living by myself. I've done everything else, but I never sorted myself out for that. I hadn't prepared myself for living on my own. I can't remember when the depression really started. It all seemed to have built up from years ago. The last place I worked I had to work really hard and when I got home I was no good for anything. I couldn't take housework again. I can manage on my own, but not anyone else's. Before I came into this hospital I would have these little do's. My daughter would ring the doctor when she would see me start to walk about shaking and rubbing my hands and she got to know how they started and she would say, 'Mother's going to have another bad do'. It was after the separation they seemed to start."

"What do you think caused your depression?"
"I thought it was all the worry I had. I knew I had achieved something and I knew I should have done it before. I worked and worked and worked. I would scrub anyone's floor for one and six. I never applied for any money from anywhere. I lived on what I earned and that was how I brought my children up. There was the responsibility of being father and mother. I don't know whether I was proud or that I shouldn't do it or what. You see, I lost the first time when they told him not to go down there. He promised faithfully that he wouldn't and Mrs Richards was there as well as me to hear him say that. We all went back on the bus to the village and as soon as he got off the bus he went down there. I lost faith, you see, I did. I mean, I've always been capable, but it's only people who have made me the way I am. It's people and what they do to you .... I wasn't mental. I was ill through other people. I lost every sense of feeling that I had had. I think as the feeling came back this pain used to start here and I used to shake and shake and shake. I think if I had sat down and thought about it and gone and got proper help I should never have got this depression. I should have had someone to understand and help me."
"Do you think that having that sort of childhood had anything to do with being depressed?" "No, I don't think it did. I made up my mind that when I grew up and had children I would bring them up differently. I couldn't give them what I wanted to give them but I did keep them together. They have all married and have managed to get homes of their own."

Q. "Did you make up your mind that you would get the things that you wanted?"
A. "Yes. I did get a few things, but the war came. I did get two new bicycles. I used to like cycling. But I couldn't carry on with my music lessons and I began to forget what I had learned. My sister's husband got my children a piano but then we couldn't afford the lessons. Then my husband took the room over and that was that." Q. "If he had come back from the war all right and had worked hard you might have had a nice house now." A. "Yes. He could turn his hand to anything. He could have been a rich man." Q. "Do you get angry now?" A. "No. I felt bitter. I got very bitter. But I don't get angry. It doesn't do any good. I mean, before I didn't know where I was when I was ill. I used to go to bed at night and in the morning I would feel terrified of getting out of bed. I just felt terrified of getting up. I think it was the pain in my head." Q. "Did

you feel safe while you were in bed?" *A.* "Yes, I was safe in bed. I didn't want to get up. I was on my own and, of course, eventually I made myself get up. I didn't want to bother. I didn't want to clean the place up. I didn't want to bother to cook meals. I kept myself washed and everything. Why I was terrified I can't discover, but I felt like that. The pain in my head was terrible. I was crying and crying and I couldn't stop. I couldn't be still. I couldn't look at the paper, watch television, nothing interested me. I used to think my face looked funny. I would imagine all sorts of things." *Q.* "Were you frightened of dying?" *A.* "No, I wasn't frightened of dying. I was frightened of being on my own, terrified. I never thought of dying. It was being on my own. If I was with company I was safe, but to be here on my own, oh it was terrible, terrible." *Q.* "What do you feel would happen if you were on your own?"

A. "Well, I thought I'd go mad. I must get away, I must get away, I said to myself, this house, I must get out of these four walls, it doesn't matter what it is as long as I'm with someone that I can talk to, that's why I must go. I couldn't stay in the house. I must be with someone. The worst Sunday I had, Joan took me down to the Garden Centre. Those flowers which really would mean, a flower means everything to me, they didn't, nothing, to me there was nothing. Nothing seemed anything, if you understand what I mean. I was just walking on the pavement and I was going with Joan. Nothing, no effects, it didn't mean anything. A flower didn't even look pretty to me. They were telling me to do things and I couldn't do them and that was that — I said, 'I can't do it' and Joan said, 'Try,' and that did worry me, her saying, 'You must try, mother. You've got to help yourself.' And I wanted to try. I'd get my knitting and I'd do a row and then I'd have to put it down, it was too much and she said, 'You must try, you must try, mother,' " *Q.* "So people were pushing you to do things — " *A.* "And I couldn't, I felt as if I was being driven and I didn't want to be driven. I wanted, I didn't know what I wanted. I wanted peace, you see, that's what I wanted. I wanted peace, I couldn't seem to find it."

So Rose went into hospital and was given ECT. "My sister came to see me and I knew her and I began to pick up wonderful. I think I did real well considering I didn't know how I had got there or anything. I can't remember anything about that. I kept saying, 'How did I get here?' and they said that it didn't matter how I got there, I was just to keep on going forward. I suppose for the first three weeks I wouldn't know much. Then I got so I could wash and lay the table and so on."

After Rose was discharged from hospital she was still not able to be as strong as she would like. "I should like a job but I couldn't take any responsibility, I know that."

Q. "Has it been in the past that if you can keep busy then the depression isn't so bad?" *A.* "Well, I did have one or two do's when my son was at home, but when I get busy I forget. I seem so short of strength at the moment. I don't know why I get weary. Ever since I have been ten I have been on the go. I hate to feel I'm not a useful member of the community. I have always been helping other people. You never realize there is going to come a day when you have got less strength. I get so tired." *Q.* "How would you feel if the doctor said that you had to give up helping other people and be waited on yourself?" *A.* "Oh, no, no, no, I don't want that. Not while I can go do I want to be waited on. While I have arms and legs I shall make myself go. I want to be useful to myself. I think to myself that I must keep going." *Q.* "What would happen if you gave up?" *A.* "That would be terrible. You don't feel a proper person if everything is done for you. If I can do something for someone else that makes me feel better. Since I have been living on my own I wonder if it's right that I should be doing just for myself. I've always been a person who has been a help to anybody."

"From what you say about your early childhood your mother taught you to work hard at a very early age, and perhaps the message she was giving you was that people will love and value you so long as you work hard." "My sister and I didn't have the choice. When I'm at home I do my garden and all that, but I think to myself, 'You're not a useful person.'"

Q. "It's not good enough just to be looking after yourself?" *A.* "No. I feel I should be doing something to help people. But still, I think that I have worked all those years and I should rest." *Q.* "So part of you is saying that you ought to sit down and take it easy and the other part of you says that you should be up and doing things for other people." *A.* "Yes, that's right. Mind you, I couldn't do any more housework. I should want something where I was with other people. I wish I could get rid of this depression and be one of those people who didn't care. Some people never seem to bother about anything and they get through. I couldn't be careless and I'm not a slaphappy person. I would love to be really free and easy. I think sometimes that I worry too much."

Rose said this to me some four months after she had been discharged from hospital. By then she had told me the story of her life and she could see no reason why she should continue coming to see me. As she had promised to visit one of her daughters to help through her confinement we did not fix a date for another meeting but left it that she would get in touch with me. Just a fortnight later her daughter telephoned me to say that her mother was very depressed. I said that I would go and see Rose the next day.

Rose's home was half of a large stone house which fronted the village high street. I did not find it immediately after I had parked my car, but Rose had been watching for me and came out onto the footpath to collect me. She took my hand and nearly cried when I greeted her.

We sat in her small kitchen which was warmed by a coal fire. The rest of the house was cold and there were patches of damp on some of the walls. Rose said that she felt secure in bed but that it was wrong to stay there. She must be up by eight o'clock, but then she felt weak and exhausted. She felt that the world was pressing down on her head. Everything looked larger than lifesize. She wanted to cry. She felt that she was still a stranger in the village although she had lived there for forty years. She wanted to run away, but where could she run to?

I listened and talked to her about the need for her to rest. I knew that my advice would not be heeded by her without a struggle since if goodness is found in hard work, resting must be wicked. So I was prepared to repeat this advice many times and in as many different contexts as I could conjure up. I doubted that this advice was given any consideration by Rose at this meeting, but it did seem that our relationship had changed. I had become a friend and not merely someone who had shown a polite interest in her. I arranged to call again the following week, but Rose telephoned me at home to say that she was staying with her sister and would I visit her there. She said that she knew that I would "bring some sunshine".

Rose's sister, Ann, had been recently widowed but she was still living in a cottage on the large farm where her husband had worked. Despite a lifetime of hard work and little comfort and the loss of the most important person in her life, Ann was gay and lively and entertained me with stories of life in this part of rural England. When she talked of her passion for local archaeology she reminded me of a schoolgirl, slim and long-legged in her gymslip, fresh from the hockey field and eager to learn. But she had never been this. Like her sister, she had left school early to fill her days with housework, in service to the mistress of the house, to her mother, her husband and her children. "We had to keep what we were interested in inside ourselves because we had our work to do," she told me.

Like Rose, she had set herself high standards in her work and she had had the intelligence and spirit to achieve them. Now, as Ann told me of the different kinds of work she had done, of the difficult war years and the terrible winter that followed the war, Rose told me of her anguish that she had no strength and so could not do the work that she must do. So again I argued the necessity of her resting. Since the rest for one's own sake was a dangerous self-indulgence, I put resting in the context of duty and applied this to both Rose and Ann. It was their duty to look after their children, and, now that the children were grown up, the way to look after them was not to cause them extra worry but to look after themselves by resting and so recovering. They promised me that they would do this.

When I went to see them the following week I took them some books on archaeology and travel, and in the following weeks these books were more thoroughly read than in all the time they had rested on my shelves. Rose now said that she felt weak and tired in the mornings but felt better as the day progressed. I argued that there is no law that forces us to do certain work before noon. Dishes can be washed and beds made just as efficiently in the afternoon as in the morning. To this novel view Rose, at last, gave some qualified acceptance, but she knew I must have been joking when I said I never wash the windows in my house.

Rose soon felt well enough to return home and in the following weeks, when I called, we would go for a walk in the woods or by the river and drop into a pub for a stout on our way home. On our walks Rose told me the names of the plants and trees we saw and described what the countryside had been like before the spraying and the combine-harvesters had arrived. "When we were children we always used to find the first aconites and the first snowdrops and the first bird's nest and I loved collecting those cones and any pinewood, little bits of pine-wood, you put them on the fire and you get a beautiful smell. We used to walk miles with the children and especially when the trains used to run past our village. There was one train at twenty to seven and one at ten to seven and I hardly ever missed them. I don't know but they always fascinated me, the steam trains. We used to walk for miles and there used to be such different flowers then, the wild orchids and we used to call them tottering johnies, I can't remember the other name, and the cuckoo flower, harebells and daisies and ever so many kinds of flowers, but ever since they've done all this spraying I think they've killed a lot off."

In late summer Rose went on a series of family visits and so the weather was getting colder when next we met. She was very pleased with what she had achieved and said, "I'm sure it's you who have put me on the right track."

Q. "But all I've done is tell you that you've got to rest."   A. "You've done something for me. I'm sure you have. You're such a nice person to talk to. I've taken notice of what you've said and I like you and I think you have done something to me, I feel totally different."

"How do you think you have changed?"

"I feel as though I'm a free person and I'm not going to let things worry me. I know I've got older and I must realize that I've got to take things much steadier. I'm hoping to live till I'm ninety or something like that. Of course, I have to talk. I am a talker and I've always been with people and I can make friends with anybody. If I had money, I would go on a sea cruise. I wouldn't like to fly but I love the water. I've always loved travel. I would travel anywhere. I love those mountain and sea books. I love them, oh, the sea it thrills me, I can't swim, I know, but I'd still go on a boat."

One day I asked her, "How do you imagine heaven to be?" "When I was a child I thought heaven was up above and, of course, I thought that everything there was beautiful, but since I've got older I think that heaven is being good and doing what you can for people to help them and if there is, well, there will be a Judgment Day, they say. Is there a devil? There must be a God because there wouldn't be such beautiful things if there wasn't a God. So I imagine heaven, if we're going to be brought before our Maker, well, I try to do the best I can and I might still have a lot to answer for yet but, I mean, these people that do bad, they'll have a terrible lot to answer for. When you think of the churches, how they were built and all these lovely chapels, the men that built these were better builders than what we have today. And they must have thought there was somebody, a power beyond just all these human people on earth. Look at the seasons, the colours, colours from flowers — the greens and everything."

Q. "So everything that's beautiful in nature is proof that there is a God?" *A.* "Yes, with nature there is, there couldn't be such beautiful things otherwise. I think that with the devil you make your own life like that because you abuse things and, you see, if you abuse things, you're going with him. I mean, like all the terrible things in the world. There must be something what's driving all these people to killing and hurting innocent people, little babies, all these people. I'm definitely sure there's heaven because you wouldn't get such beautiful colours as there is." *Q.* "Do you feel that when you die you come up for judgment then?"

A. "Yes, but it makes you wonder if people don't soon realize and be good and kind, it makes you wonder if the world might come to a sudden end, but, you see, they said it was going to be destroyed by fire next time, because there's these atom bombs, isn't there. But I want to be cremated, I do. When I was a child we used to watch them dig graves and I used to think to myself, 'I'm not going to be put down there and have all that dirt thrown on me.' I never wanted to be buried, not after I saw all that dirt, I think it will have to come to cremation because look at all the land they're taking for houses. And dying, well, I used to think, 'What's it to die?' I don't want my family to see me die because, I don't know how I shall die, but none of us know that, but I think if you've led a decent life I don't think you should be — getting old, you die peacefully like that, I think that would be lovely. But look at all the accidents that happen to people, like in Northern Ireland, they just kill them, they just open the door and shoot them. I don't think I want to be on my own when I'm dying, but, I don't know, but there is definitely, I've always maintained that there is a God because there couldn't be such beautiful things around, I mean, there's not one coloured grass, we don't know how many coloured grasses there are. There's the rainbow and there's a lot of wonderful things, when you think. There's the seven wonders of the world and the sea, that's another wonder. It moves. The sea's never still, is it? That's a wonderful thing, to watch the sea, even. You can't stop it, can you, and where does the wind come from, that's what I often think. How the wind comes, how the rain comes, you get the sunshine. All those are things that man couldn't make, could they, they can't make them things." *Q.* "Do you imagine God as being a person?"

A. "Well, that I don't know. He was on the earth, that's the troubling part. But I think when you have communion you feel more as if there's a holy spirit, I definitely do. From being a child I said my prayers. I used to kneel at the bedside with my mother. Now I say them in bed." *Q.* "When you were depressed could you pray?" *A.* "No, I couldn't get things in the right perspective. Everything seemed different. Everything looked wrong to me, nothing looked right. Whatever I did seemed wrong and another thing, I couldn't do it, I couldn't get to do it, but I think communion is the Holy Spirit."

I asked her to tell me more about why she did not want to be buried. "I'm not going down below," she said. "From being a child we used to watch them. We lived near the cemetery and when I used to see all that ground they took out and were going to chuck back on you, oh, I used to think, 'I can't stand it' and, I mean, you were dead, but I thought, ooh, I used to think, fancy, you've got to go down there and have that put on you. Of course I knew the person in the box was dead, but it still gave me that horrid feeling, ooh, I used to feel as though I was going to be suffocated. I dread being shut up and I used to think, 'I can't stand that, I couldn't do that'. I couldn't let them do that to me. So I've made it quite clear to the family that I want cremation. To see all that dirt taken out, because you're six foot down. We were only kids and we used to watch them make the grave and, my father and sister and brother were buried together and, oh dear — When I was a child we used to have pigs in a sty and we used to have suckholes, as we used to call them, where all the stuff from the sty would run down. My mother was talking to a neighbour and I came out and I stood on this grating and it gave way. It was only so big and I was only four and the grating gave and I went down and mother just caught me by my hair and of course she took me in and gave me a bath first and after the bath I still got a crack. I don't know why she hit me. I don't know whether that's where I got the fear."

Q. "Can you remember all that?" A. "Oh, yes, I remember that as plain as day." Q. "And if she hadn't caught you?"

A. "Oh, I'd have gone right down, ooh, I don't know where I'd gone and that's why I never want to be shut in a room. I never do want closing in. That's why I couldn't be like a miner. I couldn't go underground. I went to Derbyshire with Mrs Richards and they said would you like to see this — um, well, I thought we were going to walk, I didn't know it was underground, you see." Q. "Was this the Blue John mine?" A. "Yes. We had to go right down under the ground and then there was the water and a boat and they had this acetylene light. 'Oh,' I said, 'Have we got to go on that?' and she said, 'Yes' and, oh, this narrow way and when we got to the end there was this deep lot of water. I was never so terrified in all my life. I daren't show it that much but I said that next time I'll know where I'm going." Q. "How would you feel if you were locked up in a room?" A. "Oh dear, I'd get out the window somehow. I can't be shut up. I love the open. Now I'm better I feel I've got the freedom."

Freedom, cleanliness and the need to help others were recurring themes in Rose's conversation. During the conversation about her religious beliefs Rose referred to herself as "a clean worker". She recalled that the last job she had had involved some very dirty housework. "I used to come home with my knees as black as ink. I can't bear to have my knees black now. I used to come home and think, 'Black knees again, it's disgusting'. The work was piling up and I didn't have the energy to do it."

"It seems that for you, when you die, being able to face the Judgment without any fear is to be good and to be good is to help other people. So I suppose that when you started to find that you couldn't do as much to help other people, then this wasn't just a matter of not being able to do things but it had this fear that you wouldn't be satisfactory, that it wasn't good enough, you might even be getting more like the sort of people who turned to the devil." "Yes, that's it."

Q. "Do you think that this taking things easy makes any difference to what might happen after you die? Or do you think that God understands?"

A. "Yes, I think to myself, I've got my windows painted which I couldn't get done last year. I've washed my curtains and dyed them which I was going to do two years ago and I keep looking for cobwebs and I'm going to do that grate and I've scrubbed all my cupboards out and it doesn't matter how you scrub the wood in the pantry it's still brown, but, I've no, if I go, I've done what I've wanted to do and that's all that matters, and I just keep the dust and the dirt out and get my hoover on my bedroom and I keep the bathroom as clean as I can."

"So if you died and people came in here they'd see the house — "

"Well, if they said it was dirty they'd be wrong. I mean, I scrub out, I've scrubbed every bit of that pantry and I've got my door painted white and I've done all my windows which wanted doing and I'm quite satisfied now. I get my hoover out and I do the passage out and the bedroom and downstairs and every time I have a bath I wash it straight out. I keep the windows clean, I keep my clothes clean. I keep myself clean, every night I have my bath, so I know if anything happened I'm clean."

8

HELEN, CLAIRE, JANE AND MRS MONDAY

"But first I must tell you
That I should really like *to think there's*
*   something wrong with me —*
Because, if there isn't, then there's something
*   wrong,*
Or at least, very different from what it seemed
*   to be,*
With the world itself — and that's much more
*   frightening!*
That would be terrible."

T.S. ELIOT

Helen came into hospital because there seemed to be no physical reason for her loss of weight other than a refusal on her part to eat. She insisted that she ate too much. Although she was of average height, she weighed no more than ninety pounds. She resisted the regime of rest and an adequate diet that was prescribed for her and soon left the hospital, but she accepted my invitation to come and talk with me.

Although she needed to swathe herself in layers of clothes to hide the ugliness of her bony thinness, her face, with its delicately carved cheekbones underlining her soft, luminous eyes and pale translucent skin, had an ethereal beauty. She spoke in a carefully modulated voice, and, while she disclaimed any extensive education, she evinced an interest in the arts and an appreciation of learning. She seemed to be an elegant, sophisticated young woman, yet at the same time she was a vulnerable little girl.

We did a repertory grid where she talked about herself, her ideal self, her parents and her husband from whom she was now separated. She described herself as a "gluttonous pig". She despised herself, got angry with herself, felt guilty about herself, was very frightened of herself. She was a failure, she let people down, she was a burden to others, she never helped other people, she was scared to lead her own life. By contrast, the person she would like to be was someone who had willpower, never let people down, was never a burden to others, always helped other people and was never scared to lead her own life. Her mother was someone who was a failure, she let people down, she cared very much what the neighbours thought, she was a very average person, she rejected Helen. Helen in her turn got very angry with her mother; she also felt very guilty about her mother. Her father, too, let people down, rejected Helen and cared what the neighbours thought. He made Helen feel very angry and guilty, and she was very frightened of him. Her husband, Roger, was an independent person with willpower, but he was also a failure who let people down and rejected Helen. He, too, made her feel angry and guilty, and she was very frightened of him.

I asked Helen whether she would prefer to be dependent or independent. "An independent person, I think, on the whole," she said, "But it frightens me to be too independent. I think we all need other people."

> Q. "Why is it important to be independent?" A. "It shows that you are a person within your own right. An actual human being capable of leading a natural life." Q. "Why is it important to be an individual and an independent human being?" A. "There's no point in living otherwise, is there? I feel as if I must have been put here on this earth for some reason and not just to live day to day as I am doing now. There must be something more to life than there is at the moment." Q. "Do you mean that life should have some purpose?" A. "I think that you should have a purpose in life because then everything you do will be toward this purpose and that in turn should make life happier. All the things I do are for no reason whatsoever." Q. "So having a purpose means being happy?" A. "Yes. I can't see a life with no purpose being filled with pleasure. Those people who choose the difficult life, they must still be happy at it although it must be hard. They must gain more satisfaction out of life than I am at this moment. I'm not getting anything out of my life."

"Let's go back to 'dependent'. Why is it important to be dependent on other people?" "No man is an island. I suppose during the day I want a career and be independent — to help other people, and in the evening when I'm tired out, that's the time I should like to be dependent. I should like to relax with someone I could depend on. I suppose when I say dependent I mean someone I can unwind and relax with. And, there again, they're there if you need them."

> Q. "So being dependent is okay if you've got someone to lean on that you are fond of. What are the bad things about being dependent?" A. "You can be too dependent. You daren't make a move without someone pushing you which I think is wrong. At the moment it takes me half a hour to decide whether to have a cup of tea or not."
>
> Q. "You described yourself as a gluttonous pig. What is the opposite of 'gluttonous pig'?" A. "Somebody who eats sensibly and under control. They stop when they have had enough. They eat their portion sensibly with a knife and fork at all times." Q. "Why is it important to be like that?" A. "If I were like that I would eat more and look more attractive. I would feel better. From the social point of view I should be able to enjoy

life more. I'm terrified of going out to eat. I shouldn't eat a thing. I should go home and go berserk. I don't even stop to make a proper sandwich. I start off by cutting the loaf. I swallow it down without even chewing it. If I have a piece of cake I don't slice it on to a plate and then eat it, I just ram it into my mouth." *Q.* "When you say you're frightened when you go out for a meal, what do you think is going to happen? What are you frightened of?" *A.* "I don't know really. Perhaps eating in front of other people. I'm very faddy about my food, so I'm frightened of what others might think of me. I should turn my nose up at all the different things." *Q.* "What do you think people will think if you do things like that?" *A.* "I feel that they would notice me. I don't like being noticed. I don't like mixing socially at all. I'm all right if I can go to a party and stand in a corner where no one can see me at all." *Q.* "Why is it important not to be noticed?" *A.* "I'm all right now with you, but say we were at a party and the conversation got going, I should just clam up. I don't think I should have anything to give back. There would be nothing for me to talk about. Most parties I know or know of end up with someone taking someone else's wife home, or being sick all over the carpet. That would be a couple's night out. The last party I went to there was the typical rowdy, boring crowd. I try to laugh at the rude jokes, and everyone is drinking and everything like that. They would laugh at me because I didn't laugh off their jokes and get drunk every night. To those sort of people you haven't had a good night unless you wake up with a hangover the next morning. To me that isn't a good night out."

"Now you said that you don't want people to notice you and then when I said why not there was something, is there, about not having anything to give back? Do you think of this when you meet other people — that you don't have anything to give?" "I think I must be very boring and uninteresting to other people. It says in magazines if you are shy, take an interest in what other people are doing and the questions will come spontaneously, but it doesn't work. They say I am stuck up because I don't talk back. I'm shy I suppose. I think of something to say but by the time I have got it out I have muddled it up and got it back to front. Or it might be too late to say it anyway."

Q. "Are you saying that within a relationship there is the giving of something, and when you come to give it it is all muddled up and you make a mess of it? You don't get the gift across properly." *A.* "Mm. Yes, I suppose so. I'm also scared of giving to somebody, I'm scared of letting anyone know the real me." *Q.* "What do you think will happen if you do this?" *A.* "I shall be hurt again." *Q.* "How will you get hurt?" *A.* "By being rejected. I've put my trust in my parents and Roger. I'm still trying to give myself to Chris." (a friend she had recently met) "He wants to know me better. He doesn't want anything back — he just wants me. I try and knock that brick wall down and give myself to him as much as I can. But something is holding me back all the time."

"You've been hurt in the past, and you've been hurt by the people who should have looked after you." "That's what I say. I bet if you asked my parents if they rejected me they would disagree .... It scares me that Chris is getting involved with me. He's taken up with me while there may be someone else waiting round the corner. That scares me very much. He could go out and find someone with no problems and no hangups. Before, he was carefree and happy, whereas now I know he leaves me at night and goes home and worries. He knows I am going into the terrible atmosphere of my parents' home. He has this strong affection for me, and it's marvellous to know he does. I'm scared for his sake."

Q. "Why? Why shouldn't he feel like that about you?" A. "I'm not really worth it. There must be a lot more people around who can give something back. People more worthy of it." Q. "What is it that you haven't got to give?" A. "All of myself I suppose. I'm very scared of letting anyone know the real me. They might say, 'Well, there you are, take yourself back, I don't want you now.'" Q. "So there's something about you that when people get to know you it would make them reject you."

A. "I suppose there must be. I fell foul of my parents and I fell foul of Roger — " Q. "So there must be something in you that people reject rather than it's you who have met a lot of people who are themselves unloving." A. "Yes, there must be. I don't know what it is, but if I did know, then I would try to put it to right." Q. "Why must it be you? Why can't you say that you're a loving person and that you've met all these dreadful people?" A. "It's too much of a coincidence for my parents to be wrong and for Roger as well. That's like trying to put the weight on someone else's shoulders."

"But earlier this morning when we were doing the grid you said something about it takes two people for a marriage to fail. Now you're saying that as far as you're concerned it only takes one." "I suppose it was both of us that caused it to fail. I should have been able to stop it from failing. I should have been the person he wanted me to be. I should have been able to keep it going that way. I could have gone out drinking with him and his rowdy friends every night, come home roaring drunk and fallen into bed, got up the next morning feeling awful but laugh about it. I did have an untidy home. I suppose if I had accepted that was enough for me and my life our marriage would have gone on. It's because I wanted more out of life. I wanted to be happier — that's why we broke up. There was no communication whatsoever. I would say, 'Have you had a good day at work?' He would slump on the sofa with an 'Ugh', turn the telly on and that was that. I just could not communicate with him."

Q. "So, if you had been a person who enjoyed rough parties and drinking then you think your marriage would have succeeded. To be that sort of person you would have to be the sort of person you didn't want to be. You would be leading a life you didn't want to lead." *A.* "I wouldn't have been happy but it would have kept the marriage going, I suppose. It would have kept my parents happy. It would have satisfied them. It would have satisfied Roger because there would have been someone there to do his washing and ironing. I suppose people just expect the wife to be there." *Q.* "You think that if you had been the person your parents and Roger wanted you to be then that would have saved your marriage?" *A.* "Yes." *Q.* "So if you're the person you want to be the marriage would fail?" *A.* "Yes." *Q.* "So if you'd have been the person they wanted you to be and made your marriage last, then you would have been the sort of person you despise."

A. "Yes. I would have been unhappy but my parents and Roger would have been happy. I wouldn't have been all this trouble to my parents. I could tell myself that these last three years have never happened, but I could learn something from it all, I suppose." *Q.* "What have you learned?" *A.* "Not to put too much trust in people, for one thing. But I suppose I am trying to relearn that and to put trust in people. I'm learning who to trust and who not to trust. I'm learning to pick and choose." *Q.* "How much do you trust yourself?" *A.* "At the moment, not very much. Not very much at all. I wish I did." *Q.* "You must trust yourself to some degree because you made a choice. You made a choice between either being the person you wanted to be or the person that Roger and your parents wanted you to be. You were in the situation where whichever one you chose you were going to be unhappy. But the choice you made was to be yourself." *A.* "I'm pleased I made that choice. I don't regret it for one moment. I just wish I'd got it more organized so that I didn't have to go back to my parents. Part of me is very disorganized, so I don't trust myself. I want to prove that I can arrange my life. It's turned out that I am a burden to my parents and a nuisance to myself. I've ended up losing so much weight. I'm living with my parents but I feel like a lodger, not one of the family. I don't communicate with them at all. My father is the typical Irishman, but I did think there should be more between my mum and me, but there isn't. I don't know how she could have given birth to me and brought me up and then not to feel anything. I try to talk to her about it but she tells me not to be stupid and that's as far as it goes. I think if she did feel anything she would sit and talk. There seems to be no bond between us .... It would have been easy to try to fit in with Roger and his ideas. It would have been a pretence and I don't want to live in that type of world. I think that to be happy I shall have to face up to the bad things in life. To me, it's like if you've got spots, put plenty of make-up on and then nobody will notice you have spots. I should want to clear the spots up so I didn't have to wear make-up .... But I just feel I owe my parents so much." *Q.* "What do you owe them?" *A.* "Well, not moneywise. I do pay them for having me. They did take me back after the — well, I suppose I owe them for that. I would hate to hurt them. And yet I think it would be impossible to hurt them because they seem without feeling most of the time."

At our next meeting I showed Helen the analysis of her grid and asked her about some of the words she had used. "Here, where you use the words 'average person', has this got some special meaning?" "In some ways I like to be the average person. I like the normal job, the normal husband, the normal semi, and the (what is it?) the average one point nine kids, and all the ordinary things like washing on a Monday, and then at other times I think I don't want that at all. I want more out of life than all that. At the moment I don't want to settle down and have a family and all the rest of it. I would like to be settled in a job if I wasn't so skinny. I suppose I wish my mental outlook was more average."

> Q. "What's the advantage of being an average person?" A. "You're accepted more easily by other people." Q. "Do you feel that people who aren't average aren't accepted?" A. "They're not neglected, but they aren't accepted so easily." Q. "What's the advantage of not being an average person?" A. "It depends on the individual. I think you're independent if you're not average." Q. "Why is it important to lead an independent life?" A. "It's important to me at the moment. I went from home to married life, and from married life back to home, and I suppose I ought to prove that I can be independent. And yet at other times I feel I would like someone to be there to lean on and rely on."

"You described yourself as being scared to lead your own life. What are the sort of things that make you scared to lead your own life?" "I can't seem to settle at anything."

> Q. "Do you mean you can't seem to make your own security?" A. "Well, to begin with, I have to get a steady job that I am happy in. It doesn't look as if I am going to do that. When I look back I can see that when I first started hairdressing I knew that I was doing it well. Now I'm not competent at all because I have been out of it for so long. I'm not up-to-date with the new styles and everything. But I desperately want a job. I won't be content to sit around home and look after a couple of kids." Q. "How do you feel when you're actually on your own?" A. "I'm hardly ever on my own unless I go out for a walk or something." Q. "Well, suppose you went off to live in a flat on your own, how would you feel then? Does that idea frighten you? Would you find that difficult?" A. "No, I don't think so. I'm not frightened of being on my own, and I'm not frightened of the dark or anything like that. Last night we had a big flare-up at home, and after I was frantically looking in the paper for a place. Looking at it rationally I just couldn't leave until I can prove that I can hold down a steady job. From the practical point of view I have to be certain of an income coming in every month. There is electricity and gas

and all the rest to pay. I suppose that I am frightened that any big decision I make might go wrong again."

"Do you expect on the whole that things will turn out badly?" "Yes."

Q. "Has it always been like that?" A. "No, I don't think so, no. I have always been scared of exams and have expected to fail." Q. "Do you worry about — well, if you're in a train do you worry that there will be an accident?" A. "No. The thing that worries me about flying is that I get airsick. I don't think about it crashing. If it is going to crash there is nothing I can do about it so — I'm scared of making big decisions." Q. "Because you think you're more likely to make the wrong one than the right one?" A. "I wish someone or something would force me into making a decision. I have these brainwaves — like last night I was thinking that I should go to live in as a housekeeper or go and live and work in a hotel or something like that. Then when it all comes to do so, I haven't got the courage. The more depressed I get the more I find it hard to make a decision." Q. "Why do your decisions turn out badly? Is it your fault or is it other people's fault?" A. "I suppose it must be my fault. I mean, I decided to take that typing course but it's nobody else's fault that I couldn't stand it. It's my fault."

Later in this conversation I asked her how long she had been depressed. "I suppose it depends on what you call depressed," she said.

Q. "What would you use to describe that feeling?" A. "I suppose I would say very, very unhappy." Q. "How long have you been very unhappy?"

After a long pause Helen said, "I don't know. It's just every day I get more unhappy. I suppose it's shortly after I got married."

Q. "Were you happy as a child?" A. "I don't know. I always kept myself to myself. I never had a schoolfriend. I hated school parties and everything like that. I was all right until I was eleven, and then I didn't like high school at all. With my parents being Catholic I couldn't join in assemblies and religion classes." Q. "Was this your choice or your parents' choice?" A. "Oh their choice." Q. "What did you think about it?" A. "I thought it was pretty stupid. It's daft ... we all believe in God. I think it's wrong to make a child stand out and be different. When I left school I vowed I would never go inside a church again. It was because they forced me to go when I was at school. I did give it up and never bothered at all until about three months after I was married. I go every Sunday now. I don't know what I believe in. I'm not at all sure that there is a God up there that looks like a bloke with a long beard. I think I just have to have something to believe in."

We talked about different religious practices and Helen said, "When I was little we never had meat on a Friday. When my dad goes to communion at Easter and Christmas there is a great big fuss and no one is allowed to eat before they go to church. He thinks he is so great because he hasn't ate a bowl of cornflakes before he went, and yet he will be swearing and going on."

Helen went on to talk about how she ate uncontrollably at night when no one was watching. "It bothers me so much that I do act in this way. It makes me very depressed. It depresses me because I can't control myself. And I can't get a job. I see jobs in the paper — waitresses for the Wimpy Bar — there's more to life than that. I might as well pack it in now."

"How much do you feel like packing it in?"

Helen was silent for a while and then said, "I suppose I am thinking of it a heck of a lot at the moment. Sometimes I think there must be something worth living for — there must be. There's Chris and you trying to help. There must be some point in making life go on. I couldn't throw myself under a bus or off a bridge — I would just dwindle away so to speak."

> Q. "You'd just fade away to nothing." A. "Yes. Today I feel pretty miserable so I feel like that anyway. I just want to fade away." Q. "What comes into your mind when you think about dying?" A. "Oh, nothing dramatic. I wouldn't slash my wrists or anything. I just feel like curling up in a corner." Q. "When you get that picture of you curling up in a corner, how do you see that picture? Are you that actual person doing the curling up, or are you sort of standing off and looking at yourself?" A. "I am standing off looking at myself. It's not someone else I see curling up in the corner. I am looking at myself." Q. "What do you look like?" A. "A frail and skinny bag of bones." Q. "And a corner of what? What sort of room?" A. "It's my bedroom." Q. "How do you feel when you look at this?" A. "A feeling of relief. A relief that it's all over and done with." Q. "Are your parents present when you're dying?" A. "No." Q. "How do you imagine them behaving after you're dead?" A. "They are looking at 'Match of the Day' and they are saying, 'You remember Helen, our daughter — '. They would have that sort of attitude." Q. "They'll remember you but in a very offhand sort of way. Will they feel guilty about you?" A. "No, because they have done their duty in taking me back. They tell me that it's up to me whether I make a go of it or not. I wish sometimes they would turn round and say, 'Get out.' They'll never do that because to them that's turning me away. They worry what the neighbours would say if I told them that my parents threw me out. They never will actually tell me to go." Q. "So if you died and there weren't any neighbours around would they remember you?" A. "Only in an offhand manner. I think they would feel relieved. They would try to cover it up and say it doesn't exist. That's what they do whenever a

problem arises — they just try to cover it up. It might be a dirty mark on the wallpaper or it might be me." *Q.* "So does this mean that if you really did die they would be able to forget all about you? Or would it be something that other people talked about?" *A.* "Other people would remember. The neighbours would say, 'Where has Helen gone?' When I was in hospital here they never would admit it to anyone. They said I had gone away on a long holiday."

"So in some way they still had to acknowledge your absence. I suppose the fact that you have got so thin makes it impossible for them to cover up completely. How does it make you feel that you embarrass your parents?" "I resent their attitude. I suppose part of me is trying to make up to them. I am always trying to do things for them. It doesn't please them whatever I do. I am trying to make up for failing them in other ways. I resent feeling like this. They should tell me they're embarrassed and tell me to go and find somewhere of my own. The other part of me though is trying to help my mum and dad. I am always buying them things. But I know I can't buy love. This is what I'm trying to do with them."

Q. "So part of you is saying, 'Look at me and love me' and the other part is saying, 'Hey, look what you have done to me.' " *A.* "I suppose so. I try to help mum in the house and I buy her sweets. If I make them a cup of tea they will say, 'What the hell have you brought that for? We didn't want it.' Or, 'Oh, you haven't made tea have you? I wanted coffee.' It's like that all the time. It doesn't bother them, and I'm the one who ends up being hurt. But I still carry on doing it. Every day I tell myself not to do it, but I still do."

I commented, "You seem to be giving me two messages at the one time. This is only the second time you have looked at me in over an hour. You give me the impression that you want to be here and yet you don't look at me when we talk." Helen said, "I have been longing for today," and began to cry, "I like talking to you but I'm so embarrassed by how I behave — it's so irrational. I feel I shouldn't feel resentful towards my parents. I feel very guilty about feeling resentful …. There is only you and Chris that I am prepared to carry on with life for. My parents don't know how I feel at all. They don't know me. I think Chris knows me better than anybody. We went for a walk last week and it was pouring with rain and I was wearing old trousers and a jumper and my hair was its usual mess and yet he said he loved me. I suppose I find it hard to believe that there are people around who are prepared to accept me for what I am …. I hope I can go to sleep tonight, and maybe when I wake up tomorrow it will all be different."

Q. "What would you like to have changed?" *A.* "Me, and my whole life. Well, not my whole life because I would miss Chris if he vanished. I was going to say I would miss you, but it would be nice if I didn't have to come here. I suppose I would be like you and have a good job that is rewarding." *Q.* "What do you see as a rewarding job?" *A.* "I would like to be in contact with people. I would like to help people. I could never be a nurse or anything like that." *Q.* "Why not?" *A.* "I couldn't stand the dirty part of it. I suppose all this gets back to me having too many high ideals in a way. From what hairdressing I have done people have said, 'Oh you do fuss.' I like to settle people under the dryer with a magazine and coffee and to me that is all part of the job. To the other girls there the job is winding in the rollers and putting in the pins. They don't do any more. I know that is the skilled part, but I might as well be in a factory all day. That would be boring. The more bored I am the more depressed I am. I feel sorry for myself when I'm bored. That's why I think I should be doing something to help someone else. I should feel life was worth living. I hope I do find something worth living for before I fade away."

Helen said, "I think I make myself ill and so depressed because I eat so stupidly .... I know I must pull myself together and start eating three normal meals a day. I don't like meat so I don't eat that anyway. My mum used to try and force it down me. I'm scared of food making me sick. And yet I never am sick. It's the fear of being sick that's my biggest fear. It worries me because I think I shall never be able to control myself. Yesterday I had eaten so much that I felt ill and when I am like this I can't make decisions of any kind and I couldn't even decide whether to go to bed or not. I hate myself for opening packets of biscuits and giving in. I just eat whatever is there. I don't think at the time how much I am eating. I look back over what I have eaten and I am amazed at what I can get down me. I maybe have eaten a loaf of bread. If I had sat down and made myself a cheese sandwich I just wouldn't have been able to eat it."

Q. "Why not?" *A.* "I don't know. I think I am just scared." *Q.* "What are you scared of?" *A.* "I'm scared that I shall be sick. Yet I know it won't make me sick and there again I like cheese. It just seems that everything that is good for me I'm scared of eating. Yet if someone said, 'You're going to eat a loaf of bread' I should say, 'No, I can't because it will make me sick.' It's once I start that I can't seem to stop myself. After I have eaten a whole loaf I realize what I have done and get scared, and then I really do start to feel sick. But I'm not sick. I'm scared of the actual quantity that is in me. I feel as if I am carrying a baby elephant. It makes me feel so terrible physically and also I despise myself for doing it. I can look in the mirror and slap myself. I hate myself so much for doing it and for being so weak-willed. I say to myself, 'Never again,' and yet I always do. At the time I am saying, 'Stop it, stop it!' but I carry on." *Q.* "So there is someone there saying, 'Stop it' and someone there carrying on." *A.* "The person I hate is the one that carries on and is always the person who wins."

"Always when you are talking about your eating you are talking about two people," I commented. "Yes, and the person I hate is the person who eats too much."

Q. "What sort of person is that?" A. "A greedy and gluttonous pig." Q. "If you met her what would she look like?" A. "Big, fat, ugly and overweight. Horrible. Gross." Q. "Could you draw me a picture?" A. "Well, she is smaller than I am. She is bloated, bulky and gross. She is big all over. She has short legs and looks like a dumpling in her skirt. She has no poise or sophistication. She has short, stubby sort of fingers. She has bad skin and bad teeth. She has long, greasy hair. She has no personality. She has no depth. All there is to her is what you see the first time you meet her. She has no ideas and no ambitions. She doesn't like being that size. She decides she is going to slim but she doesn't." Q. "How old is she?" A. "Fairly young — about sixteen. She has no friends." Q. "What's her name?" A. "It would be a very plain name. Susan or Jane or something like that." Q. "What's good about her?" A. "I don't know. Nothing, I think. She's not bad in the way like she'll murder her mother. She's quite contented and willing to stay the way she is. She's ordinary. There's nothing particularly good about her."

I asked, "Now if you picture the other one who is trying to keep Jane in order?" "Tall with short hair. Slim but not skinny. She has a nice figure. Nice skin, hair and teeth. She has poise, but isn't very sophisticated. She is a very nice person to know and she has a nice voice. The other one would be very boring to have a conversation with. Her voice would be monotonous and she wouldn't have anything interesting to say. This one would know what is happening. She would read the newspapers. She would be able to hold a conversation. She would have confidence in her job and her personal life. She would be full of self-control. Not just over eating habits but over everything. She would look neat and tidy."

Q. "What's her name?" A. "Something unusual. Maybe she would be a Claire. I don't know why I say that because I don't like the name Claire."

I asked Helen to picture Jane and Claire together. "They would be stood side by side. They might say hello. They are strangers and they might be stood at a bus stop. It might rain but Jane is there in peep-toe shoes and skirt and jumper. But Claire is prepared and carries an umbrella and a handbag. As Jane walks she is splashing the backs of her legs. Claire would be standing there not looking at all wet and uncomfortable. She will be dressed for the weather. Jane is always unprepared. That's how I was yesterday. I had to walk home in open-toed sandals in the pouring rain. They are still at the bus stop and the bus comes along and it is Claire who has the right money ready. She gets her ticket and doesn't fall down the gangway. She just walks to her seat. Jane fumbles in her purse and doesn't have the right money. She gets her ticket and drops it. She stumbles down the gangway and drops something else. She squashes the lady she is sat next to."

Q. "How does Claire feel when she sees all this?" *A.* "She's a bit hard in some ways. She doesn't have any feelings. She just knows that she must look better because she is more in control of herself." *Q.* "How does Jane feel?" *A.* "Idiotic and stupid. It doesn't worry her so much though as to make her do something about it." *Q.* "How old is Claire?" *A.* "In her early twenties." *Q.* "If they had a conversation what would they talk about?" *A.* "Just surface things like the weather. Claire would talk above Jane. Jane would feel a bit intimidated by Claire. Claire isn't as nice as she appears because she is very bored with Jane. She wouldn't try to help her." *Q.* "You sound as if you feel a bit sorry for Jane." *A.* "Mm, I do. Yet I feel sorry for Claire too. She is just a bit too poised and confident. She tends to make people like Jane feel small. She has got everything that everyone wants so she is bound to come a cropper one of these days. People don't dislike Jane. She doesn't do anything for anyone to dislike. Most people refer to her as 'fat Jane from around the corner'. She is that kind of person. I think people would envy Claire." *Q.* "Does Claire like being envied?" *A.* "Yes, I think so. She likes to know it isn't her who looks a mess. She likes to know that people secretly admire her. She has confidence to walk to the side of a swimming pool and stand there and let people look at her. If Jane dare venture to go swimming she would sneak out and get into the water as quick as possible. If people stared at Jane she would think, 'I bet they are looking at me because I am so fat.' "

"Suppose you picture them together in the kitchen." "Even if Claire was by herself she would have a properly laid tray with a napkin, and she would eat daintily. She would spread her bread and butter properly and she would eat sensibly. She would eat the same if she was dining at a hotel or eating in her own home. She chews each mouthful properly. She puts the food on to her fork and puts it into her mouth. Jane stands at the kitchen surface and she saws away at a chunk of bread. She stuffs it in her mouth and washes it down with a mug of tea. She picks up a piece of cake and gnaws at it until it's gone, whereas Claire will cut it into pieces with her cake knife, takes a bite, and then puts the cake down until she has finished with that bite. By this time Jane will have gone through a loaf of bread and started on a packet of biscuits. She wouldn't have sat down even to eat it."

Q. "How does Claire feel when she is eating?" *A.* "Relaxed. Jane is tense. She is eating as if every bite is going to be her last." *Q.* "Does she feel guilty about eating like that?" *A.* "Yes. And she wishes she could be like Claire. The more she wishes the worse she is. Claire only prepares so much, and if she ate any more and began to feel full then she would be able to leave it. But Jane, even if she felt too full she would eat it because she wouldn't like to throw it away. She would think it was a waste."

I asked, "How long have you known these two people?" "For about a year. No, that's not quite right. I don't know exactly. But I have been behaving like Jane for just over a year now."

Q. "Do you think they might have existed in some form before that year?" *A.* "I don't know, although I can't remember or visualize Jane being little or growing up. I can visualize Claire being a bit younger. She was a nice little girl to know. She was her mother's pride and joy. She just grew up to be a very nice and confident young lady. Jane was always a very fat child and people felt sorry for her in a very mild sort of way. She has always been the same to look at. I can't remember her having a clear skin and nice eyes." *Q.* "What is going to happen to Jane?" *A.* "I suppose she will just drift on and on as she is doing." *Q.* "What's likely to happen to Claire?" *A.* "She will be successful in whatever she does."

I wondered if "Jane" and "Claire" were names that Helen had given to her "self" and "ideal self", so I suggested that we add them to the grid we had done. This showed that while there was some similarity, there were important differences. Jane did not let people down as much as Helen herself did; Helen was more frightened of herself than she was of Jane; Helen did not feel guilty about Jane and Jane did not reject Helen as much as Helen rejected herself; Jane was more of an average person who cared about what the neighbours thought; Jane helped other people which Helen did not. While Claire had many of the qualities Helen admired, she was more independent than Helen would wish to be; Helen did not love her unreservedly since she was very frightened of Claire; Claire rejected Helen; Claire did not help other people. Helen had said that she was not depressed when she could help other people and that eating gluttonously made her depressed. It seemed that both these actions stemmed from that set of attributes which she labelled "Jane".

We often talked about food. As Helen said, "I've got to the stage where just about every thought I have is about food. I am either thinking, 'There is a loaf of bread down here and half a pound of butter there — what is it all doing to me?' or 'Now what shall I have for tea?' " I suggested to Helen that we do a grid on different foods. This showed that Helen divided foods into three distinct groups which she placed at extreme points from one another. In the first group were salads, apples, cheese, boiled eggs and oranges. She described them as being food that Claire liked, that was good for Helen, that made her feel healthy, full of light and life. In the second group were toast, white bread, cake, biscuits and chocolate of which Helen would eat all that there was to eat, which made her feel guilty, which were fattening and starchy, which Jane liked, and which were comforting. The third group was comprised of meat and chips, both of which made her feel frightened.

Helen said, "I go for foods that fill me up fast. I love apples and all sorts of fruits, but I don't feel the effect of them immediately. That will be why I go for the bread and biscuits and cakes. As soon as I have swallowed the food I hate it .... At home I can hardly relax and sleep at all. Usually it's at night I start eating. I suppose I feel very insecure at night when it's dark. Most happily married couples go to bed together and they have this feeling of security. I go to bed and I can't sleep and I feel very insecure. Eating all that food is the quickest way of getting that feeling of security. But mum says the same thing every night before she goes upstairs, 'You'll kill yourself eating that before you go to bed.' "

From what Helen had described of her family's eating habits it seemed that each member of the family had idiosyncratic eating habits and that the family made eating more of a ritual, albeit an unconventional ritual, than a mundane habit. "All you ever hear in our house is diets. They have different diet sheets for every day of the week. They don't eat, yet mum always fills the house with cake and bread and crisps. My dad is a great meat eater when he does eat. I hardly ever see mum eat at all."

I asked, "When you were little did your parents use food as a comforter?" "Yes, sometimes. We would eat a lot of sweets and things like that. 'Be a good girl and I'll buy you an ice cream.'"

> Q. "If you fell over would they tend to give you a sweet rather than a cuddle?" A. "I can't remember them cuddling me. They still cuddle my little brother now. I can remember them saying, 'If you're good we'll take you to the fair.' I can never remember her kissing me goodnight .... When I'm with my parents I feel tense and nervous. They make me feel I rely on them. I don't want to do that. I felt like Jane yesterday when we were arguing. I said, 'I don't need you or your food.' I thought I should isolate myself from them in every shape and form. I thought at first that I should go without food and drink for a few days and when they saw this they would feel guilty. But I couldn't keep it up. I'm not the sulking sort."

One day I asked Helen to describe her mother to me. She cried as she said, "I know it sounds awful but in one way I wish she were dead. I wish I need never see her again. Part of me hates her. She makes me so upset. She is always rejecting me. Every little thing I try to do for her she rejects .... She doesn't talk about anything really. She talks about what her neighbour has on her washing line."

> Q. "When you were a child could you talk to them about things? If you were in trouble at school was she interested?" A. "I never got into trouble at school. I was always quiet and independent. The typical good little girl sort of thing, I suppose. They say, 'We had you for sixteen years without any fuss or bother. We don't know why you have to be such a bother now' .... She has the skill of ignoring things she doesn't want to see. She seems to be able to shut herself off from situations which she doesn't want to know about. I don't believe in covering things up all the time."

A few days later Helen's mother telephoned me to say that she was very worried about Helen. When I told Helen about her mother's call, about which her mother had not told her, Helen found it hard to believe that her mother was really concerned about her. "She's only concerned with how I look," Helen said. "She wants me to put on more weight. She doesn't like to see my skinny arms and legs. She doesn't want to understand the emotional side of my problem."

> Q. "But we can love a person without understanding that person." A. "I

don't see how you can love somebody unless you really knew them and until you understand them."

I objected, "That would make all love impossible. What about all those women whose limits of understanding are 'I must feed my family, keep the house clean and see that my children are properly dressed.' Don't they feel love for their children?" "I see these women as without love. They have a sense of duty .... When my mother worries about me it only is about how I look. She doesn't worry about why I lost weight .... I think I am craving love and affection from her. That's why I get so upset when that love doesn't get reflected back."

Q. "Yet when I give you evidence that she cares for you you reject it." A. "But it doesn't tie up with the way she acts towards me." Q. "How would you say a mother should behave if she did love her daughter?" A. "She would show a genuine interest in her. She should remember things which her daughter told her. She should accept things which her daughter told her. She should accept things from her. She should try to do little things to please her. I think she should be sensitive to her daughter's needs and wants. I should hope that if I was a parent I would be able to sense if my child wanted to talk to me. When I asked her if she had ten minutes to spare to listen to me she made every excuse to get away. If I went home and said that I had seen a nice pair of trousers in Marks and Spencers she would listen to that. But deep and emotional things she doesn't want to know about. She might be frightened by it all — I don't know. A lot of people pretend things aren't there if they are frightened by them. I suppose I think it's best to think about these things and mother thinks it's best to cover problems up." Q. "So the picture you paint of an ideal mother is someone who is sensitive and aware and she is concerned with what goes on and not just with looking after her family. That's a pretty marvellous person and there's not many of them about." A. "She is always saying that I expect too much."

We talked about how high Helen's expectations were and I remarked, "Probably when you were a little girl and she was an inadequate mum then maybe you made up some fantasies to make you happy." "Yes, I used to have a Mrs Monday. Mum says she remembers finding me in the garden when I was little and I was talking to myself. I was dressed in high-heeled shoes and I was saying, 'Come on, Helen, let's go for a walk.' Then I threw off the shoes and ran to the other end of the verandah and said, 'Oh, Mrs Monday, thank you for taking me for a walk.' Then I would put on the shoes again and I would be Mrs Monday again. There was just me and Mrs Monday. If I fell down and hurt myself I would run and get those shoes and tell them that I had hurt myself. Then I would put them on, and pat myself, and say, 'Don't cry, Helen. Your hurt will soon be better.' "

Q. "What did Mrs Monday look like?" A. "I remember she had real dark hair but other than that she was really very ordinary. She was mothering, kind, loving and considerate. She was plump and cuddly. I think she liked me as a person."

When I queried whether Helen was expecting too much of her mother, she said, "I suppose I shall have to lower my standards then."

Q. "Is it a question of lowering your standards or seeing the world as it is? Your mother is just an ordinary woman." A. "Maybe I envy her in a way. She is able to shrug things off. I see her as an ordinary human being." Q. "She is ordinary and you're expecting her to be a saint. I think you're angry with her because she isn't a saint. I remember the first time you came to see me, you were saying how good it must be to help people, and while you were saying this I could feel the saint title being put on me. If I helped people then I must be someone special who has special powers. I tried to knock this idea on the head as soon as I heard it because I'm an ordinary person. I have no special powers. So if you expect me to be a saint then you're bound to be disappointed."

We talked about the extreme views Helen had of food as well as people and Helen said, "It all boils down to a lack of security. It has been offered to me on a plate by Chris .... I seem to think that today we have clarified things a lot. I think I have to accept people for what they are."

At our next meeting we talked about her relationship with Chris. Helen was frightened that this relationship would fail as her marriage had failed. "I think I might be impossible to live with. I don't want to be a burden to Chris. I don't want him to think that he has to be tied to me. My mother says I'm impossible to live with, and Dad agrees with her. They said it would be impossible for me to live with Roger and they proved themselves right over that .... In a way I think I am testing Chris. I felt so ill after seeing you last time. Chris took me home, and in a way I think I was testing him. I've never dared tell him what I've eaten but I did do that night and I thought he would turn round and call me a greedy pig, but he understood completely. I have this birthmark on my leg and it has always embarrassed me. I purposely showed it to him to see what he would say. I have had some terrible remarks about it from other people but all Chris said was, 'What difference does that make?' He just shrugged it off. So he does know my worst side as well as my good side." I talked about how, when we have been rejected in childhood, we grow up expecting to be rejected and so often see rejection where none is intended. "I wonder if this is what I am doing with my mother. Everything she does I see as an act of rejecting me."

At the end of this conversation it seemed that Helen saw herself as being able to leave home once she and Chris had found a flat. When I saw her ten days later they had found a flat but Helen had rejected it because it was too dirty. She was distraught. "The trouble with me is at the moment the more I get tensed up at home the more I eat ridiculous things. I haven't had a proper meal for days. I will stuff myself stupid on things that I hate. I feel awful at work and I know I'm having trouble with this job. But whatever the reason I can't stop. I had a row with Mum last night and she went out. When I was on my own I went in the pantry and ate my way through two loaves and a pound of butter. I was clawing at the butter with my hands and afterwards I felt so ill that I just went and laid on the bed and cried my heart out. I wasn't even hungry. I just return to being Jane every time there is a tense atmosphere in the house. I seem to be getting worse all the time. I know all the time that I am trying to change my mum into being what I want her to be. I think this stuffing myself with food to make up for the love I don't get from my mum is a stupid excuse. There is Chris giving me his love, but that still is no substitute for love from my mum," she cried and, through her tears, talked about how difficult things were for her at work.

Eventually I said, "I was just trying to think how I felt about this. I was just listening to you telling me about your feelings of depression and instead of me feeling closer to you I felt as though I was getting further and further away from you. You seem to me to have enclosed yourself. You don't even look at me. All the time we have been talking you are looking away from me. It's not a two-way conversation at all. I feel excluded. It seems almost as if you go into your own world .... It's like you're saying your life is terrible and you don't want anyone to interfere."

"I don't want sympathy because I think that will make me more miserable. At the moment I know I am drifting alone and I want someone to sort of force my hand. I know it isn't your job or responsibility to say, 'Pack your bags and go.'"

"It's useless doing that — telling a person what to do, because then you end up playing the 'yes but' game. It's like me saying, 'Move to another place and get a flat.' You'll then say, 'Yes but I might not get a job there.'"

"You can call it a 'game'. That's all right for you, being a psychologist. You can get a job anywhere .... Sometimes when I have been here it has helped quite a lot but sometimes like today I feel as though I might be talking to a paper figure. This is my fault — you haven't altered in any way. It's the way I accept or won't accept whatever it is you have to offer me .... I suppose it does sound like a boring monologue. Every now and then I get the fleeting thought, 'Why don't I pack it all in. It would make things so much easier.' There are so many tablets lying round the house, that I'm scared that one day I will do. But I haven't got the guts to. I do feel though what's the point in going on. I think one of these mornings I won't get up for work and I shall lie there until I dehydrate or something. I won't do anything dramatic like cutting my wrists. As I feel now I feel like fading away. I suppose I am trying to make my mother feel guilty. She accused me last night of eating too much and so I said I wouldn't eat another mouthful while I was in that house. I know I was trying to make her feel guilty. She thinks that there is only one thing wrong with me and that is that I am underweight. I just go mad and eat as much as I can. I can't understand why I did the very opposite of what I had said to her. I suppose if I really had wanted to die I would have just gone up to my room and not have had anything to eat."

"The trouble with suicide is that once you're dead you have given up the chance to play all the games we play with one another. So long as you stay alive you can go on playing the game of revenge on Mum. If you actually died then that game would be over, wouldn't it?"

"Yes, I agree, it is a game of revenge. Sometimes I wish I could be really thin again. That would make her feel guilty. I could turn round and say, 'This is your fault.' But, you see, I can't stop eating and I wish I could."

"Then you come and play the game with me. You want to make me feel guilty. You say that when you ask me to help you I don't help you. And as much as you want to get better you also want to stay ill. You want to prove that I can't help you just the same as your mother can't help you. When you do start to get well it means that you have to give up all ideas of revenge. When I saw you last things looked great. You were on the verge of success. Well, success can be very dangerous."

"I'm afraid of what success is. I want to be a nice weight. I want to be able to control my eating. I want to accept my mother as she is and I want her to accept me as I am. For either of us to be happy we must lead separate lives. Success to me means getting my own flat or sharing with Chris. I am frightened of it, I suppose. I am frightened of the future and what it holds. I am frightened of failing. Once I have left my parents I am on my own because I know they will never take me back again. If it doesn't work out there is nothing to fall back on. I dislike intensely what I've got, but I do know it is a form of security .... Leaving home, sometimes I feel it would be running away from it. If I leave now part of me tells me I am running away from it all. If I left after I had come to accept my mum for what she is, that would seem better .... It all boils down to the fact that I have to make up my own mind and decide what I'm going to do with my life. I shall have to decide for myself how to set about doing what I decide .... I need something to force my hand. Something like my parents moving to a smaller house with not enough room for me. I suppose this is why I am scared of getting really better. I know if I put on more weight and look really better then my parents would tell me to go .... One half of me is saying, 'Eat up, build yourself up, get strong.' Healthy body, healthy mind, so people keep telling me. Then the other half of me is saying that if I lose weight I'll be able to stay at home. It is at least a bit of security. It's somewhere to go without having full responsibility .... The way I've been feeling these last two weeks I know I have to make up my mind."

I commented that up till recently Helen could avoid making up her mind by "hovering between independence and death" but it seemed to both of us that she was now at a point where the conflict might be resolved. Before she left I read her Cavafy's brief poem.

> *"To certain people there comes a day*
> *When they must say the great yes, or the great no.*
> *He who has the yes ready within him*
> *Reveals himself at once, and saying it he crosses over*
> *To the path of honour and his own conviction.*
> *He who refuses does not repent.*
> *Should he be asked again he would say, 'No',*
> *And yet that 'No' — the right 'No' crushes him for the rest of his life."*

9

JOE

"We invent for ourselves the major part of experience."

NIETZSCHE

Dr S wrote to ask me to see Joe, a fifteen-year-old boy. "The differential diagnosis," said Dr S, "is between an early psychosis or tense, ruminative depression ... He has an obsession about a girl at school .... Over the past year he has become increasingly irritable .... He often lies awake at night and now has homicidal feelings .... About a year ago someone broke in and killed his pet rabbits and pigeons."

Joe lived in a remote village on the bleak North Sea coast. His father had deserted his family when Joe was a small child. Joe was tall, a very thin lad who sat, hunched and bony, in a kind of mute misery. He would answer questions, however, and so at our first meeting it was possible to do a repertory grid. He described himself as being gentle to animals, imaginative, cruel towards people, wanting to be powerful, changeable in mood, likely to get out of hand. He did not understand himself, he was frightened of himself and he felt very guilty about himself. The girl he thought about all the time, Ann, he described only in extremes. She was never gentle to animals, never imaginative, never there when she was needed, never cruel to people, never wanted to be powerful, never changeable in moods, never understood him, always totally happy, was extremely frightened of him and quite unlikely to get out of hand. He would get extremely angry with her, he was extremely frightened of her, he could never talk to her, he felt extremely guilty about her, he could never trust her and he loved her totally.

I asked him what, for him, was the opposite of "cruel towards people". He said that it was "gentle, helping". When I asked why it was important to be cruel to people he said that if he was not they might get out of hand. Similarly, by being changeable in moods he made people uncertain, stopped them from getting out of hand and so he was able to control them.

I invited Joe to come again when the analysis of the grid came back from the computer and this he did. I explained to him how I had set out the graph of the grid and we discussed, by me asking questions and he replying, why he was "awkward" in dealing with his family. I summarized our discussion by saying to him, "Well, let's see if I've got it right. If you loved your family without ever putting a limit on it, you would be putting yourself in the situation where they would be expecting you to do things. If you loved them completely all the time you'd never get awkward with them. They would then feel able to ask you to do things, and one of the things they would ask you to do would be to mix with other people in a way that you don't want to mix with other people. They want you to not say what you thought. You'd have to keep your thoughts to yourself. Keeping your thoughts to yourself leads you to the situation where you think people don't trust one another."

Shortly after this I left the room to make a phone call and left the tape-recorder running. When, later, the tape was played back, Joe's voice was heard making sounds of aeroplanes crashing and wolves howling. "This tape destroys itself in five seconds," he said. "This office is bugged. This is the American Air Patrol, we are now watching the red spot on Jupiter. We are approaching planet Earth. The invasion is about to start. The year is 1988. The whole world's radar is out of action. We shall claim the planet. This is the king of the planets. Spock and the others have been down there a long time. We are now beaming down to investigate. This is the captain of the starship Enterprise. We are due to land. This recording will destroy in five seconds — bang!! Wee Willie Winkie runs through the town, upstairs and downstairs in his nightgown, and you think I'm mad!"

Joe came to see me a month later and gave monosyllabic answers to my questions about how he was getting on now that he had returned to school after being absent for several months following an incident when he had threatened Ann. Since he lived some considerable distance from the hospital and since I occasionally made visits in a village near where he lived I suggested that I call and see him at home in a fortnight's time. He agreed and then suddenly said, "Can I pop back and see you before then? Could I bring Dick with me? He could tell you what I'm like at school." So I arranged that they could both come the following week.

However, Joe had to come alone because Dick was ill. We talked about his group of schoolfriends and about his pets. I commented, "So at the moment life seems to be a lot better than it has been in the past." "Yes."

> Q. "What sort of things still aren't too good?" A. "The fact that I can't get straight off to sleep — the fact that I stay awake all night. Before, me and mum could talk about it, but we can't now. When I want to talk she doesn't want to listen and when my mum wants to talk I don't want to listen." Q. "What sort of things would you like to talk to her about?" A. "About what happened between me and Ann." Q. "When you can't get to sleep at night you think about Ann?" A. "Yes." Q. "What sort of daydreams do you make up about her?" A. "I can't say." Q. "Are they happy ones or unhappy ones?" A. "Most of them are happy." Q. "What are the unhappy ones like?" A. "They're when I plan to kill. The unhappy ones are about when I find myself killing her."

We talked about Joe's temper. I asked, "Do you stay angry for a long time or does it blow over?" "Sometimes it lasts a couple of days."

Q. "How do you feel about this? Do you think it's a good way to be or a bad way to be?" *A.* "I feel good about it." *Q.* "In what way is it good?"

A. "It's good because then people know what to expect from you. They know you'll be angry towards them." *Q.* "In what ways is it bad?" *A.* "They begin to talk behind your back. They talk about how you behave." *Q.* "Would you rather you had a different sort of temper?" *A.* "No. I would like to keep the same one." *Q.* "When you get angry with your brothers do you ever feel you are going out of control and could murder them?" *A.* "It happened once with Harry. We were messing about and started fighting. He hurt me and I shouted, 'I'm going to kill you!', and mum come running up the stairs and stopped us. I had my hands around his neck. I think I would have killed him."

My car broke down, so Joe came to see me instead. He talked about how at home he had been "playing up" by saying nasty things to his mother. Then we started to talk about death. Joe said he sometimes imagined what it would be like to be dead. I asked him what sort of picture came into his mind. "A picture of becoming a ghost. I'm walking up and down .... I'm watching all the people and seeing what they are doing. I'm seeing what they say about each other."

Q. "Do you imagine they are talking about you?" *A.* "No. They don't talk about you when you're dead, do they?" *Q.* "Would you rather they talked about you?" *A.* "I don't want them to talk about me. It would remind me of the time I was alive." *Q.* "How would that make you feel?" *A.* "Like I've been missing a lot of things. Touching people and looking after things." *Q.* "Suppose you died now and you come back as a ghost, wouldn't you expect your mother to be upset?" *A.* "Yes." *Q.* "How would that make you feel as a ghost?" *A.* "A little bit ashamed that I had died." *Q.* "So you would feel it was your fault you'd upset them?" *A.* "Yes." *Q.* "I suppose you can say it's a general rule that if you love somebody you're upset when that person dies. So are you saying that you'd prefer that your family didn't love you so that they won't be upset when you die? How much would you like them to love you?" *A.* "About half way." *Q.* "Is this why you do nasty things to them? Is this why you're nice to them for a bit and then you're nasty? So you'll sort of stay in the middle?" *A.* "Yes." *Q.* "So if you're nice to your mother all the time she might love you too much. If you're nasty to her all the time she might not love you at all. So if you're nasty to her sometimes and nice to her sometimes then she will be somewhere in the middle .... Do you ever find yourself at home with just your mother and you're happy together and there is a feeling of warmth between you?" *A.* "Yes. But I get the feeling that I've got to stop it." *Q.* "It seems to me from what we've talked about this morning that in the present, now, you're restricting your affection and the affection of other people so that in the future you won't be upset. The question is, what's the reality of that future? What certainty have you got that in the future, when you die, death will be as you imagine it?" *A*. "I sometimes wish I could die and then come back and see what it's like." *Q*. "Would you prefer to be in the present and deal with the present as whatever is happening here or to live in the present so that when you die everything will be all right?" *A*. "In the present to make sure things after you're dead are all right."

I asked, "When you say you'd be ashamed if you upset them by your death, can you tell me more about that — what this feeling of being ashamed is?" "You feel that you can't stop it and then you feel guilty and know you shouldn't have done this."

Q. "When you say you feel guilty what sort of picture comes into your mind?" *A*. "I get a picture of something that I have to do but I shouldn't have done. It's like going into a room that's supposed to be locked. You go inside and you shouldn't." *Q*. "When you say you have to do it, who or what is making you?" *A*. "Curiosity. I want to know what is behind the door." *Q*. "Who is telling you that you shouldn't go in?" *A*. "My conscience." *Q*. "What does this locked room look like?" *A*. "It's just got a big door. I unlock it." *Q*. "What's inside the room?" *A*. "A big demon. And I let it out." *Q*. "What's the demon like?" *A*. "A big, reddish cloud. A cloud with a face in it." *Q*. "What does the face look like?" *A*. "It looks frustrated and puzzled. Puzzled but pleased." *Q*. "What happens then?" *A*. "It floats out of the door and starts to do damage. It starts to smash up everything." *Q*. "Is it harming people?" *A*. "Sometimes. The cloud pulls them over and when it rises up they are dead." *Q*. "When you said it looked pleased is it because it's damaging things and killing people?" *A*. "Yes. It's been locked up for so long — it's pleased to get out."

We talked about how Joe thought there were some things about his family that he had not been told and about which he felt he could not ask questions. He said, "The family think it's nosey, wanting to know about things."

Q. "How do they act towards you if they think you are too nosey?" *A*. "They call you 'know-all'." *Q*. "So if you're too curious people won't like you. What sort of things do people object to you being a know-all about?" *A*. "Well, in an argument they argue about who is right. They make out that you're big-headed and try to make out that they know more than you do." *Q*. "How do you feel if you win an argument?" *A*. "I feel good that I won but I don't want to win all of them." *Q*. "What will happen if you win all the arguments?" *A*. "They'll think I'm too good and won't have any more arguments with me."

"This destructive cloud — we've talked about it doing bad things. What's something good about it?" "It shows me what I could be like."

Q. "That sounds as if it's something you would like to be. Why do you want to be like the destructive cloud?" *A.* "To be recognized." *Q.* "Why is it important to be recognized?" *A.* "So people can take you for what you are." *Q.* "To recognize you as an individual?" *A.* "Yes."

When Joe next arrived to see me he looked very miserable. I asked him, "What sort of things do you think about when you're feeling like this?" "Nasty things — of hurting people — I think about hurting Ann."

Q. "Do you think about hurting yourself as well as hurting Ann?" *A.* "Sometimes. I think about destroying all the things I want." *Q.* "When you have these awful thoughts are you frightened of putting them into action?" *A.* "Sometimes."

We talked about this and then I asked, "What would you like me to be able to do? Suppose I had a magic wand and could change things." "I would like you to talk to Ann."

Q. "Do you think that if I talked to Ann in some magic way everything would be all right?" *A.* "Yes. Because I want everything to be all right. Everything back to normal." *Q.* "When in your life time do you think life was normal?" *A.* "Just after I met Ann." *Q.* "How did you meet her?" *A.* "Well, she came over and asked me my name." *Q.* "When did you think she was different?" *A.* "About six months after that. I realized I wanted her for myself." *Q.* "How did she treat you?" *A.* "She didn't want to know me." *Q.* "When did you start to think that you wanted to do things to hurt her?" *A.* "About after a year." *Q.* "What is it about her that makes her special and different from all other girls?" *A.* "She's better in the way she looks." *Q.* "What does she look like?" *A.* "Like a rose .... I want her for myself." *Q.* "Some people fall in love often in their lifetime. Do you think you could fall in love several times?" *A.* "No. If she's the girl I want, no other girl will be as good." *Q.* "So if you went off with another girl she would be second best. Why is it important not to put up with second best?" *A.* "If I did I might get second best all my life. People would say he's had second best once so he can have it again." *Q.* "Do you think that rule applies to life in general?" *A.* "Mostly, yes." *Q.* "Is the reason that you come to see me that you are hoping I will talk to Ann?" *A.* "Yes." *Q.* "So every time you come here you are hoping to persuade me to do that. What does your common sense tell you?" *A.* "That you might talk to her if I'm lucky." *Q.* "If you're lucky! Don't you realize that there are practical things in the way?" *A.* "Yes." *Q.* "What are the practical things that you see?" *A.* "She would tell the headmaster and her parents, and I could be sent to another school." *Q.* "Suppose you and Ann meet by chance, what is the possibility that while you were alone together you would do something to hurt her?" *A.* "Evens." *Q.* "I couldn't do anything that would put Ann in danger."

I expanded on this and then said, "You're looking very intense. Are you thinking, 'Well, she's not going to help me with Ann, so I'm not coming to see her again'?" Joe's ambulance arrived to take him home. I asked, "When would you like to come again? " "Soon," he said.

At our next meeting I asked him why Ann was so important to him. "Because she is part of my life," he said.

> *Q.* "Suppose you had to choose between being the most powerful person in the world and having Ann love you, which would you choose?" *A.* "I would have Ann." *Q.* "What if I said the choice was between Ann not loving you and another girl just as beautiful as Ann loving you?" *A.* "I would be with Ann." *Q.* "What if I said that you can only have Ann if you are kind and loving all the time?"

Joe was silent a long time before he said, "Kind and never being awkward to Ann"

> *Q.* "It would mean that if you were kind and loving to her all the time she'd be upset when you died. How would you feel about that?" *A.* "Angry. I don't want her to be upset." *Q.* "But if you were awkward with her while you were still alive she'd be upset, wouldn't she? How is it you don't feel guilty about making people upset now?" *A.* "I will be able to make it up to them, but if I died I wouldn't be able to."

I asked him why he had chosen to see death as leading to an afterlife where he was a ghost on earth. "That way I shall know what is going on in the world. I shall be there to see what is happening."

> *Q.* "Could you imagine death as going to a perfect world?" *A.* "No." *Q.* "What would be a perfect world for you? *A.* "If everyone helped each other to get along."

I asked him if heaven were a place where people loved one another and were there reunited with their family and friends would that change the way he behaved now. He said that it would not, because then he could have the pleasure of being nasty on earth and them make it up to those he had hurt when he went to heaven. Moreover, if he was always loving to his family, "they would just ask you to do everything. I wouldn't have time to do anything for myself." As against this, when I asked him to put in order of importance the virtues of courage, truth, love, generosity, justice and humility, he put "loving" first.

The following week when we were again talking about Ann I read him a passage from *Swann's Way* where the adolescent Proust sees Gilberte. "But very soon that love surged up again in me like a reaction by which my humiliated heart was endeavouring to rise to Gilberte's level, or to draw her down to its own. I loved her; I was sorry not to have had the time and the inspiration to insult her, to do her some injury, to force her to keep some memory of me. I knew her to be so beautiful that I should have liked to be able to retrace my steps so as to be able to shake my fist at her and shout, 'I think you are hideous, grotesque; you are utterly disgusting!' " "Is that anywhere near the sort of feelings that you have?" I asked. "Yes .... I want to be with Ann all the time and with no one else. She is someone special. I would give her things."

> Q. "What sort of place do you imagine the two of you being together in?" A. "A big field. It's a big, square field with a few cows, and the grass is about two feet high. There's a pool in the middle and we are sat beside it .... I feel happy. Then I feel sad because it isn't true." Q. "Do you imagine the two of you together in other places?" A. "In a lane with a stream running down the side of it. There are trees on either side of us." Q. "These pictures, are they the start of a story which you tell yourself and do they go on from there?" A. "That's it, just the picture." Q. "But at other times do you imagine you and Ann doing different things?" A. "Yes, sometimes we talk." Q. "What would you talk about?" A. "I don't know." Q. "Do you ever imagine things like you being married to Ann and you going to work? Do you have daydreams about ordinary things?" A. "No." Q. "What for you is so special about this picture of you and Ann sitting beside the pool?" A. "It's so calm and peaceful." Q. "When these pictures come into your mind does that make you feel comforted?" A. "Sometimes it makes me feel lonely."

We talked about how he got along with the girls in his class, and it was clear that Joe could not mix with these girls, that he lacked the simplest social skills and that he had no way of acquiring these skills nor did he see the need to do so. There was no way that Joe could come to know Ann as an ordinary girl.

Joe took a great interest in dead animals and birds and would carry them about in his pockets. His mother found this disturbing, as she did his habit of laughing at the news of accidents and deaths and his inability to live peacefully with his family. Dr S thought it might be best for Joe if he came into hospital. Since Joe would be going into a ward with adults, we spent some time talking about what this would involve. Joe thought he would continue to be nasty so that "People don't get too friendly with me. I won't be there very long will I? They'll get too friendly and then I'll have to leave."

> Q. "If you've a choice of having a pleasant time with a bit of pain at the end of it or having a very boring lonely time with no pain at the end of it, which would you choose?" A. "The boring time with no pain." Q. "Lots of people think in the opposite way. They think they can't avoid

dying so you might as well make the most of life while you've got it. What would you say about that?" *A.* "You might not want to be happy." *Q.* "Why is it important to be unhappy?" *A.* "People will feel sympathy and then you can use them and get what you want." *Q.* "What if you were unhappy and nobody took any notice?" *A.* "Then you could be nasty to them because you are unhappy." *Q.* "Do you get any satisfaction out of being nasty?" *A.* "Yes." *Q.* "Which would you choose, the pleasure of having friends and your being nice to them or the pleasure of being nasty?"

Joe thought for a moment and then said, "Being nasty. People might ask me to do things that I can't do."

Q. "What sort of things do you consider asking too much of you?" *A.* "Asking me to organize things." *Q.* "The nurses will ask you to do things. How will you feel about that?" *A.* "I shall think about it and if I can do it then I will. If I can't, well, then I won't."

When Joe had been in hospital a few days he complained that the people on the ward were too friendly. "When you want to be by yourself they are always coming round. The first night I was here I couldn't sleep at all. I kept thinking about killing all the people in our ward." He described the ways he had worked out of murdering without his crime being discovered. Then he said, "It worries me. I don't want to go around killing people or even thinking about it." He told me how he had found the hospital rubbish dump and how he had built a coffin out of bricks there.

Q. "What were you thinking about when you built it?" *A.* "I was thinking about Ann. At home I have a picture of her that I drew. It's properly framed and there is an inscription that says, 'Here lies my beloved, lost in the Region of Oblivion'." *Q.* "Can you tell me how you imagine it to be?" *A.* "It's just a big, blank space. Ann is just floating about in it." *Q.* "How do you feel about Ann being in Oblivion?" *A.* "I don't like it. I want to be with her all the time." *Q.* "Do you want to die so that you can be there with her?" *A.* "Yes." *Q.* "Which of these two would be better, for you two to be together here or for you two to be together in Oblivion?" *A.* "To be together here on earth." *Q.* "Suppose you couldn't be with Ann here on earth, would you prefer her to be with someone else or in Oblivion?" *A.* "In Oblivion." *Q.* "How do you see a person showing his love to somebody else? Suppose you were with Ann and told her that you loved her. How else could you show her that you loved her?" *A.* "I would be kind to her." *Q.* "So you do see kindness and loving as going together. If someone was unkind to you, would you think that person didn't love you?" *A.* "It would depend on what sort of mood they were in when they were unkind to me." *Q.* "What sort of mood would the person have to be in for you to think that they still loved you?" *A*. "If they were nasty in a nice tone of voice. If it was a soft tone of voice." *Q*. "So if you say to Ann in a soft voice, 'I am going to kill you' she'd know that you still loved her." *A*. "Yes." *Q*. "From the way you know love do you reckon a fellow will put his girl's wishes before his own or after his own? Whose interest does he consider to be the most important?" *A*. "His own." *Q*. "So when you love another person you can be kind to that person but you put your own interests before that of the other person." *A*. "Yes .... I want Ann to be safe and happy, but with me and no one else."

Counterarguments by me did not change Joe's point of view. He talked about how he would like to frighten Ann, "to make her realize that I mean business and I don't want to be messed about".

Q. "If you did, what would you like her to do in retaliation?" *A*. "Her to say that she was going to kill me." *Q*. "Would you mind if she killed you?" *A*. "No, so long as we had some fun trying to kill each other. If I came back as a ghost I could have vengeance on her."

Joe's favourite reading was horror stories about black magic. I asked him, "Do you feel that the more you read about death and dying the more you come to understand it?" "Yes." *Q*. "Do you feel that by understanding, knowing more about death we can control it in some way?" *A*. "Yes." *Q*. "How would you like to be able to control it?" *A*. "If I was going to die I'd want to go either in my sleep so I wouldn't know about it or a quick death by being shot. I wouldn't want to be stabbed to death and get all that pain .... If I can't get what I want I'd rather be dead. If I can't have what I want, a toy or something, I destroy it so no one else can have it ..., When I die, if we do come back, I want to come back as a white eagle so that people will take notice of me next time."

When Joe next came to see me he looked very unhappy. He described how he had been thinking about Ann, how he was not allowed to see Ann and how he was "thinking about hurting — doing some injury to her, knowing that I might do it".

Q. "Is that what happens now, you start to think about how nice it would be to be with Ann and then you remember you can't be with her and then you feel angry about this and think, 'If I can't have her, nobody else will,' and then you get scared that you might carry out this idea? These are like steps down, aren't they? If you had to draw a picture of the way you're feeling right now, what sort of picture would you draw?" *A*. "From the moment I was with Ann I would start with bright red and go right down to black. From the red down it would get darker." *Q*. "How would you draw yourself?" *A*. "Just thinking." *Q*. "What sort of place do you feel you're in?" *A*. "There's this big, black empty space. It's like a great, big prison. I can move further into it, but I can't move out of it." *Q*. "Do you feel that anyone can reach you when you're in that sort of place?" *A.* "Maybe Ann could. I don't think anybody else can — something else has been getting me down. It's her birthday soon and I have been thinking about sending something ugly to her. Maybe a dead animal or something. Maybe another threat." *Q.* "When you're in this black prison, is that when you think more about hurting Ann?" *A.* "Yes." *Q.* "When you're in this black place do you want to get out?" *A.* "No, because if I do get out I start thinking about Ann and then I go gradually back in there again. Also, when I'm in this prison I think about nice things and about being with Ann. It's not as nice as being out of prison, though, and thinking about being with Ann."

I asked, "What would you say was the most special thing about Ann?" "Her personality. She is gentle and kind."

Q. "What other people have you known who have been gentle and kind." *A.* "Angela. That was when I was nine. When I was in a home. Mum got sick and had to put my brother and me in this home." *Q.* "What was it like?" *A.* "It was all right to begin with and then we met other people and they weren't so nice. They would suddenly become nasty and tell you off." *Q.* "Were there a lot of rules about what you had to do?" *A.* "Yes. You couldn't use the upstairs toilets during the day. You had to wash all the soap off your hands before you dried them. You had to wash your hands before each meal. You had to go to bed at a certain time." *Q.* "If you didn't keep any of these rules what would happen to you?" *A.* "They would send us to bed or just tell us off. And if you wanted to send a letter during the week they told us we should have done it at the weekend when they had given us our pocket money." *Q.* "And the one nice thing in the home was Angela?" *A.* "Yes." *Q.* "What did she look like?" *A.* "She had freckles and dark ginger hair in plaits." *Q.* "And she talked and played with you?" *A.* "Yes. At first I would play with my brother. He would tell me off for forever following him. So I played with Angela." *Q.* "Did you know when your mother was coming to take you out of the home?" *A.* "No." *Q.* "Then suddenly one day she turned up and you went?" *A.* " Yes." *Q.* "Did you get a chance to say goodbye to Angela?" *A.* "No." *Q.* "Could you write to her?" *A.* "No, I didn't write." *Q.* "It's hard to do that when you're nine, isn't it? So when you met Ann and thought how lovely she was you were all the time half expecting someone to come and take her away." *A.* "Something like that." *Q.* "Do you think that at some future date you might meet someone else as nice as Ann? *A.* "I don't think about meeting anyone else. I don't want anyone else. I only want Ann." *Q.* "Suppose one day you just forgot about Ann, what would you think of yourself then?" *A.* "Angry. Angry that I forgot about her." *Q.* "So part of you is saying that you must remember Ann and you must live your life around her and you mustn't do anything else." *A.* "That's it." *Q.* "There is a part of you saying that you must remember, so there must be another part that is being given that message. If that part of you was a person what sort of person would he be?" *A.* "At the moment he is a wicked person who wants to hurt her and all the time there is the kind person there telling me to remember her and how I would like to be with her." *Q.* "What will happen to you if you forget?" *A.* "If I am having a good time and I forget, then something crops up to remind me of her. It's like this morning, I was looking at a flower-pot holder and it was in the shape of a heart and it reminded me." *Q.* "Suppose you suddenly thought that you hadn't thought of Ann for twenty-four hours what would you do then?" *A.* "I would try and remember all that I know about her."

Joe did not think that he was an ordinary person. I asked him, "If you had a choice about being ordinary and meeting Ann and thinking she didn't seem anything special, or living as you are now and suffering as you are now — " "I would suffer as I am now."

Q. "Why?" *A.* "Because I don't want to forget Ann. I want to remember her for always. I want to try and be with her for always." *Q.* "Do you think that by always remembering Ann you'll end up being a better person?" *A.* "Yes" *Q.* "Is there any part of you that says, 'Oh, let's forget Ann and have a nice time?'" *A.* "Yes, sometimes, it does. But as soon as I've had a nice time I start to think about her again." *Q.* "So you're having a nice time and along comes your conscience and says, 'You're not thinking about Ann'." *A.* "Yes." *Q.* "When we give ourselves instructions to do something we usually do this because if we don't give ourselves these instructions something unpleasant will happen. What's the nasty thing that will happen to you if you forgot Ann? What are you guarding against?" *A.* "I wouldn't love her any more if I forgot about her, would I?" *Q.* "Why would that be terrible?" *A.* "It would be terrible because I do love her." *Q.* "What's so terrible about stopping loving her? Does that thought frighten you?" *A.* "A bit." *Q.* "Would it be that if you stopped loving her you would be completely alone in the world?" *A.* "Yes. I think I am only living because of Ann. Life wouldn't be worth living." *Q.* "How would you imagine yourself dying then?" *A.* "I would die of loneliness, I suppose. Not caring about anything."

Joe would argue that it was Ann's fault that he was in hospital. "I know she likes me to get into trouble and she likes me being in here where I can't do anything to her."

Q. "How does that make you feel, the thought that she likes to know that you're in trouble?" *A.* "When I'm down it makes me angry but when

I'm all right, I laugh about it — because when I get into trouble I like to get in deep — for a bit, anyway. I think it's fun to be in trouble. I like being in trouble because when I'm in trouble people notice me then. They don't when I aren't."

Growing up as the quietest member of a large family Joe had found that he attracted his mother's attention more when he was naughty than when he was well behaved. I said, "I suppose I've been taking a fair bit of notice of you, compared to the amount of notice you've had taken in the past. Do you sometimes worry that if you get better, I'd stop taking notice of you?" "Yes. Then I'd threaten Ann again so somebody would notice."

Joe became very depressed and was given a course of ECT. Afterwards he said, 'I still have the same thoughts that I did last week but maybe not so bad. I'm not on about it all the time. But still do· get it, you know. Sometimes I have thoughts of killing you. That upsets me because I like you."

Q. "I don't think you would kill me." A. "No, I don't want to, anyway. I am still thinking of sending Ann something nasty for her birthday."

Joe was worried that if he went home on leave for a day he would find some poison which he thought was in the house. He asked me, "Do you think I should try and destroy myself?"

Q. "Do you think about destroying yourself?" A. "Sometimes. I think about myself taking poison."

I asked him if he wanted me to get in touch with his mother to ask her to find the poison and to throw it away. "No. You see, if I don't get the poison to kill Ann with I will have to shoot her and that will be painful for me to have to watch her die." "It will be painful for Ann too." "But stabbing is a physical thing and I don't think I will be able to do that. But if I got desperate and I had to do it — well, then it would be terrible for both of us."

Q. "So you want to find a way that doesn't cause too much pain." A. "Yes. That's if I get around to killing her. I should like to kill her on her birthday. What a nice present."

The only films Joe went to see were horror movies. He told me about one that he had enjoyed very much. "Everything happened to this fellow in the film that has happened to me except she didn't pack him in. In the end he got killed."

Q. "What happened before that?" A. "He started killing these women off because he had been seduced by two of them and they were black. Then he met Ann and they helped each other and she didn't pack him in. She was looking for the person who was doing all these killings and she didn't know it was him. Then he told her that it was him and that he would have to kill her. He was strangling her and then this fellow came up and they started fighting and he was thrown over the cliff." *Q.* "In what way did you see yourself as being similar?" *A.* "We both had gone out with a girl called Ann and we both tried to kill her." *Q.* "What about this bit where he had been killing off all these other women?" *A.* "Oh, that had nothing to do with it." *Q.* "Who was the chap who came and saved Ann?" *A.* "A doctor." *Q.* "Had he been in the film all along?" *A.* "Yes." *Q.* "Was he the hero?" *A.* "Yes."

It had taken me a while to realize that he had told me the story from the villain's point of view. We often mistook the point of view from which one of us was telling a story. On one occasion I finished a story about one of life's ironies by saying, "I suppose all you can do is to laugh about it." Joe said, "And then in the end when you have laughed at it you can always cry about it."

As the weeks went by Joe got bored with hospital routine. He complained of being fed up.

Q. "Do you ever wish this feeling of being fed up would go away and that you could then go on enjoying living?" *A.* "Sometimes, yes. Sometimes I like being fed up." *Q.* "What do you get out of being fed up?" *A.* "Sometimes a bit of attention. Sympathy." *Q.* "Do you think if you stopped being fed up people will stop giving you attention?" *A.* "Yes, sometimes." *Q.* "But if you gave up feeling fed up don't you think you'd have a lot of other things to do?" *A.* "No." *Q.* "So being fed up sort of fills in your time." *A.* "Yes."

Joe worried that the reason he had been sent to hospital was to force him to forget Ann. I asked him, after he had been in hospital for three months, if he thought this was likely to happen. "I don't think it will," he said.

Q. "But what is it that happens to us as we get older, we don't forget the things that have happened to us in the past, but what happens?" *A.* "You lose interest in them." *Q.* "Can you think of anything in your past life that meant a great deal to you at one time but now you're no longer interested in it?" *A.* "Angela." *A.* "How do you feel about her now?" *A.* "Just someone I knew." *Q.* "So, how would you feel if sometime in the future that was how you felt about Ann?" *A.* "Be disappointed." *Q.* "Disappointed in what?" *A.* "That I'd forgot her and I don't want to forget about her." *Q.* "Why is it important to remember Ann?" *A.* "Because she is part of me." *Q.* "What part of you?" *A.* "Part of my mind." *Q.* "Suppose we sort of thought of you as two people. Suppose there's you as you are now and suppose we could have, sitting in that chair, you when you're twenty-one. And you at twenty-one only remembers Ann as somebody he knew in his past and he doesn't think about her very much because he's got friends and a job and other interests. Now, what would you think of that person?" *A*. "I wouldn't like him because he's nearly forgot about Ann. He doesn't remember her the way I do." *Q*. "Would he be the sort of person you admire?" *A*. "No. He forgets about people too easily." *Q*. "Why is it wrong to forget about people too easily? *A*. "He forgets about people because they don't become important to him." *Q*. "Do you think, if he's forgotten Ann, he would still remember you?" *A*. "No. He'd become too easy to manage, to handle." *Q*. "Who'd be managing him?" *A*. "His manager at work, his mum, they'd all be telling him what to do and how to do it." *Q*. "Are you saying that a person who forgets other people easily is a person who is easily managed by other people?" *A*. "Yes." *Q*. "What you're saying, if you forgot about Ann then all the people around you would be able to make you do things that you didn't want to do. Is that it?" *A*. "Yes." *Q*. "What sort of things would we all be trying to make you do?" *A*. "Anything that they wanted to do." *Q*. "You wouldn't be able to say no, I'm not going to do it." *A*. "Yes." *Q*. "Do you see that you only draw strength from remembering Ann?" *A*. "And other people." *Q*. "Yes, And that if you forgot about them you wouldn't have any strength at all." *A*. "Yes." *Q*. "You don't feel that you can just rely on yourself?" *A*. "No — because Ann's defied me and in remembering that Ann's defied me, I can defy other people." *Q*. "And if she stopped defying you?" *A*. "Then someone else would have to."

Later I asked him, "Do you see yourself as being an independent person?" "Sometimes, when I'm nasty."

Q. "Can you only conceive of yourself as being independent when you're nasty? Can't you see yourself as being independent, good, nice and loving?" *A*. "No. You need more than one person to be loving. You've both got to love each other." *Q*. "You feel in that situation you wouldn't be independent?" *A*. "Well, you aren't are you?" *Q*. "Do you think I try to take your independence away from you?" *A*. "Sometimes." *Q*. "What sorts of things do I do which takes your independence away?" *A*. "Like when you tried to get me to work on a ward. And then there's when you try to make me change my mind about killing Ann." *Q*. "So if you turned out to be cheerful, gay, fun-loving, outward-looking, you'll be just doing what I've told you to do." *A*. "Yes." *Q*. "Can I make you be happy?" *A*. "No." *Q*. "Can you make Ann love you?" *A*. "No." *Q*. "We can do things to one another physically but we can't force people to think certain things. We have no way of knowing what another person thinks." *A*. "I'll have a go at forcing Ann." *Q*. "How would you go about forcing her to love you?" *A*. "I don't know yet." *Q*. "If someone frightened you very much, would you feel lots of love for him?" *A*. "No." *Q*. "Do you think we ever come to love someone when all that person has done is frighten us?" *A*. "No." *Q*. "What sort of people do you think we would be able to love?" *A*. "People who are kind and loving to us. But I don't get any pleasure out of being loving and kind."

Joe often talked about one of the nurses who took an interest in him. When he complained that she had limited his reading of horror stories I pointed out that she did this because she was concerned about him. "I don't like her being concerned about me," he said. "I don't want help. I want to stop as I am."

Q. "I was saying yesterday that I felt concern and affection for you. Do you find that sort of feeling very upsetting?" *A*. "Sometimes, because you care about me. That's upsetting. I don't want to change. I want to stop as I am. You're getting too close to me. I was walking back yesterday and I was trying to think of a way I could hurt you." *Q*. "Do you think because I care for you that I expect too much from you sometimes?" *A*. "Sometimes." *Q*. "And every time you tell me about your thoughts do you want me to reject you by saying that it was a terrible thing to do?" *A*. "Yes." *Q*. "And when I don't do this it makes you feel frightened because you really don't know what I'm thinking and I might be thinking it's wicked." *A*. "Yes."

We talked about Joe's need to be punished. "I think about inflicting pain on myself. Sometimes I cut myself and pick it so that there will be a scar left. Sometimes I put the blame on myself and upset myself. It was my fault my birds got killed. I should have looked after them better. If I had built a better loft no one could have broken in. I just like to blame myself. Sometimes when I'm in the right mood I could commit suicide."

Q. "What makes you want to commit suicide?" *A*. "Sometimes it's the way I feel and sometimes it's because I blame what happened to my birds on myself. Sometimes it's because I know people will take notice of me. They will talk about me." *Q*. "Would you be around to know it?" *A*. "If I came back as a ghost I would."

We talked about suffering and Joe argued that "God has the right to make people suffer."

Q. "Do you think human beings have that right?" *A*. "If they don't they should have." *Q*. "How do you imagine God to be?" *A*. "When I think of Him I get a picture of an old man with a grey beard and sitting on a throne." *Q*. "What sort of a person do you think He is?" *A*. "I think He can be kind and gentle but moody and angry sometimes." *Q*. "Is He moody and angry when someone does something wrong?" *A*. "Yes." *Q*. "Why do you think He is like that? *A*. "I think He's just normal." *Q*. "So you think being moody and angry are normal and everyone is like that?" *A*. "Yes." *Q*. "Some people imagine God as always being kind and never angry." *A*. "Yes, but He got angry and threw Adam and Eve out of the Garden of Eden when they ate the apple. If He didn't get angry He wouldn't send anyone to hell, would He?"

We talked about God's power and I asked, "Do you think there are any limits to what He can know about?" "Yes, there are limits …. He has to think about one thing at a time. He might end up in here if He tried to think of everything at once."

Q. "Do you feel you can rely on Him?" *A*. "Yes." *Q*. "How much can you rely on Him?" *A*. "Not much." *Q*. "Some people think of God as knowing everything all the time. He's all-powerful and all-good." *A*. "He can't be all-good or else He wouldn't send people down to hell." *Q*. "Some people don't believe in hell." *A*. "There's supposed to be hell and heaven and a little bit in between." *Q*. "How do you picture the devil?" *A*. "There are two ways really. One is where he has horns coming out of his head and a tail, and the other has a face of a skeleton." *Q*. "Is he all skeleton?" *A*. "No, just the head. He must be powerful or else he wouldn't have been able to turn himself into a snake and enter the garden of Eden. And then God shouldn't have let him in, should He?" *Q*. "Do you see the devil as having as much power as God?" *A*. "He must if he can get into the Garden of Eden and get to the tree of knowledge. He turned himself into a snake so he must have some sort of power." *Q*. "Have you ever heard the saying, 'Man creates God in his own image'?" *A*. "No, but I've heard that God created man in His own image." *Q*. "When I said to you, 'How do you picture God?' what did you give me a description of then?" *A*. "A bearded man sitting on a throne. He's nice at times and moody at other times." *Q*. "Yes. He sounds as if He can be awkward. Now who do we know who is like that?" *A*. "Me for one thing." *Q*. "So when I said what sort of person is He, you described yourself." *A*. "I suppose I did."

When a young girl came as a patient on Joe's ward Joe set out to tease and upset her. I remonstrated with him and he sought to excuse himself by saying, "She is supposed to be very bad. The first time she was in hospital she was always causing trouble."

Q. "So what? You cause trouble now. Should you be punished for that?" *A*. "Should be, but I aren't." *Q*. "Why aren't you punished for it?" *A*. "Because they're afraid. They should tell me to stop but they won't, so they're afraid. Instead of them saying that he's a rotten mixed-up kid, they say he is lovely."

When I inquired about why he thought the nurses on the ward were frightened of him he said, "They might have seen me being nasty to someone else and they don't want the same treatment."

Q. "Do you think we ought to say those things to you?" *A.* "Yes." *Q.* "If we punished you because you were bad, what would happen then?" *A.* "Normally I would stop doing the things I had been doing. But the way I feel now I should carry on." *Q.* "If we punished you for having these wicked thoughts would that stop you?" *A.* "No .... This ECT, is like punishing me."

Often, when we talked about Joe's attitudes about Ann he would argue "it's her fault that I'm in here because I'm obsessed by her. If I hadn't met Ann, if I hadn't asked her to go out with me, I wouldn't have ended up in here." He applied the same reasoning to excuse himself for losing his temper with a nurse and throwing a bottle at her. "She got me mad. She worked me up emotionally to do it. If she hadn't got mad I wouldn't have thrown a bottle at her so it was her fault." I pointed out some flaws in his argument and said that he had behaved like a three-year-old. This made him very angry but he sat still and then asked, very quietly, "Can I swear at you?" "If you want." So he did, and then we went on with our conversation.

Joe's mother felt that he was not making an effort to get better, and she told him that she would stop coming to see him if he did not improve. This upset Joe, so I asked him if he thought it would help if he and I had a talk with his mother. He thought that it might and so the three of us met. She gave him a lot of advice which he either ignored or rejected rudely, but when they declared their love for each other they both cried. The next day Joe and I talked about our meeting and I said, "Your mother is a very gentle person, isn't she?" "Yes. That's why I love her so much."

Q. "And she values other people." *A.* "Mm. I don't." *Q.* "I noticed that when we were talking about killing your pets and killing people she said that you could replace pets but you couldn't replace people, because people are individuals. Some people forget that. They say that other human beings aren't important." *A.* "Well, they aren't, are they?" *Q.* "Your mother was saying that when you were a baby you were very, very good. You didn't need to be picked up. She actually said she only picked you up to change you or to feed you. Have you heard that before?" *A.* "Mm — two or three times." *Q.* "What do you think about that?" *A.* "Well, if she says I was quiet I suppose I was quiet, but I am getting my own back now." *Q.* "When you were little and quiet did that mean that you got more or less attention from your mother?" *A.* "I am getting more attention now. More than I ever had before." *Q.* "Do you feel that if you went back to being good and quiet your mother would stop taking notice of you?" *A.* "We would sit quietly there watching television for hours and she wouldn't mention my name or anything."

One day Joe told me that when he was talking with a young woman, a patient on his ward, he had asked her if he could strangle her. She agreed, perhaps thinking that it was a game, and he had begun to do so, stopping only when she became unconscious. "I thought she was dead," he said, "She came round again — luckily."

Q. "How did you feel when you thought she was dead?"   A. "I thought, 'Oh God, she's dead,' and that's all. I didn't do anything to see if she was all right or nothing."   Q. "Why did you say 'luckily she wasn't dead'?"   A. "Well, I wouldn't be here if she was dead, would I? I might be in Broadmoor .... I don't think I would have minded if I had killed her. I wouldn't feel guilty or anything. I wouldn't feel ashamed. It happens every day — people get killed .... Why didn't I help her when she became unconscious?"   Q. "I don't know — why didn't you?"   A. "I don't know either and that's why I'm asking you. Maybe it's the way I was feeling at the time. She reminded me of Ann .... But now I have tried to strangle someone I am frightened I will try again."

We discussed this and I suggested that, "so long as you go on thinking that by killing people you can become more important there is always the possibility that you will kill somebody. It's really a question of whether you're prepared to give this up." "I don't think I am. If I did I would just be nothing."

Q. "You really want to feel important because at heart you're a murderer?"   A. "Sometimes, yes. It keeps people away from me. You don't get involved with anybody, do you?"   Q. "It does seem to me to be a bit extreme."

Often, as we argued the rights and wrongs of killing Ann and other issues, Joe would sigh and say, "I'll kill her in the end, you know."

I asked him whether living on a mixed adult ward had satisfied his curiosity about many things. He replied, "I have still got a lot to find out. I have to find out if I kill Ann."

Q. "That isn't something to find out. It's something you can choose to do or not to do."   A. "Yes, but I have to find the guts to do her in first."   Q. "It sounds as if there is something you're frightened of. What is frightening there?"   A. "I might be halfway through it and realize what I am doing and then stop. Then I won't be able to do it. I think I should shoot her. It will be much more quicker. I could stab her — no that's too painful, isn't it?"   Q. "When you say those things what would you like me to do?"   A. "Listen. I would like you to try and analyse it."   Q. "Do you think that if you stop saying these things to me I shall stop trying to analyse you?"   A. "I think it will build up and build up until I do something."   Q. "So you think that in some way talking about it reduces the possibility?"   A. "Yes. It is sort of getting it out of my system."   Q. "After you have talked about these thoughts do the thoughts get less?"   A. "Sometimes — I get impulses and I can't control them. I have been thinking of killing you."   Q. "Well, that doesn't make any difference to me, does it?"   A. "No, I don't think I would hurt you because you're helping me to get over my problems."   Q. "So if you did kill me you'd be

very much on your own." *A*. "Yes. I can talk to you." *Q*. "I suppose
you feel like killing me when I don't seem to be taking much notice of you
or am being critical of you." *A*. "Yes. I could have killed you when you
said I was acting like a three-year-old child."

While he did not like being compared to a three-year-old, Joe could say, "I don't
want to grow up to be a man." When I inquired why, Joe thought that it could be
because he was frightened of the world outside the hospital.

Q. "What frightens you?" *A*. "Everything — no, not everything. Getting
a job and living at home. I would be expected to do my share of the
work." *Q*. "Are you afraid that if you changed and got along better with
people, they would say that you have to leave hospital?" *A*. "Yes." *Q*.
"When you were at home — before you ever thought you might come in
here — did you worry about growing up?" *A*. "I thought I might lose
my friends if I grew up. I liked being a child as well. You're waited on if
you're a child." *Q*. "So even then you would have liked to have stayed a
child all your life?" *A*. "Yes, but I didn't mean to be in a place like this."

On another ocassion I asked Joe, "Why are you frightened of growing up?" "I'd
have to go into the outside world and mix with other people."

Q. Why is that frightening?" *A*. "I don't know. It was all right at school
because I was in my own little world and I can do what I want. But with
work and meeting people, I don't think I'm capable of doing that." *Q*.
"Perhaps if you grew up you'd find you'd become capable of it?" *A*. "I
don't want to." *Q*. "Why not?"

Joe sat and thought for a long while. Then he said, "It would shatter my
fantasies."

Q. "You'd have to give up your fantasies?" *A*. "Yes. And become
someone who was at work, meeting people, having to make new
friends." *Q*. "What sort of person would you have to become?" *A*.
"Pleasant, caring, helping person." *Q*. "To do that you'd have to give up
your fantasies and you're not prepared to do that?" *A*. "No, because if I
was, I wouldn't be me, would I? If I was prepared to give up my fantasies,
I wouldn't be here, would I?"

Sometimes Joe justified his threat to kill Ann by claiming that this would make a
man of him. I asked, "Does growing up mean becoming a man?" "No. It means
going out to work and being sociable. It means being friends with people."

Q. "How is that different from when you say, 'When I kill Ann I'll become
a man?' What does becoming a man mean?" *A*. "I would have done

something to prove my manhood. I wouldn't be able to call myself a normal, ordinary person. I would be able to say that I was a homicidal maniac."

This made me laugh and Joe joined in. I said, "I can imagine Benny Hill saying that." "If I was like that I should be special and therefore get special treatment. People would shudder at the sight of me. They would be afraid for fear I should turn round on them."

Q. "So in that way you would still be looked after as if you were a child. It would be nice to stay a child for the rest of your life. But obviously this isn't going to happen. When you're physically grown up people won't accept you as a child any more. So one of the ways to get people to look after you and treat you as a child is for you to become a homicidal maniac." A. "Yes. But I would get sent to prison. But I would be like a child then because they look after you there, don't they? .... I need a mother." Q. "And you don't want to give up needing her, even if your mum was a warder in a jail?" A. "Yes." Q. "So when you say you want to kill Ann to prove that you're a man what you're really saying is that you want to kill Ann to prove that you're still a child." A. "Yes, I think that's it. It could also prove that you're a man." Q. "In what way?" A. "Having the courage to do it." Q. "Which would take the most courage, to kill Ann or to live your life like an adult?" A. "Live your life like an adult." Q. "So killing Ann isn't all that brave." A. "But it still takes courage to do it."

As the months went by Joe ceased to be depressed and became much more involved with the people he met in the hospital. By the time his seventeenth birthday approached he had discovered that he could feel affection which did not include jealousy and possessiveness, that to love someone is to be kind and understanding. However, this love he saw only as relating to other people, not to Ann. His love for Ann still contained jealousy, possessiveness and a desire to destroy her. As Joe became less depressed he began to express his anger more immediately, by breaking windows rather than by carrying out rituals to do with death. The staff on the ward were very tolerant and supporting, but his temper and his delight in ghoulish affairs distressed many of the other patients. So Joe was moved to a less permissive ward where the staff had established an atmosphere of kindly tolerance, support and humour within a framework of firm rules. One of these rules was that every patient, as soon as he was well enough, should work. Joe went to work on a geriatric ward and found that there is a pleasure to be derived from doing a job well and helping other people. Then he began working outside the hospital as an unpaid helper in a centre for the physically handicapped. One day when he and I were together, laughing about the inanities of "Star Trek", he suddenly said, "I've given up the idea of killing Ann. I've decided it isn't worth it."

A few weeks later I gave Joe a copy of this chapter and when he had read it we discussed what he thought of it and how he had changed. He thought it was a good description of "my state of mind when I was murdering people in my mind".

Q. "How are you different now?" A. "I'm much more calmer. I can sort things out for myself. I can sit down and think things over. Not rush in and do them straight off. And I don't go around saying I'm going to kill people. I still think about it sometimes but I keep it to myself." Q. "What sort of thoughts do you have about Ann now?" A. "They aren't the same thoughts as I had before. When I think about killing her I say, 'Don't be so stupid.' " Q. "What has happened to make you change?" A. "My mother for one thing. I can accept new responsibilities. My mother saying she wouldn't have me back if I didn't try to get better made me buck up my ideas. I'm thinking about getting myself discharged now .... I get closer to people that I did before. I find it much easier to do things for people." Q. "How much do you want to be the most powerful person in the world?" A. "Not at all now. I'll stop as I am." Q. "Why is it not a good idea to be the most powerful person in the world?" A. "You won't have many friends if you're powerful. Telling people to do this and that. Then other people get jealous of you. So it's better to stop as you are and have friends. I'm glad I've changed from what I was like."

I asked him if the image of the powerful reddish cloud was still important. "I no longer believe in the red cloud," he said, "It's gone." I asked how he felt about Ann now. "Ann's still someone I would like to know but I don't crave over her like I did before."

Q. "How would you feel if you read in the paper that she had married someone else?" A. "I'd say hard luck it wasn't me. Anyway, when I find another girl I think I'll forget all about her." (Joe had discovered that the world was full of beautiful girls.) Q. "Do you think it's right or wrong to forget about her?" A. "It's right and it's wrong. It's right that I haven't got these feelings and the wrong is it's a pity to lose someone you've had all your life."

I asked if he still thought it necessary to get into trouble in order to draw attention to himself. "Getting into trouble's stupid," he said, "I get plenty of praise at work."

Q. "Do you think it's possible to be an independent person and still have close relationships with others?" A. "Yes." Q. "What are the chances that sometime in the rest of your life you'll kill someone?" A. "No chance." Q. "Do you feel frightened of being grown up?" A. "I know what it's like now. I've seen other people and I've grown up myself." Q. "Is it better than being a child?" A. "Yes. You learn to do things for yourself. When you're a child you have things done for you so you don't learn from it."

"If you had your life to live over again and you could go back knowing what you know now, what would you do differently?" "Everything. I wouldn't get so depressed."

"What were the sorts of things that made you depressed then?"

"My animals being killed and seeing people being killed on television. I'd have to stop watching programmes like that, stop reading horror books. Watch cartoons that make you laugh. And once I met Ann and she said she didn't want to see me anymore I'd make that the end of that so I didn't have to go through all this rigmarole again."

"Do you feel you've gained anything out of this experience?"

"Yes. I've gained a lot. I've gained experience of being in hospital, growing up myself, being on my own. I've gained a lot. Made friends, new friends. But you can't beat your old friends. I'll be glad to get back home."

10

KAY

"It's hard to make other people realise
The magnitude of things that appear to them
petty;
It's harder to confess the sin that no one
believes in
Than the crime that everyone can appreciate.
For the crime is in relation to the law
And the sin is in relation to the sinner."
                                              T.S. ELIOT

To the psychiatrists who had treated Kay over the past ten years, Kay was an epileptic who also got depressed. To Kay, her fits were a rare and minor inconvenience. It was her depression that filled her life with torment. Kay was married with two teenage children. She always looked attractive and well-dressed, since she chose her clothes with care and taste and, to hide her ravaging turmoil, she, like Prufrock, always took the time "To prepare a face to face the faces that you meet".

Kay said that she had become depressed when the fits had started ten years ago. This depression had lasted two years and then disappeared when she got a part-time job in a shop. All went well for two years and then she had begun to feel depressed again. She had some small seizures which were treated successfully but, despite the anti-depressant drugs, the depression stayed. When she had a seizure, "I can always see my husband in the background and I am always trying to get to him. I feel as though I am in a whirlpool. I want to get to him and I can't. I'm at the top of this tunnel and he's at the other end, and I'm trying to get to him and everything is going round and round and buzzing and buzzing. It's a real quick whirlpool."

Over the months, as Kay and I talked together, I came to see that Kay's description of what she experienced in a seizure was an encapsulation in an image of what she saw her life to be. She saw herself in a turmoil, a deep whirlpool where she, confused and weak, could not pull herself out and so reach her husband and the outside world. In our conversations I often felt the swirl of this whirlpool for, as I tried to follow one line of inquiry through to a conclusion, she would make one statement and then shortly follow with its complete opposite. The contradiction was for her a source of dread and confusion. She had no notion that such contradictions can be seen as balance and harmony, thesis and anti-thesis, and why should she when the capacity to espouse the opposite opinion quickly enabled her to dismiss all advice and to frame an endless series of questions which left the person questioned in a dilemma, the outcome of either alternative being one with which Kay could castigate herself. "Aren't I the worst patient you've ever had, Dorothy?" she would say. If, in reply, I agreed that she was, then this would confirm her worst fears and raise the question as to whether my ability could be stretched to helping her. If I disagreed, then this made clear that she could, indeed, get worse.

In the following account I have put together her comments on a number of important topics. These comments are drawn from more than thirty two-hour conversations that took place over a year. We had many other unrecorded conversations. As time went by some new themes emerged and the whirlpool seemed, to me at least, to be a little slower, but the unresolved contradictions remained.

The most common topic was how Kay felt when she was depressed. "I just can't sit," she said, "I'm up and down. I don't know. It just doesn't feel like home any more. I keep getting up and going in the kitchen. I have cigarette after cigarette. Then I can't be bothered to do anything. Jack wants to start decorating and I say, 'Oh don't talk to me about decorating' .... I was just saying to mum this morning I don't think a murderer would have gone through what I've gone through .... I think I was happy all the time the children were growing up. We were both happy. We had the ups and downs that everybody has .... It's just this guilty feeling of marrying Jack and not being in love with him at the time — that's how it all started. It started after a fit. It brought back the thought that I didn't love him when I married him. I might just have had that thought at that time or it might be that I have always had this at the back of my mind."

"Why is it important to love people?" I asked. "Well you get so much out of it, don't you, really?"

> Q. "What sort of things?" A. "I'm happy to see them come home at night. Just shutting the curtains at night. Making the place all cosy and warm about teatime." Q. "The sort of feeling of security?" A. "Yes, I loved that. When we are all sat down together I'm happy. Now I walk round the house like a stranger. I start one job and then I'll do another. Then I drop things. I can't concentrate on what I'm doing."

I asked Kay what she was frightened of. "I think I shall either end up in a mental hospital or I shall die. I don't know what is at the end of it. I am frightened really .... When you think of dying you just dismiss it, don't you? ... I feel as though I am right at the bottom and I just can't be bothered to get out. I feel that perhaps I'm not trying. I'm not trying because I just couldn't care less. I do sometimes know that I'm not trying."

> Q. "What would happen if you didn't try?" A. "I think I would break everyone's hearts. I should land up in here — in hospital .... I feel

sometimes — I don't act silly — like a naughty child. It's so ridiculous. I feel like a stupid, naughty child. I always want my own way. If Jack ordered me not to do something I'd be real mardy with him and wouldn't speak to him. I do think that I act spoilt. I want my own way all the time. But I shall have to give something to receive. I've got to give love to receive it. I think someone who didn't want their own way all the time would be a considerate person. I don't think I'm considerate at all. I should like to be. I can't have my own way all my life, can I? I've been ruined and I know I have .... I always spite myself, really. In the holidays we would always go away for one week and the other spend at home and go out for days. The second week, and I used to do it regular, I would argue with Jack and for the second week I would be miserable. We would be going out and I wouldn't talk to him and I wouldn't give in. I would spite myself. That's the sort of person I am. I have always been stupid." *Q.* "Even when you were a little girl?" *A.* "Yes. There were two sisters lived next door to us and they had straw hats and I didn't and I was so spiteful I pulled one apart. And I remember her mum coming round to our house and I was frightened to death. I suppose I was jealous because I liked it. Mum sort of stuck up for me." *Q.* "Did you feel at the time that this was what she should have done?" *A.* "I think she should have given me a damn good hiding."

"I'm not a worrier," said Kay, "The only thing I worry about is this depression .... When I'm depressed I think of all the bad things. There are twice as many good things to think about but I can't remember. I can't seem to think of anything good that I have done at all. I feel as if something is going to happen. I can't describe it. You know when someone tells you something really bad and your stomach turns over .... I don't want to talk about death when it's about anyone who is close to me. Mind you, I haven't lost anyone yet. Jack has lost his mum and dad, but he's lucky because he's got over his heartache and I've got mine to come. I do worry a lot about losing my mum and dad. When I'm depressed I don't want to visit mum very much. Normally I am popping down there as often as I can. When I feel depressed I feel that I could walk out of the house and leave them all. I don't know where I would go but I would leave Jack and the kids and Mum and Dad. I feel as if my home and family mean nothing to me. When I'm depressed no matter what anybody did it wouldn't suit me. When I'm depressed I cannot talk about another thing. If you started to talk about yourself I wouldn't be listening. I'd be waiting to butt in and talk about myself .... Depression is just something that comes over me — like a black cloud."

Q. "Do you get a picture of a black cloud?" *A.* "No — sometimes I get a picture of me laid out on the floor dead. I'm not dead because I've taken something. I've died naturally because I've had enough. I get a slight picture of that really." *Q.* "When you say you get a picture of you lying on the floor, are you standing back looking?" *A.* "No, I'm looking up at them, I think. I'm laid on the floor and Penny comes home from school and it frightens her to death. She loves me so much. You say, do I think about dying, well, it has crossed my mind a couple of times. It never crossed my mind to take anything. I always wanted to die naturally."

On a later occasion Kay said, "This morning I woke up like it. I feel so guilty and my face goes so hot. I just feel as though I've done something."

Q. "You feel you have done something wrong?" *A*. "Yes, and then I start to think about when I got married. That is the whole thing behind all this. Whichever way we turn, that will always be at the bottom. I just wake up and I'm not interested in anything. I go all hot and my stomach turns over as if I have done something really wrong. My mouth goes dry and I feel like — like when you're waiting in the dentist's chair." *Q*. "You feel as though someone is going to punish you?" *A*. "I think I am being punished by the depression. I don't think I am going to be punished by someone coming in and giving me a damn good hiding. Depression is my punishment and I can't get this out of my mind .... This is what I think — to get better from this depression I have got to love somebody. By loving this one person it will keep me going and in the end I shall love everybody as I get better .... I am being punished because I have done something wrong. I am suffering because I have done wrong by marrying Jack. I see myself dying or ending up in here. I can't see any future at all. I can't really draw a picture because I can't really see one. Everything seems black." *Q*. "Where are you in this blackness?" *A*. "Struggling to get out. I don't know where I am and I know I am trying to get out of it. I want to get better and then I think that I can't get better. It's impossible and I just can't get better. I'm in such a tangle. I'm in such a mess. Whichever way I turn I can't get out. I can't explain the blackness but I'm in a hell of a mess and I want to get out. It doesn't matter which way I look I can't get out — it's impossible." *Q*. What would happen if you stopped struggling and stood still?" *A*. "If I stand still I think I shall sink lower and lower and lower. I think that my physical health will catch up with me and I shall die.

Yet on other occasions she would say, "I think by getting in a panic I get into a worse state."

"Am I going to live like this for the rest of my life? I shall maybe have a few good days and a few bad days and be like that for the rest of my life. I will be such a bore because it must be awful for the people you live with. When I am good I am very good, right back to normal, but I have only to think about my depression and I am back. Yesterday I wasn't too bad and I was standing at the bus stop and talking to a friend and she was saying about a family get-together they had last Saturday and, do you know, it all came back. It was as simple as that. She was saying about this super

family party and my heart seemed to miss a beat. That's how I used to be. I would
always have a family party at Christmas time. Now I couldn't be bothered. It just
came back like that. But if I don't think about it — it's funny, isn't it? ... I feel I am
suffering more than a murderer is suffering. In the end a murderer forgets and it all
goes away from him. I don't think I should be suffering as much as this. There are
plenty of people who have done what I have done .... I think I am awful. I think I
have thought so much about how awful I am that I have become that awful I
know I have caused it all myself. I shouldn't get you to help me when I have done it
myself."

Q. "You feel you don't deserve help because you did it to yourself?" *A.*
"Yes." *Q.* "If you fell down the stairs in the shop because you hadn't
been looking where you were going, would you feel it right for someone to
help you then?" *A.* "Yes, I think I would then." *Q.* "So why is it
wrong for me to try to help you now?" *A.* "I'm causing all this bother.
I'm making everyone unhappy. You're spending all this time with me. I
honestly don't think I deserve people to help me. And yet I really want
someone to help me .... Surely somewhere I must have a little bit of a fight
in me. I do want to get better but I can't see myself getting better." *Q.*
"Do you think you deserve to get better?" *A.* "Well, I didn't at one time,
but since I have been talking to you — I mean. I haven't murdered
anyone, have I? ... If I thought I was never going to get better well, I don't
know. But I don't want to do it. I don't think I dare do it." *Q.* "Why
wouldn't you dare do it?" *A.* "Well I don't like pain. I can imagine the
stomach pump. I think in a case like that the nurses wouldn't be
overpleased with you. But to die naturally — I would be out of the tangle
.... It's always at the back of my mind. I think I shall have to come in here.
I see the patients going into the canteen and you can tell them, can't you? I
see the clothes, they wear and I wonder, 'Do I look like that?' I think if I
did land up here it would kill my mum .... I think I am the only person
who is like me — not loving my husband and children. I know I'm not the
only one that suffers from depression, but it's my guilt — it's worse than
the depression. I think it's my guilty conscience that brings on my
depression. I feel the guilt first and then the depression. I start to feel guilty
and then I start to feel unhappy. No one can cure a guilty conscience.

"I know if I go to bed depressed I shall be depressed in the morning too
.... When you're depressed you don't see the trees blowing. When you're
depressed everything seems so still and dead. You lose interest .... Still,
you're doing your best, Dorothy, aren't you? I shall really have to learn
how to change. This is another thing that also worries me. I sometimes get
to a pitch — I know it sounds awful — and then I'm just not interested in
getting better. I think that I really can't help myself and that I shall go to
bed and just lay there and die. It sounds morbid but that's how I feel. And
every time I get depressed I think, 'I won't tell Jack.' But then every time I
do. I can't help it. I can't hide anything from him. When I'm depressed I

have to tell him. I wish I had the willpower not to tell him. Why should I tell him every time? I would be better if I could hide it and then when I do tell him, what can he do anyway? Nothing." *Q.* "What's wrong with telling him?" *A.* "I'm just saying that I don't seem to have much willpower. I suppose it's just my way, isn't it? Jack wouldn't tell me if he was ill." *Q.* "And you think that's good?" *A.* "Yes." *Q.* "Why?" *A.* "Well, it shows he loves me and doesn't want to worry me." *Q.* "So you telling him shows that you don't love him?" *A.* "Well, not partic — yes." *Q.* "Does he take it like that?" *A.* "I think he gets a bit fed up. I often wonder what he is thinking. He says it doesn't worry him but I know that if he was like me it would drive me round the bend .... I wonder if it would bring me to my senses if he said he couldn't stand any more. I wonder if it would make me pull myself together or make me worse and I would kill myself or I might end up staying in here. I'm not sure which way I would turn. I think I require a heck of a lot of attention .... Mum says sometimes she gets really depressed. She wouldn't tell me because she knows what condition I'm in. Everybody treats me as if I'm glass .... Actually I don't know what I want. Everything is just in a circle. It all doesn't make sense. Whichever way you turn you are stuck. At the bottom of it I don't want to make a life of my own and I don't think I would be very good at it anyway. Actually what I've got now is what I have always longed for, for Jack to be loving and considerate. It annoys me to think that I am wasting my life .... I feel I have no choice when I am down. I think one part of me wants to be depressed. There is just nothing I can do about it. Sometimes I'm not even interested in getting better." *Q.* "When you say that one part of you is choosing to be depressed, so you choose to be depressed." *A.* "Yes I think I must do. There is just that little bit of me that wants to get better and all the rest of me wants to be depressed. There is nothing I can do about it. Perhaps it's the only choice I've got, because the part of me that wants to get better is so small. The largest part of me wants to be depressed. Getting better is right at the bottom and there is nothing I can do about it. I don't think I really choose to be depressed. I have no alternative. I just get depressed."

Kay often wondered, if her childhood had been different, "I should have been a better person today .... I think my mum loved me too much. I can't understand why my mum loved me so much. She can't understand me and I can't understand her. She puts me on a pedestal all the time."

Q. "Does this make you feel that 'She wouldn't love me if she really knew me'?" *A.* "No, I don't feel about it that way. I'm a bit — I enjoy praise. It gives you a nice feeling to be praised. I think I like to be the centre of attraction as well. So I'm not a very nice person at all, am I?" *Q.* "Do you think it's wrong to want praise?" *A.* "No, I like praise." *Q.* "Sometimes we like what's wrong. It's like you like smoking. You say you like praise and being the centre of attraction, but do you think it's a good thing?" *A*. "I think it's good if I give the same back." *Q*. "Like praising other people?" *A*. "Yes. And also I'm a bit nasty, really. I'm a little bit of a nasty person .... I think I take people for granted. If Jack does something round the house I will never say, 'Thank you. That's super.' I don't notice. I'm so ungrateful. I do appreciate it really at the bottom of me." *Q*. "Why do you think it's important to be grateful and not to take people for granted?" *A*. "I don't know really. I suppose it's because if I do anything for people I like them to say thank you to me. I think this is because I used to be so grateful. It makes the other person feel better if you say thank you." *Q*. "In what way do you think they feel better?" *A*. "Well, it makes me feel better." *Q*. "We can feel better in lots of different ways. We can feel better if we feel we are safe. We can feel better if we feel that other people like us. We can feel better if we feel we have done the right thing. We can feel better if we feel we have made up for something we have done in the past." *A*. "I think the last one, really." *Q*. "Making up for what you've done in the past?" *A*. "Yes, that one. It's like me marrying Jack without loving him."

At work, Kay said, "Although I say it myself, I know I am liked. I like to be liked."

Q. "If you had to choose, which would you prefer, people liking you or people respecting you?" *A*. "Liking me, I think." *Q*. "Why is it important to have people like you?" *A*. "Because it makes you feel good. It makes me feel good and it gives me some satisfaction to think I made those people happy. I like to be popular and liked. On the other hand, if I don't like someone I can be nasty as well. I suppose I am like all women." *Q*. "Some people daren't risk someone not liking them." *A*. "I couldn't be nasty to anyone I liked. If they did something to me I should feel nasty, but I couldn't be nasty to them. If I had a good friend and she did something to me I don't know if I dare be nasty to her. You should be nice to everyone, really. I don't think I'm straightforward enough."

Kay would often say, "I have known love and I haven't got it any more. It annoys me when I see everyone around me happy and I'm feeling so miserable. I'm jealous because they are happy. If I see a couple even our age, and they are holding hands, I think I am envious. I don't think I have ever been in love." Again and again Kay would say that the reason she was depressed was because she had married Jack without loving him. "The reason I married was I was twenty-two and I thought I was going to be left on the shelf. I never had a lot of boyfriends, but I used to go to quite a lot of dances. I never used to get a lot of dates. At work we would get invitations to these RAF do's. I would often end up the only one without a boy to walk me to the bus. I used to feel awful about it."

Q. "Was being left on the shelf a really terrible thing?" *A*. "Yes. I felt as though I had been missed out. I thought I would stay a spinster all my life." *Q.* "Would that be terrible?" *A.* "Yes. And as much as I wanted children I wanted my mum to have grandchildren." *Q.* "Did you feel you weren't like everyone else?" *A.* "Yes, Jack and I had been friends for years and mum liked him and in a way — I'm not blaming them — in a way we were nearly pushed together. I knew the morning I got married that I was only marrying him for marrying's sake. I remember walking down to the gate to meet one of my bridesmaids. I knew then that I didn't hate him but I knew I didn't love him. But I was pleased to think that he had chosen me. So with a silly thing like that I don't think I can expect anyone to help me or get me better .... When I was first married I would spend hours just looking at my rings. I would be on the bus and hold it up like this so that I could see it through the bus window. I know it sounds childish but I used to think it was wonderful. I think I wanted those rings more than I wanted Jack. It hasn't been all unhappy, but when I was unhappy he would break my spirit. I would hate him then. He never once said he hated me." *Q.* "Do you feel angry with Jack and your mother for pushing you into marriage?" *A.* "No. It's my silly fault for taking notice of them. I don't see wrong in other people, because I'm too busy seeing wrong in myself. I hadn't got the guts to tell them to go to hell. I should have married who I liked. But I thought I wouldn't have another chance. I don't think that there was really anyone for me. I have nothing to look back on, have I?"

Kay spoke of what she had done in marrying Jack without loving him as being "a silly thing". What she meant was that it was a sin. "I can't forgive myself for not loving Jack. And if I can't forgive myself, who the hell's going to forgive me?" When I read her the passage from Eliot's *The Elder Stateman* she recognized immediately what Lord Claverton meant. She had kept her sin a secret for many years. "Now I've let my secret out I think, 'Oh, everyone knows now that I married Jack without loving him.' I don't think they believe me. He says he'll never believe me as long as he lives. I often wonder, 'Should I have kept that to myself?' It was my secret, really, I wouldn't have told anyone if it hadn't have started to make me ill. I shouldn't have told anyone — I should have just lived with it. But if it makes you feel ill you've just got to say it, haven't you?"

Q. "How do you feel when you reveal your secret and no one is impressed?" *A.* "I don't think that folks believe me. Mind you, I think you believe me."

Later in the same conversation she said, "I'm not positive you believe me altogether." Two months later she said, "For a long time I couldn't believe you understood and believed me. I couldn't make up my mind. I thought you did and then I would think, 'I don't know whether she does or doesn't.' I think I have been better since I have known you better. I mean, we are really like friends. All the time you were talking to me it was going in sort of thing but it wasn't registering."

Kay talked a great deal about her husband. "I'm special to Jack and I realize that now. I didn't think I was at one time. I used to tell him he thought more about his pub than he thought about me. I used to hate that place and wish I could have put a bomb under it. At nights after Steven had been playing me up I wanted to talk to Jack about it and get things straight. I never did seem to get things straight, and if I had I don't think I would be like this. But, you see, within five minutes we would be arguing. Jack thought that to give him a damn good hiding was the correct way to bring the children up. I do too, to a certain extent, but the psychological way is better. I think you ought to let them know you always love them. I think they play up sometimes because they think you don't love them. Steven was a little bit like that and all he was doing was shouting out for attention .... If I got angry back it was very difficult. I wish now that I had stopped him, but I never wanted to interfere in front of the kids. I would wait till they had gone and then begin to discuss it but he would get furious ... and then there was the way he spoke to me. When Mum came down I used to say that he showed off. He would belittle me and shout at me because he knew that Mum didn't like it. Then when Mum had gone I used to start. Mind you, I'm just as nasty a person, and I can say some awful and nasty things as well. I used to hate being showed up especially in front of Mum. If, at one time, there wasn't a spoon in his saucer he would say I was a devil. He must always have a spoon. It's little things like that. "Where's the bloody spoon?' he'd say. I'd say, 'Act your age,' and he would go berserk."

Q. "How did that make you feel?" A. "Sometimes I didn't care, but I usually felt fed-up. One thing would lead to another and then he would clear out. I would stay at home moping. I've said, 'I hope you crash into the first brick wall you see' and things like that. Jack can be nasty but he wouldn't say things like that. If he went for a drink I would say, 'You'll find me in a heap on the floor when you get back.' Anything to stop him going out. I tried to frighten him. It was punishment for going out. The thing is, I could never seem to get back at Jack. It didn't matter what I said, it never seemed to bother him. That's why I used to say these nasty things. I would be trying to hurt him. I really would have liked to be laid out on the floor when he came home. He has admitted that I have worried him at times but he never showed it. If he had have done, I don't think I would have been so nasty .... I mope when I get angry. Jack just goes out for a drink. Mind you, while I've had this depression I don't think he's said anything bad to me at all." Q. "It sounds as if you've won the argument." A. "Yes, He'll do anything for me now. Mind you, he has always been kind right down at the bottom of him. He just never showed it. You could certainly say I've won the argument."

As well as lying on the settee and imagining Jack returning to find her ill or dead, Kay "would just stop speaking. Because I detested him at the time. It would go on for a day or two and after that I would wish I were speaking. He would say, 'You silly thing. Why aren't you speaking? You know you've got to speak in the end.' I enjoyed it. But I didn't enjoy it for long. I've gone on for over a week, but after two days I wished we were speaking. It's a wanting to get back to normal, really. After a couple of days I wouldn't feel the same and I wouldn't eat the same either .... Since I have been like this he has said 'If only you knew how much you have hurt me.' But he's never shown me. If only he had have shown me that I had hurt him in a way I should have been pleased to think that in some way I had hurt him, but I think we would have had a better relationship. But I just wanted to see that I had hurt him. I wanted him to feel like I did. Sometimes I would break down and cry when he had upset me, but I didn't want him to go that far. I just wanted to know that I had hurt him. But he never did .... Sometimes I wanted to say I was sorry but I just couldn't." Kay described how they had quarrelled and to hurt him she had refused to go to his firm's dinner dance, a function she very much wanted to attend. "I lay on the settee and I was all miserable with myself. I wanted to go, but I couldn't tell him."

Q. "What did you want him to do when you said that you weren't going?" A. "I was laid on the settee and I wanted him to come and say, 'Please come, please come, darling.' And he didn't, you see, and it shook me. That was three years ago, and looking back, that, I think, was the start of this depression. I should have said nothing and should have gone with him. We should have been all right then .... I think we were happy when we were fighting, no, I suppose we weren't. At least I didn't feel like this, did I? Every time we had a fight I would tell him, 'You'll send me to a mental hospital.'" Q. "So if you did end up here as a patient you'd have won." A. "Well, yes, I suppose so .... Mum said the other week,' If ever I hear Jack shout at you again I shall tell him.' She tells me that he has helped to cause this depression. She said to me, 'When I come home after being in your house, I say to your dad, however Kay sticks to Jack I shall never know.' That didn't make me feel any better I can tell you. I wish she'd never said it." Q. "Why not?" A. "Because I knew it was true, mind you, I have never thought of leaving him. I have said so in the heat of the moment. But I have never thought seriously about leaving him. Then I was like this, and he has started to be nice to me. I don't think I would have liked to have left him. It just seemed as if it was 'me and Jack' and that was it." Q. "What do you think would have happened to you if you never stood up to Jack?" A. "Well, I might have done better. It might have made him feel small. Or I might have become just a servant to him."

Kay described Jack as being "independent" since he would not talk to anyone about his difficulties. "He doesn't talk to anyone," she said. "I think of somebody as independent as that, it's not normal."

Q. "In what way do you think it's normal?" A. "I think that everybody needs somebody to talk to. You can't keep everything inside you. Jack would have actually to be dying before he told me that he was ill. When his mum died he never shed a tear. To me that wasn't normal. I mean, you just can't lose a mother and not be upset .... Jack likes his own company and I don't. I don't think it would bother Jack if nobody spoke to him. He's just happy in his own sweet self. He would sit there with his record-player all afternoon and not bother."

As much as she argued with Jack, she needed him. "When I'm depressed I get to wondering what is going to happen to me, and then I get very frightened. That's the time I cling to him .... When I get a new dress I put it on for him to see and he says whether he likes it, or not. I like his opinion, but if he said he didn't like it, it would sort of put me off that dress. It would be nice, if I was all dressed up for a dinner dance and looking my best, if he took me in his arms and said I looked lovely. It would be nice, but that's not Jack. He buys me nice presents. It's, well, I know I'm forty something now, but some men hold their wives' hands or even just touch, but Jack wouldn't do anything like that. He often calls me darling when we're on our own but never when anyone's there. I would love him to just come over and put his arm around me. I think that would be lovely. It needn't be all sex but just little things like that. I think a man who loves a woman without it being sex all the time loves more than a man who wants sex all the time .... I always remember us going to Brighton on holiday. I always wanted to go in the biggest and poshest hotel on the front. Jack would say, 'I'm not going in there. I shan't feel right.' Jack is just a bar man — spit and sawdust sort of thing. He often calls me a snob because I like nice places .... I have always known that I was never madly in love, but I know it has always been Jack and Kay. I have always thought of us as a couple. Everything in our house we have chosen together, even the curtains. I have relied on him just as much as he has relied on me."

Kay described how one night, as they were driving home, Jack had reached out and taken her hand. I asked her if she had told him how happy this gesture had made her. She said, "Do you know, I didn't think about that. I never really thought to tell him .... He's romantic in one way but not in another. We can lay in bed and love one another without sex. At night he always says, 'Goodnight, sweetheart.' I know that might not sound much to you but I think that's lovely, really. Nobody else would hear him say that. It's just between him and me. He would never go to bed and then to sleep without kissing me. I think to lay in a man's arms and to have a cuddle is wonderful."

Q. "What about sex?" A. "Oh no, no, no, I should run to the other end of the bed. I shouldn't want him to touch me. If we have had an argument I take it to bed with me and I'm horrible. I definitely wouldn't kiss him. If he had been bad to me then I shouldn't let him have sex. That was the first thing I would take off Jack .... I'm not a sexy person. And I have the feeling that I wouldn't be sexy with anyone. My mother tells me she has never been sexy. I think if I'd have loved him more I would have enjoyed it more. I have sort of done it for him. At one time it used to please me to think that he'd enjoyed it. He didn't satisfy me and I used to pretend.

With reaching a climax and all that sort of thing, I think I could count it on two fingers. He tells me about this wonderful feeling that he gets and I don't get it. He says, 'It's wonderful,' and I know that it should be wonderful. I have spoken to friends about it and I don't know if they all tell the truth, but I should say that more don't enjoy it than those that do. When I hear someone say they don't enjoy it, very often that pleases me. I think, 'Well, I'm not on my own.' I think it's normal to be as I am, really .... My mother never mentioned sex to me. She was embarrassed to talk about it. Then when I started to suffer with depression we did sort of start getting round to it." Q. "Did you discuss it with her when you were getting married?" A. "Never! No." Q. "What about when your periods started?" A. "No, no, she never told me. When it happened Mum just gave me a sanitary towel but she didn't say anything. She didn't mention that I would have to be careful when I went out with boys or anything like that. She would say to other people, 'I let her go to the camp dances because I trust her.' I wouldn't dare do anything wrong."

Even though Kay's mother had wanted Kay to marry Jack, she and her son-in-law did not always get along well together. "Every time even now, when I say, 'Shall we go down to Mum's?' he will sigh and moan and groan about it. So I say to Jack, 'You rotten thing, Jack. And after all the things I did for your mum, and now you're awful to my mum. You're bloody rotten.' I can't help feeling he's being unfair. I enjoyed doing things for Jack's mum and I always hoped that when my mum was old and infirm that Jack would be considerate to my mum. I think that Jack has got set in his ways and I don't suppose I will change him, and I don't suppose he will change me. I suppose this depression has changed him. He treats me like a piece of cotton wool now .... I will say something to him like 'I fancy going out tonight,' and he will say, 'Will it make you feel any better?' and I say, 'I don't know,' and he'll say, 'Well, what's the point in going if you don't know whether it will do you any good?' That wipes the idea out of my mind. He will say, 'All right, we'll go,' but by then I don't want to go. He has broken my spirit. Jack doesn't get excited over anything. By not getting excited I think you miss a lot. I haven't had that thrill and excitement for such a long time. I have this feeling that my spirit gets broken. I get squashed down and I think I will get like Jack and not care about anything .... I think I pretended for so long that I was happy. I was pretending up to two years ago. I didn't want him to know that I didn't love him as much as I should. I would tell him I loved him but sometimes when I did this I was lying .... I would get a hiding if I told lies when I was little .... Everyone at work seemed happy and loved their husbands so I felt I had to be the same."

For Kay, "The mother is the mainstay of the family and everything is built around the mother .... I was married three years before I had Steven. All the other girls started to have babies, so I must have a baby. I didn't want him so much, but I loved him when I got him. Mind you, I was terribly disappointed it wasn't a girl .... To dress Penny and Steven and to take them out nicely dressed and all clean that would give me a load of satisfaction. That was ever so important to me. I loved to be praised and that's why I kept them looking so nice .... Looking back to the time when I had Steven and I was home I think I must have been terribly depressed. I was ill because I had this milk fever and I think I was depressed as well. Looking back I think I have suffered depression a lot of times .... When the kids were small we were ever so happy. If either of them was ill at night I never had to get up. I used to make out I hadn't heard them and I knew Jack would always get up. He has been a good father but I think he has broken Steven's spirit just as much as he has broken mine. He would go out to play and Jack would tell him to be in by nine. It would maybe be half-past and Jack would thrash him and send him to bed. He wouldn't think that the child never had a watch. I mean, what's half an hour when you're playing? I would never say anything. When I think about that it makes me feel depressed. I know I used to clout him many a morning with a hairbrush, but when he came home from school I was all right with him. I had forgotten all about it .... I could never get at Steven and I could never get at Jack. Steven would be singing again in less than five minutes. That used to make me worse, I used to say, 'Do you know what I have hit you for?' I had to go to remind him. I love Steven but I have never been able to quite understand him." Steven joined the Army and when he was away, "It can start me off being depressed by someone asking, 'How's Steven?' I get this guilty feeling right here and I think, 'Oh God. I haven't thought about him for days.' I think I worry because I don't worry enough .... At least Penny still gets excited so we haven't broken her spirit. I can't make my mind up about Steven. I don't know whether he is happy or not. I have always wanted him to tell me he likes the Army and all he will say is, 'I'm in, Mum, aren't I?' He and Jack are the greatest mates now they have ever been. I always wanted Jack to take him fishing and footballing or anything like that but Jack doesn't do those sort of things. It's all right being matey now but I would rather they had been mates when Steven was small."

Kay described Penny as being "independent". "What hurts me is whenever there was a trip going anywhere I would go with mother. We were friends and before she became ill we would go everywhere together. Now I would like to be like that with Penny but I know I won't be because she is a very different kind of person. I think I have been looking forward all these years to having the same sort of relationship with Penny. It's a disappointment to me." Kay often berated herself for not loving Penny. "Why should my daughter be the one whose mother doesn't love her?"

Kay talked a great deal about her parents. "I always thought I had got the best parents in the world. Mine were better than anybody else's." But, "I think I dread Mum and Dad dying more than anything else .... I can't imagine Jack ever dying .... If it had been anyone but you who had started to discuss dying I should have told them to shut up. I would just want to dismiss it from my mind. Mum always put me on a pedestal. She is always telling people what a good daughter I am. I'm not the good person she thinks I am. Mum loves me so much she can't see any bad in me. I don't love my kids so much that I can't see any bad in them .... She sits at the window all day long and she can see me coming round the corner. She says, 'I love to see your beaming smile and that's how I want you to be again.' Then she says, 'This isn't you at all.' I walk in at my mum's and she says, 'Now then, how are you?' and straightaway I feel depressed. Mum is saying, 'Oh, no, not again!' She always says, 'We'll have to send you back and shake you up.' ... When I tell her about not loving Jack she wonders am I in my right mind. She wonders if I am saying these things because I am depressed."

When Kay was depressed she was, she said, much nicer to her family. "I never started to kiss my mum until I felt depressed. I often wanted to."

Q. "Why didn't you kiss her before?" A. "Because I was too embarrassed. I couldn't show my feeling to my mum." Q. "In some ways your depression has helped your relationships, hasn't it?" A. "Yes, definitely. Three weeks ago my dad bought me some daffodils and I was so pleased with them that I said, 'Well, Dad, I shall have to give you a kiss for that.' Do you know, I couldn't remember kissing him for years and years and years. In our family we were close and there was love but we didn't express it. Mum'll say, 'I'll give my right arm for you, duck. I wish I could feel like you for a week. I want to suffer with you for a bit.' That makes me feel so guilty. She says I'm not to feel guilty but I do .... One of the reasons I never worked full-time was because of mum. I can always remember a girl once telling me that she was going to go to work full-time because she was sick of going to her mum's. I remember telling my mum about Doris. She said, 'Isn't that disgusting?' .... They've spoilt me absolutely, but not to make me nasty. Even to this day I would not answer my mum and dad back, even if I thought they were in the wrong. They say when a child's spoilt that it doesn't have any respect for the parents, but that's not true."

Nevertheless, Kay did get angry with her mother. "When I'm at Mum's I can't knit, especially if I'm doing a pattern, and I can't read a book because all the time she wants to talk. I understand her being like that, but sometimes I think, 'For goodness sake, shut up.' I'm her only daughter and if anything happened to my dad first I shall be expected to have my mum. I'm not going to be able to be patient with her. My mum repeats herself so often. Today when I go I know she will like this suit. I bet you she will tell me half a dozen times that I look nice in this suit. Then she will say, 'Your hair looks nice. I don't know how you do it.' I feel guilty about feeling like this and all the time I am wanting to say, 'Shut up'. But I can't be nasty to her. It would hurt her too much."

Q. "When you were a child were you afraid to get angry with your mother and be afraid to show it?" A. "I used to cheek her when I was a teenager. It would upset her and we would both end up crying. When we were first married we lived at Mum's and I had the feeling that Mum was jealous of Jack's mum. We tried to treat them both the same. Mum and I had this awful row that lasted for quite a few days and we both ended up sobbing our eyes out. I don't think I have had more than three arguments with my mum, really. I was the only girl in our family. I remember when I was six my first brother being born and I was terribly, terribly jealous. I wouldn't go in the room and my mother was so upset, and I remember my mother saying to my father, 'Oh take her up town and treat her. She feels out of it.' So I have got a jealous streak in me .... I started work straight from school on my fourteenth birthday. I can remember saying to my friend, 'Just come to our house and have a look at my mum, because I think she is having a baby.' I was quite ashamed of her. I've often thought about that and how I used to hurt my mum. It hurt me when I saw that she was expecting. I thought, 'We shall be like the rest of them now — poor.' "

Kay remembered being given "a damn good hiding" when she ruined a new dress. Her aunt had tried to stop her mother from hitting her but as Kay said, "I'm a bit like that myself. If Penny came in with her dress all torn I would make a big issue out of it. I wouldn't be able to help it." As a child, "coming home after doing something wrong I knew I would get a damn good hiding. I suppose when I feel scared now it's because I can remember feeling scared at times. It's the same feeling I have that I had when I was a child and had done something wrong. I think, although I love my mum, that she had been stricter with me than she had with my brothers. Jack always says that Mum was jealous of me. Whenever we had a party (and we used to have quite a lot at one time) Jack said that Mum was jealous. I would have people to tea and Mum would say, 'You are a fool, going to all that trouble.' I remember when Steven was christened she was terribly jealous in a way although I can't describe it. She spoiled my day a bit by being jealous. She is jealous of anyone taking me away from her. She had made me feel rather sad on several occasions when I should have been happy. I have been upset when she had been jealous but I always think it's me who is the bad one."

When Kay told her mother that the reason she was depressed was because she had married Jack without loving him, "she just didn't believe me". Kay had not told her of her doubts when she was engaged to be married because "Mum would have been so upset and she would have worried about what other people think". A few years before she was engaged when Kay used to go dancing she had had a frightening encounter with a man about which she dared not tell her mother. But she feared that her mother would know by looking at her. "Have you always had the feeling that she could read your thoughts?" I asked. "Yes. If I go there today she'll know immediately how I am straightaway. I can't put on an act for her. She knows immediately I feel ill. I know her heart will turn over when I walk in and she will say as I go in, 'My heart just turned over.' I am frightened of what I shall do to her. I think, 'My God! Shall I kill her with how I feel?' If she died tomorrow I should think I was to blame." Kay usually told her mother about what she and I discussed each time we met. But as she got to know me better she dared to make remarks which were critical of her mother. Then she would say, "I daren't tell my mother that we have been talking about her this morning .... I usually think afterwards a lot when we have been talking about Mum. I think what a dreadful picture I have painted of her. I feel awful about it sometimes. I hope I haven't painted her bad. The only thing she is guilty of is loving me too much."

"Dad has always got to be giving. He will go and buy me cigarettes and I have much more money than he does …. I don't think I have ever heard my dad grumble. He just goes through life his own sweet way …. As soon as we start to discuss me and my depression, off he'll go. It's as though he doesn't want to listen …. I don't think he does know me. I know Mum knows me inside out …. Dad rang up and I had to tell him I couldn't come because Jack was working and I felt so guilty. Then he said the same old thing which makes me feel awful, 'Don't worry about not coming. As long as you're all right, your mum and me, we're all right.' I know it's a nice thought, but it makes me feel more guilty …. Mum has told me that when I first married and she would come and visit me, Dad wouldn't speak to her for days."

> Q. "Is that where you picked up your not speaking?" A. "Yes, it is. He's not so bad now." Q. "Was he like that when you were a little girl?" A. "Yes.
> "Mum says that she prays for me every night. I think I only pray when I am in trouble so He won't answer my prayers anyway. I never pray when I'm all right. It's awful, really, isn't it? I usually say the Lord's Prayer and then God bless Jack, Mum and Dad, Steven and Penny and all the people in the world who need you, and that includes me. It's more or less what I said as a child. I like to go to church but I don't go because of God, I go because I like the atmosphere and I like the service. If anyone asked me if I believed in God I don't know what I would say really. I do pray sometimes when I'm depressed, but I do always thank Him when I am feeling a lot better. I think I always forget about Him when I'm depressed. I am too wrapped up in my thoughts when I'm depressed. But I do always thank Him when I'm feeling better. It just comes automatic. Then after a couple of days I start feeling rough again." Q. "Then do you get mad at Him?" A. "Yes".

Once when we were talking about death I asked her, "If you can have a picture of you dying and then of being dead, what sort of picture comes into your mind?" "There is just the coffin. There is everyone there just stood looking at me and crying. I'm lying in the coffin. I'm looking up and seeing everybody looking down — Jack, Mum and Dad and the kids and that's about all."

> Q. "How do you feel?" A. "I should be dead and I would look up at them and want not to be dead any more." Q. "How do you feel about them being upset?" A. "Oh, I feel terrible about it. I feel awful about it. Sometimes I say to Jack I would like to die first and then sometimes I think that I would like to die second." Q. "If you die first you don't have to put up with the pain of losing him?" A. "That's right." Q. "But there again, if you go first, you know that you are hurting him." A. "Yes. It seems a bit silly, doesn't it?"

We spent a lot of time in discussing how people behave in arguments. Kay said, "If someone does something wrong to me, I wouldn't tell them, I wouldn't have the guts. I just wouldn't speak to them again …. I sometimes think that I can't forgive."

Q. "Are you prepared to forgive Jack and your mother for what they have done to you?" *A.* "I don't think I am. That's what worries me. I have always appeared to be a forgiving person, but deep down I have never been like this. I have never forgot — never! If Jack and I had a row I would go and make him a cup of tea. As I was going upstairs to bed with this tea I would think to myself, 'When I get to bed I'll put my arms round him and tell him I'm sorry.' But I could never do that. I just couldn't. So my not being a forgiving person hasn't helped at all." *Q.* "Why is it important not to forgive?" *A.* "I realize I should forgive people but I'm just too bloody stubborn to be bothered. I do know it is the right thing to do. But I feel so stubborn. It's stupid and I feel like a child. Jack and I would have a row and I would get into such a state, I would think to myself, 'I hate you. I really do.' And do you know the feeling I have now is the same as I had then, the feeling that we have just had a row. I am just too stubborn to forgive him." *Q.* "Why is it important to be stubborn?" *A.* "Dorothy, I can't think. I think it's my nature. I think it was born in me." *Q.* "If there has been a big row between the child and mother and the mother has won, the only thing that child can do to protect itself is to think to itself, 'I'll never forget that. I'll never forgive her for that.'" *A.* "Oh, that rings a little memory bell in my mind. I was in my early teens and it was over a pair of nylons. I can't remember what happened at all and all I can remember is running upstairs shouting, 'I hate you, I hate you.' I remember lying on the bed and I was kicking and screaming. I always seemed to be able to lose control of myself." *Q.* "So are you saying that if you weren't stubborn you might go right out of control?" *A.* "I think so. I don't think I am in control of myself sometimes. I feel at the moment that I am just in control. I am just bearing life. It's a struggle." *Q.* "We all have to maintain ourselves or else other people will overwhelm us. When you're nearly overwhelmed by someone (and this has often happened to you with Jack and your mother) how do you defend yourself?" *A.* "Be stubborn. Since I have been married to Jack I have been more stubborn with him than I have with Mum. I would never give him the satisfation that he had won. I would never tell him I'm sorry."

Although Kay occasionally mentioned friends, her whole life was taken up with herself, her husband, children and parents. She had no hobbies apart from an occasional interest in knitting and a dancing class. "I have never belonged to any clubs, really," she said. "What about parent–teacher associations or church groups?" "I always think there is a lot of cattiness in those sort of things." As far as television was concerned, "We were watching a film about Helen Keller the other night and I looked at Jack and Penny and I knew there would be tears and there was. I'm not a bit emotional in that way. I can't get so wrapped up in a film that I am living in it." The only job Kay had ever fancied was nursing. "If I had my time again I would love to do nursing. I like helping people. I know I only see the glamour, there are lots of dirty jobs to be done. But there are all those poorly people in bed and they are dependent on you. You're important to them." However, "I soon grow tired of things. I know I wanted children because everyone else was having children but sometimes I think the newness has worn off. A new idea and I'm all for it. It's like with the telephone. I was absolutely crazy to have a telephone and when it came I thought it was wonderful. Saying to friends, 'Give me a ring,' was super. Now the damn thing rings — I have grown tired of it. I used to love going to work. Now the novelty has worn off. About four years ago there was a first-aid course and I said, 'Oh yes, put my name down.' I thought it was wonderful. I went a couple of times and then after that I was sick and fed up with it. I have thought of taking up different hobbies and I have even thought that I would take a lover if I thought that it would do me any good. I think the novelty would wear off though. I don't know what would happen if I met someone who turned me on. Mind you, I have never, ever been turned on in my whole life .... I have no ambitions at all. I would love to have an ambition. I would like to stop biting my nails but I can't even do that. I would like something to aim at .... I am only happy when things are going for me and when I'm getting my own way. I can't take the rough with the smooth. I want everything to be smooth."

In our conversations there were rarely any silences. If one occurred Kay would say apologetically, "I can't think of anything to talk about today." I asked her, "If you and I were sat here and we weren't talking what would you think I was thinking about you?" "You would think, 'She's come to a full stop. She doesn't know what to talk to me about.' You should think that I had told you everything I had to tell you and that was it."

Q. "Having told me everything, what happens then?" A. "I think that you might not want to see me any more." Q. "So if you stop talking you have said everything that needs to be said and then I might say, 'Well, goodbye.' A. "Yes. It's also I should feel a fool. What's the point in us both sitting here saying nothing. I think it's embarrassing." Q. "When you're out with Jack and there is just the two of you do you feel you have to keep talking?" A. "It's boring if you don't. But really I don't know what to talk to him about. If we were just sat there I should feel that I had to say something. I suppose it's because I would feel that he would be thinking that I was a bit off it. He would maybe think I was hiding away from him. When I'm depressed I'm not interested in anyone else. When I am really depressed I'm quiet and withdrawn. I go into my shell and I don't talk. I have nothing to talk about when I'm depressed. Mum was telling my aunt, 'Kay's not well today, I can tell. It's because she is so quiet.' " Q. "Does your mother always see you as a person who talks a lot?" A. "Yes .... I find sometimes I must talk about my depression. But today I don't want to talk about it because I want to forget it. If I was in a good mood and not depressed at all I should hate it if someone said, 'Do you love Jack?' That would bring everything back. I think I push it to the back of my mind. I don't want to be reminded of it."

Kay was well aware of all the contradictions that she presented. "I don't know whether the word is insecure or what. How can I describe it? Say I bought something new for the house and I can't make up my mind whether I like it or not. I like Jack to say whether he likes it. For weeks after I am saying to myself, 'Oh, I don't know if I like it or not.' I hear people say, 'Yes, I like that. I'll have that.' And I can't make up my mind. If I went to buy a dress I should ask the assistant what she thought I looked like. I like someone to say, 'Yes, that looks nice.' I am like that all through life. I think, I'm not able to make my mind up about things. But I do think the fights have made me feel insecure. I don't know what I want .... There is one thing that frightens me and that is when you stop seeing me I think I shall fall back again. And yet I don't want to be relying on you too much."

Sometimes we talked about whether she should leave Jack. "I am still looking in the paper for bedsitters. If I moved I know I should be dead within a week. I can't look after myself .... Mum would say I'm independent but I don't think I am. Jack is independent. I suppose if I was married to someone who was less independent I would feel more independent .... My mum and I have been so close. She is definitely part of me. She is more part of me than Jack is. Now you understand how I feel when I don't want to go to Mum's when she is part of me. We're so close and yet she is so far away now .... If I am feeling all right and then start to feel depressed I don't associate it with my mum. I'm just not interested in her no more."

Q. "So when you feel depressed you feel you're cut off from — " A. "Everybody." Q. "But you feel cut off from part of yourself which is your mother." A. "Yes." Q. "So when I say that you're to become more independent what I'm really saying is that you're to remain cut off from your mother. I'm saying, 'See your Mother as a separate person.' It's a very threatening thing to say. I'm saying something which sounds like, 'You must remain cut off.' " A. "Jack has always thought I have been too attached to my mum. I'm sure if he could hear us now he would think to himself, 'I always said you were too attached to your mother.' " Q. "You must have resented it every time he said that." A. "I did. I hated it .... I don't think I have ever grown up. What's the answer, Dorothy? Is it to become independent of her?" Q. "At the moment you can only become independent of her by being depressed. What do you think about that?" A. "It's mainly true, I think. But I think everyone is attached to their mum."

We explored all these issues many times over the months. Then Kay one day said, "Do you know, we are getting to the real bottom of this problem. And I'm really getting scared. It's a horrible feeling. I have never experienced it before. I have such a lot to say but I don't know how to explain. I think we have come to the point where we are getting to the root of it. And when it comes to it, I don't really want to change

.... It's not very often that I go home and think over what we have talked about, I think in a way I try to forget it. I know this doesn't sound very nice, but the more I talk about it the worse I feel."

> Q. "Well, you do go round and round things. You don't think about these things, so you can't sort things out, but I see you as being that sort of person. You're not the sort of person who sits and thinks about what is happening inside you." A. "No, I have never been that sort of person. But thinking brings it all back to me .... If my mum knew the way we blame her — mind you, she has some idea because she remembers all the good hidings she gave me when I was little — she would be heartbroken." Q. "If you thought your mother was to blame you would feel guilty." A. "But I know my mum isn't to blame. I am to blame." Q. "Well, I think we have agreed that being depressed is because of the sort of person you are. It's not her fault. It's the way you react to her." A. "Yes, I understand that. But it's true what you say — I have never been a person who will sit and think. I have never thought about how I feel. I have never been that type of person .... I know you're not calling my mum. I know you're just pointing a few facts out. I suppose they are true, yes, I don't want to believe the truth. I just blame myself. I can't help it."

Sometimes I talked to Kay about how some people lived with their depression so that, instead of fighting it and feeling guilty, they organized their lives so that when they felt depressed they could be depressed. Kay rejected this, "I can't just be depressed. I feel so horrible I have to get out of it .... I have never thought of marriage as coping — everything has come easy to me. I have never had to try .... I think another thing that helps me be like this is that I always grow tired of things after a while. This has been part of my pattern through life. I know it has. I feel as though I have no stamina in me — perhaps this depression is a challenge to me — perhaps I am tired of fighting it."

> Q. "You're at the stage where you realize you have to accept this challenge and fight it through to the end, or — " A. "Live in misery for the rest of my life."

Kay described how when she was knitting, she would complete a garment quickly so it could be worn the next day but she would not finish a garment just for the sake of finishing it. I said, "You're in a similar situation now. It's difficult for you because you don't know when or what the end's going to be .... Why is it important not to finish?" "It's the easy way out. I just put it out of the way in a cupboard. I try to forget about it."

> Q. "And say it's not there. Well, what had happened with us, you come up here and for a while we talk pleasantly and that is all right for you, but after a while I start to put you on the spot. I ask you to assess yourself. I

challenge you in the sense that I am saying to you, 'Look at these things,' I am saying, 'Let's go on and pursue this difficult task.' Then this challenge started to get difficult and you weren't sure where it was going to lead."   A. "I am terrified of finding out that I'll never get right. If I knew that the outcome was going to be all right in the end I would know then that it's worth striving for .... I just want to be happy. All I want now is to have an interest in the five people who mean the most to me. And I want it to happen quick. If I thought that at the end everything would be all right then I would work towards it. I have never thought about the future before. I just lived from day to day."

It seemed to me that Kay had reached a point where she had to make a choice to press on to something new or to remain depressed. I read her Cavafy's poem of "The great yes, or the great no". Kay said, "I feel as though I am at that point, but I don't know if I can get interested in it. You see, I'm fickle, really." But on another occasion she could say, "I might become a real nice person after all this. I might even become more considerate. Being depressed does make me more aware of other people. I am more interested in people. When I was normal I would get on with my business and I would never be really interested in anyone else. I look at other people now and I find I am wondering how they are feeling."

11

DAVE

"Other men are sharp and clever,
But I alone am dull and stupid.
Oh, I drift like the waves of the sea,
Without direction, like the restless wind.

Everyone else is busy,
But I alone am aimless and depressed,
I am different,
I am nourished by the great mother."

LAO TSU

Dave came into hospital after he had taken an overdose. He was nineteen. His parents had separated when he was twelve and each had married again. He had completed an apprenticeship but soon left this work and began to drift from job to job. He drank a good deal and it was while he was drunk that he had taken an overdose. Dave was a wiry young man of very striking appearance. He had inherited his father's strong Balkan features and his mother's auburn hair. He liked eye-catching clothes, but most noticeable of all were the panthers tattooed on each arm. These animals were springing up his forearm, their red claws seeming to dig into his flesh.

At our first meeting we did a Rorschach ink blot test and a repertory grid. The Rorschach showed him to be intelligent, introverted and depressed. On the fourth card he saw "a monster from out of space. I'm stood down here and it's towering above me. It is powerful and dangerous." On the grid Dave described himself as unadventurous, selfish, unstable, sick of the same routine, wanting his own way, aggressive, drained-out, dominant and kind. He was very angry with himself and frightened of himself. ("Drained-out" and "fed-up" were Dave's words for being depressed.)

At our next meeting I asked him what he meant by the word "adventurous". "I mean travelling and getting about," he said. "It's go climb a mountain or something like that."

    Q. "Is it the opposite of sticking to the same old routine?"   *A.* "Yes. If I had to stick to the same old routine it would get me down."   *Q.* "Why is it important to go after adventure?" *A*. "It stops depression coming on. You are busy getting about and doing different things. If you stick to the same old thing then tomorrow will be booked. It is planned before it even comes." *Q*. "Why aren't you more adventurous?" *A*. "Once you have been caught by the police you're a failure. When you take to violence at a football match, or beating someone up in the street, if you don't get arrested then you're okay, but once you get caught then there is always the risk that it might happen again. You begin to think twice about it. But once I have had a drink then I don't care. I get out and think, 'Christ, what have I come here for?' Then I just sit down and drink. Some nights you can go out and enjoy yourself without drinking a lot. I go to this disco and I know the DJ now and all my mates are there, and I know all the birds there, but I'll go another night and it all seems flat somehow. If I am going somewhere I look forward to going so much and then when I get there eventually it doesn't seem right, and everyone enjoys themselves except me."

Dave described how he always expected people to be nasty and hurtful. If a person was nice then "It's a nice surprise," and if a person was nasty then "My defences are up ready".

Q. "Do you get angry if people try to put one over you?" *A*. "I can give abuse but I can't take it. I just get very annoyed. I can give it to my mates but I can't take it back. It's taking the mickey like. I don't mind when I'm doing it to someone else, but when it's my turn I resent it. I swear a lot more and just clear off like. If they get on to me real bad then I can't forget about it and I think about it for a couple of days." *Q*. "Would you like to be the sort of person who could brush it off?" *A*. "Yes, because like I am — well, it's like sulking, ain't it? You get broody and that makes me feel immature." *Q*. "So part of you is brooding and the other part is telling you not to be stupid. *A*. "But the brooding part seems to be overpowering the other part. It's like my probation officer — he can really get me going. He was on about my fine, and I'm supposed to pay five pounds a week, and I'll never forget what he put in that letter. 'I'll see you on Thursday with five pounds in your hot little hand.' I kept that letter at home — I never chucked it away. I shall never forget about that. I never really understood it and that's why I got narked about it." *Q*. "Did you feel he was getting at you?" *A*. "Yes, and then I knew his secretary had typed the letter as well." *Q*. "Do you see it as a bit of a put down?" *A*. "Yes. Fancy writing a letter like that! Then he reminded me that I was under a money supervision order and that if I didn't pay every week I should be in more trouble. When I hadn't the money I wouldn't bother to go to see him. I usually got a letter from him every week, anyway. And then at the bottom of that letter he said, 'May I take this opportunity to wish you a Merry Christmas.' Does that sound ridiculous to you?

Anyway, then Christmas was coming up and I thought I would be in the nick for non-payment of fines so I went and paid some. I took a tenner in when I owed twenty and then I missed two weeks again. I try to carry it as far as I can before owt serious happens. It's like not paying the electric bill until you get the demand."

"On this grid you described yourself as being very selfish. What do you call selfish?" "I'm all right Jack. I think of my own interests first."

Q. "What do you call people who aren't selfish?" *A.* "They are kind. Mind you, you can't say that about everybody. On some jobs you've got to control yourself. You might be selfish for all I know but you can't show that to me. It's not just on, is it?"

We talked about how he had enjoyed reading *The Exorcist*. "It never dulled off although it never got overexcitable. It was consistent all the way through and that's why I was interested. In a film you get a climax, don't you. It's like these pop concerts, after the show they start the smashing up. I mean, I know I like doing things like that sometimes, but — I did it once and it cost me all this money. I had to stop it. Sometimes I suffer — I don't know what brings it on — but I think the word is agoraphobia. I just don't like to go out because I am a little bit scared. It doesn't always affect me. Just sometimes. I can't seem to find an explanation for it." (Later we did find one explanation. He described how his nervousness kept his anger in check.) "It's like when I'm in the ward I say I can't be bothered to go to the canteen. It's not that I can't be bothered, it's that I don't want to go out. I was all right at school. It never affected me then."

Q. "When did it start?" *A.* "When I found that I had to be responsible for myself. It's been more frequent these last six months. When I was doing my apprenticeship — I was training to be a moulder — when I was eighteen I went on to piece work."

Dave described this work in detail, then said, "I had a labourer and I was responsible for him as well. The chargehand would watch us but he would never interfere. I'm not bragging but we always made a good job. He would say, 'Well done lad, you've made a good job of that.' That was good coming from him because he wouldn't socialize, not even with the tradesmen. He adopted the attitude that he was the manager and that was it. For him to say something like that to me — that boosted up my ego. But I haven't had that feeling for a long time. I like people to tell me that I have done a good job. It gives me that extra bit of interest."

I asked if he could describe a picture of the feeling of being unable to go out. "I can't really explain it that way. We have a dog and I couldn't harm that dog, but I feel that I could go out in the street and kick someone's head in. I can be like that and yet I wouldn't harm the dog. I could hate someone and really want a fight with him. Whether I beat him or not was beside the point. Yet if I was walking past and saw someone fight that person I would go to his help and try my best for him. I think to myself, 'What's going on?' I would want to hurt the person who was hurting that person. I don't like to see someone get beat. I would give him one for giving the other person one. Then my mate might join in, and then there's a whole line of people fighting one another. Then it all comes back that it was me who started the trouble and not the two who were fighting from the start. I like to get in trouble with someone. I don't mean just to have a fight, swearing and being violent. Then five minutes later I am sorry and go and apologize, and then ten minutes later I think, 'Well, why should I feel sorry?' Then you resent apologizing. Something will set me off — a row with the old lady or girlfriend trouble. I can go out to the pub feeling fine and yet I can change moods just like that going from A to B."

Dave described how he found it difficult to talk about himself in the psychiatrist's case conference. "Some people — there is just a barrier between you and them and that's it. You do your best but it doesn't always work. That's how I am with some people. You don't communicate, but that doesn't mean you hate them. It's just that you have no affection for them .... I keep meaning to phone my mother up every night. I have only phoned once. There isn't much communication between us anyway."

Q. "How much communication is there when you're at home?" A. "I couldn't say I sit down and talk to her. I don't have real long conversations with her. She will say things like, 'What will you have for tea tonight?' I never get into a really deep conversation with her. She will ask where I have been at night and if I have had a good time. It's just general talk." Q. "Would you like to talk to her more?" A. "No, I'm happy as it is. It's the same with my dad. I suppose you could say that we never had a family group therapy session. It's not like a ward meeting where you all decide to express your opinions on one thing."

A week later we talked about Dave's worry that if he went home he would again want to kill himself. I asked him what picture he had when he thought of suicide. "Well, nowt really. You don't think into the future, do you?"

Q. "What do you imagine?" A. "You take a load of tablets and you fall asleep. That's it. Full stop. I don't believe in coming out of it and going to heaven or hell, because I don't believe in any one of them. I would have a good bottle of spirits and a load of tablets. I wouldn't bother about where I was going to end up." Q. "What would you think about?" A. "I shall have to start with not being found out, shan't I. I shall just be content with that. When I take tablets, I don't wake up. It's a coward's way out — taking an overdose. I couldn't shoot myself or slash my wrists, because I would be fully conscious of what I was doing. There would be physical pain too. I couldn't jump out of a block of flats. I would know what was to happen in advance. It would deter me. I shall never try to hang myself. It might not work the first time. I should be left hanging there with a dislocated neck. I should think twice about shooting myself through the head. Ugh! Oh, yes, there is drowning — that doesn't appeal to me. There would be something telling me to swim to the surface and I would panic and try to get back. And yet when it was too late I would be glad in a sense. I would have achieved what I wanted to. It's the thought of not doing the job properly in other words. I couldn't take the risk of not doing it properly." *Q.* "What about jumping off a very high building?" *A.* "I think I might still be alive when the impact came. Some people think you die of fear on the way down. I would want to be sure I was dead before I hit the ground. In that split second when there was the thud you must feel something. It might be all a blur like when you fall off a bike. You don't feel anything when you fall but you know what's happened when you hit the ground." *Q.* "So it's partly not wanting to go through a lot of physical pain and partly this perfectionist idea. You want to do it properly." *A.* "Yes, that's it. If a job's worth doing, it's worth doing well." *Q.* "So you think that taking a lot of alcohol and taking a lot of tablets is the most efficient way?" *A.* "It depends on the circumstances, I suppose. You'd have to have it all planned out. If I hadn't been sick when I was unconscious I wouldn't have been here now. It wasn't my fault I was sick. But I did arrange it. I took the tablets out of the bottle and then I put the bottle away. I had a drink and then staggered and put that away. I had to make a good job of it, like. Then I just sat in this chair and I can't remember anything after that. I had waited till everyone had gone to bed. I didn't know I had been sick but they found me and told me I had afterwards. It ruined a good plan, didn't it?" *Q.* "How did you feel when you came to?" *A.* "A bit of an idiot. It's hard to explain. I didn't want sympathy from anyone. It's just like me not to be able to do anything right."

I asked, "Why was it important not to let anyone know?" "I didn't want to draw attention to it. If you put it down and someone else reads it, you only cause more misery. I didn't want to blame anyone and I didn't want to draw attention to myself. It's like you hear of people who take overdoses — they will have maybe thirty minutes before it works and in that time they rush to the phone and tell someone. I didn't want that to happen. I was serious at the time. I meant to do it."

Q. "Are you saying that you don't phone anyone and you don't leave any note because you don't want anyone to be upset?" *A.* "Mm." *Q.* "Or guilty?" *A.* "I suppose upset and guilty and let down. One is as important as the other." *Q.* "Why is it important not to get others upset or guilty?" *A.* "Well, you're doing enough to yourself without upsetting others, aren't you? The fact that my parents might find out would deter me, but not enough for me not to do it. It's my superego overpowering my ego. It's as though my willpower is stronger than the rest of my body. But my parents would be upset in a different way if I did that same trick again.

For one thing they would say, 'That treatment he had wasn't worth while.' They would turn round and say, 'We thought he had got over it and had got back to normal.' They would feel let down and upset." *Q*. "How do you feel when you know your family has been let down?" *A*. "It deters you as I said before." *Q*. "Yes, but how do you feel inside?" *A*. "Guilt. But not enough to stop me. I look at guilt as — say I go out with a girlfriend, right? Well, if I see one I like better I will pack up the first girl and go out with the second but I still feel guilty about it. I am selfish on my part, but I still feel a bit guilty. I suppose I have to put it in those terms. I can understand it better that way." *Q*. "Are you saying then that when you commit suicide you are really leaving your parents and taking on something new?" *A*. "Yes, I suppose you could put it like that. I can't think of a better way of putting it …. Everyone hates getting drunk because afterwards they suffer for it. But you don't realize that at the time. It's like suicide in a way. At the time you don't regret doing it. You want to do it, but if you're still there afterwards it's like one big hangover. It's been wasted. Then the next morning you can't remember what happened and you wonder if you've said anything to upset anyone. You wonder if you have been acting stupid. Then you feel guilty about it. But you don't feel guilty enough not to do it again. A couple of nights later you might go out and get even more drunk. The guilt only lasts as long as the hangover does." *Q*. "When you had that feeling of guilt, how do you actually experience it?" *A*. "I think in advance about what the other people will think if they eventually find out. I think for them before they find out and start thinking for themselves." *Q*. "Sort of, 'If I do that, they will feel like this, and then I will feel guilty.' " *A*. "Yes. I am thinking for them and for myself before I had done anything. I am doing it for myself and I am doing it for them as well. In between thinking of what I think and what they are going to think there is a gap and that gap is filled by guilt, although you can't measure it. That's the only way I can understand it. If I plan to do something wrong I am all the time wondering what my parents will think when they find out. Between me planning to do something and me wondering what they will say there is this gap and it's a gap filled with guilt. Does that make sense to you? It does to me." *Q*. "Yes. This is what I meant earlier when I said we couldn't imagine ourselves as being dead, because what you described then was what you would feel if you were still alive. You say that you kill yourself, your parents find out and then you feel guilty. This feeling of guilt can only occur after you're dead. So in some way you are still thinking of yourself as still being alive. You have to be somewhere to be able to feel guilt, don't you?" *A*. "Yes, I understand that better now it has been put that way. It must be true …. I was just looking at that picture up there. What is it supposed to represent?"

The picture was a poster from East Berlin which represented industrial progress in

North Vietnam. It was in the artistic style of the Far East, but featured tractors and cranes instead of junks and temples, piles of earth instead of delicate willows. Dave pointed out that the picture was, in effect, divided in two horizontally. "The bottom part is the old part and the top part is the new part with all the cranes and such. I was thinking that all those people at the bottom had to be used before the top part of the picture could be completed."

> Q. "You've seen something in that picture that I have never seen before." A. "When you imagine the two together it makes more sense. I'm pleased you understood and realized what I said. There is more feeling in the top than at the bottom." Q. "Whoever drew it has put his power station right in the middle of the picture at the top there." A. "It's like giving his own autograph, isn't it? It's a way of really showing his power. He wanted more of his name up there to give people proof of it. I probably want to say the same thing myself. If I do a good job I want more than my name on it. I want people to be able to say they knew who had done that job."

At our next meeting Dave had just returned from a weekend at home. "I'm wondering what I am doing in this place some mornings. I think, 'Surely there is someone who needs my bed more than I do.' "

> Q. "Do you feel guilty about being in here?" A. "Yes. I think most people do to hear them talk. When you're not physically ill and you're in a good mood it just gets you down like that. You just think, 'What the hell am I doing here?' Then some days you're glad to be here. You don't have to accept any responsibility here. It's all done for you. All I do is make my bed, take my tablets and eat my meals. But sometimes I don't appreciate it. They say they know what's best for me and I don't appreciate it so I go against them sometimes …. I don't want to get too dependent on others. I want to manage for myself. I'm a bit mixed up. I want to be fully independent but I don't …. One of a person's biggest dangers is himself, anyway, I've found that out."

The question of responsibility led on to the question of marriage. "A man works all week and then lobs his pay packet over to her, like. I couldn't see myself doing that yet. I just like freedom and having a good time. I've had a couple of chances of getting engaged and settling down. But when you get serious, too serious, they try to hang on to you. The affection I feel towards them fades away dead quick. You have to meet her so many times a week …. I've got to trust her just as much as she has got to trust me. You might have a night off from your girlfriend to go out with your mates and you might meet another bird. Then there's something in your mind telling you off. Then the attracted part of you is there telling you that she's all right and free and you're getting on all right, so — you only have to meet a couple of girls like that and it puts you off your girlfriend. That's happened loads of times. I compare them. I like to find out the worst in them …. I can never keep a girlfriend for long …. Where I live, if you're not married by the time you're twenty-one they think that there is something wrong with you …. I'd rather see a girl in casual clothes, with no make-up, just neat and tidy. If I asked her for a date and she went home and changed then I'd fall for her all the quicker …. I think a lot of women when they've married and finally got their man they let themselves go …. I like her to have personality, to be sensitive. The type that would be easily upset if you said something wrong about her. It shows that she shows physical emotion. It means that she thinks something of you. It's like a test, you see. I tell them I'm two-timing them just to see what they will turn round and say. Some will brush it off and say they're two-timing me as well. But if she's the sensitive type she'll get upset. The tears will flow and you know she's genuinely upset by what has happened. I think my ideal woman would be a sensitive, semi-dominant person. One who could cope but also be sensitive. I wouldn't stand over her, demanding her to do this and that. I would be just free and easy. I would be concerned."

Dave's brother had married at seventeen. "Then he got into trouble with the law. A few months in prison and he came out acting the big, hard convict. He was always bragging about being on the inside. I'd say, 'Shut your mouth, you're talking like an idiot.' He would say I wouldn't be able to take it. He says I'm mental and that it would get me down. I tell him that he might by physically stronger than me but not mentally stronger. When my dad gave him a good hiding he would always sob his heart out. I would never cry. They always thought there must be something wrong with me because I didn't cry so they would give me a bigger belting. They just wanted to see tears. I wouldn't cry. I worry a lot. I think if I had cried I would have got rid of all the emotions quicker. They say it's good to have a good cry but I can never do it. I tend to keep things in my system a lot longer. If you upset someone and they cry, they get over it. Others you might think have ignored you, but they haven't, they're like me and they keep it inside them. It doesn't turn to tears, it turns to anger and then depression …. People who cry do nothing for me. I'm not sympathetic towards them. If they're crying and it's doing them some good, why should I give them extra sympathy? It's like going up to someone who is crying and they say, 'Leave me alone.' So you do. There are times when you can act too kindly and make things worse. You get immuned to leaving them alone."

Q. "If you had cried would your father have felt more sympathetic?" A. "Oh no. I should have felt degraded. I'd rather bang my fist up against the wall and give it a good crack." Q. "Do you find that when you're angry you keep on and on thinking about it?" A. "Yes. I go over and over it time and time again. I can be physically hurt. The pain is there, but there again it isn't. It's not my dad hurting me, it's I've let them hurt me. They can hurt me physically but I won't let them hurt me emotionally. I won't cry or break down …. If I saw a girl sitting in a pub crying I would go up to her and buy her a drink and then go and sit down where I was before. People who act sympathetic to those who are crying get on my nerves. I've seen my old lady crying sometimes. They say, 'You must hate both of them because you don't show any feelings.' It's just that I don't express it. I went to live with my grandma to get out of the way .... I think my dad got more enjoyment out of hitting my brother than out of hitting me because he would cry and I wouldn't. I can remember my dad thinking he hadn't hurt me so he hit me again. If I'd cried the first time he would have hit me no more. But I still didn't and that put me in a narky mood for a couple of days. I remember him telling my mum, 'There's no point in hitting him. You're not getting through to him. The only way we can punish him is by stopping his pocket money and stopping him going out.' So I always used to be hard up as a kid and I was always stopping in, locked in my bedroom." *Q.* "What do you think a parent should do?" *A.* "I suppose they've got the right to punish if the kid's done something wrong. Just because I'd accepted their punishment doesn't mean that I've got to conform to their rules of crying."

One punishment which Dave did not accept was the fine the magistrates imposed for the damage he had done. "I was disgusted at being fined that I wouldn't pay it. When they said, 'We're going to be lenient with you' I was right disheartened. I just wanted the normal punishment that I thought everyone else would get. I thought I'd got off with it too light and that's why I never found the interest to pay my fines. I went to court twice for not paying my fines and they still didn't do nowt about it. They put me on a supervision order. I resented not being punished. I was disgusted with what I had done."

Q. "Did you feel that if you had been punished you would no longer feel guilty?" *A.* "Yes. I expected to go to prison." *Q.* "So by being fined you felt more guilty?" *A.* "Yes. What I did in a way was to punish them for not punishing me hard enough. It's not that I didn't have the money." *Q.* "Was the feeling of guilt the sense that something's now going to happen to you because you've done this. It's a sort of sense of fear and you have the feeling that this fear will go away once the punishment's come." *A.* "Yes." *Q.* "Was it like this when your father stopped hitting you and stopped your pocket money instead — that this wasn't a proper punishment?" *A.* "He gave in too easily, that's why." *Q.* "He should have kept on till he made you cry?" *A.* "I thought he gave in too easily, that he was a bit soft." *Q.* "You despised him a bit?" *A.* "I did a bit."

One day when we were talking about Dave's workmates I asked, "What would happen if you started to talk about being depressed?" "I don't know. We don't use that word. We say we're fed up. Depression is a word we don't use."

Q. "What if you said that you were so fed up you wanted to kill yourself?" *A.* "They would tell me to get on and do it. They would laugh it off." *Q.* "If you feel really fed up who can you talk to?" *A.* "When I'm really fed up I don't talk to anyone. I have never discussed things before I came in here. I can talk to my parents to a certain extent. But you get to the stage where you're talking to them and you know they don't understand how you feel. They're nodding their heads in agreement but they don't understand .... My mother knows if there is something wrong. Even if I act normally she knows. She will offer to phone and say I won't be in to work. She will suggest I go out for a bit." *Q.* "What was she like when you were little?" *A.* "She never had one special child. She had the same amount of affection for all of us."

After a month in hospital Dave was discharged. Before he left he said to me, "Next time — if there is a next time — I could cope with the situation better. This feeling is like a house that has been broken into. It hurts the first time, but before the next time happens you install an alarm system." I arranged for Dave to come and see me each week. On his first visit I gave him a set of cards on each of which was written the name of a virtue and asked him to put them in order. He said, "I would put courageous first, then hard-working. Then to be fair and just. To be loving. To be truthful. To be generous."

Q. "How did you work that out?" *A.* "I think a person needs courage more than anything else. You need courage to live. And if you're going to live then you've got to work hard. If you're married you've got to be fair and just. To be fair and just you have to be loving. That falls into place nicely, I think. Truth's a funny word, isn't it? I would put fair and just in front of being truthful. Some people don't think you're fair all the time if you tell the truth. When you've courage you can get over your difficulties. You can find a way round them. That's why I put it at the top." *Q.* "Why did you put generous at the end?" *A.* "I'm not very generous. You can't afford to be generous. I'm generous in spasms. To be generous I should think means to be giving all the time." *Q.* "Why is it important to work hard?" *A.* "If you are not working hard it makes it difficult to fit in with the others. You've got to work hard to get owt out of life. The harder you work at it, the better you might do. I don't just mean in terms of money and wages." *Q.* "When you're too frightened to go out to work, how does that make you feel?" *A.* "I'm a coward and I try to think it won't happen again. I try to hide away from the facts. It's just the fear that I might wake up one morning feeling there's just no point in getting up. That starts it. I don't feel hungry and she does something for me to eat — that's when it usually starts. 'Isn't my cooking good enough?' I'm dropping all the time, you see. I want to go out and yet I can't be bothered. You know what I was telling you about last week about what it would be like when I got home? Well, it's started. She doesn't realize she does it though. Maybe it's me who can just pick it out. She asks me where I'm going. She tells me not to have too much to drink. She tells me who to go out with. At mealtimes she says I must eat. She is trying to do her best. I suppose it keeps her happy. You get the feeling that she is trying to be sympathetic but not to show it. It's funny really. It is to me anyway at the moment. I might not laugh about it tomorrow though."

At our next meeting Dave was reluctant to talk, "I can't understand why anyone my age should get depressed. It should only happen to old or married people .... I think if I stopped coming here I would maybe stop thinking about it so much .... I feel obliged to come because you want to help me, but I don't want to come. Shall we leave it, and me get in touch with you some time? When I feel like being helped .... I'll see you in a month's time." A month later he said, "Me and my mother aren't getting on too well. I reckon I am slipping back again. I seem to be falling back into that familiar pattern again. That's why I phoned you the other night. I went out for a drink and I had quite a lot. I was fed up and I was thinking about it. I was all right to start with when I came out of hospital. I've proved myself wrong. The old lady reckons I have started back downhill again. She says I'm argumentative again. I don't mean to be .... I think she is jealous because I have more freedom than she does. She was already married and had a kid when she was my age. She married to get away from her mother .... While she's nagging at me and trying to get through to me it keeps her happy. If it keeps her happy I'll have to keep on doing that. I wouldn't tell her to shut up because that would upset her. If I tell her I am narked, she always says the same thing, 'You can't stand being told what to do.' She always says that as soon as I start saying something back. I can't argue with her. She is too used to it. She doesn't understand so I don't ever talk to her about it. I tell her I'm all right. She thinks I have been ill so I go into hospital and then they send me home and so I should be ready for work .... I get nervous when I go out now. That's cured when I have a few pints. Temporarily." It seemed to me that Dave was asking to come back into hospital. We talked the matter over and then I contacted a doctor who admitted him.

Shortly after he had returned to hospital Dave talked about how he wanted to escape from boring routines. "I'm getting away from something. I can't see no goals to go for at the moment. I keep running but I don't get any nearer. There is a goal at the far end and I am running towards it but never get any nearer. The faster I run, the more it seems to move back."

> *Q.* "I often have that sort of dream." *A.* "Do you know, I had a dream last night and in it I felt pain. I was rolling down this hill and I kept going faster and faster. I was rolling over rocks and I couldn't put my hands over my face to protect myself. There was this big rock and I rolled over it and it went in my mouth and it felt like a piece of soil. I could feel the blood in my mouth. There was this bloke coming towards me and he picked me up and then dropped me down again, and I started rolling again. I glanced round and saw this bloke and he came over and put his hand out and I reached for his hand and he started to lift me up and then he let go and I started to roll again. I didn't see him no more. I don't know what happened after that." *Q.* "A minute ago I was asking you to give me an image of what it's like when you're fed up and you were saying about the

football pitch and then the memory of the dream came back. In both of these images there was a sense of hopelessness. You're moving but you've no control over the movement." *A.* "You're much better at putting it together than I am .... If I had told the doctors about the dream they would think I was cracking up. They'd put me in a straitjacket .... Do you think I shall get better as I get older? I can't see any change, not at all .... I can force myself to keep under control. I can sometimes force myself to be happy, and sometimes it works as well. I can think myself into being sick and fed up. The trouble is it's too easy. But it takes more effort to make yourself happy than it does to get yourself into a state.... " *Q.* "Could we think again about that football field where you're running and never getting to the end. Are you in yourself running down the pitch or are you standing off looking at yourself?" *A.* "I think I am watching myself. When I see I'm not getting any further I just stop. I will try again some other time. That part of me that is watching just tells me to stop." *Q.* "What does that part do when it is stopped?" *Q.* "It goes back to that part that is watching." *Q.* "Do they become one again?" *A.* "Yes. I'm not getting anywhere so I just give up. I just lose interest. My main concern right now is that I might get fed up with being here. I should discharge myself when I have had enough. I should go home and regret it as soon as I was out of hospital." *Q.* "So by coming into hospital you're put in a situation where you're expected to run. You have to make an effort to get towards this goal." *A.* "That's the whole point of coming in, isn't it?"

Dave saw women as being the inferior sex. "I don't think it's right to see a bloke washing up or doing the washing. I downgrade the men who work in offices because I know a woman could do that job."

Q. "If you downgrade a man for doing what you think is a woman's job then you must also downgrade a man for having feelings like a woman — like crying." *A.* "Yes, this is what I'm getting at." *Q.* "How do you feel if you discover that someone is feeling sorry for you?" *A.* "I don't like it. Especially if they don't understand anyway. If they don't understand you can't really call it sympathy. I ought to be the one who is sorry for them because they don't understand." *Q.* "Do you feel that if someone is sorry for you then you are in an inferior position? And that really they are looking down on you?" *A.* "Yes, this is it. I haven't got a lot of pride but what I've got I like to keep by me .... My mother is always saying, 'I never did owt like that when I was your age.' It makes me feel out of it. They tell me I'm so different to how they were all the time. When they keep on saying that to me I feel as though I'm not part of them. I look back on them and they weren't so perfect. Fourteen years they stuck together and after all that time they split up. They turn round and say I'm not like them. I'm bloody pleased I'm not .... I actually asked her once if I really did belong to them both and she said, 'Don't be so daft. Of course you do.' Then we get, 'We thought all our problems were over when you started work and got grown up.' They throw it all straight back at you. If she really understood she wouldn't talk like that. They just seem to treat me differently. You get things like, 'I was never in trouble with the law when I was your age and neither was your father.' My dad was killing blokes when he was fourteen. He saw his mother and father killed by the Germans. They put them up against that wall and made him watch. That didn't crack him up. He was real hard, my dad. Some of the stories he can tell are unbelievable. He has had it ever so rough but he has never cracked up .... My parents were always rowing and falling out before they split. I got sick of hearing it. The old man used to say it was her fault and she used to say it was his fault. I was more or less getting brainwashed by each parent. It depended on who was talking to me. I just accepted the fact that they were accusing one another. I just lost interest. I lost the attachment to them. I went to my grandma's and then when everything was sorted out I went to live with my dad. Then as soon as I started work I got out again. I just lost interest. It wasn't good but I felt independent because I had made that decision. I was there eight or nine months with my grandma and I saw my mother once in that time. Then my dad kept on saying that he wanted me back. Once my brother turned sixteen he did nothing but get into trouble with the law. Then him and me had a row with dad and he kicked us both out. I would be just over fifteen then. It didn't bother me a deal. I lived in digs and caravans and flats and then I stayed with him again for a couple of weeks. It would never work out .... I have had to be fairly emotionally hard to cope with it. But I never blamed either of them .... I was able to work regular when I was living away from home. I enjoyed going to college. I got on fairly well with my trade as well. I would see the end-product of what I had started to make. I would feel proud when I walked through the factory shop and saw my castings all made up with the machinery and all packed up ready for the customer. But then I just got fed up. I probably got fed up of being independent."

A week later we returned to the question of why Dave would not cry. I asked him if he could change his views on crying. "No chance," he said, "I wouldn't be able to accept it. I wouldn't be able to change like that anyway. I should get more of a thrill out of doing something else. You might have a good cry and you might feel better afterwards but I bet you still feel 'het up' afterwards. I can get over it faster physically."

Q. "Why is it important to get over it quickly?" A. "I don't know. It will be because I've always been like that, I suppose." Q. "Suppose for some reason you were in that state and you couldn't get over it — what would happen if you had to stay upset?" A. "If I knew that I had to be upset for a long time I would put an end to it. Commit suicide or something." Q.

"Why is it so terrible to be upset?" *A.* "You're no good to yourself and you're no good to anyone else." *Q.* "What happens when you're no good to anyone else?" *A.* "Other people get that impression before you actually get it yourself. The people at work might say, 'Oh, don't mix with him. He's always moping.' " *Q.* "So if you stay upset for a long time people will reject you?" *A.* "Well, you'd be branded. I've seen it done. I've seen it done with people I went to school with, people I have worked with and with people I know now. That's why. It's a dead loss if you mope all the time and if you get really bad about it." *Q.* "Is this what would happen in your home when you were young?" *A.* "I had brothers and sisters around me and I would think that I couldn't be upset for too long because they were there enjoying themselves and I was missing out. Why should I mope just to draw attention? ... One of the things that upset me a lot was the fact that we would move quite regular. I would just get attached to a place — it wasn't a case of leaving behind my friends — I would grow attached to the place and we would go somewhere new. I used to really hate moving school. I always seemed to take a lot longer getting into the swing of it than everybody else did. I used to worry about it a lot." *Q.* "Did your parents understand this?" *A.* "I don't think I told them. I can't remember ever telling them. I just took that bit longer to adjust. And I can do it very easily and quickly now. I can get used to something very quick now. The magic goes, doesn't it? I get into the swing of things so fast — " *Q.* "That you soon get bored." *A.* "Yes." *Q.* "What you're saying to me is that it's bad enough being upset, but when I'm upset I'm in danger. It's dangerous and so I have to stop being upset." *A.* "It might be dangerous being upset to someone else some day." *Q.* "So if you stayed upset you might have a go at someone." *A.* "Yes. And if I couldn't, then it would be on me. That's how I am when I bust things up. That's what happened to that kid last week who really bugged me. That time I walked through that showroom window I was full of dope and I had had a few drinks. Most people in that condition would have gone home and crashed out on the settee and listened to some music or something. But that wasn't good enough for me. I had to do something more physical."

Ten days later Dave cut himself. "I could have smashed someone else, but I just wasn't in the mood. I was sat at the other end of the lounge where they couldn't see me. I got the nail scissors out and just started to cut away."

Q. "What were you thinking about?" *A.* "I was just feeling fed up, that was all. I wanted to see how much pain I could stand before it actually hurt me .... I wasn't in the mood to damage anyone else. No one had done anything wrong to me, so why should I pick on them? ... I'm just thinking too quick all the time." *Q.* "Is it too quick or too unpleasant?" *A.* "A bit of both actually." *Q.* "What are the sort of thoughts you're having that are unpleasant?" *A*. "Probably reality. Just facing up to things. I just don't know what I want to do …. When I get physically violent my body seems to do it before my mind tells it to do it. Last night I was getting enjoyment out of doing it which was overcoming the pain. There was satisfaction there that I hadn't smashed the ward up or upset other people."

Two days later Dave cut himself again. "I didn't feel anything while I was doing it. There was so much anxiety and energy built up inside me that I didn't feel a thing. There was more pain when they cleaned it with spirit than there was when I did it. The nurse said, 'Why didn't you tell someone how you felt?' There was no one there to talk to at the time, anyway. I wasn't going to waste my time talking to someone who — well, you know how I feel about talking to people who don't know what they're on about."

In the conversation that followed Dave talked about how his parents and his grandmother had quarrelled about where Dave should live after his parents had separated. "I let my grandmother down by not stopping there. I was feeling sorry for my dad because my grandma was blaming him. Then all the time my mum was blaming my dad. It was my fault all this trouble had started. I started it all by telling my dad that I didn't want to go back to grandma's …. If I talked to my dad it was my mum's fault and if I talked to mum it was all his fault and I was just split between them. Instead of getting involved with one of them, I just got fed up with it. I wasn't upset, I just got fed up. I suppose you could say I got depressed with it …. When I was going to my grandma's dad took me to the bus station and he said to me, 'Do you realize that you're the only one who can get your mother and I back together again. If you were taken ill and said that you couldn't get better without the two of us together again, that's the only way it will happen.' "

Q. "Did you feel that you ought to try?" *A*. "Well, I didn't really accept it at the time." *Q*. "Do you feel sometimes that you failed and that you should have tried to get them back together?" *A*. "I suppose I should have done, but at the time I could only think about myself. I was looking forward to living at my grandma's …. I do think about it now and I do feel more guilty now than I have ever done before. I don't see why I should feel guilty because my dad hasn't lost anything by it. He has remarried and they have started a new family. It's just one thing that I can't forget …. I always remember me seeming to get away with more than my brother used to. I used to feel quite chuffed about it at the time. If I did something which my brother also did, they would say to him, 'He has only copied you and your ways.' So every time I did something wrong he would be brought into it somehow." *Q*. "So it was your fault he got punished." *A*. "Yes, they reckoned I had copied him. If I would get into trouble with the law all they would say was, 'You're taking after your brother ….' " *Q*. "Did you feel that you were stronger and wiser than your father?" *A*. "Yes, on certain things. I found I could talk my way out of things. I don't know what you think, but they always thought that I had a good vocabulary. I was always able to get round things by putting them in a different way .... If there had been a tattooist here last night I should be covered in tattoos by now. I should have got rid of the anxiety through pain. They don't prescribe tattooing here in hospital. I would have tattooed myself but I'm not much of an artist with razor blades."

Q. "Cutting yourself, smashing up furniture and hitting someone else are all the same sort of thing, a safety-valve. If you didn't do those three things something much worse would happen. What's the very worst that could happen?" *A.* "I suppose cutting myself so much that I bled to death, or taking an overdose. I suppose the worst thing is that I would crack up. Get really mental. I might end up as a cabbage. And being a cabbage I might still be able to realize that if I had relieved that anxiety all this madness need not have happened." *Q.* "So it's not death you're frightened of, but going really mad." *A.* "Or getting to a stage where I was beyond repair without being mad. I would be the same person as I am now sat here but I would never be able to do anything right. I would look normal but I could never lead a normal life. I would never be able to decide things for myself. I wouldn't realize what I was doing. You see, I don't feel like this all the time. I just get moods. When I get this mood, that's when the build-up starts. I can be completely normal one minute and then the next I don't know what I'm doing." *Q.* "Are you saying that because you have this capacity to cut yourself that you also have a capacity for going mad?" *A.* "Yes, and to be anxious enough to be able to do something." *Q.* "So it is both a safety-valve and proof that you could go mad." *Q.* "When I get to the stage where I'm scared to cut myself I shall know I'm on my way to getting better."

When Dave came to see me a fortnight later he had been drinking. He said, "I'm getting worse. I feel somebody different, rejected maybe. I didn't seem to fit into the pattern at home. So I'm not going home again .... I just feel like going berserk this afternoon. I'm trying to control it .... I feel really down. I'm close to crying but I can't do it. It's against my will to do it so I'm not going to do it." Later that afternoon the doctor on the ward decided that Dave should be moved to another ward where he would be under closer supervision. Dave went to this ward, decided that he did not like it and discharged himself. He was unable to get in touch with me before he left, so when I discovered what had happened I arranged for him to come to see me each week.

We often talked about his mother. Dave complained one day, "She just isn't acting normal. She's all right like this but I know it's not her usual self. She won't argue with me. She doesn't even ask me where I've been. It's too good to be true. With her acting different she thinks she can expect me to act different as well. But she'll break down one of these days because I get on her nerves so .... She seems so false .... I don't like the closeness of it. She's too close. It would make me feel inferior because she's acting so responsible.... "

Q. "Do you think I am nice to you so that'll make you do what I want you to do?" *A*. "Not all the time. Sometimes I do. Mind you, I usually know what to expect from you."

We went on to talk about death. Dave said, "I wouldn't say I was really bothered about dying. I think about it often enough. I just think about what everyone will think about when I'm dead. I'd like to be there to see what happens. I'd like to see the shock on their faces when they found out. I can see the old lady's face."

Q. "How do you think she would take it?" *A*. "This is what I would like to see. I don't know how she would take it. Not just her face — my dad's as well. I don't know what to expect and that's why I'd like to be there to find out." *Q*. "How would you feel if they were terribly upset?" *A*. "I would probably feel guilty about dying." *Q*. "How would you feel if they were indifferent?" *A*. "That would prove to me what they really were." *Q*. "How would you feel then?" *A*. "Probably more tranquil. I would find out the truth. It would set my mind at ease." *Q*. "Because then you needn't feel guilty?" *A*. "Yes." *Q*. "Wouldn't you feel lonely then?" *A*. "I might do a bit. I'd feel dejected by it. I'd get over it, I suppose. People don't worry, do they? I hope they don't anyway." *Q*. "Which would you prefer, for there to be an afterlife or to be just finished?" *A*. "Just finished. You might let yourself in for something you don't understand if there was life after death. You might find yourself having to live the same situation over and over .... " *Q*. "We all have to go through death alone. You never know when or how." *A*. "You can help the matter. You can do that by bringing it forward." *Q*. "Suicide is the only way you can bring death under your control, isn't it?" *A*. "If I took a load of tablets I would just go to sleep and that would be it. And you never know, I might have a terrible end in store for me. I might have an accident at work. I could die of cancer. Suicide might be the easy way out."

On another occasion Dave told me about an argument he had had with his mother. I asked, "What would happen if you told her you were sorry that you had had that argument?" "I wouldn't. She started it. I won't apologize for anything that I haven't done .... She forgets about it straight away but I don't."

Q. "So you brood on it." *A*. "Yes. While we were arguing she made me a cup of coffee. I can't weigh her up .... I can't apologize. It would be like giving in. There's something that tells me not to." *Q*. "What would you think of yourself if you did forgive her?" *A*. "I'd failed, I suppose. I'd have given in to her." *Q*. "Is there anyone else that you'd never give into?" *A*. "I think it would be best if I didn't give in to you." *Q*. "What would be giving in to me?" *A*. "Telling you everything. If I told you everything I'd get dependent on you to sort things out for me." *Q*. "Do you think I can sort things out for you?" *A*. "I don't know. If I told you everything and then you couldn't I'd feel let down."

Even though Dave felt that he could not forgive his mother it worried him that he did not feel that he was part of the family. He would have liked the security of them being "around me. I'm sort of in the middle and they're around me, looking after me, like".

Q. "Whereas, the way you see it, they're over there while you're — " *A*. "Stood out on my own. There's four in that corner," he gestured towards one corner of the room, "And there's me in that one." He pointed to the corner diametrically opposite. *Q*. "If you're in one corner and your family in the opposite, what are you thinking about?" *A*. "It just depends what mood I'm in at the time. If I'm feeling all right then I'm not really bothered if I'm on my own in the corner. If things aren't going right I think about it much more. You get oversensitive about it and feel paranoid about being on your own as well." *Q*. "What are you thinking about your mother when you're in the corner on your own?" *A*. "That she's all right but she just doesn't understand. Until she can understand properly she'll never know how I feel. If I tried to talk to her I'd be talking to someone who didn't understand anyway." *Q*. "Why is it important that she should understand you?" *A*. "She'll know I'm not bluffing then. When I get bad I just go to bed and she thinks that I am getting out of something. She hasn't said nothing. It's just the impression I get. She disbelieves me." *Q*. "Suppose, in this picture, you're in one corner and your mother's in the opposite corner and she said that she believed you, what would happen?" *A*. "I suppose I'd go and meet her halfway. If I went straight to her corner I'd probably take advantage of it. If I met her halfway I haven't got so far to fall back." *Q*. "What do you mean, you'd be taking advantage of her?" *A*. "With me knowing that she understood everything I could probably get away with a lot more than I'm getting now, in terms of going out, spending my money, things like that. But I don't particularly want to do that." *Q*. "How do you feel when you take advantage of your mother?" *A*. "Not very good." *Q*. "Does that make you feel guilty?" *A*. "Yes. It's bound to, isn't it?" *Q*. "So when you're over in the corner on your own you feel frightened and lonely and if you're in the corner with your mother you feel guilty." *A*. "Yes — sick, isn't it?" *Q*. "So what you want is to be somewhere in the middle." *A*. "If she said, 'Yes, I think I know what you mean', then I could stand in the middle and talk to her, but she says, 'I don't know what you're on about' and I'm back in my corner." *Q*. "Why is your mother so easy to take advantage of?" *A*. "Probably because she feels sympathetic." *Q*. "So, if a person feels sorry for you, you can take advantage of that person more easily." *A*. "Yes, but I feel guilty about it as well." *Q*. "Suppose you were in this corner on your own and your mother said that she understood you and you shifted over to her corner and she started to show you affection, how would you feel about that?" *A.* "I wouldn't like it." *Q.* "Why not?" *A.* "Not the soppy —" *Q.* "Would it embarrass you?" *A.* "Yes. I'd rather meet her halfway, shake her hand. It's not affection that I really want. It's to make sure that she understands me. If she understood me completely she wouldn't be so affectionate." *Q.* "What makes you say that?" *A.* "Because she'd realize she uses affection as a sort of fallback. If she can't do nowt else, she can be affectionate, even if she doesn't understand. If she understood a little more and was less affectionate it would be better for me." *Q.* "What's embarrassing about your mother's affection?" *A.* "Being hugged and cuddled at my age. Scared other people might be watching as well. Also I feel when she's offering me affection like that she's looking down on me. She's the big mother and me a little kid." *Q.* "What would people think if they saw her being affectionate to you?" *A.* "They'd think I was soft. A mother's boy." *Q.* "Why is it so bad to be soft, a mother's boy?" *A.* "Because it is. I've been brought up against it." *Q.* "What will happen to you if you're the sort of a man who's a mother's boy?" *A.* "Probably won't be able to live without her for a start, get that attached to her." *Q.* "Do you feel it's dangerous to become dependent on another person?" *A.* "Yes, at the moment I do."

I asked, "Are you worried about being dependent on me?" "I am, at times. You're in a better position to accept it, though, than the others are. It's part of your job. I'd rather be dependent on you than on my mother. You understand more than her. It all comes back to the same thing of understanding. And you can cope with it better. If I feel too dependent on you I'll just stop coming for a while."

Q. "There's another alternative. To become able to cope with dependence." *A.* "Yeah, but there's an easy way out, isn't there?" *Q.* "But the easy way out is giving up the relationship, isn't it? Do you see me in one corner and you in another?" *A.* "No. We're about halfway, I think." *Q.* "But if we started to move to my corner —" *A.* "I'd get a bit wary, I think." *Q.* "What do you think would happen if you went over to my corner with me?" *A.* "For a start, I'd be back in hospital." *Q.* "Do you think I'd bring you back in?" *A.* "It depends how I was. If I went back in that corner with you I'd give up all responsibility. I'd have to do what you said. So if you said, 'Go back in hospital', I'd have to do that and that's what I don't want." *Q.* "So off in your own corner you have to be responsible for yourself and you don't feel you can manage this. If you were right over in my corner you'd have given up all responsibility and I'd be able to tell you what to do. So you have to be somewhere in between — although, somewhere in between is where I think I operate from, because I can't do anyone any good if I take all the responsibility. The image I always have about myself in this sort of relationship is one about when you're teaching anyone to swim. You can never teach anyone to swim if that person hangs on to you tight and so what you do is that you get the person out in deep water where he can't touch bottom and you hold out one hand like this, just enough to keep him floating. You won't sink in deep water anyhow, but the person learning to swim doesn't know that. Then you say to the person, 'Move your arms and kick your legs', and then, when you see that he's doing it at about the right speed, you take your hand away like that, and the person swims and discovers he can swim in deep water. In therapy the person's already in deep water and I come along and prop him up, but I don't let that person cling to me. If that happened we'd both go down. I just sort of keep the person at arm's length but supported and give instructions, 'Try this. Stop yelling.' A person in deep water is only in danger of drowning if he thinks he is in danger of drowning, and a person who is depressed is only in danger of dying, of going mad, if he thinks he is in danger .... You work along the lines of 'If I allow my mother to become too affectionate to me I'll become dependent on her, and if I become dependent on her then I'll be upset if anything happens to her, so to avoid this I will be completely on my own and if I'm completely on my own then I'll be very lonely and frightened, and the more lonely and frightened I become the more terrible the world looks to me, and the more terrible the world looks to me the more frightened and lonely I become.' That's what madness is. That, increased to infinity."

Late one night Dave telephoned me to say that he had taken the bottle of tablets that had been prescribed for him that day. He said that he was phoning to say goodbye. I persuaded him to tell me where he was and with the help of the psychiatrist, the social services and the police Dave was rapidly taken to the general hospital. The psychiatrist who saw him there returned him to the psychiatric hospital as an involuntary patient. Afterwards Dave said to me, "I felt compelled to ring you. I don't know why I did that. I thought I had to tell someone. I didn't tell anyone at home because I didn't want them involved. I thought I should tell you seeing as I had got to know you so well. I didn't expect you to do anything. I just wanted to tell you. I was disgusted when the ambulance came along. I thought you had let me down."

Dave described how he had been unable to tell me, on the last time he had seen me, how "I just felt really deep down depressed. I don't know how to describe it. It's just about as low as you can get, I suppose."

Q. "When you get that low and you had to draw a picture of it, what sort of picture would you draw?" A. "Black clouds. There would be a storm brewing. It's like that picture over there," (this was the picture he had commented on before) "black clouds with flashes of lightning." Q. "Where are you in that picture?" A. "At the top where the lightning is." Q. "So you would be in the midst of it?" A. "I am at the brink of it." Q. "And it's about to roll over you?" A. "Yes." Q. "What will happen when it rolls over you?" A. "The same as what happened two days ago. It's stupid, but I would do it again." *Q.* "So you're on the edge and this storm is coming and then it comes over you, and then what happens?" *A.* "I feel it would miss me in a way. I think it's going to go round me instead of through me." *Q.* "When you get really down does it go through you?" *A.* "Yes." *Q.* "This storm, now a storm is something we can't control. This mood, this feeling that comes over you, you feel you can't control it. It takes you over." *A.* "Yes." *Q.* "When you're on the edge of the storm, do you feel that you want the storm to come or the storm to go away?" *A.* "It depends how I feel at the time. If I'm feeling happy then I want it to blow over. When I'm feeling down I just want it to go through me, like it has done before." *Q.* "Does the storm frighten you?" *A.* "No. If it frightened me I wouldn't do the things I've done." *Q.* "So it's friendly?" *A.* "It's helpful." *Q.* "If the storm was a person, what sort of person would it be?" *A.* "One of greater strength than me. It would be something more powerful. Something that could dominate. It would put me in a position where I had to do as it commanded." *Q.* "This person — the storm — is it a man or a woman?" *A.* "A powerful man. I don't think a woman could be powerful enough to be able to do it. In some cases I suppose a woman could, but it would depend on how I felt about her. I would say it was a dominant man. It's a figure that stands over you and looks down on you as if he's saying that he's going to conquer you. You give in. There is no resistance to it. You accept it. You accept what it's going to do and therefore you go along with it." *Q.* "Are you glad he's there telling you what to do?" *A.* "Most of the time." *Q.* "And in some way he protects you?" *A.* "Yes. He's more powerful than I am. He can command." *Q.* "How would you feel if he went away altogether?" *A.* "A bit lost." *Q.* "Would you feel lonely?" *A.* "I suppose so, yes." *Q.* "How long have you had this figure around with you?" *A.* "A couple of years. It's never been as predominant as it is now. It's becoming stronger all the time now. Each time it's getting stronger." *Q.* "What does he look like?" *A.* "Bald-headed and muscular. He has dominating eyes. He is overlooking someone like that." *Q.* "What, he had his hands stretched out?" *A.* "Yes, and there is lightning coming out of his fingers. He is looking down on me. I'm getting the full concentration, sort of thing." *Q.* "Is he very much bigger than you?" *A.* "Yes. I am like a shadow to him." *Q.* "How does he feel about you?" *A.* "He has to dominate me. I'm the only subject there so he has only me to concentrate on." *Q.* "But while he dominates you, does he care about you?" *A.* "I suppose so. I have never really thought about it. He cares, but he frightens me. I suppose that's his way of making sure I take notice of what he does." *Q.* "What if you turned around and walked away?" *A.* "I wouldn't turn away." *Q.* "Why not?" *A.* "Because he's so powerful." *Q.* "He could even stop you?" *A.* "Yes. Once he's overlooking me, that is, I can't do nowt." *Q.* "Can you tell him to go away?" *A.* "No, he wouldn't take any notice.

He's too powerful. I would lose my speech." *Q.* "If he went away and left you, would you try to get him back?" *A.* "It would depend on how I felt. If I felt okay, I would let him go, and if I felt down I would go after him. He would come back. He usually does." *Q.* "And you care about him?" *A.* "Yes." *Q.* "Does he want to destroy you?" *A.* "I don't think so. It's just that I am overcome by what he does. I can't stand his full strength. He's got more strength than he realizes. I can't always cope with the full amount." *Q.* "You can't tell him that he's too strong?" *A.* "I'm powerless. I have no speech." *Q.* "What would happen if from somewhere you got more strength?" *A.* "I'd take no notice because I might upset him and he'd go away for ever. That's why I wouldn't want to answer him back." *Q.* "So if you tried to get enough strength to wipe him out you would then feel very guilty." *A.* "Yes." *Q.* "Could you try to persuade him that it would be a good idea if he let you grow up and be independent?" *A.* "No, not really, no." *Q.* "Did your father let you grow up and be independent?" *A.* "I think he accepted it. He understood it. He was pleased. He always treated me like a man ever since I was old enough. If I told him I had been in a punch-up he would be pleased I could stand on my own two feet. He was pleased I have been able to make decisions for myself." *Q.* "How old were you when he started to treat you as a grown-up?" *A.* "Once I started to vote, I think. When I voted he was dead chuffed." *Q.* "And it was round this time when this — " *A.* "Figure started to be more dominant in my life, yes." *Q.* "It's almost as if your father let you grow up, but your image — " *A.* "Stopped me. I can't think of anything else to say now. I've said more to you today than I have said for a long time."

At our next meeting Dave said, "My father says that if I had shown more emotion when I was little I would never be in this position. He said that if I had given in easier I wouldn't be where I am today."

Q. "Why didn't you give in when you were young?" *A.* "It goes against — I don't know what to call it — religion. It was my way of showing that what they said and did to me had no effect on me." *Q.* "If you had cried then what would your parents have done?" *A.* "They would probably have thought that they had won. It would have been an achievement for them. Their punishment would have worked. I beat them all the time, and that's why they got so mad with me. They expected me to cry the day I got sent to my grandmother's. But I didn't .... My brother always made out that he was harder than me physically. He's taller and weighs a lot more. But he wasn't. He was ever so soft-hearted. He would put on this act that he was brave but it didn't matter because I was always braver than he was." *Q.* "Did that make up for you being smaller?" *A.* "Yes." *Q.* "Were there times when you would have liked to have gone to your mother and told her that you were sorry and you could make up then?" *A.* "There were times, but I wouldn't give in. I'm in no position to feel sorry and say I'm sorry." *Q.* "There is still that voice inside you that says hard things to you and makes you do hard things to other people." *A.* "Yes. And I have been in here twice so it's not working so good, is it?"

I read him T. S. Eliot's lines about conscience, "This silent and severe critic". Dave said, "He knows what we're on about then. It must be good to be a poet. You can sort out your problems by putting them down on paper." One day when he came to see me and I was called away for a while I gave him an illustrated edition of the *Tao Te Ching* to read. When I returned he showed me the poem, part of which heads this chapter, and said, "I think he's written about me." I asked him what was meant by the last two lines of the poem. "The great mother is the power within me and I'm nourished by it. That's how I looked at it."

The only book that Dave had read was *The Exorcist*. "I'm not sure about believing in the devil, but I do believe in evil."

Q. "Would you say there was an evil force inside you?" *A.* "Yes, I would say quite a bit." *Q.* "That figure you were telling me about the other day, do you see that as being an evil force?" *A.* "It's hard to explain because it's different from time to time. When I'm feeling depressed it's bad and when I'm feeling okay it's okay too. It just gives me a sense of confidence when I'm okay. When I'm depressed it makes me feel worse and sort of puts that cloud over me. When I'm in a good mood, like nothing can stop it. Then if I was having a bad day, it would be just as powerful only in the opposite direction." *Q.* "So it's a force for both good and evil." *A.* "Yes." *Q.* "What happens when you feel really very angry and you want to hit out?" *A.* "I usually can't. There is something that stops me and that's when I start to inflict myself. I have thought about doing something really wrong, and I have felt that I haven't been able to commit what I really wanted to do. If I wanted to punch a bloke I should want to punch him until he was half dead. Then I couldn't do it, so I don't do it at all. There didn't seem to be enough power in me." *Q.* "Do you feel that this power comes from this figure?" *A.* "Yes." *Q.* "So you really couldn't do without this figure." *A.* "If I did I would be a coward." *Q.* "You can't conceive of living on your own." *A.* "No. Sometimes it gives me too much power, and that's what I mean when I say I can't carry things out when I really want to. It's like me being a speedway rider. I have the power to do it but I can never see me getting around to doing it .... "

I asked, "Do you believe in ghosts and seances and things like that?" "I believe in ghosts. They're evil spirits. They don't come from somewhere else. They are in our minds. The evil spirits are in everybody's minds. If you use your imagination you can bring them out to reality. If you imagine them enough then you can actually see them. I had a bad trip once when I was on drugs and this evil spirit chased me for about eight hours. The spirit belonged to me. It was the shadow of my body. It suggested evil things. It really scared me. That's what put me off that stuff .... "

> Q. "Some people see spirits tied up with what happens to us after we die. Do you see them like this?" A. "I don't believe in life after death, so therefore I don't think spirits have any control over it. I think people who commit crimes know more about spirits than other people. They get the so-called devil in them and then they do something wrong. There is something inside them telling them they have to do it. It's like when people say they have no control over themselves. A person can't explain why he committed the crime and so he comes to think there is something inside him that made him commit the crime. He resorts to believing in spirits." Q. "When you get angry do you think that's when you get taken over by the spirit?" A. "I get angry in two ways. I can get angry and get over it or I can get angry and excited as well. If I get excited with it, that's when things go wrong. You feel you can't stop. If you don't understand why you're like this and you go out of control then you tend to think there is some force making you like this. If you can't control yourself then you're bound to think it's something's fault. You feel irresponsible for your own actions. That can make you feel down a bit. You feel guilty about not being able to control yourself .... " Q. "When you talk about an evil force, where would it come from?" A. "I think my own thoughts make it up."

Dave wanted to leave hospital and so we would discuss how he would need to feel for him to be able to survive outside. One day when he said that he was not depressed I asked him what he could do to ensure this feeling of well-being. "Don't know," he said. "It's automatic. You just get that feeling. Something's being poured back into you, that's all. It's hard to describe. If you could measure it in terms of liquid it's like a liquid, feeding yourself on a liquid and sometimes you can have a big intake."

> Q. "Where does it come from?" A. "Don't know. It just comes from life in general if it's treating you all right. Just get it from life itself." Q. "Sounds like a baby, feeding." A. "Yes." Q. "Are you thinking of life being a sort of mother figure?" A. "Yes." Q. "In that sort of picture, it's a passive thing, you haven't much control over what happens. Would you prefer to have control over it?" A. "Yes. As it is I have to accept it as it comes."

But as time went by Dave came to see that he did have control over at least some of the factors that made him depressed. Before he went on leave from the hospital he could say, "I've grown wise to my own mistakes. I wouldn't do it again. I can stop it happening again by not drinking too much."

Dave's images contained the idea of a powerful figure and a passive figure, but he always angrily and aggressively rejected the possibility that he might have homosexual feelings. "I don't think nowt to queers. I won't even speak to one. I might get labelled. There are enough women in this world without there being any queers. I've got no sympathy for them." While he was in hospital Dave met a girl, got engaged and broke it as abruptly as he had described himself as always doing. To Dave sex was something you did but never discussed, and so he was not able to indicate that he wanted the girl to be as active in lovemaking as he was. Then he met a girl who not only understood this but loved him too. "We have some great times together," he said. He found that he could return her affection, that he could accept the responsibility of being a parent, of working as a skilled tradesman. But he still needed some time to be alone.

12

CAROL

"Which way I fly is Hell; myself am Hell;
And in the lowest deep a lower deep
Still threat'ning to devour me opens wide,
To which the Hell I suffer seems a
Heaven."

MILTON

Dr A was a very mild and gentle man, so I was surprised when, in writing to ask me to see Carol, he mentioned that the last time she had seen him she had been very angry with him. Carol, he said, "suffers from a neurotic depression with a good deal of anxiety". Over the past four years she had had ECT, sleep treatment and a variety of drugs, all of which had produced only brief improvements.

Carol and her husband, Bob, came to see me. Carol was small and compact. She could change rapidly from appearing as a vulnerable and diffident schoolgirl to an implacable and uncompromising woman. Yet again she would show herself to be practical, warm, friendly and amused. She and Bob had just returned from a holiday which they had enjoyed. Carol had joined Bob and their children in all the holiday activities, and the account they gave of their enjoyment would have made them seem like a very jolly and happy family had not their conversation been interspersed with references to their quarrels, "our magic moments" as Bob called them. Carol and I arranged to go on meeting. The second time we met Carol did the Rorschach test which she said she enjoyed. She saw many different things in the blots, some lively and happy, some which reminded her of the difficulties she and Bob had in their sexual relationships.

The Carol who came to our next meeting was a different person. She moved and spoke like a tired old woman. She described how, after a few weeks of being active, she had now plummeted down into the depths of depression. We did a grid, but Carol had few ideas to offer and those that she did were full of self-hatred. She described herself as a bitch, someone she hated, got frightened of and got very angry with. She was not active at all, not kind, but someone who wanted things to be just right. Her mother was like her in wanting things to be right. Her mother, husband and children made her very angry.

It was now apparent that Carol did not simply live a life punctuated by periods of depression but rather she lived on a continuum which ranged from intense activity down to near immobile depression. I drew a line to represent this continuum and asked her to name the extremes. The active end was when she wanted everything to be "shipshape and Bristol fashion", the immobile end was "in the pit" where "I prayed for help and the worse I got. The more I cried out the more I seemed to cry out." The mid-point was the ideal which she never reached, where she was "placid, easy-going, able to listen to Bob and the children". For the following five months Carol kept a chart of the changes along the continuum to see if there was any pattern to these changes but none became apparent. As we talked over the next twelve months it became clear that these changes in mood related to how she saw herself and her world.

"When I'm up," said Carol, "I can do anything. I know it's silly, but I was making chutney·at four o'clock the other morning and I was so tired the next day .... I'm on twenty-four hour call. I've been working day and night. It's not fair. I feel pressurized. I'm working myself to a frazzle .... When I'm swinging up I am always thinking, 'This is fine but how long will it last?' I know I should enjoy it while it's there but I am waiting for the next let-down. And then it comes and I think I panic and I go from being on a reasonable keel to being nasty.I'm nasty and I shout and then I could throw things. I feel so angry, mainly with myself. I am bitterly angry with everyone and not really knowing why. Then I can see my mother in me. I panic. It's like a volcano. I feel I'm going to erupt." At such a time, Bob said, "I am completely at a loss to know what to do to be right. There are arguments all the time."

"When I'm in this condition," said Carol, "I can only be pushed so far. When I'm pushed too far I come smack down again. After so long I just opt out and go down into the deep depression again, when I want to sleep and let the rest of the world go by. I've got to have a release, I've got to stay down until I've had a rest. Nothing enters my head. I stay here till I possibly feel I can cope. Then I fly up again. When I start to think the pressure starts again. When I'm down there I'm in my own home. I'm safe and secure. Bob has to take over. I feel quality at being like this. I'm just hopeless and helpless. Nobody would want to be down here, it's so terrifying .... I have this feeling that if I hadn't have gone down into this depression I either wouldn't be here at all or I would have done something drastic. No one seemed to really understand or take any notice. The doctor kept trying out different pills on me and it was always 'Oh, you will get better'. Four years ago we had a summer like this last one. I remember all of the family being at the swimming pool. I was sitting on the grass and I was just staring into space. I can remember not wanting to hear and not wanting to see. I can remember now how vividly I felt then. Everyone about me was enjoying themselves and I just wanted to sit and be encased. As far as I was concerned I don't think I was there. I don't think anyone got through to me. If they spoke I didn't hear them. That was one of the times when things were really very bad. But then it got even worse after that. Then I came in here. After a while in here I felt that I should have to get out or be in here forever. The depression did lift. I was absolutely on top of the world. So I went home. Then it all blew up again .... Yesterday I wasn't too well and we were sat down at night and suddenly it all erupted like a volcano. I said, 'I can't stand any more of this. I am ruining four lives, not one. I can't see any other way out. I shall have to do something about it — drastic.' 'Oh, don't be silly,' says Bob. 'I'm not being silly. I'm being sensible.' I cried and I said that there was no point in going on any further. I had had all the tablets in the world and nothing could solve anything. Working it out afterwards I could see that if I had taken my own life, and with my Christian beliefs, I knew I would be somewhere looking down on those I had left behind and see the suffering I had made them go through. Then I was thinking that the only way out was to pump the children full of drugs as well. I should have to take them with me. Then I thought it wasn't fair to take their lives as well as mine, and then I was thinking was it fair to leave them? Their existence would be very bare. I was telling Bob all this and he said, 'After all the trouble I have taken with those children to bring them up.' 'Well, that means you don't need me.' 'No, no, no, I didn't mean that.' Next day the vicar asked me if I had any problems with the children. This is it — there seems to be nothing. There is nothing to cause it. It's just me. I don't know why. I don't want to be like it. And if I was as strong-willed as I used to be then surely I ought not to be like it. But this strong will seems to be in the wrong places. It centres round things that aren't really so important. I don't think life is worth living, but I know to be dead would be no release for me, not with my beliefs. There would be no relase on the other side. It's a band that is getting tighter and tighter and tighter. There seems to be no way out. It doesn't matter how I say my prayers, how I go up to take communion or whatever I do as regards the spiritual world, there's a block, I can't get through. We can't communicate and that worries me an awful lot — when one has been able to — I have been able to communicate and now I can't."

To help Carol sort out her thoughts I encouraged her to write, so from time to time she would bring me passages that she had written. One of these she called 'Help!',

"What is this self, this me?
  Why do I want to change me?
  Why can't I accept me?
  I just don't like me, why?
  Others seem to accept themselves,
  Why can't I? Am I so different?
  Questions, questions, where are the answers?
  Why do I swing so fiercely from a too high mood,
  Down to the miserable depths?
  Why can't I be the happy medium?
  When in a high mood I'm told
  'That's better, more like your old self'.
  Horrors. I Don't Want To Be My Old Self.
  Little do they know what lay behind the 'Old Self'.
  Misery, bewilderment, anxiety, unrest,
  Disappointment, all hidden behind a mask,
  Which is still put on even now,
  To face the outside world."

Once when Carol was talking about the pressure that she felt I asked her if she could turn this feeling into a picture. Carol answered immediately, "My mother. Yes, it's behind three parts of everything. It always seems to stem back to that. It's in my mind. Honour thy father and thy mother. Whatever I try to rationalize, everything that's happened, my mother is behind it. And I'm so bitterly ashamed at having to say it. Because they brought me into the world and if they hadn't I wouldn't be here and I must be here for a purpose. They probably haven't got much longer on this earth. I know my first duty is to my husband and my family. I've thought it the best thing to do is to keep away from my parents but one can't do that because of the grandchildren. They think the world of them. So I don't know what to do. My mother is the most generous, kind person in one way and in another she can just say two words and then down you. I think my mother wouldn't like anything more than to see our marriage break up. She's a mischief-maker. The more trouble she can cause the happier she should be. She's moan, moan, moan all the time. She only thinks of herself. She's not interested in anyone else's problems unless she can make trouble. She is a suspicious-minded person. I saw my mother in town yesterday. I was walking down High Street and who should be walking towards me but my mother. I thought, 'Oh God!' Anyway, the boys had been up the week before to see her and she was saying how sensible Andrew was. Then she said, 'You can't get anything out of Peter. He just lays on the floor with a comic.' She only likes them to go up there so she can find out what's going on. Then she was going on about the next-door neighbour. I was trying to change the subject. I was telling her how much Peter enjoyed games at school. 'That's typical of Bob's family,' she said, 'His mother will run a mile for a bit of pleasure.' I was thinking, 'I shall have to get away.' Luckily someone else came up then and I told her I would have to go. She won't let you relax for two seconds. She won't let up about anything. She has this thing that everything happens to her. She thinks obstacles are put in our way. She's always saying, 'If there's a snag in owt we get it.' I know it's fatal for me to spend time with her. In no time at all I'm like this. I wish I could turn off and just not listen. She does not understand. When I get depressed she says, 'You want to pull yourself together. You'll have your marriage breaking up.' If she sees me having a rest, she doesn't understand that that hour and a half I have after dinner to lay down refreshes me, empties my mind so that I can carry on. It's always, 'Oh you lazy so and so.' That's her attitude. She doesn't have to say it because I can see it. She buys the boys things and says she gets pleasure out of getting them things. Does she, or is it her way of hanging on? The last two or three times we've visited she has been quite nice. She has been extra nice which makes me suspicious."

Carol's father had been ill over recent years. "My dad always worked hard. Everything he had he put into his work. My mother always said that his work came first .... I can go to him now and take his hand and I feel that I've forgiven him. I can't touch my mother. I can't kiss her. I can give my dad's hand a squeeze. My mother doesn't like that. To catch a glance from her when I do that, if looks could kill I'd be dead. She's terribly jealous of that." "What's the main thing that stops you forgiving her?" I asked. "The fact that she can't see any further than her nose end."

Q. "What would happen if you did forgive her?" *A.* "It has happened before. I think that she's becoming kind and understanding but it doesn't work because when she does become kind and understanding she starts ferreting in. Then she starts bringing the nastiness round. She tries to poison my mind against my husband and all the other relations. She pushes everyone else out."

Carol and her mother did not agree on how she had brought up her children. "I would tell them once, I would tell them twice, and third time they got one. I didn't do what my mother did. My mum used to belt me with a razor strap. I use my hands. I never got away with a thing when I was a child .... The only pleasure my folks got out of me was when they conceived me. Still, I shouldn't blame them for how I am. Now I have gone and done the same thing. I have planted two kids in this world and unfortunately they have half of me in them. I hate to think about that. I don't think I will ever change .... I had always said I didn't want an only child. An only child is a lonely child. I reckon that if my mother had had six children then she wouldn't have had time to row with my dad. Right up to when I was about eleven I thought all grown-ups carried on like my parents carried on. Then after that I would go and visit girlfriends and meet their parents and I used to come away wondering why my parents couldn't be like that. Then I realized that we were odd. I can remember her nagging me when I was younger and me getting at the bottom of the stairs and saying as soon as I was safely out of reach, 'Nag, nag, nag'. I don't know how I dare used to do it. Then there came a time when I realized that I hadn't to take part. I didn't want to enter into it. I would take no notice. If she had fallen out with dad she would want me to side with her but I got so that I had no interest. Things got worse then because if you didn't agree with her then she made your life ruddy hell."

Carol still needed her mother. As she said when her mother did not visit her at Christmas, "Part of me was disappointed and part of me was relieved. My mother asked a fortnight ago if the boys could go and stay. Bob took them on Friday night and I thought I would go when he went to fetch them on Saturday. They'd had a marvellous time, etc., etc. 'Nan is funny', etc., etc. I know it's childish of me but it makes me angry. Why couldn't she have been fun with me? Why does she now want to do all the things with the boys? It makes me angry and it makes me feel bitter. I suppose I should let her enjoy them. While they were away I was always asking Bob to get them back. In the end I said, 'When are you going to fetch them back?' 'I'll go in a few more minutes.' 'Go now. They are my kids and I want them back.' Suddenly I must have them back. I think if she had them too long she might do Andrew some harm. I know it's irrational. I know when I react it upsets Andrew."

I commented, "It sounded to me as if you're jealous of the boys getting what you never got. Then very quickly you felt guilty about feeling jealous of them. You felt this guilt in the sense that something might happen to them."

"Yes, and more to Andrew. It wasn't the clothes, it was the fact that she could find love in her. I didn't think she knew what love was and therefore she couldn't give me any. Anything she does that makes them happy I am thinking it makes me miserable because why couldn't she be like that with me? It would have made my life easier. My mother would stuff me with food but that wasn't what I really wanted. She gave me things but she never gave me what I wanted, security and love. When I see she has got those capabilities and she can give them to the boys, then I think why did she have to make my life so miserable, why did she have to enjoy getting me in tears about what a terrible childhood she'd had and why did she have to put that burden on me? It hurts to think that she has got that capability of affection and really never was able to show it to me without there being a danger attached to it of some kind. She was always generous with me, she never wanted me to lag behind, she always said, 'I never had so and so,' and she always wanted me to have what she didn't, when I really don't think that's altogether good. Even with the things she gave me, I used to get, 'If you hadn't had that, I could have had so and so.' Well, okay, why didn't she have so and so? Why did she have to let me have the things and then say, 'Look what I've gone without to let you have.'?"

Carol felt that her mother looked down on Bob and his family. "She'll say about Bob and his family, 'They're not our sort.' I say to her, 'Well, what are our sort?' She couldn't answer that. I didn't marry Bob because she didn't want me to. Don't get me wrong, but I should never have found someone good enough for her. She used to say, 'Let her marry a dustman. So long as she's happy I don't care.' If I'd have taken a dustman home I can imagine what it would have been like. I still think that if there was a split in our marriage it would somehow please her. Bob says this is all the good reason why we should try harder .... I don't think Bob and I talk enough. If only we could develop a relationship of talking. My parents were never like that. They were never on the same wavelength. Bob and me are like that. We just don't seem to be on the same wavelength. Sometimes when we've been watching television I suddenly say, 'Oh, talk to me,' and he'll say, 'What about?' 'Anything.' I'm appealing to him and he says, 'What about?' "

Bob's family was different from Carol's. Bob said, "I'd always seen my father kiss my mother when he went out to work."

"I'd never seen that in my home," said Carol, "When I saw them do that I laughed .... My sex education was nil. When I asked my mother questions all she said was, 'It's a duty. It's part of the bargain of marriage.' I hoped when we got married it would be different but it wasn't. It's her behind me all the time. She'll say, 'I don't know what they see in it. Men get more out of it than women do.' I have kept thinking about this and I remember when we were engaged we used to talk about this, and we both decided that it really wasn't like that. There is just this at the back of my mind now, 'There you are, see.' My marriage is important to me, the most important. But I want it to be *all* right, not just outwardly to other people. I want in my marriage what my mother never had — a good sex life and a happy relationship. There are bound to be times when you don't agree. I suppose I want a fairy tale, a lived happily ever after marriage. I can't get it into my thick skull that it doesn't happen like that. I'd like us to have a good sexual relationship. I'm a perfectionist. If a thing isn't right it's got to be chucked to one side or something's got to be done to get it to perfection. Our honeymoon was a flop. I sometimes wish we were just starting out — that we were courting now. We both felt it was something kept for marriage. I would hate to think that Bob had gone about with girls. I think if we had made love before we were married and it hadn't worked out we maybe shouldn't have got married. I suppose it isn't the most important thing. It is important. Well, I think it is anyway. I think if we could get that part of our marriage on a better basis other things might come right. It's all a strain. Bob used to say things like, 'I don't suppose you're in the mood.' 'No, I'm not.' I wasn't in the mood because I don't think that was the way to approach me. If he put his arm round me I would say, 'Oh, you're feeling like that, are you?' The way he does it is wrong. I think it's my fault really. I just don't seem to be able to relax. I feel tensed up. It's like a job of work that has to be done the hard way. If only I could relax. I like to play with him but when he starts to touch me I have to say, 'Don't do that.' Yet I also want some enjoyment out of it. It's like everything else with me — if it's not perfect then it's no good. Bob keeps saying, 'Practice makes perfect' .... I don't seem to see a lot of women my age but I find that it is something which is never talked about. Are some women (what can I say?) very sexy? Do women vary? I don't see it. I always thought that men were more inclined that way than women."

"How would you feel if I said, 'No, they are not. Women are just the same as men'?"

"I should think, 'Well, what's the matter with me?' This is it, see, because Bob will say to me, 'I don't know what's the matter with you.' I'll say, 'How do you know about other women?' How does he know about other women? He only knows what they talk about at work. I don't know why I am awkward with him. It's like this morning when he brought me here. We drove up to the door, and he put his face across to mine and I said, 'I'm not going to kiss you. I'm not in the mood.' That was a rotten thing to do and it wouldn't have hurt me. I always feel it's unfair if I don't feel that way to encourage him. It's just that one thing leads to another."

"Do you mean that if I'd looked out of the window and watched you kiss him goodbye there might have been something else to see?"

"He would have thought, 'Oh, that's nice.' He is coming back here to fetch me. If I'd have kissed him he might have slapped his hand on my knee or something. If he was to do that I should say, 'You can come off that for a start.' I mean it's so rare for us to — er — well, naturally if I was to give him any encouragement he would take me up on it. I'm sure he's not sex-starved. He can't be. He thinks he is. How does he know? He might say things like, 'Other people don't go on like we do.' How does he know how other people go on unless he's in the house and hears them. I don't like it and I don't want it. I think men must be different. They seem to put their ordinary lives completely out of their heads and change. I can't seem to function. And then there is this phrase he will use. 'There is nothing that will turn you on.' I get so mad I have to tell him, 'I am not a bloody tap.' I just can't understand the language. You don't turn things on and then turn them off as far as I'm concerned. The last couple of times we — I can't call it making love — I have felt that I am just something that has to be used. I have been in such a state afterwards that I think he thinks that it is just not worth bothering .... Bob says I shut myself off and this is partly true. Then if I do begin to open out I have this awful feeling that I'll get hurt. We can make love and then maybe only two hours later he can say something quite nasty. I think to myself, 'How can he be so nasty when something like that has just taken place?' When that happens I bitterly resent him and I think I hate him as well. I think the best thing is to keep myself shut off. I know really that isn't the solution .... It's switch off the telly and go upstairs and switch on the tap. Mind you, what feelings I've got are very muddled. I don't seem to get strong feelings. That's frustrating. I don't seem to feel love. But if it's not there I can't make it come and that makes it worse. Bob just says, 'Put your armour on.' I want to feel to love him. I suppose I could take part, but when there's no feeling, it's really awful to me. I think what these — er — prostitutes are — probably haven't any feelings at all. They just do it without enjoying it."

One day when we were discussing her relationship with Bob and with her mother I said, "You feel left out when your mother has an important relationship with another person, like your son. You have the same feeling about Bob. You can't bear the idea of sharing him with somebody else."

"Yes. I don't want him myself but I don't want anybody else to have him. It's rather a nasty thing, isn't it? I can't really say that I don't want him myself, but there is no feeling. He says that I never loved him from the first. He thinks that's the trouble. I don't know what to think. My argument is that I don't think I know what love is. Anyway, there are so many aspects of love."

I told Carol the story of the Lady and the Tiger. "Once in ancient Rome there was an Emperor who delighted in devising new games for his circus. In one of these a prisoner would be put in the arena and shown two doors which opened into the arena. Behind one door was a beautiful lady and behind the other was a hungry tiger. The prisoner had to choose which door would be opened. If he chose the one which opened to reveal the lady he would then be married to the lady and he would be given his freedom. If he chose the door to reveal the tiger he would be killed then and there by the tiger. Now the Emperor had a daughter and she fell in love with a man who was an enemy of the Emperor. When their love was discovered the Emperor had the man imprisoned. He then announced that this man would appear in the arena to make the choice between the two doors. The princess could not save him, but she could bribe the gaoler to tell her behind which door was the lady and the tiger. The princess was in the Royal Box when her lover was brought into the arena. He looked at her and she signalled to show which door he should choose. Now, if you were the princess and Bob was in the arena, which door would you tell him to choose?"

"The first thing that came into my mind was to choose the tiger because if I couldn't have him then no one else could. What a decision to have to make. Thinking twice, it might be best to see him happily married. I don't know."

Carol told the story to Bob with the adjustment of him in the Royal Box and her in the arena. She reported that Bob had said, "I don't think I'd like to see you mauled by a tiger. I'd choose the chap and then I'd go out and slay him and then I can have you." (When I had posed this problem to Joe, with him in the Royal Box and Ann in the arena, he unhesitatingly chose the tiger. He said he expected Ann to make the same choice.)

So Carol and Bob were determined not to let one another go. But they could not live peacefully together. As Carol said, "From what I do it would be enough to drive a lot of men away. Maybe I have this sense of insecurity that I have to push him to see how much he can stand. I find that when I have something to worry about it is always there and I am always thinking about it. But Bob seems to be able to dispense with anything that is a worry. He seems able to forget it. That makes me angry because if it's a worry that is between us why should he forget it? When we were first married I used to hate him sometimes. The only way I could show him there was anything wrong was to be nasty. I couldn't get through to him in any other way. I used to say, 'Let's sit down and talk.' It would end up in a battle royal or with me in tears. But what do you do when you're being hurt? I suppose I should have let myself go into a cabbage. But as for hurting him, nothing seems to get under his skin. He just lets it roll off his back. They were always a family who would insult one another."

Sometimes Bob would come with Carol to see me and lively discussion would follow. They often argued about their arguments. "What I say to you just rolls off your back," said Carol. "What you say to me goes in. I harbour it and bear a grudge." "Why do you want to hurt me?" "Because you've hurt me. It's an eye for an eye and a tooth for a tooth." Bob turned to me. "We both think we retaliate and nobody starts it." "You're like a brick wall," said Carol. "Does she hurt you?" I asked. "Yes." "Oh aye, yes, you say that flippantly," said Carol. "I can't afford to have a breakdown." "You can't afford to show your feelings," said Carol. "No good me bursting into tears." "What would happen to you if you did?" I asked. "She would think she had scored over me. Then she'd think, 'Oh, I've got him. Now he's down I'll keep on belting him.'" "Any sign of weakness would be a danger?" I asked. "I think so, yes. I feel if I showed that I was in any way hurt she'd immediately jump on that and as soon as she found a spot sort of work on it .... As far as I see it, Carol is a very strong and dominant person and to the same extent I'm the same. As things are at the moment, for the last two or three years, whatever I've done or said has been wrong. She's always telling me, 'You shouldn't do this' or 'You shouldn't do that'. Just as she speaks to the boys when she's telling them to put their clothes away. You might just as well say, 'This is how I want you to be and this is how I want our lives to be and that's it.'" "I never get my own way," Carol interjected. "Of course you do. We both get our own way in certain things." "It's difficult to have a discussion with you. It's like getting blood out of a stone," she said. "Probably we don't discuss things enough. Carol's more interested in directing the kids, telling them to get washed and that sort of thing rather than talking about other sorts of things." Later in this discussion I commented, "To be an adult you can't indulge your temper. You can't have the sheer pleasure of just letting fly. You have to find other ways around it." "Does that mean being an adult you should never lose your temper?" demanded Carol.

Carol and Bob would fight while they were with me and would tell me of their fights at home. But they showed clearly that they cared about one another. The problem for Carol was, "I just seem to have this thing in me. I have to hurt or be hurt. The minute I put my defences down nearly always something happens and I get hurt. I might be looking for it — I don't know. I don't know how to cope with being hurt. I'm afraid to give out too much love, to give fully for fear of being hurt. I can't relax. Bob can be kind and gentle, but if I wag the red rag at him, he can respond. I've seen so much of that in my parents' home. Even now he says, 'If you don't calm down, I'll hit you.' I'll say, 'You try and see what happens to you.' Underneath I'm terrified. Instead of bursting into tears I put on a hard outer shell. Underneath I'm hurt. With my experiences as a child I tend to think that anybody who says anything a bit off is getting at me — because of what went on at home and all things got twisted round and anything you said there was always a double meaning to it. I have got a sense of humour but it gets lost." "What would happen at home if you showed your mother you were hurt?" I asked. "She wouldn't care. It doesn't do to show my mother that she's hurt you. The more she thought she'd hurt you, the more she'll carry on. That's why when we go to my mother's I've got to put on this simple act — 'I'm a quiet little mouse' attitude. It would be no good bursting into tears in front of my mother. If I shut off those things, if I don't see and I don't hear, then nothing can hurt me. With Bob, I withdraw and I continue to withdraw. But by doing this I'm really crushing my love. If only you can give out it comes back. I do try, but the slightest thing and I dash back into my shell. It's the only way to be. I'm safe in here. What I've got I'll keep. And what have I got really? If I don't give out I can't expect to receive. My trouble now is a matter of trust. I find it very difficult even with Bob. I can trust him but it doesn't come easily. And as for my mother I wouldn't trust her as far as I could kick her. Trust is one of the most important things really. I can't trust my feelings because they're forever changing so where does one start? It's very difficult. I was thinking about this only last night because I was remembering that only after knowing you a short while I asked you if I could trust you. I thought I might have upset you by asking you that. It was strange because no one used to call on me and then I met you and suddenly people kept knocking at the door. I wondered why that had happened all at once. One of my mother's favourite sayings was, 'Beware wherever you tread'".

Q. "What does the word 'trust' mean to you?" A. "Complete loyalty. It's like when I say things to you about Bob. He knows I talk to you about him, but I never tell you anything that hasn't already been said to him." Q. "Do you see it as a whole thing — like you either trust altogether or not at all?" A. "Yes, it's got to be total. Total." Q. "This sets you a hard task, then, doesn't it? If you found out that Bob wasn't as loyal as you wanted then all your trust has gone." A. "Yes, that is it, I suppose. For me a friend's a friend and an enemy's an enemy."

Carol had a good friend, an elderly woman who lived near. "She's a good woman. She's God-fearing. She's everything I would want of my own mother and to talk to her, I always come away feeling better and that I should try and give out more of this, well, it's love which exists around her, with her, with all her family, it wells up in her and when I get it, it brings out my better side, thought for others, feelings. I go home and I feel better. Something makes me feel like helping others. I've been horrible all the week, rotten, not fit to live with. I know this. Then when the boys come in from school I start to shriek at them. Then that feeling's all gone. It can be there for the outside. It can be there for me when I'm on my own. But I can't seem to do it inside of my own family. I'm screaming and going on like someone gone crackers. Why do I keep on doing it? But I suppose with my friend we do seem to treat one another politely, which I don't do at home. But if you can't let yourself go at home where can you let yourself go? Bob says to me, 'How can you come in from church and start ranting at the kids?' Why shouldn't it be so? Why shouldn't I rant at the kids? They make a mess, don't look after their clothes. I looked in Peter's wardrobe and all his ironed clothes were on the floor. Peter blamed the metal coat-hangers. It looked as though his clothes had been in a beggar's press. That was one of my mother's sayings. I threatened to sling their clothes in their bedrooms but really they know I wouldn't do it. Everything I do is destroyed, really. As soon as I do it they undo it. I can dust and sweep all day and the house looks lovely and then by the end of the evening I think to myself, 'Why did I bother?' I don't really want to be lazy. I don't enjoy being lazy. I think my solution would be to have some knitting laying around and then at least it would look as though I have been productive. Even if I didn't touch it, it would be there. If anyone came they would be able to say, 'She's busy anyway.' You're not busy if you're sat watching television or reading a book. They are time-wasters." I commented, "When you measure your virtue by the work you do that means that you think that you yourself are of no value." "Yes, well this is how I feel."

> Q. "This is why you wear yourself out and feel so tired. You're trying to do the impossible, aren't you?" A. "Yes, I suppose so. I was only saying last night that I would be better out and away from them all because I am only making their lives a misery. Anyway they were saying that I was their mum and I did see to their clothes and I did feed them and I thought, 'That's not much of a value, is it?' "

But hard work meant more to Carol than merely justifying her existence. For her, "Only the best is good enough. I always set a standard which I couldn't achieve. I had to be an ultra-super housewife and everything had to be in its place. My mother was the sort who would flick the cover up to see if there was any fluff under the bed so I had to try harder."

Bob had not been brought up to appreciate Carol's standard of hard work. She said, "I always say, 'Peter's just like his father's family. He'll always find the easy way out.' My mother always said, 'The easy way is never the best way.' In that family they all do seem to take the easy route. I've had it instilled into me that the easy way isn't the best."

> Q. "You have to suffer?" A. "It seems so. If you've done it the hard way then you've done it properly. I don't know why I think like that." Q. "How do you feel about it now you're an adult?" A. "Well, it's silly really. I remember thinking when the children were small I was maybe too strict with them, but I didn't know how to be any other way. I have told

my sister-in-law that I worry in case something goes wrong with the boys when they are older and they blame me for their mistakes. 'Why worry?' she said, 'We all make mistakes.' She says I can only do my best. It must be smashing if you can be like that." (On another occasion she said of this sister-in-law, "I can't understand how she can get into such a sloppy way of living.") "Mind you, I have learned a lot since I have been ill. You always find that anyone who is willing gets put on. What was it Bob was saying this morning? He was saying, 'Will you bring those shopping bags with you when you come? I have to remind you about everything nowadays.' I thought, 'Yes, and I'm learning, because at one time I would have had it all planned and he was the other way round. He was the one who would have gone out and not cared if the windows were closed and things like that. I am beginning to learn now that if you take on responsibility, the more you'll get put upon. I am beginning to get a bit sharp now. In fact I act daft. At one time I used to think, 'It's my duty to do this and that.' " *Q.* "So it was your duty to do everything and to do it the hard way." *A.* "If it wasn't done the hard way it wasn't done properly. Stupid, isn't it really."

Carol felt that she had not done as well as she might because "To become a housewife and mother one's given no training whatsoever. Me and my conscience. I still worry about what I've done." But "whichever way you do things, someone has to criticize. If a kid looks a ragtag who gets the blame really? Most of society wouldn't say, 'Okay, that kid chooses to be a ragtag.' The majority of people would think, 'What does that kid's mother think she's doing sending her kid out looking like that?' I think to myself it reflects back onto me. You know that Peter is the untidy type but I can't accept it. Ordinary people can't accept that either. The ladies who polished their windows every day and the ladies who scrub down their entrances every day, they couldn't understand why he looked so untidy. They would think, 'What is his mother thinking about sending the boy out like that?' " She was, as she often said, "super-sensitive". Carol was just as critical of other people. "I suppose I judge people. I'm pretty quick at making up my mind — likes and dislikes which is wrong, really, because if you dislike someone you should try harder to like them, but for usually, if I dislike someone for no apparent reason, the longer I know them the more I find out why I dislike them. And then not liking is not trusting."

Q. "Do you feel that your first impressions tend to turn out right?" *A.* "Nearly always. Three out of four times."

She had her own opinions but "everything's all right if I keep quiet and don't say anything. If you've got a point of view you should shut up. Peter had this tape-recorder for Christmas and over the holidays we had a lot of fun with it. The other morning I was listening to a tape we had made at Bob's mother's house and I noticed that everytime I opened my mouth to speak someone else started up too and it seemed to me as if no one wanted to listen to what I had to say. 'What you have to say isn't important' was the message I seemed to get from this recording." We often talked about this problem. I commented, "It seems to me from what you say you're surrounded by people who don't listen to you. On occasions Bob doesn't listen and then there's your psychiatrist, your GP and your mother. They don't listen." "Why don't they listen? Do you think I go on so much that they don't listen any more. If I have an opinion about something surely they should listen. Even when I'm not right I've got a right to my point of view. Surely I have the right to express what I feel. I get the feeling they are saying, 'Shut up, belt up' to me. If they think that they might as well stick me in here and wait for me to become a cabbage. Even your own folks think that because you've been in a psychiatric hospital that you're mad. I don't trust them while they're thinking like that. When I'm waiting at that bus stop I seem to think that the ordinary members of the public seem to be wary of us. They think, 'She's come from over there. Better watch out.' " Because people would not listen to her Carol felt that her questions were not being answered. "I always seem to want to know. I think I have a right to know. Blooming doctors! They think we're only the patient and therefore we have no right to know. I'd like to know what goes on inside me. I'd like to bring my brain out and get everything out and put it back in order. I'd like to fit everything back in its proper place and start all over again."

Not long after Carol first came to see me she asked me, "Can I trust you completely? Is what I say to you being passed on? I've just had some social workers to see me and I feel I've been in the witness box." She often expressed a dislike for my tape-recorder. When I asked her why she said, "In case I say something I shouldn't. I'm frightened I would drop a clanger. Say somebody robbed this place."

Q. "But what could happen then?" A. "I don't know. Slung in gaol. It's evidence." Q. "What, evidence that can be used against you?" A. "Possibly, yes." Q. "You're entitled to be critical of whatever goes on in the Health Service because you're a customer and customers are allowed to complain."

But her fears persisted. "Although I have been coming here for a year and we have gone a long way I find that I am still a bit frightened of you. Bob said last night, 'Here she comes. She looks quite ordinary, you know.' I'm still — well, there is still a bit of difference. I said to Bob, 'I know Dorothy is on leave next week. I wonder if I rang her up in the week she would come to tea. I wonder if I should do that.' 'Well she can only say yes or no.' I thought I shouldn't be able to cope. What should I do for tea? The more I thought about it the more inadequate I felt and in the end I couldn't do it. There would have been a terrible panic situation. Sometimes there are things that I should like to ask you but I think that I shouldn't ask. I noticed last night you said something about your hair and Kay asked straight out, 'Which hairdresser do you go to?' I thought, 'She isn't afraid to ask sort of personal things.' I'm just afraid to step over that line. This doctor–patient relationship makes me afraid to step where I shouldn't step."

Q. "What are you afraid might happen if you stepped over the line?" A.

"Possibly — er — it's difficult to say. There must be a line for you. I don't know where that line is." *Q*. "Well, there is a line for everybody, isn't there? We're all adults involved in different things. We all have different commitments and so on. If you had an appointment to see me and that morning Peter was taken ill and you rang to cancel seeing me, I wouldn't say how dare you break your appointment and put Peter before me. That would be me stepping over the line you had drawn." *A*. "You always make it sound so simple."

Much of Carol's conversation concerned the health of her and her children and the continual difficulties she had with various doctors who had failed to live up to her expectations. I asked her, "Do you think that doctors and other people in authority should know everything and should be able to protect you?" "Yes."

Q. "And to do that, should they also be very powerful?" *A*. "Yes."

I pointed out that while there is security in knowing that the people who look after us are omiscient and omnipotent, there is also insecurity, for people powerful and knowledgeable enough to protect us are also powerful and knowledgeable enough to harm us. If we see people in authority as being ordinary human beings, lacking complete knowledge and power and able to err, then we may be less protected by them but we are also less in danger from them. "I've never looked at it like that," said Carol, "because I've always looked up to anyone like a doctor. I've always put them higher than the ordinary level. I've always thought that they should know. It's their job so they should know."

Q. "When you say, 'They should know' that carries with it the idea that you'll get angry if they don't know." *A*. "Yes. But if I could work out that Peter should have another check-up, why didn't they?" *Q*. "The only answer is that they're human beings and like all human beings they don't always do their job properly." *A*. "I only see things one way. I don't seem to be able to see another point of view. That's really, partly it."

Like all people impressed by authority, Carol had a need to defy it. When talking about being in hospital Carol said, "I always feel like being a real rebel and when the nurses say, 'Come on,' if I dare, just sit there and really defy them and say, 'I'm not,' but I wouldn't dare. I would cause too much trouble. Mind you, I might enjoy it, but I doubt if anyone else would."

Q. "Why is it important to be a rebel?" *A*. "Possibly to show a will of my own. That I'm not going to be pushed, because that — know up to a point you've got to be helped, but there's a difference between being helped and being made. I remember when I went in hospital I wanted to be quiet. I didn't want to stick shells on tins. I had plenty of occupational therapy at home. I'd come to hospital to get better. But you've got to watch yourself in there or you'll get into lumber."   *Q*. "You want to be a rebel but you're scared that if you do do this you'll get into trouble."   *A*. "Yes. I think that's why I tend to rear up at home with Bob because I think to myself, 'I'm not having that. That's not fair,' when I don't suppose it matters that much but I've got to make my point. I know sometimes that I'm being terribly awkward. It's like last night. Bob said, 'Which programme do you want to watch?' I said, 'You choose, because whichever one you want I shall want the other just so I can be awkward.' 'Why?' 'Because I just want to be.' I knew damn well I was just being awkward. That's ridiculous."

It was also immensely pleasurable. Time and time again when Carol was telling me about how awkward she had been her eyes would light up with glee and she would exclaim, "Oh, I am awful! I am rotten, I know." She treasured her resentments just as much. "I think I can forgive, but I don't think I could forget. This is my trouble. I never forget. With us when the air gets heated between us we tend to bring all these things back. I've got to have something to fire at Bob when he starts on me. I'm grateful that Bob has put up with me. But gratitude can only go so far. You get to the point where you're just taken for granted. I've realized that after thirteen years of marriage I was never a person that could say I was sorry. That was a lot of our trouble. I keep things inside and build up a resentment."

One day Carol told me how she had managed to go to town by herself. "I walked to town which was a brave thing to do because I haven't been to town for quite a while and to go on my own was a bit brave."

Q. "What do you find frightening about going to town?"   *A*. "I don't really know. Whether it's the crowds — the jabble of people and all the voices. Sometimes it can be a feeling of insecurity and I need somebody with me to hold my hand. Something might happen to me — fainting in the middle of all those people and being trampled. Thinking about it, it's the same kind of fear I used to have from going to the secondary modern school. When I was about eleven this fear came on me. Assembly in the morning used to be a dreadful ordeal for me because in the hall you get everybody crowded in. I used to have this terrible fear that I should probably faint. It used to happen to other girls. Suddenly somebody would drop just like that and I had this terrible fear of it happening to me. I was probably frightened of making a fool of myself. It never entered my head to opt out. I always tried to get near the end of the line. I felt safer then. I always had the same feeling when I went to church. I used to stand and grip my toes to keep the blood circulating. I was a fat kid and I was very conscious of it. I was as fat as I was long. I'd cause such a stir-up if I fainted."

Carol had fainted in public only once. On her first admission to hospital she had had the injection to prepare her for ECT and was standing in the corridor, waiting her turn, when suddenly she fainted. She fell on her face and smashed her front teeth. Her fear of fainting became even greater when next day she was asked by the staff if she had staged a faint to draw attention to herself. However, one benefit did derive from this incident. Instead of having to follow the ward programme of activities she was allowed to sit quietly in her room and watch the birds. This gave her the strength to face the outside world. Back home she sought this kind of peace in sleep. "To me, sleep is a release. When I'm not well, if I can go to sleep and not dream, I can wake up and everything's clear, and I feel better, but if I go and have these stupid dreams I think I wake up worse than when I went to sleep, so then I go off to sleep again to see if I can wake up the next time on a different plane. I like to dream nice dreams. I don't like these muddled ones. I can't make sense of them." One of the muddled dreams which worried her concerned a visit to a fortune-teller. "My turn came to go in and I remember asking her a question which made her very angry, and I had to beg for forgiveness in terror of my life. Then all the people and the fortune-teller were around us and were laughing and mocking us. I woke up very frightened and disturbed."

Carol often told me anecdotes of family life in which she had expected the worst and was not disappointed. On a visit to a neighbour, "I was just waiting for Peter to smash that Chinese lamp. I was thinking all the time, 'He will do it, he will do it.' Anyway he knocked over some plastic ornaments — but I knew he would." When I asked her how she knew these things would happen she said, "Premonitions. More often than not when I've thought of something it's happened."

Q. "Does that worry you?" A. "No. I think it's an advantage in one way. I think there must be something in it. I get a sort of feeling. You can't always say directly what's going to happen. It's an inspiration that suddenly comes over me that there might be some trouble. It doesn't worry me. In fact, I think it's an advantage." Q. "It allows you to start worrying sooner." A. "Possibly. When the car didn't pass its test I wasn't a bit surprised. I could not get out of my mind about the accident my cousin had. Whether somebody's giving me a bang on the head and giving me these premonitions! I wish they'd give me nice premonitions — so that things would still be all right — so I didn't have to guard myself."

So Carol lived in a constant state of fear. She was also in a constant state of guilt about her bad temper. "My guilty feeling make me punish myself and the more guilty feelings I get the more irritable I become. It's a vicious circle."

Q. "Do you ever forgive yourself for losing your temper?" A. "No. I always have it all at the back of my mind .... I'm trying to get away from myself. I'm striving to be different, to be calm, placid, all the things I'm not. But, as fast as I try to shake things off, something seems to pop up to hold me back or to hinder me. It seems to be all these frustrating things that make me irritable and worked up. There always seems to be something, somewhere or someone who's holding me back. I don't know who it is or what it is. I just can't win whatever I try to do. These things, they're only drops in the ocean, really, but to me they seem like mountains. I've got to face up to them. I let myself in for them. All these things with doctors and dentists and hospitals. Like with Peter, I wanted him examined again and now it's come through it's like another hurdle to be got over. Something to worry about. Like my mother says, 'The more you try the more you may'. I never get over one mountain and think, 'I'm there,' because looming up in the distance there's something else. There's never a clear view in front. If ever I've thought to myself 'Things are going quite well. We seem to be on a quite level plain,' lo and behold something happens and there it is again, a great big mountain. It's tempting Providence."

Life then was a series of mountains to climb, in the endeavour to get everything right, to find a clear and open plain. When Carol described her image of mountains and valleys it seemed obvious that she was using the name of a geographical feature when she said "plain". However, when she told me of how she envisaged heaven, it seemed that this plain also incorporated its homonym "plane", with its meaning of a grade of development. The reason she had to get everything "shipshape and Bristol fashion" in this world, on this plane, was "if I pop off everything will be in order. There won't be any mistakes or muddles. In the next world I'll look back on what I've done wrong. Then I would try and do my best to help those that were on this world to help them get shipshape. I'd feel I still had a job to do. I feel we're on this earth for a purpose. I don't think we die and that's it. It's the Christian religion, life after death, and I feel when you go on to the next world you are there and you are helping those in this world. I think that by helping those in this world you are then getting yourself on a higher plane possibly in the next world. I don't believe that one goes straight up to God, wherever God is. But I feel that one even in the next world has to work one's way. It's in stages. What one does in this world helps towards the next and then what you do in the next, helping down in this world, helps you towards greater things. There is no end of worlds. 'In my Father's house there are many mansions.' "

Q. "Eventually you get to the final stage?" A. "If there is a final stage. But possibly there isn't. There could be rebirth." Q. "And do it all again?" A. "Maybe." Q. "So you're working on what you're doing here in this world with a view to what's to be done in the next world." A. "Yes, I'm trying to." Q. "That's why, today, on the first day of the summer holidays, you're making a list of the clothes the boys will need next term?" A. "Yes." Q. "Suppose I told you that you're to rest. You're not to do these things, and then you died." A. "I should still hope I could get back and help. I think possibly dying is like being born. You don't remember being born, do you? So you won't remember dying. My earliest recollection is when I wouldn't go for a walk with my father. He gave me a good slap. You don't remember dying until something suddenly clicks and you start work. I don't think God punishes so long as you ask forgiveness. I think I shall wake up in heaven and someone will say, 'Look down and see what you can do to help.' " *Q*. "How do you think your family will feel when you die?" *A*. "Very sorry. I think it would cut Bob to pieces. I've got the feeling that Bob will get to the age his father died and he'll go. When Bob's father died, Bob's mother said, 'They're not a long-lived family.' All I want is that I shouldn't be left. I have a terrible fear of that. I've never been right since his dad died." *Q*. "Do you see yourself as joining Bob in heaven?" *A*. "Definitely. In time. I don't think it happens straight away. Probably I would have to do a little work because he'd be on a higher plane if he went first. Sort of find him by working. I feel that what you sow here you reap in the next and what you sow in the next you reap in the one after that. If I chose to die by my own hand I would be stopped by the possiblity that I wouldn't get to where I wanted to go because I had done that which I think is wrong."

When I suggested that other people saw the afterlife in different ways Carol said, "I can't see anyone else's point of view. I have got my set idea of what it is. I don't think that when you go up there that you're working all the time. There must be tranquil places. To me, if somebody's died of a nasty illness, say cancer, obviously when they get up there they can't set to work straight away. There would have to be a period of hospitalization to repair them, to heal them. I think that God forgives you if you are truly sorry, but you've got to be truly sorry. You sin in fact if you snap at your next-door neighbour or land out at your kids when they don't deserve it. When you take your frustration out on others. It's all those sort of things that are sinful. They're terrible. I'm bitterly ashamed of them. I feel terribly guilty about it."

Q. "You feel that God has made a record of all this?" *A*. "I do, yes, I do. You know how I feel that a lot of my trouble is because of my mother. Well, I feel that one day she's going to go up there and she's going to look down and she's going to see things in a different light and she'll see the reason why things are like they are now and that's really why I just can't turn round and tell her. It wouldn't be right. I would be recorded up there." *Q*. "Do you feel that when she dies and goes to heaven she'll make things more difficult for you?" *A*. "No, they'll not let her do that. Because those that are up there, they're there to help. And they wouldn't let her do that. I feel if I can manage to keep quiet now and hold my tongue and hold my temper, I feel that when she goes she'll be able to see things differently. She's going to be able to look down and realize then what, why and wherefore."

Like Carol, Bob believed in a life after death. He believed that he would become a spirit which went to another sphere. People who lived a Christian life would go to one sphere and evil people to another, but contriteness for one's sins, however late, could save. He believed firmly in the existence of good and bad spirits. People who helped others were guided by good spirits, but cruel people were guided by evil spirits. However, the good spirits were always as strong as the evil spirits. He saw life as constantly renewing itself and when something died, something else was born. He saw himself fitting into this pattern and his children as a continuation of himself. Seeing life in this way, he would never desert his family no matter how difficult Carol might be. It was an optimistic philosophy, but his separation of spirit and body played some part in the misunderstandings which arose when he and Carol tried to be lovers.

Carol believed in good and evil spirits and feared that, "I had got some evil in me. If evil has a chance to creep in then it will do so. It can take over the good. But I don't think you're altogether aware of it. Evil to me is cold and it creeps. Unless you have some strong force of good inside you or helping you, evil can take you over. Evil can't be warm, that is, not unless you become overcome with evil and then you will enjoy it. There is the comfort of being evil."

Q. "If you painted a picture of evil, what would you paint?" A. "Ice and snow and black and grey. The devil with horns and spikes. It would be black. Anything that could drag you down." Q. "If you painted a picture of being depressed, of being in the pit, what would that look like?" A. "A very deep pit. Bottomless, well, not entirely bottomless but so steep you couldn't climb out. Much as you tried, the more you tried to grovel your way up, the more you would slide. Grey and nothing, like you see when a volcano's erupted, all the lava, when it's died down, all that sort of clinkery, burnt-away, nothingness, no life, nothing colourful in it at all, no colour or anything like that. The darker it was, the worse it would be to me." Q. "If you painted a picture of that force of good, what would you paint?" Q. "Warmth, sunshine, flowers, greenery — all the beautiful things — all the things you get pleasure out of looking at — not material things — I mean the trees and the birds, the flowers, the sun and the stars. A new-born baby, that's good, that's warm and good to me. And children — little children. By the time you're five there might be a nice warm mum at home, but you already know a bigger boy who kicks you. A few years ago I could go by and never see any beauty in anything. Bob would say, 'Oh, look, isn't that lovely!' All I could see was black."

As time went by Carol found that, while she still became overactive and then depressed, her experiences were no longer so extreme. She came to realize that her depression was "only me crying out for someone to take notice of me. That was the only way I could make people understand that I could stand the pressures. It was me who was always on duty. I am frightened to death that when I get better they will just sling everything back on me. I'm frightened they will think I'm better and that's it. It really shook me to find that out about myself — to find out that I'm as frightened of getting better as I am of getting more depressed." Once, when all she could see was black, Carol wrote a prose poem which she called "My Experience of Depression".

"Oh, the torment, the agony, waiting for the daylight hour.
Knowing when it comes, one is even more alone,
Busy housewives, hurrying tradesmen, watching, seeing but not being able to compete.
Despair, distress, anger, frustration.
All hope gone.
Trying to work out why. *Muddled thoughts, not belonging to myself, not wanting to belong.*
No feeling, just cold, cold ice.
Life goes on, but without me, I, not really *seeing or caring of the world about me.*
The seasons come and go and I cling helplessly to my own four walls.
Safe sometimes, but so afraid, but of what?
Sometimes sleep brings blessed relief, sometimes torment of dreams. Real or just fantasy?
Trying to cope, knowing the useless mess I am making.
Tears flow endlessly, not of sorrow, but of the inability,
shame and disgust of my useless self.
Why? Why? There is no answer.
Pills to pep one up, pills to calm one down.
Am I a human being or just a robot?
Five years of my life gone, where?
Desperately clinging to the hope that something or someone will help me.
Pills, treatment, pills, more pills, different pills.
'Oh, you will get better.'
'But when? How?' I say.
They say, 'Just carry on.'
Do they really know how hard it is to do just that?
Then out of the darkness comes a ray of light, someone to listen, someone who does understand, and helps me sort out my muddle.
Helps me back slowly to being a person.
It takes time, there is no limit.
I have bad days, sometimes weeks.
The road back to health is hard, but the outlook is brighter, if not altogether secure as yet.
If only one could take those who don't understand on a quick trip through the experiences I have written down,
it might help to dispel their fears of us.
Then perhaps they wouldn't be so quick to give advice on the best way to get better."

13

THE GROUPS OF PROPOSITIONS WHICH ENCLOSED THEM

> *"If Mrs. Guinea had given me a ticket to Europe, or a round-the-world cruise, it wouldn't have made one scrap of difference to me, because wherever I sat — on the deck of a ship or at a street cafe in Paris or Bangkok — I would be sitting under the same glass bell jar, stewing in my own sour air."*
> SYLVIA PLATH, *The Bell Jar*

We can consider depression to be that experience which accompanies the selection from the set of possible groups of propositions of a person's language structure of that particular group of propositions whereby the person sees himself as being cut off from and as choosing to be cut off from interactions with others, both people in his external reality (e.g., wife, friends) and figures in his internal reality (e.g., his God, happy memories of his dead mother, his good self, his successful future).

When we operate with a group of propositions which allows us to interact with our world, we experience a sense of the outgoing of the spirit, a sense of the force of life, a sense of freedom and movement which may range from mild placidity through vigour and vitality to immense and marvellous joy, relish and delight. Such an experience is accompanied by some degree of confidence, creativity, optimism, courage and benevolence. When we operate with a group of propositions which enclose, we feel that we merely exist, that we are diminished, constricted, isolated, inhibited, helpless, despondent, anguished, barren, desolate, fearful, pessimistic and bitter.

The propositions which enclose concern:
not trusting others,
envying others,
wanting revenge on others,
rejecting others,
feeling unloved, unloving, unforgiving, unforgiven,
feeling ignored by others, disparaged by others, unable to communicate with others, not understood by others,

feeling confused, in conflict, incompetent, different from others,

feeling that other people are dangerous, that one is disliked, that one cannot be loved for oneself alone but only for what one does, that one's burdens are greater than anyone else's,

feeling that one is bad, abnormal, mad, ugly, that one cannot change,

feeling disappointed with one's past life, that nothing good can be expected in the future, that the world is uninteresting, that it is dangerous,

fearing other people's anger, the power of others, rejection by others, loss of individuality,

fearing that one will go out of control, go mad,

fearing to become attached to others, to be seen to be happy, to do anything less than perfectly, to make a decision, to excel, to be an individual, to be self-assertive, to reveal oneself to others, to change,

feeling guilty because one is disliked, gets angry, makes others angry, distresses others, has not met one's responsibilities to others, has not lived up to one's own expectations,

fearing isolation, chaos, annihilation, death.

It is possible to go through the conversations, reported here and identify those statements which together serve to enclose each person. It is obvious that these statements are so interlinked that, while we may refer to each set by means of a spatial metaphor, "propositions which enclose", "a network of sentences", it would be impossible to represent accurately their relationships to one another in any diagrammatic way, to reduce the relationships to three dimensions. Nor is it possible to show the relationships by means of logic without making this account infinitely long. Some statements which can be deduced from other statements can themselves be premises, and as such all coexist. It seems, as Russell (1956) has suggested, that it is impossible to have a logically perfect language. Many of the relationships between the propositions would need to be examined by means of modal logic, the logic of possibility and necessity. Statements like "If my mother had loved me, how different my life would have been" refer to a host of possible worlds. Again, the link between propositions can be by metaphor, by image or by an ambiguity which requires an Empson to analyse. When Kay declared, "I think everyone is attached to their mother" she implied, perhaps, that "attached" means both "loves" and "part of", and by this one statement described and justified her lack of independence. Again, when Kay cried, "Why should my daughter be the one whose mother doesn't love her," she presented the paradox that the mother who does not love her daughter is also the mother who resents that her daughter has been singled out for the deprivation. This resentment implies a concern by the mother for the girl, even if it is no more than that of injured pride, that some aspect of herself (her child) has suffered damage.

There are propositions that we rarely bring into full consciousness or, when we do, we rarely question them, for we regard them as axiomatic in our structure of the world. A group of propositions need not come into clear consciousness for us to act on them. Nevertheless, it is possible for us to explain our actions in terms of these propositions. Of all the various groups of propositions available to us, some groups are more available, more persistently used than others, though changes from one group to another can be abrupt.

The following are lists of the groups of propositions which served to enclose each of these nine people. Each list is probably not complete, since we did not cover every aspect of each person's life. The meaning of each statement could, of course, be expressed in a number of ways. "I don't trust other people" could be put as "I think that people are not trustworthy". These lists are illustrative rather than exhaustive.

Joan's Group of Propositions
I don't trust other people.
If someone dislikes me it must be my fault.
If someone gets angry with me I don't want to have anything more to do with that person.
If I discuss my angry feelings I shall become angrier.
If I show my anger I may go out of control.
A good person never gets angry.
I am different from everyone else.
There is something wrong with me.
I have never been normal.
If I did not get depressed something worse would happen to me.
People take no notice of me.
I don't want people to notice me because I am so big and ugly.
My husband does not love me the way I want him to love me.
My mother does not love me.
My dream of becoming part of a large, loving family will never come true.
I must never get attached to anybody.
If I loved someone I should be hurt when I lost that person.
If I loved someone that person would have power over me.
If I depend on anyone that person will reject me.
I prefer to be depressed than to form close relationships.
In a close relationship the other person would expect me to give up being myself.
In a close relationship one person always tries to destroy the other.
By being a martyr I can avoid being destroyed by guilt.
No matter what my husband does I feel hard done by.
When I am depressed my husband is nicer to me.
My relatives do not allow me to be myself.
My husband does not like to see the children or me enjoying ourselves.
I have no choice; my burdens are thrust upon me.
When life gets too complicated I can escape by becoming depressed.
I cannot change myself.
Some great, beautiful thing is missing from my life.
I cannot find an ideal mother.
I must revenge myself on my mother and my husband.

238

Mary's Group of Propositions

If I decide to do something myself someone will get angry with me.

I must do things properly.

It is wrong to owe money.

People who are careful with money are not concerned with what people think or whether they are hurt.

If I am careful with money people do not like me and if I am not careful I feel frightened.

I want to keep on the right side of everybody.

I feel guilty if I upset anybody.

If I behave like my sister people will not like me.

If I bother too much about other people I lose my individuality and people use me.

If I don't bother about people they won't like me.

Everyone uses me as a doormat.

People give me things they don't want as presents and that puts me down.

If anyone gets angry with me that person no longer likes me.

If anyone gets angry with me it is my· fault.

I must not defy my father.

My father is very powerful.

It is dangerous to excel at anything.

It is better to be an ordinary person than a special person.

My father wants me to be a special person, the sort of person he wants me to be, so he can feel proud of himself.

My father makes me very angry but I am afraid to let him know this.

My father always tells me what to do.

Fathers should be obeyed because parents know best.

I feel sorry for my father because I know he cares for me.

My mother would not dare to protect me from my father.

I feel guilty about being happy when my mother is unhappy.

My father is jealous of anything that makes me happy.

People who take things seriously do things properly.

I envy my sister because she always finds life easy.

If Robert really cared for me he would be more serious.

The outside world is dangerous.

I am safe at home.

I feel guilty if I am away from home for long.

When I die I want to be forgotten so that I shall not feel guilty about upsetting my family.

If my family do not feel upset at my death it will mean that they do not love me.

If Robert gets upset I feel guilty and if he doesn't get upset I feel unloved.

I have lost my baby.

If I have another baby I am afraid it will be taken from me.

John's Group of Propositions

If I am not tidy I shall not be accepted by others.

If I don't conform I shall be rejected by others.
If I am a domineering person people will dislike me.
If I care about other people I worry about other people.
When I worry about other people I get depressed.
If I use other people I shall be like my father.
If I don't help other people I shall be like my father.
If I am like my father I shall argue with other people.
If I argue with people I hurt them and feel sorry for them.
If I argue with people I get punished.
If I leave my family I have nowhere to go.
If I am on my own I cease to exist.
If I have a panic attack in a certain place I can't go there again.
If I go near deep water I shall panic.
If I go up high buildings I shall panic.
If I go again to a place where I have panicked I may cease to exist.
If I left my family I couldn't go back.
If I run around in circles I feel guilty because I am not achieving anything.
If I am cremated I shall be wiped out and forgotten.
If I don't love my family they will forget me when I die.
If I have lead a good life it still does not compensate me for having to die.
If I am kind and good that will not stop me from dying.
If I forget Paul then I shall be forgotten when I die.
If I take up a burden I have to carry it on my own.
If I can't talk to someone about my problems I get tensed up and depressed.
If I get depressed I am letting people down.
If I get depressed I can't talk to people.
If I do not earn enough money people will attack me.
If I have too much money I shall be greedy.
If I am greedy I shall be like my father.
If I am like my father I won't trust my wife.
If I don't trust my wife I shall despise myself.
If I don't save my money I shall anger my wife.
If I get angry I get upset.
If I get angry I feel a fool and can't face the other person again.
If I don't think about the pros and cons of an argument I put myself in danger.
If I win an argument I am putting someone down.
If I hurt another person I feel hurt myself.
If I am hurt I feel helpless.
If I had a job I liked I would not earn enough money.
If I am in a routine I lose my freedom.
If I lose my freedom I become frightened.

Rose's Group of Propositions
I don't want to change: I am honest: I stick up for myself: I would never lie: I am a good worker.

I liked playing the piano but I had to give it up.
I would have liked to have stayed on at school.
I would have liked to have been an engine-driver.
I would rather work in the open air than be shut up in the house doing housework.
I was not allowed to be what I wanted to be.
My mother preferred her sons to her daughters.
My mother was not fair to me.
I am afraid of my father.
I thought that my husband would look after me but he didn't.
My husband could have worked hard and been successful.
My husband preferred other women to me.
My husband broke his promise.
My husband lied.
I would not give in to my husband.
My husband spoiled my life.
I lost all my feelings.
Perhaps my husband never loved me.
When I got my separation I knew that he would never come back.
I hoped everything would turn out all right.
I want to run away but I have nowhere to run to.
If I left the children I would feel guilty.
I wanted my children to have a better life than I did.
My best friend is dead.
I never planned my future.
I never asked for help unless I could pay for it in some way.
I am frightened to be on my own.
To be good I must be useful.
It is wrong to look after myself.
Heaven is being good and doing what you can for other people.
I must do my best so I can meet my Maker on Judgment Day.
There must be a God because there wouldn't be such beautiful things if there wasn't a God.
Being shut in is like being in a coffin and buried under the earth.
I must be clean when I meet my Maker.

Helen's Group of Propositions
I despise myself.
I am frightened of myself.
I am a failure.
I let people down.
I never help other people.
I am scared to lead my own life.
I have no will-power.
I feel guilty about myself.
I am a burden to others.

My mother rejects me.

I am angry with my mother.

My father rejects me.

I am frightened of my father.

My husband rejects me.

I am frightened of my husband.

Life must have a purpose.

I have no purpose.

I am frightened to eat in front of other people.

I am frightened of what other people think of me.

I am boring and uninteresting to other people.

If I let anyone know the real me I shall be hurt again.

I am not worth loving.

If I had to become the person my husband wanted me to be I should despise myself.

I cannot communicate with my husband.

I don't trust other people.

I cannot communicate with my mother.

If my mother loved me she would understand me.

I am frightened to make a decision.

It is my fault that my decisions turn out badly.

I always keep myself to myself.

I can't control my eating.

I can't lead the life I want to lead.

I want to fade away and die.

My parents have me at home only because they care what the neighbours think.

My parents would be relieved if I died.

I have high ideals.

I hate myself.

The food which comforts me makes me feel guilty.

An ordinary person is able to ignore important things.

I think important things should not be ignored or covered up.

I am not an ordinary person.

Ordinary people are accepted by others.

My parents say that I am impossible to live with.

If I don't eat my mother will not be able to ignore my misery and she would feel guilty.

If I left my parents they would never take me back.

If I were well my parents would ask me to leave.

I cannot accept full responsibility for myself.

Joe's Group of Propositions

Animals are better than people.

I do not understand myself.

I am frightened of what I might do.

If I am not cruel to people they might get out of hand.

242

By being changeable in mood I can stop people from getting out of hand.
I must limit the love I feel for my family and their love for me or else they will expect too much of me.
If my mother does not love me too much she will not be upset when I die and so I can avoid feeling guilty about dying.
If I upset people now I can make it up to them but if I upset them by dying I can't make it up to them.
It is dangerous to feel guilty.
It is dangerous to be curious.
If I am destructive I shall be punished.
If I am destructive I shall be recognized as an individual.
If I take second best now I shall be given second best all my life.
If there is an afterlife then I can come back as a ghost and find out all that I want to find out.
I enjoy being nasty.
I must avoid the pain of being separated from the people I care about.
I can do this by not caring about anyone.
By being unhappy I can control people by making them feel sorry for me.
To love someone means to possess that person.
If I cannot have something that I want I destroy that thing.
If I cannot have Ann no one else shall have her.
If I cannot get what I want I would rather be dead.
I must remember Ann for always.
If I stopped loving Ann I would die of loneliness.
Ann likes to get me into trouble.
I like being in trouble because then people notice me.
A person who forgets people who were important to him is a person who is easily managed by other people.
If I forget Ann other people will be able to make me do whatever they want me to do.
I can be independent by being nasty.
A loving person is not independent.
God has the right to make people suffer.
God is moody and angry and sends people to hell.
The Devil is as powerful as God.
People are frightened of me.
By being a potential murderer I feel important and keep people away from me.
I don't want to grow up.
If I kill Ann I shall be treated as a child.
If I kill Ann it will show that I have courage.

Kay's Group of Propositions
I don't love my family.
I am in a turmoil and I can't get out.
I committed a sin when I married Jack without loving him.

I shall end my life in a mental hospital.
I am a naughty child who is about to be punished.
I am spoilt.
I am not considerate of other people.
I spite myself.
I deserve to be punished.
I cannot forgive myself.
Depression is my punishment.
I want to leave my family.
I cannot manage on my own.
If I stop struggling I shall die.
I don't deserve to be helped.
No one can cure a guilty conscience.
My family treat me as if I'm glass.
One part of me wants to be depressed.
My mother loves me too much.
My mother does not understand me.
I feel guilty about my mother.
I want to die so that my family will be sorry.
I don't do things for people and so I can't make up for what I have done.
I want to be liked so that I can make up for what I have done.
I am jealous of people who are happy.
If I hadn't married Jack I would have been a spinster because no one else would have
wanted me.
Jack has broken my spirit.
Neither Jack nor my mother believe that I have committed a sin.
They do not understand how I feel.
I feel guilty because I should have stopped Jack from punishing Steven so much.
I would like to be ill or die so as to punish Jack.
I want to hurt Jack.
I stop talking after an argument with Jack and I won't say that I am sorry.
Jack does not show me what he feels.
I need other people to tell me what to like and not to like.
Jack does not love me the way I want him to love me.
Sex is disgusting.
I looked after Jack's mother so that he would look after mine but he does not do this.
I pretended that I loved Jack and I was punished for lying.
I want to be like other people who are happy but there is something wrong with me.
I can never get at Steven.
I don't understand Steven.
I feel guilty because I don't worry about Steven.
I wanted Jack to be mates with Steven when he was young but he wouldn't.
Jack has broken Steven's spirit.
I hoped that Penny and I would be close but she is independent.
I dare not think about my mother's death.

I dare not argue with or criticize my mother.
My mother told me that sex was disgusting but she still had my brothers.
My mother was jealous of me and spoilt things for me.
My mother was jealous of anyone taking me away from her.
My mother is part of me.
My father does not understand me.
If I die before Jack I shall hurt him and I don't want to do that.
If Jack dies before me I won't be able to manage on my own.
I cannot forgive because I am stubborn.
By being stubborn I protect myself.
I have no ambitions.
I can't accept the rough with the smooth.
I am insecure.
I try to forget things that are unacceptable.
When something is difficult I give up trying.

Dave's Group of Propositions
I am unadventurous.
I am unstable.
I want to dominate and be dominated.
I want my own way.
I expect people to be nasty and hurtful.
I resent people criticizing me and teasing me.
I brood over things that annoy me.
I am frightened to go out.
My fear stops me from letting go of my anger.
I am unable to be responsible for myself.
I get blamed for things I did not do.
I cannot afford to feel sorry and to apologize.
I don't communicate with my parents.
It would be an achievement to kill myself.
I like to complete a job properly, but I can't do anything right.
I feel guilty about being selfish.
If I kill myself I shall be deserting my parents as I deserted them before.
I don't want to depend on others.
I am a danger to myself.
I don't trust women.
No matter how much I am punished I won't cry.
Instead of crying I get angry and this makes me feel drained-out.
I have no sympathy for people who cry.
When people are sympathetic to me I feel degraded.
I won't let people hurt me emotionally.
I ought to be punished when I do something wrong.
I don't communicate with my mates.
I am not a generous person.

I am a coward.

I am frightened of being close to my mother.

I am trying to reach a goal but I get no closer to it.

I am ashamed of doing anything that a woman does.

I am not part of my family.

My parents do not understand me.

I want to be as brave and hard as my father.

I lost my attachment to my parents.

I must be independent.

If I get upset and don't get over it by hitting out or killing myself I shall be rejected by other people or go mad or be damaged beyond repair.

I no longer get attached to places.

I quickly get bored with places and activities.

I feel guilty because I let my grandmother down.

I feel guilty because I should have saved my parents' marriage.

It was my fault my brother was punished so much.

If I committed suicide I would be able to find out if my parents really cared for me.

By committing suicide I can control my death.

I cannot forgive my mother.

If I forgave my mother I would be giving in to her.

My mother does not believe that I cannot work.

If I was close to my mother I would feel guilty because I would take advantage of her.

When my mother is affectionate to me I feel inferior.

It is dangerous to be dependent on my mother because that will make me soft.

I am in the power of forces outside my control.

I am disgusted by any suggestion that I have homosexual feelings.

It is wrong to talk to a woman about sex.

Carol's Group of Propositions

I hate myself.

I want everything to be perfect.

I cannot accept anything that is not perfect.

When the pressure gets too great I must withdraw and rest.

Life is not worth living but there is no relief on the other side.

I cannot communicate with God.

My mother makes trouble for me.

My mother is concerned only about herself and not about me.

I am frightened of my mother.

The more my mother thought she had hurt me the more she would try to hurt me.

My mother does not understand me.

I know what unpleasant things my mother is thinking, even if she does not say them.

When my mother is nice to me I feel in danger.

I cannot touch my mother.

My mother tries to turn me against my husband.

My mother is jealous of my affection for my father.
I cannot forgive my mother.
I cannot change.
I wish my mother loved me.
I am angry and bitter with my mother because she did not love me.
I am jealous because my mother gives my sons the love she never gave me.
My mother gave me things and then begrudged the giving.
My mother expects me to be perfect.
Bob and I cannot communicate.
My mother told me that sex was a duty which wives did not enjoy.
My marriage is not what I hoped it would be.
I will not share Bob with anyone else.
I don't like Bob to touch me.
I feel used by Bob.
I resent Bob.
I don't know what love is.
I have to push Bob to see how much he can stand.
I get angry with Bob because he does not worry about the things I worry about.
If I did not argue and stand up for myself I would become a cabbage.
Bob is impervious to what I say to him.
When Bob is nasty to me I am hurt and I bear a grudge.
I want to hurt Bob because he has hurt me.
I have to hurt or be hurt.
I don't know how to cope with being hurt.
I am afraid to relax my defences.
People try to hurt me.
If I shut things out I won't get hurt.
I don't trust other people.
Trust means complete loyalty.
Everything good I do is destroyed by others.
I can only value myself because of the work I do.
The easy way is never the best way.
If you've done something the hard way then you've done it properly.
The more responsibility you take on the more you'll get.
It is my fault my children aren't perfect.
I am criticized by others for not being perfect.
If I dislike someone I know I am right in my opinion.
My relatives take no notice of what I say.
People expect me to be silent.
I am frightened of people in authority.
People in authority should know everything and be able to look after me.
I am angry with people in authority when they fail to do this.
I want to be a rebel but I am afraid of what might happen.
I enjoy being awkward.
I forgive but I don't forget.

Because I don't forget I always have ammunition to fire at Bob.

If I am too grateful to Bob I shall be taken for granted.

I cannot say I am sorry.

I build up my resentments.

I am frightened to go into crowds in case I faint and make a fool of myself.

I always expect the worst.

I have premonitions of trouble.

It is an advantage to have bad premonitions because then I can be on guard.

I feel guilty about my bad temper.

I don't forgive myself for my bad temper.

There is always something to stop me achieving what I want to achieve.

I must get everything right in this world in preparation for the next.

By getting things right in the next world I can then go on to the next world after that and so on.

There is no end of worlds.

What you sow in one world you reap in the next.

God will not punish you so long as you feel guilty about what you have done.

I am afraid that Bob will die before me and that I shall not only be alone here but I shall never catch up with him in the other worlds.

I fear I have evil in me.

I fear that I may be taken over completely by evil.

By becoming depressed I make people take notice of me.

By becoming depressed I could get Bob to take over most of my responsibilities.

I am frightened to get better in case people expect me to take on responsibility again.

PART 3

General Considerations

14

SOME COMMON PROPOSITIONS

Images and Metaphors

" ... *as I walked back across the field I said now I am meeting it; now the old devil has got his spine through the waves .... Reality, so I thought, was unveiled. And there was something noble in feeling like this, not at all petty.*"

18th September, 1923

"*the end of* The Waves .... *I have netted that fin in the waste of water which appeared to me over the marshes out of my window at Rodmell when I was coming to the end of* The Lighthouse.*"

7th February, 1931
VIRGINIA WOOLF (1953)

The image of a fin appears often in the writing of Virginia Woolf. What she called "my vision of a fin rising on a wide, blank sea" her biographer, Quentin Bell, called "a signal of disaster", since it was so often associated with an episode of what was considered to be her manic-depressive illness. Quentin Bell saw a link between her illness and her creativity since Virginia had written, "One sees a fin passing far out .... I hazard a guess that it may be an impulse behind another book".

Virginia Woolf understood the nature of images. She saw that the important images in our life are formed when "in earliest childhood any turn in the wheel of sensation has the power to crystalize and transfix the moment upon which its gloom or radiance rests" (1967). This is like the moment of projection which Cassirer described. In such images the person is both passive and active, the victim and the aggressor, since *all* the image is part of the person. Such an image represents forces which are both dangerous and beneficial. To Virginia, the image of the fin was central to the experience which was called illness and to the experience which was called creativity. As she saw it, to give up one was to give up the other.

In *To the Lighthouse* Virginia Woolf showed the creation and persistence of an image which had the power to determine both a career and a persistent unhappiness. At the beginning of the book, six-year-old James, playing happily beside his mother, has his hopes of visiting the lighthouse dashed by his father. Years later, when he does set out for the lighthouse with his father, "James kept dreading the moment when he would look up and speak sharply to him about something or other. Why were they lagging about here? he would demand, or something unreasonable like that. And if he does, James thought, then I shall take a knife and strike him to the heart.

"He had always kept this old symbol of taking a knife and striking his father to the heart. Only, as he grew older, and sat staring at his father in an impotent rage, it was not him, that old man reading, whom he wanted to kill, but it was the thing that descended on him — without his knowing it perhaps: that fierce sudden black-winged harpy, with its talons and its beak cold and hard, that struck and struck at you (he could feel the beak on his bare legs, where it had struck when he was a child) and then made off, and there he was again, an old man, very sad, reading his book. That he would kill, that he would strike to the heart. Whatever he did — (and he might do anything, he felt, looking at the Lighthouse and the distant shore) whether he was in business, in a bank, a barrister, a man at the head of some enterprise, that he would fight, that he would track down and stamp out — tyranny, despotism, he called it — making people do what they did not want to do, cutting off their right to speak. How could any of them say, But I won't, when he said Come to the Lighthouse. Do this. Fetch me that. The black wings spread, and the hard beak tore."

He remembered a scene where "there was none of this gloom and none of this throwing of hands about; people spoke in an ordinary tone of voice .... It was in this world ... something, he remembered stayed and darkened over him; would not move; something flourished up in the air, something arid and sharp descended even there, like a blade, a scimitar, smiting through the leaves and flowers even of that happy world and making them shrivel and fall.

" 'It will rain,' he remembered his father saying. 'You won't be able to go to the Lighthouse.'

" ... The strain became acute. For in one moment if there was no breeze, his father would slap the covers of his book together and say: 'What's happening now? What are we dawdling about here for, eh?' as, once before he had brought his blade down among them on the terrace and she had gone stiff all over, and if there had been an axe handy, a knife, or anything with a sharp point, he would have seized it and struck his father through the heart. His mother had gone stiff all over, and then, her arm slackening, so that he felt she listened to him no longer, she had risen somehow and gone away and left him there, impotent, ridiculous, sitting on the floor grasping a pair of scissors."

Virginia Woolf's writings contain many images to do with water. She spent much of her childhood near the sea and it is perhaps no mere coincidence that she chose to die by drowning. Turgenev saw death in images of the sea. In *Spring Torrents* he described Sanin's *'taedium vitae'* and fear of death. "He saw himself sitting in a small, unsteady boat, staring at the dark silt of the sea bottom, where he could just discern shapeless monsters, like enormous fish. They were life's hazards — the illnesses, the griefs, madness, poverty, blindness .... Here he is, looking at them — and then one of the monsters begins to emerge from the murk, rising higher and higher, becoming ever more clearly, more repellently, clearly, discernible .... Another minute and its impact will overturn the boat." In *On the Eve* Turgenev writes, "Death is like a fisher who catches a fish in his net and leaves him for a while in the water; the fish is still swimming but the net is round him, and the fisher will draw him up — when he thinks fit." A few months before his death Turgenev said to a friend, "I was on the sea bottom, and I saw monsters and concatenations of the most hideous organisms, which no one has yet described because no one has ever come back to life after such a spectacle." (Schapiro, 1972)

The childhoods of Virginia Woolf and Turgenev are sufficiently well documented for us to know that each person had ample opportunity to form painful and frightening images. Recent research in child development suggests that babies have the capacity to give structure and meaning to their environment, particularly the appearance and sound of people, much earlier than had been supposed. Of course, loving adults have always smiled and cooed at babies, but what happens to the baby whose environment includes angry looks and threatening gestures, or immobility and silence? What kind of images does he form?

We all carry the images from our childhood. Sometimes we are unable to bring these images into clear consciousness, to describe them in words, perhaps because they existed before we were old enough to communicate by language, perhaps because we are not in the habit of inspecting our images. Sometimes we hesitate to inspect these images and to describe them to others since we fear that we are mad or may be considered to be mad. All we are aware of, or complain of, is the anxiety that these images provoke. This psychiatrists then describe as "anxiety state" or "free-floating anxiety". Whatever anxiety is, it is never free.

Each of the nine people described here has recalled enough from his childhood to suggest that each had ample opportunity to form the images which have such control over his life, since the images both frighten and fulfill. These images are part of the structure by which each person seeks to organize and to control his world. Of course, some parts of his world, like the existence of death, are difficult to frame into a comfortable pattern, though all of us try. Goethe explained death in terms of the daemonic. As he told his friend Eckermann, "Every exceptional man has a certain mission which he is destined to accomplish. When he has done so, his presence on earth in that form is no longer necessary, and Providence puts him to some other use. But since everything here below happens in a natural way, the daemons keep tripping him up until he finally succumbs. This is how it was with Napoleon and with many others. Mozart died in his thirty-sixth year, Raphael at about the same age, and Byron was only a little older. But they had perfectly fulfilled their appointed tasks, and no doubt were due to go, if there was to be anything else left for other people to do in this world .... The daemonic is that which intelligence and reason cannot account for. It is something external to my nature but to which I am subject." (Luke and Pick, 1966) Goethe was eighty when he said this. His structure of his world maintained his sense of his own worth, while it relieved him of the pain of mourning the early deaths of men of genius whom he admired.

The meaning that we place on death determines so many of our actions. Carol's determination to do everything perfectly and her anger and frustration at failing to do this which, to Bob, seemed most un-Christian, were all determined by her religious beliefs. The behaviour of the first Christian Roman Emperor was equally puzzling. Bainton, in his *History of Christianity*, records that "Some have assumed that Constantine's faith sat lightly upon him, since he was not baptised until he lay on his death bed. But this was not unusual: the Church taught that baptism washed away all previous sins, and in Constantine's time the prudent usually postponed receiving the sacrament until all their sins had been committed."

In my conversations with these nine people the images would appear in different guises, in dreams, in pictures seen in inkblots, in interpretations of works of art and in metaphor. Dave's metaphors were often of power. "The brooding part seems to be overpowering the other part." Helen saw Chris handing her security on a plate. For John "to cry" was "to break", to go to pieces, to lose existence. Kay said, "Everybody treats me as if I'm glass." In such a way she imaged her family as looking down at her, not touching, when she was dead and cold as glass. Glass, too, is fragile and does not respond to fingers that might explore it. Untouched, glass can retain its perfection.

Our metaphors are grounded in our earliest experience and grow outward from there. Thus "as if I'm glass" represents death, isolation, fragility, perfection, love given and love received. But it also represents an ordinary, real object. It is thought and reality in one. As Maurois said of Proust, "The artist ... realised ... that all valid thought has its roots in daily life, and that the 'role' of metaphor ... is to give strength to the Spirit by forcing it to renew its contacts with the Earth, its mother."

Conscience

> *"What is this self inside us, this silent observer,*
> *Severe and speechless critic, who can*
> *terrorise us*
> *And urge us on to futile activity,*
> *And in the end, judge us still more severely*
> *For the errors into which his own reproaches*
> *drove us?"*
> Lord Claverton in The Elder Statesman
> T.S. ELIOT

Colin Woodmansey set out to answer Lord Claverton's question when he wrote, "When a young child is engaged in a battle of wills with a parent who is determined to win, punishment and rebellion provoke each other in turn until a point must be reached beyond which the child dare not go. But then 'the child is at an impasse, at the end of his resources' (Dicks, 1939); for, however great his fear of reprisals and his urge to withdraw, he cannot just switch off at will the angry impulses compelling him to fight back each time he is punished. On the contrary, the greater his feeling of persecution the greater will be his anger and the greater his difficulty in controlling this.

"The child's own belligerent self, then, by preventing his escape from danger, will appear as the principal cause of his own suffering; so he will now feel towards himself the very hostility that — for the same reason — he previously felt towards his punishing parent, and condemn himself as he was first condemned by his parent, with whom, therefore, he may even come to feel that he is in alliance against his own rebellious self. The child, being now divided against himself, is no longer striving against his parent; and, because it thus extricates the child from the external fight (the memory of which is eventually repressed) this process is likely to become habitual, and the splitting of the ego permanent. Evidently there is now installed that 'critical agency within the ego ... (that has) ... cut itself off from the rest of the ego and come into conflict with it' : namely, the punitive superego." (Freud, 1921)

We have all gone through this process; we all have that critic, our superego, our conscience. Some of us have consciences who are firm but accepting friends who assure us that we shall do better next time, that our efforts will be successful, that happiness is our just desert. But some of us have no friend in our conscience. It whispers that we have sinned, that we shall fail because we deserve to fail, because "the Gods," as Virginia Woolf said, "must, when they have created happiness, grudge it" (1953). We give a special name to the fear that our conscience inspires — guilt.

The demands of a punitive conscience create boundless guilt and interminable conflicts, as the experiences of these nine people showed. Joe was torn between the kind person who wanted to be with Ann and the nasty person who wanted to hurt her. The consciences of Joe and of John commanded them to remember and this they had to do, despite the unhappy consequences. Rose's conscience valued her so little that she saw herself as being acceptable only when she was helping other people. When her children no longer needed her care and she was too old to work for others she had no way of appeasing her conscience. Dave's conscience told him that he should have saved his parents' marriage and, when he failed, punished him as Dave felt that he deserved to be punished. Kay's conscience told her that she deserved to be depressed. Carol's conscience set her the impossible task of achieving perfection. Helen's conscience forbade her to eat and Mary's never to upset anyone, while Joan's conscience urged her on to martyrdom.

The guilt that these people felt was not merely a painful sensation, the equivalent of the painful sensations that one experiences in the course of pneumonia or scarlet fever. The guilt related to specific acts of commission and omission, to the expectation of deserved punishment and to attempts to propitiate, to recompense. The keen observer could trace the connection between certain childhood experiences and the actions, provoked by guilt, of the adult. Leonard Woolf wrote of Virginia's father, Sir Leslie Stephen, "this fortunate man, whose bank balance was virtually impregnable, never stopped worrying himself and his children about money. He lived in a perpetual fear of bankruptcy, convinced every Monday morning that he was being ruined by what were called by Victorian fathers and their women folk the household books ... he sighed and groaned over the enormous sums they were spending on food, wages, light, coal — at this rate ruin stared them in the face and they would soon be in the workhouse." Later Leonard Woolf records that "one of the most troublesome symptoms of (Virginia's) breakdown was a refusal to eat ... she would maintain that she was not ill, that her mental condition was due to her own fault — laziness, inanition, gluttony. This was her attitude to food when she was in the depths of the depressive stage of her insanity. But something of this attitude remained with her always, even when she appeared to have completely recovered. It was always extremely difficult to induce her to eat enough food to keep her well .... Left to herself she ate extraordinarily little .... Below the surface of her mind ... there was, I felt, some strange, irrational sense of guilt."

The morality we learn in childhood is, as Oakeshott said, "a vernacular language". It is in this language that our conscience berates us, that we express our guilt or our excuses. "It was my fault my birds were killed," said Joe, "I should have looked after them better. It is Anne's fault that I am in here."

Even as our conscience berates us we can be performing the devious manoeuvres to repair or maintain our self-esteem. Reilly, in *The Cocktail Party*, speaks of the harm done by people who want to feel important, who

> *"are absorbed in the endless struggle*
> *To think well of themselves."*

It seems that there may be no limit to what we are prepared to suffer in order to be able to explain, to justify our actions in terms more noble than simply, "I wanted to do this". What better justification than in what Virginia Woolf saw in herself and described as "the queer, disreputable pleasure in being abused — in being a figure, in being a martyr" (1953). History is full of noble martyrs. The Slavs, at their defeat by the Turks at Kossovo, were among the noblest of them all. As Rebecca West records, "They knew that in this matter they were virtuous, therefore it was fitting that they should die." Such reasoning is commonplace amongst those people who see suicide as the logical and necessary outcome of their lives.

If suffering implies virtue, then by suffering we can think well of ourselves and so increase our sense of our own importance. Bainton recounts how, when Jerusalem fell before the Babylonians in 587 BC "The captive Jews sat by the waters of Babylon and wept. Why had Yahweh abandoned his people: as the psalmist sang, 'My God, why hast thou forsaken me?' When the Assyrian had just begun his oppressions, the prophet Isaiah answered this lament by asserting that the calamity was a chastisement for Israel's sins and that the Assyrian was the rod of God's anger. To propose that God was using this great empire to discipline a few tribes who had been faithless to his covenant was an audacious assumption. Israel put herself at the centre of world history, and by so doing she made her God the God of all the world, and the mightiest empires of the world but devices in his plan for his chosen people." The decision to view the disaster and suffering in this way seems to be an important factor in the survival of the Jews as a distinct group of people, but it also served to strengthen the link between the ideas of suffering and virtue which became a cornerstone of the Christian religion. In the third century AD "a graded system of penance was evolved in which the number of years of exclusion from the rites of the Church depended on the gravity of the offence. The concept of penance was developed as a sequel to baptism, which was believed to wash away all previous sins. Since baptism could not be repeated, martyrdom was regarded as a second baptism, a baptism of blood, remitting all the sins committed since the first baptism .... For those who had sinned after the original baptism and who might not suffer martyrdom, penance was available." (Bainton, 1967)

In martyrdom the person was considered to give up his will and to submit to the will of others. ("I have no choice," said Joan.) In *Murder in the Cathedral* Thomas à Becket, in his last sermon, explains this to his congregation. "A martyrdom is always the design of God, for His love of men, to warn them and to lead them, to bring them back to His ways. It is never the design of man; for the true martyr is he who has become the instrument of God, who has lost his will in the will of God, and who no longer desires anything for himself, not even the glory of being a martyr." The Fourth Knight, after the murder, puts another point of view. "There can be no inference except that he had determined upon a death by martyrdom ... when he had deliberately exasperated us beyond human endurance, he could still have easily escaped: he could have kept himself from us for long enough to allow our righteous anger to cool. That was just what he did not wish to happen; he insisted, while we were still inflamed by wrath, that the doors should be opened. Need I say more? I think, with these facts before you, you will unhesitatingly render a verdict of Suicide while of Unsound Mind. It is the only charitable verdict you can give, upon one who was, after all, a great man." Did Thomas à Becket sacrifice himself to the will of God or for his own greater glory? Does the woman who says that she has no choice but to sacrifice herself for her family do this because of a selfless concern for others or to give to herself a greater sense of her own importance? Is it either or both? How sensible is it to claim that "I am responsible for my family's happiness"? Perhaps there was something that Dave, at twelve, could have done to help his parents stay together. Perhaps if Kay had loved her husband when she married him her life and that of her family would have been entirely different. How can we decide if a sense of guilt is rational or irrational? Who is wise enough to judge? Any judgment we make can be made only from the standpoint of our individual value system. What to Kay was a sin appeared to me as no more than the foolishness of a young woman. Questions of morality are infinite and allow of no absolute and unequivocal answers.

This does not mean that we should give up asking these questions or content ourselves with simplistic answers. Our culture, our language, is full of concepts to do with guilt, reparation and propitiation, redemption, suffering, martyrdom, sin and virtue. A depressed person will describe some of his experience in these terms. To label this as no more than evidence of a symptom of an illness is to denigrate not only this person's experience, but the experience of all the people in the history of the human race who have pondered upon the meaning of life and who have tried, however unsuccessfully, to construct a morality by which we might live.

When we form our individual notions of what a good person is, of the person that we would like to be, we may set ourselves an impossible task since we have framed our definition in irreconcilable terms. We may strive to be an invincible individual who submits to the will of others, or a virtuous libertine, or a humanitarian egoist. Thus to succeed in one part of our definition is to fail in the other. Our conscience can never be satisfied.

The way in which we talk of our conscience, our superego, the way in which we frame our sentences when we talk to ourselves, "You shouldn't have done that",

"You must try harder", often leads us to think and act as if there are two people inside us, our ego and our superego. We tell a friend about our misdemeanours and if the friend says, "That's all right. I do the same myself" we, in the guise of our superego, think, "What a wicked person he is". If the friend says, "That was a terrible thing to do" we, in the guise of our ego, cringe under the blow and have the satisfaction of feeling aggrieved. In this way we can resist any attempts to take our suffering away from us. What we forget is that it is our language that gives the illusion of our body being inhabited by two people. We can describe our self as being made up of two selves or any number of selves, and by such a description illuminate some aspect of our experience, but all our experience all together is of one self, oneself. The child, "divided against himself", is in the situation described by Alan Watts as "it is as if I have been absorbed in a tug-of-war between my two hands, and had forgotten that both were mine".

The more a person becomes involved in this tug-of-war, absorbed in his guilt, the greater becomes his self-involvement, a continual self-inspection, a looking at everything from his own point of view. There is no time to be interested in other people or things except in how they reflect one's own situation. That mode of thought which began in interaction with others can so develop that it hampers to the point of destroying one's relationships with others.

Relationships with Others

> "Lucasta: 'How afraid one is of ... being hurt!'
>
> Colby: 'It's not the hurting that one would mind
> But the sense of desolation afterwards.' "
>
> T.S.ELIOT, *The Confidential Clerk*

In our efforts to avoid this sense of desolation that can eventuate from our relationships we often act in such a way that our relationships are impaired even further. Kant observed that moral principles can only be established through interaction with others. The accounts given by the nine people here show that the principles which they establish through their interaction with others, in the long run, did not draw them into closer contact with others nor preserve them from that sense of desolation.

Joe and Joan thought that they could avoid the hurt and desolation by limiting their love. They saw love from others as a threat to their independence. These principles ensured their loneliness. Rilke once observed that a man ceases to be lonely once he learns to make loneliness his home. Rilke's life suggests that this may be true, but perhaps a necessary prerequisite for this acceptance of the loneliness which is every person's lot is the experience of some personal success and the existence of love and friendship, all of which Rilke had available but Joe and Joan did not.

When one has learned, as Joe and Mary had learned, that other people are dangerous, one needs to construct an image of a perfect, changeless world, as Joe had done in his idyllic scene of Ann and himself in a meadow. But such a world does not protect one from daily encounters with people. In *The Waves*, Rhoda, who later killed herself, says, "I shall edge behind them as if I saw someone I know. But I know no one. I shall twitch the curtain and look at the moon. Draughts of oblivion shall quench my agitation. The door opens; the Tiger leaps. The door opens; terror rushes in; terror upon terror, pursuing me. Let me visit furtively the treasures I have laid apart. Pools lie on the other side of the world, reflecting marble columns. The swallow dips her wing in the dark pools. But here the door opens and people come; they come towards me. Throwing faint smiles to mask their cruelty, their indifference, they seize me. The swallow dips her wings; the moon rides through blue seas alone. I must take his hand; I must answer. But what answer shall I give? I am thrust back to stand burning in this clumsy, this ill-fitting body, to receive the shafts of his indifference and scorn, I who long for marble columns and pools on the other side of the world where the swallow dips her wings .... There is, then, a world immune from change. When I have passed through this drawing room flickering with tongues that cut me like knives, making me stammer, making me lie, I find faces rid of features, robed in beauty .... There is, then, a world immune from change. But I am not composed enough .... What I say is perpetually contradicted. Each time a door opens I am interrupted. I am not yet twenty-one. I am to be broken. I am to be derided all my life. I am to be cast up and down among these men and women, with their twitching faces, with their lying tongues, like a cork on a rough sea. Like a ribbon of weed I am flung far away every time the door opens. I am the foam that sweeps and fills the uttermost rims of the rocks with whiteness; I am also a girl, here in this room." (Woolf, 1974)

Suffering and deprivation do not ennoble the young child. Such experiences establish envy; they prevent the person from being able to share, as Kay, Carol and Joe describe. Such experiences develop the love that

> "seeketh only Self to please,
> To bind another to Its delight,
> Joys in another's loss of ease,
> And builds a Hell in Heaven's despite."

The opposite of refusing to share can be to sacrifice oneself. But, as Yeats said,

> *"Too long a sacrifice*
> *Can make a stone of the heart."*

When we have learned what a good relationship can be and then we lose that relationship through death, we sometimes try to deal with the sense of desolation by forming the principle of never forgetting, as Joe and John did. Proust, when writing of how he mourned his grandmother's death, described their experience. "For as the dead exist only in us, it is ourselves that we strike without ceasing when we persist in recalling the blows that we have dealt them. To these griefs, cruel as they were, I clung with all my might and main, for I realised that they were the effect of my memory of my grandmother, the proof that this memory which I had of her was really present in me. I felt that I did not really recall her save by grief and should have liked to feel driven yet deeper into me these nails which fastened the memory of her into my consciousness." (1967b) Proust's metaphor of the "nails which fastened the memory into my consciousness" with its evocation of the crucifixion captures the sense of pain, guilt, salvation through suffering, keeping faith, which prevented Joe and John from allowing their memories of Ann and of Paul to recede into the past.

When a person is depressed he seems, to others, to live in the past. He himself will complain that he cannot stop himself from remembering painful events. But it seems that these ever-present memories are not imposed on him by some autonomous force. They are there because they are memories which he feels he ought not to forget. They may be ways of holding on to someone whose existence, if only in memory, is essential to one's own continued existence. Or they may be ways of reassuring oneself that one has not forgotten a vow made long ago, "I shall never forgive you". A young child who finds himself completely in the power of an adult who is threatening and dangerous fears that he will be annihilated, destroyed as an individual by that adult. If he is old enough to know that another person, no matter how powerful, cannot know what he is thinking, then he can enjoy in his thoughts the revenge he dare not show in action. Sometimes he plans the revenge he will carry out when he is older, and so he will not forget he vows never to forgive. The idea that by forgiving one loses something of one's identity can be so basic to his way of relating to others that it becomes an unbreakable rule which prevents the development of the acceptance and understanding which is an integral part of a good relationship.

Sometimes having been hurt leaves one with the desire to hurt someone else. When Kay and Carol said that they wanted to hurt their husbands, this was not a mere blindly striking out but a kind of reaching out to another, a seeking of proof that the person on whom one depends is actually like oneself, a person able to be hurt. But, since each woman had little understanding of her husband, she did not realize that he did not react to hurt in the same way as she did and that he saw her as dangerous, so that no matter how much he was hurt, he dared not show any weakness. Had she known him better, she would have known that he was hurt.

Suffering does not necessarily promote understanding. If anything it militates against it. Those who have suffered see life as at extremes. Like Hitler, Joe could plot murder and then weep sentimentally over his love for his mother. Deprivation can leave the person longing for an impossible perfection as Joan, Carol and Helen longed for an impossibly perfect mother. Deprivation involves the person in a ceaseless round of self-observation, leaving him no time or desire to observe others disinterestedly, even, or perhaps especially, those people who are most important to him. Joe had no concept of Ann as a real person, a fifteen-year-old schoolgirl. Mary envied her sister Fay for always being happy, yet a casual observer could see that Fay was an anxious person. Not understanding, they found much which they could not forgive.

When a child receives a great deal of punishment from a parent or from a teacher whom he sees as in his parents' place, the child suffers not only pain of the punishment but also the pain of knowing that he is being punished by the person who should be his protector. If he continues to see his parent or teacher as being a bad person for inflicting such pain on him, then he has to see himself as being alone, without protection. To save himself from this second desolation he may decide that his parent or teacher was right to do what he did. In the words of Anna Freud, he "identifies with the aggressor". When he grows up he can be heard to declare, "I was thrashed when I was a boy and it never did me any harm". To preserve a good image of the people who had punished him he must refuse to question whether the punishment did do him any harm. He must push away any memory of the hurt and desolation.

The harm that identifying with the aggressor seems to do in the long run is to inhibit the development of insight and understanding. A person who has defended against hurt in this way is able to sympathize with suffering in those he sees as deserving sympathy, but in forbidding himself to introspect he has lost the key whereby we come to understand ourselves and so other people. As a result, he finds his own behaviour puzzling and to cope with this he develops a set of rigid rules for himself. Equally, he expects other people to conform to the rules which he follows, and when they fail to do this and persist in acting in ways which he misinterprets he feels mystified and cut off from others.

Rose was one such person. She had identified with her strict father. His strictness, his rules, had all been for the best. She fled from introspection into the company of others, where she maintained not so much a dialogue as a monologue. She could not tolerate to be alone and silent. Her descriptions of other people were mere sketches, accounts of what the people said or did, not of the way they hoped or feared. She had formed no theory as to why her husband had behaved as he did, but simply observed that he had broken the rules. She measured her worth by what she did for other people, but did not allow herself to see that her way of helping people was to avoid putting herself under any obligation to them and thus she was able to ward others off, to avoid the desolation of rejection. Except where she said she could have worked harder, she was sparing of self-criticism and self-questioning.

Endogenous depression is defined by psychiatrists as that which arises in a person whose personality, prior to the illness, was normal. Perhaps those people who earn the diagnosis of endogenous depression are those people who find it impossible to discuss with another person or even with themselves the matters which cause them the greatest pain. People with this diagnosis often find that their depression is relieved by a course of ECT. The reason for the success of ECT may not lie merely in the metabolic changes brought about by the ECT but in the fact that the person finds himself supported, cared for, in a way which he finds acceptable — love, comfort, reassurance given to him with a minimum of explanation required from him.

But Rose, like all the other people in the group, valued being able to talk to someone who listened. All these people changed in ways they found beneficial in the course of these conversations. Perhaps the conversations had something to do with this.

Change

> "I meant, there's no end to understand a
> person
> All one can do is to understand them better
> To keep up with them; so that as the other
> changes
> You can understand the change as soon as it
> happens,
> Though you couldn't have predicted it."
> Colby in The Confidential Clerk
> T.S. ELIOT

It would be satisfying to be able to explain how and why each of these nine people changed over the time they talked to me. During this time I made many predictions and spun many theories, but in the end came to agree with Colby. Why one person abandons one set of propositions and selects another set, only that person can tell. The most I could do was to recognize the change and so behave in what I hoped was an appropriate way.

It was easier to tell why a person did not change, why he would persist in operating with a group of propositions which cut him off from others and so ensured a continuance of the miseries of depression. As Virginia Woolf wrote of her own experience, "there are some compensations ... the dark world has its fascinations as well as its terrors" (1953). Each of the nine could describe the compensations and the fascinations of their experience, arising out of the implications of their propositions and out of the behaviour of their relatives, who often became kinder, more attentive, when the person was depressed. Propositions to do with personal vanity are always difficult to change when to do so means that we are to see ourselves as an unremarkable person in a world which is indifferent to our existence.

To change we often have to come to see our relatives differently, and this can be extremely difficult. The propositions that the nine people here used to describe their relatives were not the result of an overactive imagination. Many of the actions of the relatives, judged by people other than the sufferer, would still appear as hurtful, irritating or rejecting. The only way in which they could alter the propositions by which to judge their relatives was to develop a degree of disinterested tolerance, to distance themselves from their relatives, to see that people often behave in ways which we find irritating and hurtful but which spring from reasons which need not have any connection with us. Joan came to see her mother not as a dangerous witch but as a lonely old lady. Carol became indifferent to her mother's lack of affection for her, while Dave came to understand that much of his mother's irritability stemmed from her ill-health and not from a desire to persecute him.

Similarly, it is not easy for relatives to see the sufferer as being different when he attempts to change. As an obese person often finds, when he decides to diet, his relatives think of him as fat and do not want to change their perception to one of him as thin. Their attitudes can often prevent him from carrying out his purpose. In the same way, when a depressed person decides to change it often happens that the relatives, at the same time as they want the sufferer not to be depressed, do not want to go to the trouble of changing their own ways, and so they behave in such a way as to drive that person back into his isolation and depression.

So as not to make this book exceedingly long, I have not shown how in our conversations we went round and round that group of propositions which I have called the group of propositions which encloses. As time went by, each person became able to select another group of propositions and to operate in this, but then something would occur in each person's life, an argument in the family, a reminder of death, a fear that his life was changing too rapidly, and that person would fly back to the enclosing set of propositions with its attendant certainties and miseries. Over the time that we were talking together some of them, Mary, John, Helen and Dave, had people who were very important to them enter their lives and they had to adapt their set of propositions to this new situation. Mary, at last, had a child that was not taken from her, and this gave her the courage to do things which she could not do on her own. John found someone who understood him and who did not enclose him. Helen found someone who could prove to her that he loved her. Away from her parents' home her problems about eating disappeared. Dave found someone to care about and a renewed pleasure in carrying out a skilled trade.

If Rose remained on her own for too long she rapidly became anxious and depressed. She and her sister acquired a bungalow where they could look after one another and could keep the house as clean and neat as their father had ordered, but Rose found it hard to adapt to the change of home. Kay and Carol, whose circumscribed lives within their families allowed them to continue making the sorry round of their enclosing propositions, were pushed by me into Depressives Associated, a group of people who try to help one another to deal with depression and who try to inform the general public about the nature of depression. Joe found how much a person can help himself by helping others. Joan was the only one of the nine who, without changing her lifestyle, changed the way she saw herself and the world.

The experience of depression is the experience of the effects of isolation, of living in a frightening and dangerous world. In this century many people have had this kind of experience in the course of long-term imprisonment in solitary confinement and some of their number have attempted to describe not only what happened to them but also what stratagems they devised for survival. Cohen and Taylor recently surveyed the studies of psychological survival and concluded that "repeated affirmation by survivors suggests the first rule for any handbook on survival : *understand what is happening to you*".

The same rule applies for those who wish to survive the experience of depression. Unfortunately, so many depressed people, when they try to discover what is happening to them, are told that they have an illness which only a doctor can understand. Books on depression are rarely enlightening. What one needs in this situation is someone to talk with, someone who will not give advice and produce solutions, but who will help to unravel the complexities of one's thinking and feeling and to look at possible alternatives, someone whose presence ensures that the isolation is not complete.

When we use our language to structure our world we are creating a form which we call our life. This form contains our memories of our past, our hopes and expectations for our future, our image of ourselves as we see ourselves and as we think others see us, and our image of our activity in our world. We try to create a form, a life, which gives us a sense of mastery, of satisfaction, but sometimes we do not succeed. We create, instead, a form which gives us pain. Sometimes we can change the form we have created by entering into that kind of relationship which is called therapy. There are as many kinds of therapy as there are people to act as therapists, but therapy, in general, might be defined as the process whereby another person tries to help the suffering person to find a form which gives him a sense of mastery and satisfaction, and so relieves his suffering. Therapy is the process whereby two people try to build a thing which they do not know about, out of materials that they are not sure they have, a thing which they may not recognize when they have completed it; indeed, they may not know when they have completed it and, even if they do, each will see a different thing. To some extent, the therapist is the canvas on which the person paints his picture, but at the same time he is engaged in imposing his own picture on the artist. If therapy was simply like an artist creating a picture or a scientist improving the functioning of a machine, then we might be able to compare different therapies and therapists by comparing the pictures or machines they produce, but, as yet, neither aesthetics nor scientific method have evolved a technique by which to evaluate the forms created by the cooperation of the person and his therapist. Only the participants can judge. (This is not to say that we should not try to understand what happens.)

15

CONCLUSIONS

*"What makes the biological machinery of man
so powerful is that it modifies his actions
through his imagination. It makes him able to
symbolise, to project himself into the
consequences of his acts, to conceptualise his
plans and to weigh them one against another as
a system of values. We, as men, are unique, we
are the social solitaries, we are the creatures
who have to create values in order to elucidate
our own conduct, so that we learn from it and
can direct it into the future."*

JACOB BRONOWSKI

These words are from the last broadcast Jacob Bronowski made before his death. He called this talk "People Are Different from Rats". He would also say that people are different from machines, that they are more than bodies that are attacked by illness.

Because we have imagination, because we develop systems of values, because we can project ourselves, through our imagination, into other times and places, when we try to study ourselves we are faced with a far more complex task than when we study machines or bodies of animals. We can think of ourselves as if we were a machine, a body, or an animal, and we make some interesting discoveries within this framework, but such discoveries can never be anything more than partial answers to our questions about the nature of human beings. We may discover that in a human body under certain conditions certain metabolic changes take place. If we want to relate this finding to the question of why a human being behaves as he does, we then have to discover how the particular person who is undergoing this metabolic change perceives what is happening to his body and how he fits this perception into his system of values. Metabolic changes alone cannot account for our behaviour. A person develops his system of values through his interaction with others, not merely those in his immediate environment, but those whom he meets through all the media of communication. To understand why a person behaves as he does we need to discover how he perceives his own world (not the world as we see it, but the world as he sees it).

To understand why a person does what he does we should ask him under such conditions where he is disposed to tell us. Of course, a person will not talk freely and openly about himself if he believes that by doing so his questioner will think him mad, bad, stupid or inferior. None of us will talk freely to someone whom we see as being in a position of power over us, being able to consign us to gaol or to a psychiatric hospital, or to restrict our freedom in any way, or to take away our livelihood or to withhold benefits or privileges, or to draw our God's attention to our misdeeds. None of us will talk freely to someone who sees himself as superior to us, who will criticize, belittle and reject us. Free and truthful discussion is only possible between people who see each other as equal members of the human race.

Because we are so frightened of one another, because we so often want to be seen as more important, more powerful than other people, we rarely find ourselves in a situation where another person feels able to talk to us freely and so to explain how he sees himself and his world and thus behaves as he does. Other people, then, are puzzling to us and, rather than admit our bafflement, we lump them into large groups and stick labels on each group, groups like "psychiatric patients", "delinquents", "attempted suicides", "drug addicts", "the youth of today". We then attempt to explain the behaviour of these people by saying that they each contain some "thing" which causes and so explains their behaviour. The "thing" may be a "depressive illness", and "EEG pattern indicative of a brain dysfunction", a "death instinct", a "weak ego", a "recessive gene", "extraversion" or, if we have not learned that kind of jargon, we can say, "He got it from his father's side of the family". Our interest in the "thing" we have created can serve to hide from us the realization of how little we understand ourselves and other people. Until we learn to talk together without fear we shall not be able to progress in understanding the human race and its world.

Our progress in understanding ourselves and our world is not a matter of one day discovering The Answer. It is a matter of asking questions to which a good answer is one which allows us to frame a better question and from that an answer which creates another question and so on till we are no longer here to ask questions.

I have spent a great deal of time, far more than is reported in this book, in talking with depressed people and in observing what happened to them in the course of their treatment as psychiatric patients. I have also talked with many people who are not depressed. What I learned created for me many questions and few answers. I have tried to present some of these questions here and to offer answers which are framed, not as solutions, but as formulations from which better questions might come. Wittgenstein once remarked of St Thomas Aquinas that he did not make much of his answers, but he thought that his questions were good. I should be pleased to have the same said of this book.

Basically, I am questioning whether in the experience of depression there is an order of events similar to the order in a physical illness. For instance, the presence of a measles virus is followed by the symptoms of chills, fever, coryza and red macules. In a depression it is said that there is a metabolic change which is followed by the symptoms of a despairing mood, guilt, loss of confidence, loss of sexual drive and other symptoms. Could not there be another order of events such that a person sees himself and his world in such a way that he finds himself unable to escape from his isolation which itself intensifies his fear? The fear and the isolation, if prolonged, produce metabolic changes which can, to some extent, be mitigated by physical means. A depressed person will often complain to his psychiatrist that he feels guilty about not loving his family or that he and his wife cannot enjoy sex, only to be told by the psychiatrist that the guilt will disappear or the enjoyment of sex return when he has recovered from the depression. This answer is confusing, since the depressed person knows that he has always been inclined to limit his affections or that the enjoyment of sex can hardly return to a place where it has never been. This seems to me to be analogous to the situation where a prisoner in a cell complains about the walls and locked door of his cell, only to be told by someone outside that these will disappear once he stops being upset. To maintain that depression is an illness often seems to lead psychiatrists into situations where they use their language to obscure rather than to reveal reality. Proust, who, as a lifelong invalid, knew doctors well, once remarked, "Medicine, when it fails to cure the sick, busies itself with changing the sense of verbs and pronouns." (1967b)

To understand what a person says and why he says it we have to look at the social activity which provides the context for what is said. For instance, it is not surprising that doctors interpret certain phenomena as evidence of illness, since their education has been directed at training them to categorize using illness terms. It is, indeed, in their interest to define phenomena in the illness categories, for such categories bring the phenomena into the doctor's control. Presented with the same phenomena, architects would define it in architectural terms (e.g., "High-rise flats cause depression"); clergymen would define it in religious terms ("The depressed person is separated from God"); the sociologist in sociological terms (e.g., "Depression is the sign of alienation in a consumer society"); the anthropologist in anthropological terms (e.g., "Western culture is a depressive culture"); the behaviourist in behavioural terms (e.g., "Depression is an example of learned helplessness"), the psychoanalyst in psychoanalytic terms (e.g., "Depression is a desperate attempt to compel an orally incorporated object to grant forgiveness, love, and security"); and, of course, the personal construct theorist, whose own biases are well demonstrated here. All of these interpretations have a certain validity and a certain usefulness. In some contexts the categories into which we divide the phenomena, the propositions by which we evaluate them, serve to elucidate the situations, to allow us to progress freely and usefully. The same propositions in another context can only serve to confuse and hamper. When a person is so severely depressed that he is physically exhausted and his torment allows him no rest, to treat him as being ill seems the most sensible and effective alternative open to us. When he returns to physical health and can think about and discuss his predicament, to treat him as having an illness serves only to confuse him and to hamper his progress. The way in which certain propositions alter in their usefulness depending on the situation can be seen within a person's life. For Rose, the propositions which stood her in good stead during her working life were the ones which caused her such pain when she could no longer work.

Sometimes the context in which a person speaks is one which makes it necessary for him to lie. It would be naive to think that everything these nine people told me was an exact statement of the case as each of them saw it. No matter how much they might have wanted to trust me, experience had taught them to be careful, and the more important I became to them the greater was the risk of my disapproval. But lying is a difficult art, for the only way we can form a lie is out of our own experience. Thus each lie we tell tells something about ourselves. Even when we lie by omission, these gaps in our accounts serve to illuminate what we have presented. We cannot present anything other than ourselves.

What forces us to lie, to pretend to other people and to ourselves that our experience is different from what it is, is fear — fear of what others may do to us and fear of what we may do to ourselves, fear of our guilt, fear of fear itself.

Throughout the accounts of the people here runs the theme of fear, fear of being angry, fear of making others angry, fear of being rejected, fear of losing control, fear of death, fear of ordinary places, things, activities. They fear the future, their memories are of being frightened, their images are those of fear. They are like the people described by George Eliot, "men who have always been pressed by primitive want .... To them pain and mishap present a far wider range of possibilities than gladness and enjoyment: their imagination is almost barren of the images that feed desire and hope, but is all overgrown by recollections that are a perpetual pasture for fear." The "primitive wants" of which George Eliot speaks are mainly material needs. There is no doubt that poverty increases fear, but it is also obvious that we can live in ease and plenty and still fill our lives and the lives of our children with fear. It would seem that everything that is evil in this world comes from someone being afraid. Courage is the first virtue, because without it no other virtue is possible. So long as we bring children up in conditions that make them afraid, so much of the experience of human beings will be the experience of depression.

A friend, a psychiatrist, told me that he had experienced depression. I asked him if he would write an account of what had happened and this is what he wrote.

> "You asked me to write something along the lines of my own experiences of depression with particular regard to the components of anxiety, fear, and experiences of unreality. Such feelings are not easy to describe: our vocabulary — when it comes to talking about these things — is surprisingly limited. The exact quality of perception requires the resources of poetry to express.
>
> "What I remember telling you was the onset of my first (and most shattering) depression, together with the strange, frightening feelings that I had, somehow, to contend with. First, I had to accept the certainty of having become depressed. I remember feeling very isolated. For a while I became convinced that I was set apart. Everyone else seemed so well and confident. I marvelled that they (including my wife) were able to get through the day. I dreaded being left alone, and not, I think, because I feared succumbing to the temptation of killing myself (I was, in fact, far too slowed-up to do anything as complicated as that), but because isolation was intensified to an intolerable degree when the house was empty, and the time, as a consequence, hung more heavily than ever. My first inner response to the

realisation of being depressed (an experience at that time utterly new to me) was something like, 'My God, it's happened to me'. It seems now, on recollection, quite a melodramatic moment, but I assure you that I felt like a man who has been told that he has cancer, and that there's little or no hope. My position — or rather the feelings that convinced me that I was in an unusual position — at that time of senior psychiatric registrar intensified my isolation. The psychiatrist who is ill is in a very difficult situation: but I have commented on this elsewhere (Wakeling, 1975). However, I will just say this: my professional status caused me to feel not merely isolated, but positively trapped as well. The onset was quite sudden. Nevertheless, the night before I felt strangely anxious. I could not account for this feeling which again was new to me. Naturally I had felt anxious before but had always been able to satisfy myself — correctly or otherwise — as to the cause. But not this time. An unpleasant sense of dread filled me which three or four pints of beer did nothing to shift. In fact I might as well have drunk water. I went home and went to bed early. At five o'clock (I remember the time) I awoke into a different world. It was as though all had changed while I slept: that I awoke not into normal consciousness but into a nightmare. I got up and dressed, came down, then broke into tears and told my wife that I couldn't face going to work. I didn't. But I remained at home for only a short time: forcing myself back to work before any treatment had begun, and trying, of course, to convince myself that it would go away. It didn't. After much truly agonised cogitation I eventually plucked up the last remaining ounce of courage left to me and approached a nice, kind colleague who not only was a good friend but also knew little psychiatry. I found him — as they say — non-threatening, but, above all, kind. I wanted kindness, sympathy and the rest. He prescribed something for me, and said these reassuring words, 'I really am surprised — you don't look depressed to me.' It seemed inconceivable that I should look, apparently, normal.

"This brings me to the next experience — the horrible feeling that everyone could see that I was depressed. I dreaded meeting people. I was exquisitely vulnerable: like feeling that I was made of glass (not literally — I wasn't deluded).

"I told you of my feeling about Rembrandt : of how his pictures to this day possess a menacing quality, a gloomy depressing quality. I used to sit at home tears streaming (I wept more then, I am sure, than in the whole of my childhood) desperately trying to distract myself from the hellish state of seemingly perpetual misery I lived in with music and books. Perhaps I was drawn to Rembrandt by the strongly religious content of his work — and especially perhaps by the depiction of Jesus's sufferings. The guilt and atonement attracted me morbidly, I am sure. Music was the greatest comfort, but I could not endure light, happy music. I derived what can be called a truly cathartic support from music that expressed a mood in sympathy with my own. It sounds, I know, like a neurotic self-torture, but I assure you that it kept me going. At that time ordinary objects — chairs,

tables and the like — possessed a frightening, menacing quality which is very hard to describe vividly in the way that I was then affected. It was as though I lived in some kind of hell, containing nothing from which I could obtain relief or comfort. My wife was wonderfully supporting but even she seemed far away and inexplicably able to achieve what appeared to me to be miracles of confidence and initiative such as shopping and seeing to the children. I have lived then in blackness, grief, vulnerability and despair. Time itself changed. The day went on for ever; the nights lasted for centuries. And yet I do not think that I once thought of killing myself. I was too much retarded. I remember trying to read. It would take me an hour to finish a line. And yet I could recall nothing. I was able to sit almost motionless for hours. Actually, it was later — much later — when I was back at work and by then taking tablets and just about able to function that I took an overdose. One awful thing about my depression was the tremendous sense of guilt that I was unable to attach to any memory, or action or any part of myself. I was all feeling at that time and no thought — not real thinking, only a slow-motion kind of guilty rumination. Certainly I had no hope that the future would bring me relief, let alone happiness.

"The history of that depression is a long and to me painful one. Other depressions followed. They have been of the greatest value to me. As a consequence I have lost most of my former fear of death. I know now that I can get the better of depression and therefore I am not now afraid of depression. I know that I will not plumb the depths again — not those same depths, at any rate. I have experienced a far better, truer understanding of myself. I have become much nearer to my feelings. I have felt the sense of having been re-created. All that sounds rather pretentious, I know, but I can only say that it has been like that. Naturally the part that depression played in my development has been enhanced by others. Without others I would have gone under. I remember becoming dependent upon certain friends and acquaintances from whom I tried to get back some reflection of myself that would convince me that I still existed as a person and not — as I felt myself to be — a transparent, vulnerable concoction of moods. Depression is not — as I have eventually and painfully learned — something to sweep under the carpet: to deny, to forget. It is an experience that brings great misery and causes a great waste of time, but it can be, if one is fortunate, a source of personal wisdom and worth more than a hundred philosophies."

REFERENCES

Auden, W.H. (1974), "Unpredictable but providential", in *Thank You, Fog*, Faber & Faber, London.

Bainton, R. (1967), *History of Christianity*, Vol. 1, Penguin and American Heritage Publishing Co., pp. 116, 20, 108.

Bannister, D. (1970), *Perspectives in Personal Construct Theory*, Academic Press, London.

Bell, Q. (1972), *Virginia Woolf*, Vol. 2, Hogarth, London, p. 109.

Black, M. (1962), "Models and metaphors", in *Studies in Language and Philosophy*, Cornell University Press.

Bragg, M. (1976), *Speak for England*, Secker & Warburg, London, p. 3.

Bronowski, J. (1975), "People are different from rats", in the series "Journey round a twentieth century skull", *The Listener*, 3/7/75.

Carney, M.W.P., and Sheffield, B.E. (1973), Letter to the *British Journal of Psychiatry*, **123**, 723.

Cassirer, E. (1946), *The Myth of the State*, Yale University Press, New Haven, p. 14.

Cassirer, E. (1953a), *The Philosophy of Symbolic Forms*, Yale University Press, New Haven, Vol. 1, p. 284, Vol. 2, p. 240, Vol. 3, p. 108.

Cassirer, E. (1953b), *Language and Myth*, trans. Susanne Langer, Dover, New York, pp. 8, 25, 15, 13, 36.

Cavafy, C.P. (1966), *Complete Poems*, Hogarth, London.

Cheadle, J., and Morgan, R. (1972), "Does the chronic psychiatric patient understand plain English?", *British Journal of Psychiatry*, **120**, 553–560.

Cohen, S., and Taylor, L. (1972), *Psychological Survival. The Experience of Long Term Imprisonment*, Penguin, p. 138.

Dicks, H.V. (1939), *Clinical Studies in Psychopathology*, Arnold, London.

Douglas, M. (1966), *Purity and Danger*, Routledge & Kegan Paul, London.

Douglas, M. (1973), *Explorations in Cosmology*, Penguin.

Eliot, George (1861), *Silas Marner*.

Eliot, T.S. (1917), *The Love Song of J. Alfred Prufrock*.

Eliot, T.S. (1932), "The metaphysical poets", in *Selected Essays*, Harcourt Brace, p. 247.

Eliot, T.S. (1935), *Murder in the Cathedral*.

Eliot, T.S. (1943), *Burnt Norton*.

Eliot, T.S. (1950), *The Cocktail Party*.

Eliot, T.S. (1954), *The Confidential Clerk*.

Eliot, T.S. (1958), *The Elder Statesman*, Faber & Faber.

Empson, W. (1969), *The Structure of Complex Words*, Chatto & Windus, London, p. 339.

Ey, H., Bernard, P., and Brisset, C. (1963), *Manuel de Psychiatrie*, Masson, Paris.

Flach, F.F., and Draghi, S.D. (1975), *The Nature and Treatment of Depression*, Wiley, New York, p. 3.

Foucault, M. (1974), *The Order of Things*, Tavistock, London.

Frazer, J. (1960), *The Golden Bough*, Macmillan, London.

Freud, S. (1921), *Group Psychology and the Analysis of the Ego*, standard edition, p. 18.

Freud, S. (1957), *Collected Works*, standard edition, Hogarth Press, London.

Hopkins, G.M. (1948), *Poems*, Oxford University Press, London, pp. 107–110.

James, J. (1976), "Makes your heart bleed doesn't it?", *The Listener*, 29/1/75.

Jaspers, K. (1963), *General Psychopathology*, trans. from 7th edition by J. Hoenig and M.W. Hamilton, Manchester University Press, London.

Jung, C.G. (1975), *Man and His Symbols*, Aldus, London, p. 5.

Kant, I. (1953), "What does it mean to orientate ourselves in thought?", quoted by E. Cassirer in *The Philosophy of Symbolic Forms*, Vol. 2, Yale University Press, New Haven, p. 93.

Kelly, G. (1955), *The Psychology of Personal Constructs*, Vols. 1 & 2, Norton, New York.

Kendell, R.E. (1975), "The concept of disease and its implications for psychiatry", *British Journal of Psychiatry*, **127**, 305–315.

Kendell, R.E. (1976), "The classification of depression: a review of contemporary confusion", *British Journal of Psychiatry*, **129**, 15–28.

Kraepelin, E. (1921), *Manic-Depressive Insanity and Paranoia*, trans. M. Barclay, *Livingstone*, Edinburgh.

Lao Tsu (1973), *Tao Te Ching*, trans. Gia-Fu Feng and Jane English, Wildwood House, London.

Lewis, A.J. (1934a), "Melancholia: a historical review", *Journal of Mental Science*, **80**, 1–42.

Lewis, A.J. (1934b), "Melancholia: a clinical survey of depressive states", *Journal of Mental Science*, **80**, 277–378.

Luke, D., and Pick, R. (1966), *Goethe: Conversations and Encounters*, Eckerman 11.3.1828, p. 179, 2.3.1831, p. 229, Oswald Wolff, London.

Maurois, A. (1962), *The Quest for Proust*, trans. G. Hopkins, Penguin and Cape, p. 201.

Mendelson, M. (1974), *Psychoanalytic Concepts of Depression*, Wiley, New York.

Meyer, A. (1951), *Collected Papers of Adolf Meyer*, Johns Hopkins Press, Baltimore.

Newson, J., and Newson, E. (1976), "Intersubjectivity and the transmission of culture: on the social origins of symbolic functioning", *Bulletin of the British Psychological Society*, **28**, 446.

Nietzsche, F.W. (1966), *Beyond Good and Evil*, trans. W. Kaufmann, Random House, London.

Oakeshott, M. (1975), *On Human Conduct*, Clarendon, London, p. 78.

Piaget, J. (1971), *Structuralism*, trans. C. Maschler, Routledge & Kegan Paul, London, pp. 5, 19, 38.

Plath, S. (1976), *The Bell Jar*, Faber & Faber, London, p. 196.

Proust, M. (1962), in *The Quest for Proust* by A. Maurois, Penguin, p. 30.

Proust, M. (1967a), *Swann's Way*, Part 1, Chatto & Windus, London, p. 194.

Proust, M. (1967b), *Cities of the Plain*, Part 1, Chatto & Windus, London, pp. 222, 64.

Richards, I.A. (1934), *Coleridge on Imagination*, Kegan Paul, Trench, Truber and Co., London, p. 231.

Rilke, R.M. (1946), *Selected Letters of Rainer Maria Rilke, 1902–1926*, trans. R.F.C. Hull, Macmillan, London, pp. 386, 263, 205, 367.

Rilke, R.M. (1968), "The first elegy", in *Duino Elegies*, trans. J.B. Leishman, Hogarth, London.

Rimbaud, A. (1870), *Voyelles*.

Riviere, J. (1936), "A contribution to the analysis of negative therapeutic reaction", *International Journal of Psychoanalysis*, **17**, 304–320.

Rowe, D. (1971), "Poor prognosis in a case of depression as predicted by the repertory grid", *British Journal of Psychiatry*, **118**, 297–300.

Rowe, D. (1976), "Grid technique in the conversation between patient and therapist", in P. Slater (Ed.), *Intra-personal Space*, Wiley, London.

Russell, B. (1956), *Logic and Knowledge*, Allen & Unwin, London, pp. 195–6.

Russell, B. (1964), *The ABC of Relativity*, Allen & Unwin, London, p. 12.

Russell Davis, D. (1970), "Depression as an adaptation to crisis", *British Journal of Medical Psychology*, **43,** 109–116.

St. Ignatius (1936), *Spiritual Exercises*, First Week, "Discernment of the spirits", trans. J. Rickaby, Burns Oates and Washbourne, London .

Schapiro, L. (1972), "Critical essay", in I. Turgenev, *Spring Torrents*, Eyre Methuen, London, p. 180.

Slater, E., and Roth, M. (1970), *Clinical Psychiatry*, Bailliere, Tindall and Cassell, London, pp. 31, 78, 194, 35.

Slater, P. (Ed.) (1976), *Intra-personal Space: the measurement of Subjective Variation by the Grid Technique*, Wiley, London.

Steiner, G. (1975), *After Babel. Aspects of Language and Translation*, Oxford University Press, London, pp. 50, 29, 226, 83.

Toynbee, A.J., and Urban, G.R. (1974), *Toynbee on Toynbee*, Oxford University Press, London, p. 54.

Tsvetayeva, M. (1974), *Penguin Modern European Poets*.

Turgenev, I. (1972), *Spring Torrents*, trans. L. Schapiro, Eyre Methuen, London, p. 10.

Turgenev, I. (1973), *On the Eve*, trans. C. Garnett, Heinmann, London, p. 152.

Vico, G. (1948), *The New Science*, trans. from 3rd edition.

Wakeling, P. (1975), Letter in the *British Journal of Psychiatry*, News and Notes, pp. 13–14.

Wakeling, P. (1976), Personal communication.

Watts, A. (1974), *The Way of Zen*, Penguin.

Watzlawick, P., Weakland, J., and Fisch, R. (1974), *Change. Principles of Problem Formation and Problem Resolution*, Norton, New York.

Well, S. (1976), quoted by M. Laski in "Triggers to ecstacy", *The Listener*, 25/12/75, p. 81.

West, R. (1941), *Black Lamb and Grey Falcon*, Macmillan, London.

Whorf, B. (1956), "Language, thought and reality", in *Selected Writings of Benjamin Lee Whorf*, Carroll, Cambridge, Mass.

Wing, J.K., Cooper, J.E., and Sartorius, N. (1974), *Measurement and Classification of Psychiatric Symptoms. An Instruction Manual for the PSE and Catego Program*, Cambridge University Press, pp. 10, 155, 154, 151.

Wittgenstein, L. (1961a), *Tractatus Logico-Philosophus*, trans. D.F. Pears and B.F. McGuinness, Routledge & Kegan Paul, London, pp. 12, 72, 56.

Wittgenstein, L. (1961b), *Notebooks*, Blackwell, Oxford, p. 94.

Woodmansey, A.C. (1966), "The internalization of external conflict", *International Journal of Psychoanalysis*, **47,** 349.

Woolf, L. (1965), *Beginning Again*, Hogarth, London, p. 92.

Woolf, V. (1953), *A Writer's Diary*, Hogarth, London.

Woolf, V. (1967), *To the Lighthouse*, Hogarth, London.

Woolf, V. (1974), *The Waves*, Penguin.

Yeats, W.B. (1947), *The Song of Wandering Aengus*.

Yeats, W.B. (1960), *Easter 1916*.

INDEX